The
Jane Addams
Reader

The
Jane Addams
Reader

Edited by

JEAN BETHKE ELSHTAIN

BASIC
BOOKS

A Member of the Perseus Books Group

Published by Basic Books,
A Member of the Perseus Books Group

Designed by Cynthia Young

Library of Congress Cataloging-in-Publication Data
The Jane Addams reader / edited by Jean Bethke Elshtain.
   p.   cm.
Includes bibliographical references and index.
ISBN 0-465-01915-3 (alk. paper)
1. Addams, Jane, 1860–1935—Political and social views.   2. Women
social workers—United States—Biography.   3. Women social reformers—
United States—Biography.   4. Hull House (Chicago, Ill.)—History.
I. Elshtain, Jean Bethke, 1941– .

HV28.A35 J36   2001
361.92—dc21
[B]

                                                    2001043839

02 03 04 / 10 9 8 7 6 5 4 3 2 1

To the memory of

Christopher Lasch who

first stirred my interest

in Jane Addams

Contents

PART TWO

PART THREE

ACKNOWLEDGMENTS

Thanks to John Donatich, president of Basic Books, for the idea of combining my intellectual biography of Jane Addams, *Jane Addams and the Dream of American Democracy* (Basic Books, 2002), with a new reader incorporating large chunks of Addams's writing drawn from her many articles as well as from her books, nearly all of them out of print. JoAnn Miller, my editor, and her assistant, Jessica Callaway, played indispensable roles. My primary indebtedness is to my son, Eric P. Elshtain, who tracked down even the most obscure references so that at least some of the many names and incidents mentioned by Addams that she could, at the time she wrote, assume her readers would know, might be made intelligible to the contemporary reader. My husband, Errol L. Elshtain, helped with computer complexities and organization.

PERMISSIONS

ONLY ONE OF JANE ADDAMS'S BOOKS—*Twenty Years at Hull-House*—has been in print continuously since original publication. Her groundbreaking book and the one that first drew her to national attention, *Democracy and Social Ethics*, was reissued by Harvard University, Belknap Press, in 1964, edited, with an introduction, by the distinguished American historian Anne Firor Scott. The copyright with Harvard University Press covers Scott's material, which is not quoted directly here. Most of Jane Addams's writing, save for that which appeared in print after 1923, is in fair use. Excerpts from *The Excellent Becomes Permanent* (1932), *Early Years at Hull House* (1935), and *My Friend, Jane Lathrop* (1935) used with permission Simon and Schuster Publishers. There are Jane Addams archives and collections in a number of sites, most important among them being the Swarthmore College Peace Collection and the Jane Addams Memorial Collection at the University of Illinois–Chicago. The massive and by now indispensable Jane Addams Microfilm Project, the Jane Addams Papers (edited by Mary Lynn McCree Bryan and published by University Microfilms of Ann Arbor, Michigan, in 1985), makes available to scholars the extant documentary and archival material, including copies of her published essays and books. The University of Illinois–Chicago was most helpful in sorting out copyright issues. The Stephenson County Historical Museum in Freeport, Illinois, includes some early Jane Addams correspondence, and the little museum in Cedarville, Illinois, devotes a room to Jane Addams and the Addams family. The museum contains many items, including Jane Addams's traveling medicine kit, samples of her hand-knitting and her dresses, as well as a copy of John Bunyan's *Pilgrim's Progress*, given to her by one of her school teachers. The bibliography of the printed works of Jane Addams is included as copied from John C. Farrell's *Beloved Lady: A History of Jane Addams' Ideas on Reform and Peace* (Baltimore: Johns Hopkins University Press, 1967). It is reproduced with their permission. "Tolstoy and Gandhi," *Christian Century*, vol. XLVIII (November 25, 1931), appears with permission of *Christian Century*. "Our National Self Righteousness," *University of Chicago Magazine*, vol. XXVI (November 1933), appears with permission.

CHRONOLOGY OF THE
LIFE OF JANE ADDAMS

1860	Laura Jane Addams born September 6, in Cedarville, Illinois
1863	death of mother, Sarah Weber Addams
1868	remarriage of father, John Huy Addams, to Alice Haldeman
1877	enrolls in Rockford Female Seminary
1881	graduates from Rockford Female Seminary (later renamed Rockford College)
1881	death of father
1881	registers at Woman's Medical College, Philadelphia
1882	awarded bachelor's degree from Rockford College
1882	health breaks down; winter of invalidism
1883–1885	tour of England and Continent
1885	baptized and joins Presbyterian Church
1887–1888	second trip to Europe
1888	attends springtime bullfight in Madrid
1889	goes to Chicago in January to look for a "big house"
1889	doors to Hull-House open September 18
1891	Edward Butler, Chicago merchant, gives $5,000 for an art gallery at Hull-House; Jane Club, a cooperative boarding-club for girls, founded at Hull-House
1893	coffeehouse and gymnasium built at Hull-House
1894	Pullman Strike

Note: This chronology closely follows that in Christopher Lasch, ed., *The Social Thought of Jane Addams* (Indianapolis, Ind.: Bobbs-Merrill, 1965), pp. xxix–xxxi.

1895	appointed garbage inspector for the 19th ward
1896	visits England and Russia; meets Tolstoy
1898	opposes United States' acquisition of the Philippine Islands
1901	defends anarchist Abraham Isaak, who was arrested following assassination of President McKinley
1905	first of many summers spent in Bar Harbor, Maine, with companion Mary Rozet Smith
1905–1909	member of Chicago School Board
1907	delegate to first National Peace Congress
1909	appendicitis
1912	delegate to Progressive national convention and member of platform committee; seconds nomination of Theodore Roosevelt
1914	First World War begins
1915	attends first congress of Women's International League for Peace and Freedom, in the Hague
1916	tuberculosis of kidneys; one kidney removed
1917	breaks with many Progressives over United States' declaration of war on Germany
1919	presides over second congress of Women's International League for Peace and Freedom, Zurich; tours postwar France, Holland, Germany; blacklisted by Lusk Committee, New York legislature
1920	votes for Eugene Debs for U.S. president
1921	attends third congress of Women's International League for Peace and Freedom, in Vienna
1923	travels around the world
1924	attends fourth congress of Women's International League for Peace and Freedom, in Washington, D.C.; votes for LaFollette for U.S. president
1926	attends fifth congress of Women's International League for Peace and Freedom, in Dublin; heart attack
1928	votes for Herbert Hoover in U.S. presidential election, due to his role in famine relief in postwar Europe
1929	attends sixth congress of Women's International League for Peace and Freedom, in Prague; resigns as president; elected honorary president for life

1930   awarded honorary LL.D., University of Chicago

1931   undergoes surgery (seemingly successful) to remove tumor; receives Nobel Peace Prize (with Nicholas Murray Butler)

1932   votes for Hoover again

1935   dies in Chicago on May 21, of cancer; buried in Cedarville, Illinois

HULL-HOUSE FIRSTS

First Social Settlement in Chicago

First Social Settlement in United States with men and women residents

Established first public baths in Chicago

Established first public playground in Chicago

Established first gymnasium for the public in Chicago

Established first little theater in the United States

Established first citizenship preparation classes in United States

Established first public kitchen in Chicago

Established first college extension courses in Chicago

Established first group work school

Established first painting loan program in Chicago

Established first free art exhibits in Chicago

Established first fresh-air school in Chicago

Established first public swimming pool in Chicago

Established first Boy Scout troop in Chicago

Initiates investigations for the first time in Chicago of: truancy, typhoid fever, cocaine, children's reading, newsboys, sanitation, tuberculosis, midwifery, infant mortality, social value of the saloon

Initiates investigations that led to creation and enactment of first factory laws in Illinois

Initiates investigations that led to creation of first model tenement code

First Illinois Factory Inspector: Hull-House resident Florence Kelley

First probation officer in Chicago: Hull-House resident Alzina Stevens

Labor unions organized at Hull-House: Women Shirt Makers, Dorcas Federal Labor Union, Women Cloak Makers, Chicago Woman's Trade Union League

---

Note: From the Centennial Annual Report of the Hull House Association, Chicago. (Note that although the association does not hyphenate *Hull-House*, Jane Addams always did; and I have followed her usage.)

A RETURN TO HULL-HOUSE

Taking the Measure of an Extraordinary Life

JEAN BETHKE ELSHTAIN

THE STORY OF JANE ADDAMS SEEMS at first glance an uplifting tale of do-goodism fired by the charitable impulses of a woman who fashioned a highly personal approach to social theory and to solving social problems. There are critics who go farther and argue that Jane Addams, and all she stands for, was a method to reconcile new immigrants to lives of poverty and exploitation and to their contemptuous treatment by America's dominant classes. Others claim that her creation, Hull-House, represents a "prescientific" way of approaching social work that gave way before far more reliable methods. Within the purview of the professional-client approach to social problems—one that Jane Addams eschewed—the key questions revolve around managing a client population. But Jane Addams was up to something else. She aimed to create citizens, not manage clients. Her ideal of the settlement as a "place for enthusiasms" where the social classes engaged one another in acts of "mutual interpretation" strikes many contemporary critics as murky and naïve, if not altogether disingenuous.

The time has come to challenge these distorting interpretations and to try to see Jane Addams and Hull-House in fresh ways, through Jane Addams's own eyes. This is no easy job for many reasons. Reigning images of American womanhood shifted dramatically during the twentieth century. In her own lifetime, Jane Addams witnessed the emergence of the flapper and sexual rebel even as she herself represented the first generation of college-educated women determined to lead lives of action even though they had not yet won the right to vote. Since Addams's time we have seen women emerge as Rosie the Riveter, as consumers, as mainstream homemakers, as victims of a feminine mystique, as striving career women, as sexual liberationists, even as soldiers.

In her era, Addams neither celebrated domesticity nor condemned it; rather, she sought to balance what she called the "family claim" against a wider "social claim"—all in the interest of service and duty. She would extend the boundaries of home to include the city, believing, as she did, that housekeeping inevitably meant dealing with the wider forces that intrude into every domicile, for good or ill. For her, a too-narrow compass of domesticity was not a balanced human life, but neither was that of the striving careerist who disdains tending to the tasks of minding and mending the small world of caring for basic human needs. Were she among us yet, she would be appalled at our collective falling away from civic commitment, for she had struggled for the freedom to choose a vocation centered on action in service to others. The fact that women could not vote did not stay her hand. There were many things women could and should do. The advice she and other young women were given—to live essentially private lives as the mainstays of nineteenth-century domesticity—she found not so much unworthy as too limiting, whether for college-educated women like herself or for an immigrant mother or young factory worker. Women were required to juggle complex and often competing claims if they were to be faithful to the family claim as well as to the larger social claim. A complex balancing act was required. Seeing the world through the prism of both duty and compassion, through social responsibility and witness-bearing, life was, for Jane Addams, a pilgrim's progress. Her moral earnestness, her powerful evocation of maternal imagery—despite the fact she never married or had children of her own—likely fix her in our minds as a rather old-fashioned figure. It is time for a reconsideration.

Jane ("Jennie") Addams was born Laura Jane Addams on September 6, 1860, in the small town of Cedarville, Illinois. She was the eighth of nine children of John Huy Addams and Sara Weber Addams and one of four (three girls, one boy) to reach adulthood. Her mother died when Jane was two years old, and young Jennie was cared for by her older sisters until her father married Anna H. Haldeman in 1867. Haldeman, a widow, had two children of her own, one of whom, George, became a constant companion to, and an important influence on, his stepsister. John Addams was the most distinguished figure in the town of Cedarville, population 750. A formidable man of Quaker background who preached self-reliance, honesty, and devotion to duty, he prospered as a miller and a banker and served eight terms in the Illinois state senate. He was a friend of Abraham Lincoln's and one of the founders of the Illinois Republican Party.

Early on, John Addams became and then remained the primary influence on his daughter's life. His political heroes were Abraham Lincoln and the Italian patriot and republican Guiseppe (anglicized as "Joseph") Mazzini. His daughter shared his heroes, particularly the martyred sixteenth U.S. president. The childhood ties Addams forged to the legend of Lincoln as a symbol of all that was great and good, as the man who had "cleared title" to the American democracy, were reconfirmed throughout her adult life. In the active shaping of her life story, Addams tied her principles, her struggles, and her public accomplishments to the legacy of Lincoln. Imbued with driving ambition and a sense of destiny, for herself as well as for her country, Addams was a member of the first generation of American college women. She entered the Female Seminary—later Rockford College—in Rockford, Illinois, in 1877, acquiescing to her father's wish that she go to a school nearby. She had hoped to attend Smith College, where she had been accepted, but that ambition was postponed and then abandoned altogether.

Addams found herself immobilized after her father's untimely death in 1881 at the age of fifty-nine. She was torn by a deep social, moral, and psychological conflict: the struggle to balance the family claim against her own ambitions and a wider social claim. Her famous essay, "Filial Relations," which appeared in *Democracy and Social Ethics* (1902), describes this conflict as both necessary and tragic. "The collision of interests, each of which has a real moral basis and a right to its own place in life, is bound to be more or less tragic. It is the struggle between two claims, the destruction of either of which would bring ruin to ethical life."[1] It took her eight years to work out this delicate balance, a time during which she was diagnosed with a condition called "neurasthenia," which afflicted many young, educated, middle-class women whose pathways to action were blocked by external impediments, internal conflicts, or both. Jane Addams sometimes referred to the torment of a "baulked disposition" as a way of characterizing an inability to act. In *Twenty Years at Hull-House,* she writes vividly of finding herself unable to "formulate my convictions even in the least satisfactory manner, much less . . . reduce them to a plan for action. During most of the time I was absolutely at sea so far as any moral purpose was concerned, clinging only to the desire to live in a really living world and refusing to be content with a shadowy intellectual or aesthetic reflection of it."[2]

Jane Addams's time in purgatory ended when she found a way to put her social convictions directly to work on behalf of others. Along with her good friend, Ellen Gates Starr, she founded Hull-House in 1889. Hull-House was a political and social solution to nearly overwhelming personal distress, as Addams notes in another famous essay, "The Subjectivity Necessity for Social Settlements," first presented as a talk in 1892. She makes clear that the settlement house movement was as much for the benefit of the idealistic young people who undertook it as it was for those they lived among and served. In the case of Hull-House, this was the population of the bustling Nineteenth Ward of Chicago, an extraordinary mix of immigrants—Italian, Greek, Irish, Russian Jews, Germans, and others. Hull-House was an experiment in urban sociology. Its activities were shaped by Jane Addams's dream of improving the quality of life for immigrants by offering them art, drama, and music as well as public baths, baby care, job training, and classes in English and in citizenship. Hull-House was a setting for enthusiastic social engagement. It quickly became the great national symbol of the settlement house movement and of a version of the Protestant social gospel in practice. By 1905, Jane Addams had become a national hero and a symbol of democratic humanitarianism.

She wore her crown as the most beloved woman in America lightly even as she took her public role very seriously indeed. For Addams, power meant responsibility. Hull-House would be her home for forty-six years, until her death on May 21, 1935. At that point America was in the throes of the Depression and Franklin Roosevelt's New Deal, watching with apprehension as the menacing shapes of national socialism in Germany and communist totalitarianism in the Soviet Union grew more visible on the horizon. For many, Hull-House's day had already passed by the time of Addams's death. Newer modes of "social provision" and what came to be known as the "welfare state" superceded what Hull-House at its height had represented—a lively experiment that included a day nursery, kindergarten, playground, Boys and Girls Clubs of all sorts, cooperative boardinghouse, theater, music school, multiple reading groups, a Labor Museum of immigrant crafts, courses in cooking, sewing, a butcher shop, a coffee shop, and a bakery.

In *Twenty Years at Hull-House*, Addams describes the all-purpose nature of the settlement: "From the first it seemed understood that we were ready to perform the humblest neighborhood services. We were asked to wash the new-born babies, and to prepare the dead for burial, to nurse the sick, and to mind the children."[3] The needs and shifting demands of Hull-House enabled Jane Addams to exercise her remarkable gifts as fund-raiser, organizer, public arbitrator, and great public citizen. She wrote prolifically for scholarly journals but primarily for mass-circulation magazines, including *Ladies Home Journal* (a politically serious magazine at the time), *McClure's*, and *American Magazine*. She was one of the first, and remains one of the most important, among a group of social thinkers committed to communicating to a general audience that we have come to call "public intellectuals." One essay after another flowed from her fertile pen, as did eleven books. She kept up a schedule of speeches and public appearances that left her contemporaries breathless in her wake.

Addams and the capable women—and a few men—who both lived and worked at Hull-House and were known as residents, created American urban sociology as the empirically rigorous study of the conditions of urban life—a contribution sealed with the publication of the *Hull-House Maps and Papers* in 1895. Addams and her colleagues used data on tenement conditions, the existence of sweatshops, and the relation of tenement crowding and unsanitary conditions to rates of preventable diseases and ailments to press for dozens of reforms over the years. In such efforts, Hull-House allied with other reforming groups, individuals, and organizations. Nearly every piece of major reform in the years 1895–1930 comes with Jane Addams's name attached in one way or another, including labor and housing regulations, employment regulations for women and children, the eight-hour workday, old-age and unemployment insurance, as well as measures against prostitution, corrupt politicking, and vice and for public schools, public playgrounds, and the creation of juvenile and domestic court systems. Jane Addams was the first woman president of the National Conference of Charities and Corrections (1909); the first woman awarded an honorary degree from Yale University (1910); and the winner of the Nobel

Prize for Peace (1931), an award she shared with Dr. Nicholas Murray Butler, another leader of American antiwar efforts and president of Columbia University. Her name is linked to the creation of the Urban League and the National Association for the Advancement of Colored People as well as woman's suffrage.

Addams's college years—she was valedictorian of her class—had been spent in a high-minded, self-critical search for meaning and purpose. During her time at Rockford, she met and became fast friends with Ellen Starr, with whom she shared her early hopes and dreams and who became her partner in the founding of Hull-House. Addams's letters to Starr reveal her as both idealistic and practical. She was determined to forge a link between abstract ideals and concrete actions. The urge to be useful and to embrace a worthy vocation was her passion and, for a time, her torment as she found the path to action blocked. Convinced that women had their own voice and their own claims to authority and knowledge, Addams spent a lifetime putting that conviction into practice and into words. She was insistent that women should never abandon what she came to call "the long road of woman's memory." Ellen Starr was but the first of many close female friends and colleagues. The most important friend in her life was Mary Rozet Smith, who joined the Hull-House effort in 1892. From a wealthy Chicago family, Smith became not only an important benefactor of Hull-House's efforts but also Addams's friend and companion until her own death in 1934. Self-effacing, Smith preferred to stay out of the limelight, instead doing what she could to help support and care for Addams, who frequently ignored the admonitions of friends to slow her pace and to get more rest.

One reason for the enormous success of Hull-House was that remarkable group of women and men who, inspired by Addams, joined her effort. She had the capacity to generate collegiality and long-term loyalty. The names of her associates are a veritable Who's Who of American reform, including Florence Kelley, Julia Lathrop, and Dr. Alice Hamilton. Kelley moved into Hull-House in 1891 and was recognized immediately as a formidable figure. She went on to become the chief factory inspector of Illinois. Lathrop battled for the creation of juvenile courts successfully and was named to head the Children's Bureau in Washington, D.C. Alice Hamilton oversaw medical investigations in the Hull-House neighborhood and was a pioneer in investigating occupational hazards and industrial diseases. She also tried to tend to Jane Addams's medical needs but found that Addams was a very difficult patient who routinely ignored doctor's orders. Philosopher John Dewey, recognized as the great proponent of that strand of philosophy called "pragmatism," was an associate and resident for a time and a great admirer of Addams's work and her writing. Famous visitors were drawn to Hull-House and lectured there during their visits to Chicago, from the great writer and psychologist William James, to Sidney and Beatrice Webb (the leaders of British Fabian socialism, a brand of democratic socialism that repudiated Marxism), to the famous Russian Prince Kropotkin. By 1915 Addams's public reputation seemed virtually unshakable. She had access to all the powerful men of her time, including the president of the United States. Then came World War I, turning Jane Addams's world upside-down. Her defense of anarchists and immigrants who were under assault as potentially disloyal, as well as her brave and lonely devotion to pacifism that set her in opposition to many who had been her closest and most ardent supporters (including John Dewey), placed her outside the American mainstream and brought down upon her head a tide of derision and abuse. When World War I broke out in 1914 but before America's own entry into the conflict in 1917, Addams helped to create the Woman's Peace Party, which called publicly for continuous mediation of the conflict. In articles, speeches, and books, Addams traced what she considered women's historic commitment to preserving and sustaining life, and she placed this ancient and perduring commitment in opposition to what she scored as militarism. She embraced a version of feminism that counterposed it to the war mentality. As she wrote in *The Long Road of Woman's Memory*, "It would be absurd for women even to suggest equal rights in a world run solely by physical force, and Feminism must necessarily assert the ultimate supremacy of moral agencies."[4]

Called a traitor at worst and a naïve, gulled woman at best, and then denounced as a Bolshevik, Addams stood her ground, but not without intense and often tormented self-questioning. In a democratic society, she asked herself, does one really have the right to stand apart from all the rest, particularly when one's country is at war? In the decade following the end of World War I and the Russian Revolution, America was gripped by an anti-Red hysteria. Jane Addams's name appeared regularly on lists of subversives, but she never reneged on her commitments to basic civil liberties and pacifism. After the antiimmigrant hysteria had run its course and America moved into the 1930s and confronted the crisis of the Great Depression, public hostility toward Addams softened, and her reputation was largely recouped. Her recognition for the Nobel Prize; her endorsement of Herbert Hoover for U.S. president (largely because of his heroic efforts to feed the starving masses of Europe after World War I, an effort with which Jane Addams was associated); her indefatigable commitment to public service; and her undying faith in the goodness displayed routinely by ordinary people—all helped somewhat to restore her to her earlier niche as America's foremost public citizen.

Jane Addams died from inoperable cancer on May 21, 1935, at the age of seventy-four. Her death prompted an extraordinary outpouring of public grief and tribute. Some compared her to Lincoln. Perhaps the most famous of all the eulogies in her honor is that of Walter Lippmann, who wrote: "She had compassion without condescension. She had pity without retreat into vulgarity. She had infinite sympathy for common things without forgetfulness of those that are uncommon. That, I think, is why those who have known her say that she was not only good, but great. For this blend of sympathy with distinction, of common humanity with a noble style is recognizable by whose who have eyes to see it as the occasional but authentic issue of the mystic promise of American democracy."[5] Jane Addams is buried in the Addams's family section of a small cemetery in Cedarville, her hometown. An obelisk lists her, at her request, simply as one associated with Hull-House and with the Women's International League for Peace and Freedom.

Following her death, Jane Addams's reputation went into a slow but decisive eclipse. The received wisdom on her life and work narrowed. The complex and capacious activities of Hull-House were described routinely as social work and Jane Addams as a social worker rather than a great public citizen. The view surfaced that she was not an original thinker, that her work was derivative, that she was "more important as a publicist and popularizer" than as a theorist of any real originality.[6] Indeed, a number of critics converged on this view.[7] In standard social and cultural histories, Addams was either not mentioned[8] or referred to only cursorily.[9] One exception is Christopher Lasch's introduction to his edited volume *The Social Thought of Jane Addams*[10] and the chapter Lasch devotes to Addams in *The New Radicalism in America, 1889–1963.*[11] Lasch, almost alone among critics and commentators, called Addams "a theorist and intellectual—a thinker of originality and daring."[12] Lasch is critical of the antiintellectualism he finds in some of her work—I do not see this strand so clearly—given her enthusiasm for applied knowledge. But his serious consideration of Addams as a social thinker of continuing importance is one on which to build. Addams's brand of interpretive social thinking bears within it a powerful cultural and political critique that is, at one and the same time, a constructive vision of American democracy. Jane Addams believed that public citizens, writers, and intellectuals had a duty to criticize and to affirm. They could not just tear down. They, too, had to build.

One can think of her writings as part of a process of complex social revelation, putting on view much that is both tragic and terrible yet revealing, at the same time, human integrity and perseverance even under circumstances that many of us would find insupportable. Addams's favorite form was the essay. Her books are essays revised and arranged thematically in order to create a coherent and pleasing work. This should not be taken to mean that she simply cobbled together what she had published previously. Her writerly sensibilities and aesthetic sense would not allow that. She was a stickler for form, striving to achieve inner thematic continuity in her texts.

Her work also embodies a stance of dignified reticence, much out of fashion in our say-everything, say-it-loud era. One commentator described her style as "neither self-effacing nor brassily self-absorbed," which seems just about right.[13] This same critic continues: "Addams never sounds shrill, paranoid, or self-pitying, but rather seeks to restore equilibrium by framing social problems in an ethical context."[14] Unlike so many social reformers who became prisoners of their own dogmatic ideology and rhetoric, Addams was able to stand back from what she was doing even as she was doing it. For her, critical assessment and interpretation was a part of the doing, not an activity sundered from action. She tells us that by instinct she tended toward moderation.

It was this reputation for evenhandedness that made it possible for her to do so many civically courageous things. In 1901, for example, she stood up for beleaguered anarchists when the police, overtaken by public fear and hysteria, swept up suspected anarchist immigrants in a huge dragnet following the assassination of U.S. President William McKinley by self-described anarchist Leon Czolgosz. Opposed to anarchism, Addams was also opposed to extremism in the defense against anarchism. She was one of those rare persons who strives to maintain the warp and woof of the fabric of civic and moral life in ways that keep it both sturdy and beautiful—beautiful so that we might love what we ourselves have helped to create. Just as she would do this work of weaving, she would ensure that the tensile threads between generations do not break, not even under the upheavals and frequent bitterness of the immigrant experience. Her life's work was this weaving together of past and present in order to create a better—not perfect, as she was no utopian—society. Her many books, essays, and speeches progress to that end through a method she called "sympathetic understanding."

Jane Addams's most famous work is considered a masterpiece of American autobiography, *Twenty Years at Hull-House,* from which excerpts are included in this reader. Published in 1910, this beautifully sustained effort helps the reader to appreciate Addams's unusual powers of description and her method of interpretation. Addams was already a celebrated public figure when she wrote her autobiography. Her reputation as a writer was growing given the books she had published to wide popular acclaim: *Democracy and Social Ethics* (1902), *Newer Ideals of Peace* (1907), and *The Spirit of Youth and the City Streets* (1909). After the publication of *Twenty Years at Hull-House,* she wrote a follow-up autobiographical volume—*The Second Twenty Years at Hull-House* (1930)—as well as *A New Conscience and an Ancient Evil* (1912), *Women at the Hague: The International Congress of Women and Its Results* (1915, coauthored with Emily G. Balch and Dr. Alice Hamilton), *The Long Road of Woman's Memory* (1916), *Peace and Bread in Time of War* (1922), *The Excellent Becomes the Permanent* (1932), an unusual collection of eulogies, and *My Friend, Julia Lathrop*, published posthumously in 1935. The last is a story of a friendship and much more, including yet another attempt by Addams to depict the early history of Hull-House. If one considers that these books and her more than 500 published essays, speeches, and editorials were all written *in medias res*—in the thick of an exceptionally busy, public life—the number and the quality of her works is astonishing.

Jane Addams's writing style, vividly on display in her books with a strong narrative story-line, like *Twenty Years at Hull-House, The Spirit of Youth and the City Streets,* and *The Long Road of Woman's Memory,* is a rich composite of symbols, injunctions, purposes, and meanings derived from a social gospel forged from Christianity and from America's greatest democratic thinkers and citizens, foremost among them her beloved Abraham Lincoln. Lincoln is widely acknowledged not only as the greatest of presidents but as the greatest writer among presidents. Addams would emulate his rhetorical skills. In telling her own story, she locates it within the greater story of America itself as a society called, in Lincoln's words, to respond to the "better angels of our nature." For Addams, the life of citizenship is a moral claim. Morality is no remote abstraction but a living, breathing reality.

Several apparent paradoxes in Addams's thought surface in her writings, including dual commitments that set her apart from those who were unambivalent celebrants of the progressive spirit. One example is her battered but never repudiated belief in an evolutionary move toward more inclusive and pacific social forms, on the one hand, and, on the other, her equally unwavering depiction of the pathos of lives swept up, like so much human debris, by imperious waves of industrialization. When Jane Addams celebrated progress, she did so as an expression of her democratic faith based on a particular reading of Western history. But when she told the story of history's castaways, she did so from their point of view, from inside their despair and their often stupefied sense of alienation that forced many into silence, madness, or self-destruction.

Addams's ambivalence about the world that industrialization wrought is rooted in her social morality and compelled by her commitment to a social theory anchored in attunement to particular cases. No abstraction has credibility, she argued, unless it is rooted in concrete human experience. Her immersion in the particular, an ability to articulate wider meaning through powerful depictions of individual suffering, joy, hope, and despair, sets her apart from all who write abstractly about human life—including the moral life. She believed one can never wring out of remote abstractions a sense of the thickness, complexity, and sheer messiness of human life. One example suffices to convey Addams's ability to portray the terrible suffering the early wage-labor system trailed in its wake and, as well, to illustrate her descriptive powers and her extraordinary eye for detail. She pens a searing word-portrait of a lone woman caught in a terrible dilemma. Addams turns a social fact into a potent piece of writing:

> With all the efforts made by modern society to nurture and educate
> the young, how stupid it is to permit the mothers of young children
> to spend themselves in the coarser work of the world! It is curi-

ously inconsistent that with the emphasis this generation has placed upon the mother and upon the prolongation of infancy, we constantly allow the waste of this most precious human material. I cannot recall without indignation a recent experience. I was detained late one evening in an office building by a prolonged committee meeting of the Board of Education. As I came out at eleven o'clock, I met in the corridor of the fourteenth floor a woman whom I knew, on her knees scrubbing the marble tiling. As she straightened to greet me, she seemed so wet from her feet up to her chin, that I hastily inquired as to the cause. Her reply was that she left home at five o'clock every night and had no opportunity to nurse her baby. Her mother's milk mingled with the very water with which she scrubbed the floors until she should return at midnight heated and exhausted to feed her screaming child with what remained of her breasts.[15]

Here Addams undertakes a task at once ethical and political. It was her conviction that only a tug on our human sympathies and affections could draw us into the moral life and keep us there. This life has no fixed reference point but evolves as an ongoing engagement with competing human goods and purposes. "Pity, memory, and faithfulness are natural ties with paramount claims,"[16] claims run over roughshod when mother's milk drains out into scrubwater and an infant goes hungry as a mother toils alone in an office building late at night. At the same time, claims of the wider society—Addams's "social claim"—also have legitimacy.[17] The social claim should not demand harsh work for low pay that forces workers to ignore the needs of their families; rather, it should help us to see ourselves as active, productive members of a wider community. Our moral lives are distorted if we focus on this social claim to the exclusion of ties of kinship and friendship, even as they are distorted if we draw the circle around domesticity so tightly that there is room for no one, and nothing, else. The pathos of the scrubwoman in Addams's vignette is that she has no chance to balance out these competing claims; rather, she is forced against her will and, therefore, against the just and preemptory claims of the needs of an infant, into the world of ill-paid, lowly regarded work. She is denied the opportunity to make her way in the world as well as the opportunity to pay attention to the legitimate family claims in her life.

For Addams, a livable human ethic was embedded within the density of our moral lives. Life is complex. Often our choices are not between clear-cut good and evil but between competing goods. So our ethics must be as complex as life itself. What stays Addams from sliding into moral relativism, on the one hand, or moral absolutism, on the other, is her dual commitment to empathetic understanding as the surest route to social knowledge and to a form of compassion linked to a determination not to judge human beings by "their hours of defeat."[18] The requirement that the social commentator make a sympathetic attempt to interpret, to understand, and to criticize in a way that also turns back on the observer herself, demanding a form of self-interpretation and self-criticism as well, lies at the core of Addams's social theory. She would be with others in their hours of defeat as well as their moments of triumph, rather than to "do for them" from a lofty perch above their struggles.

Human nature being "incalculable," in Jane Addams's account, there can be no single, fixed interpretive entry point into the human condition: Neither economic man, nor morally uplifted man, nor psychological man, nor any other one-dimensional substitute for the complexity of varied human life. (And "man" here is meant generically, although often it is clear that historic thinkers—certainly *not* Addams—meant to take what it is that men do, or are said to do, as definitive of the human condition as such.) Addams was aware of our human tendency to backslide, as it used to be called, to fall short of any norm of perfection. At the same time, she calls upon us to strive toward something more perfect than what it is we have or who it is we are. What staves off moral anarchy and flux, for Addams, is that rootedness provided by her social ontology, the very ground of her discourse. She gives prescriptive force to a vision of human solidarity that links human beings across societies and through time; that has its base in widespread and basic emotional experiences central to the human condition but provides at the same time for individual distinctiveness and cultural diversity. As individuals and societies we can come to know ourselves, Addams insisted, *only* to the extent that we realize in our own lives the fundamental sociality of our natures. Cultures as well as persons would fall into stagnation and dullness without those perspicuous contrasts offered to us by those different from ourselves but sufficiently like us that, looking at them, we recognize a common human condition.

Hull-House was the living embodiment of Jane Addams's social phi-losophy. That experiment was never intended primarily as a charitable institution or as a definitive solution to the assorted evils of uncon-trolled industrialization. Addams's "subjective necessity" compelled the creation of Hull-House and precluded any simple accounts of its pur-poses or her own. Addams became acquainted with the settlement house movement that began in mid-nineteenth-century England in 1887–1888, during one of her extended trips to Europe. Inspired by the writings of social theorists and reformers like John Ruskin and Thomas Hill Green, settlement beginnings were humble enough. In 1875, an Oxford tutor, Arnold Toynbee, moved to Whitechapel, a derelict part of London, in order to witness terrible social conditions firsthand. Ten years later, the first social settlement, named Toynbee Hall, was founded.

Addams visited Toynbee Hall, which by 1887 was a bustling center of activity that included everything from soup kitchens to adult educa-tion classes. Seeing all of this with her own eyes helped to reinforce an idea that was already taking shape for Jane Addams, namely, that she and several friends should find a big house in a congested quarter of Chicago and make their own attempt at "settling." Addams and her compatriots needed Hull-House, and that is why it was created—to open up a life of meaningful action to young women "who had been given over too exclusively to study."[19] In serving, one would reveal oneself. One must understand both the subjective and the objective poles of Hull-House as an attempt to put into practice "the theory that the dependence of classes on each other is reciprocal."[20] Hull-House was not, Addams declared, "philanthropy or benevolence, but a thing fuller and wider than either of these, as revelation that, to have mean-ing, to be made manifest, must be put into terms of action."[21]

The first settlements in the United States—the College Settlement in New York and Hull-House in Chicago—opened in September 1889. The settlement idea seemed especially well suited to democratic ideals, and it spread rapidly. At the height of the settlement house movement, there were hundreds of social settlements all over the United States, concentrated primarily (though not exclusively) in urban areas. Ad-dams worked and reworked her definition of the settlement throughout her life. The prose of the Hull-House charter is remarkably prosaic: "To provide a center for a higher civic and social life; to institute and maintain educational and philanthropic enterprises, and to investigate and improve the conditions in the industrial districts of Chicago."[22] But she and her companions learned "not to hold preconceived ideas of what the neighborhood ought to have, but to keep ourselves in readiness to modify and adapt our undertakings as we discovered those things which the neighborhood was ready to accept."[23]

Small wonder, then, that Addams called the settlement a "place of enthusiasm" that should "never lose its flexibility, its power of adaptation, its readiness to change its methods as the environment may demand." The things that the neighborhood was ready to accept were rich and varied, encompassing drama classes, play groups, music societies, well-baby clinics, nutritional courses, day nurseries, and the famous Hull-House Labor Museum designed to reveal the skill and craft of immigrant parents and grandparents to their Americanized children and grandchildren, who were often ashamed of their origins and their Old World heritage. To this one must add the Working People's Social Science Club and Hull-House's role in pioneering the investigation of social conditions, including housing, hygiene, medicine, employment, child care, transportation, truancy, and alcohol and drug use. In her writings, Addams details this complexity and offers an exhilarating sense of a shared adventure. The firmness of her commitment to social interpretation and to politics as one chief way people in a complex, heterogeneous society reveal themselves to one another shines throughout. What also emerges is the tension between providing a forum where immigrant cultural distinctiveness can be displayed and preserved and studying this population through the methods of the new social science.

Jane Addams created for herself a demanding, all-absorbing vocation. Those around her observed that somehow her energies rose to meet every occasion. She was on call around the clock. Here, for example, is a testimonial drawn from the *Boston Transcript* of April 23, 1903:

> Chicago people look to Jane Addams of Hull House in many emergencies. The other night the little woman was roused at midnight to meet a committee of firemen in the parlour. Stables had been burned in the neighborhood and horses were injured but not killed. There is a city law which requires a special order of court to shoot a horse within city limits. This order of court could not be obtained

until morning. Horses were suffering with no hope of relief but death. "Miss Addams, can't you give us an order to shoot them?" asked the burly fireman. "I have no legal authority but I will take responsibility," said the little woman. They drove with her to the place and she stood by to see the horses shot.[24]

Labor strife and neighborhood tragedy also called her out. When three Italian boys were shot by a policeman in front of the Polk Street School, Hull-House secured legal assistance for the family and pushed for an investigation. Fifteen witnesses stepped forward to declare that the shooting was unjustified.[25] The issue would never have been joined without Hull-House's mediating role, one that enabled issues to be protested and adjudicated without stirring up more violence. Indeed, Jane Addams detested strikes that stirred up animosity and created a warlike atmosphere. Her sympathies were most often with the strikers. But because she was evenhanded and fair-minded, she was called upon frequently to arbitrate disputes. During a major strike at the Deering, Illinois, plant of International Harvester, the manufacturer of large farm equipment, women strikers asked Jane Addams to hear their grievances so that they might, with her help, "be able to get the factory inspector to take up their case, as they say the factory is not complying with state factory law."[26] Jane Addams did as she promised—she listened to the grievances and made the grievants' case. The result was the formation of a union with some 800 female members.

We are aware of the decline of the Hull-House/settlement model in the wake of the creation of schools of social work built on the "scientific"/management model that stressed professional social provision rather than the engagement of settlement workers and immigrants as citizens and citizens-to-be. As well, with the coming of the New Deal, the state took over more functions, and social provision was increasingly staffed by government-paid case workers. One's evaluation of the settlement idea depends, in part, on one's approval, or disapproval, of the professional social worker model. Efficient management became more of a watchword and slogan in contrast to helping immigrants meet the requirements of citizenship or offering a place for enthusiasm, debate, and social interpretation. In light of recent criticism of the welfare-state model, from both the left and the right, some are calling for a reconsideration of the settlement house idea as an alternative to overmanaged welfare bureaucracies that seemed to perpetuate dependency rather than to help people to stand on their own feet as dignified citizens.

Jane Addams was ahead of her time in insisting that the poor should not be isolated or kept marginalized in separate sections of a city. She argued, instead, that the poor should be drawn into the stream of life through making available a wide variety of public goods, from direct assistance in emergencies to the creation of safe public spaces for play and recreation. She insisted that the settlement idea was no goody-goody, sentimental model of social reform but rather a tough-minded yet sympathetic creation that benefited those who created the settlement as well as those who were drawn to its activities and possibilities.

To be sure, there are critics who find Addams's settlement model wanting as well. They decry it as an instrument of social management or control, a way to "homogenize" an immigrant population and to smooth over the rough edges of social injustice. But many of these so-called social-control approaches are patronizing to the immigrant poor, representing them as a pliable population to be molded as social reformers see fit. Addams had more respect than that. Following the bitter experiences of the World War I era, she was sufficiently skeptical about overweening concentrations of power, including the state, to seek to serve its purposes uncritically, whether as an individual or through the institution she pioneered. Of course, her complex civic and philosophic stance involves a number of tensions—for example, the tension embedded in her celebration of the settlement as a place for enthusiasms, on the one hand, and her focus on the need to adjust immigrants to their new positions in industrial life, on the other. But she would tell us that the tension is simply *there* in the complex reality of life in the immigrant city and that there is no way one can paper it over by offering too slick an interpretation of it.

The honesty of Jane Addams's vision is refreshing in our era of sound bites and relentless spin control—all the attempts to manage the news and to reduce public debate to whoever offers the most quotable quote or clever insult. Were she alive today, she would put to us the same questions she put to her contemporaries: What kind of story do we tell about the America of our own era? Do we emphasize power and empire? Or do we stress a narrative about a society striving to be fairer, more decent, and capable of setting many places at its civic table? What are the current lines of class and social division? What institutions help to form us as decent, ethical beings? What possibilities exist for dynamic mutual interpretation of Americans separated by class, region, and race? As an advocate of nonviolent social change, Jane Addams urged face-to-face debate, even confrontation, in order that each side could listen to the arguments of the other.

There is much to question and to challenge in Jane Addams's social thought, but there is also much to learn, particularly about how a brilliant writer and creative social thinker does social theory from the inside out. Her writing retains a remarkable freshness after all these years, in part because we are still struggling with so many of the problems she and her generation confronted, in part because we have not yet figured out how to deal with stubborn poverty or how to strike the right balance between diversity and commonality or how to be fair to the one and respond to the needs of the many. She is also, in many ways, a remote figure: in her devotion to duty rather than self-seeking pleasure; in her thorough going commitment to a moral stance; in her celebration of citizenship and her lofty view of the call to civic life.

We worry, rightly, that contemporary America does not provide the social soil to nurture such persons any longer given the decline of our civic culture. As paternalistic and stifling as the world of Jane Addams's era could be for its young women, it nevertheless instilled in many a conviction that a human life is one lived with purpose, dignity, meaning, and honor. To see in the dissolution of that way of life only liberation from unacceptable constraint is not tenable. Jane Addams helps to take the measure of what we have lost as well as what we have gained. We cannot call up or return to the civic culture of an earlier time. But perhaps we can remember and attempt to recall its best features and think of how we might call them to mind yet again. Rereading Jane Addams renews our acquaintance with a writer of great clarity who was gifted with the capacity to convey deep human emotion without mawkishness or cheap sentimentality. She helps to deepen our capacity for empathy and understanding, and she stirs within us an awareness of human limits and vulnerabilities.

Though Jane Addams has had her day, she has yet to receive her due. It is my hope that those who take the time to read her words will discover not only a writer of great descriptive power but also a distinctive voice representing the American experiment at its best: energetic, hopeful, generous yet aware of the pathos attendant upon life in a society that is always changing, always pressing on to the next frontier. Jane Addams understood that with each gain there is also a loss. The reflective citizen recognizes this and finds a creative way to deal with the tension. She offered so many shelter in the storm and stress of tumultuous change. Out of this engagement, we can reacquaint ourselves with one of the greatest public citizens of the twentieth century.

Notes

1. Jane Addams, *Democracy and Social Ethics* (New York: Macmillan, 1902), pp. 76–77.

2. Jane Addams, *Twenty Years at Hull-House* (New York: Macmillan, 1912), p. 64.

3. Ibid., p. 109.

4. Jane Addams, *The Long Road of Woman's Memory* (New York: Macmillan, 1916), p. 129.

5. Cited in Allen Davis, *American Heroine: The Life and Legend of Jane Addams* (New York: Oxford University Press, 1973), p. 291. Lippmann's eulogy was widely syndicated, appearing in newspapers throughout the United States.

6. Thus Allen F. Davis in his biography, *American Heroine: The Life and Legend of Jane Addams* (New York: Oxford University Press, 1973), p. xi.

7. Daniel Levine, *Jane Addams and the American Liberal Tradition* (Madison: The State Historical Society of Wisconsin, 1971; reprinted Greenwood Press, 1980), p. x.

8. E.g., Henry Steele Commager, *The American Mind* (New Haven: Yale University Press, 1959).

9. E.g., Ralph Henry Gabriel, *The Course of American Democratic Thought* (New Haven: Yale University Press, 1956), p. 360.

10. Indianapolis: Bobbs-Merrill, 1965.

11. New York: Vintage Books, 1965.

12. In his introduction to *The Social Thought of Jane Addams*, p. cv.

13. Herbert Leibowitz, *Fabricating Lives: Explorations in American Autobiography* (New York: Alfred A. Knopf, 1989), p. 136.

14. Ibid., p. 140.

15. Jane Addams, *Twenty Years at Hull-House*, pp. 174–175.

16. Ibid., p. 20.

17. Addams implies but never develops fully a theory of the child's developmental emergence as a moral being. She recognizes that early neglect may lead the individual to remain forever impervious to life's gentler aspects and that compelling a child to complete tasks beyond his or her normal growth is often

cruel and can be disastrous. She poses a concept of sublimation, urging that blind appetite be transformed into worthy psychic impulses by moral motives. For Addams, child development is an evolving education of the heart.

18. Jane Addams, *A New Conscience and an Ancient Evil* (New York: Macmillan, 1912), p. 137.

19. Jane Addams, *Twenty Years at Hull-House*, p. 85.

20. Ibid., p. 91.

21. Ibid., pp. 121–122.

22. Ibid., pp. 111–112.

23. Jane Addams, *Forty Years at Hull-House* (New York: Macmillan, 1935), p. 132.

24. Clipping from Swarthmore College Peace Collection, Addams holdings. Jane Addams subscribed to a clipping service, so there are notices clipped from newspapers all over the United States, indeed, the world, in this collection.

25. Clipping from the *Chicago Post*, May 19, 1899.

26. Clipping from *Chicago Inter Ocean* as reported in the *Chicago Tribune*, April 19, 1903.

Part One

Introduction: "The Snare of Preparation" and the Creation of a Vocation

Jane Addams's gifts as a writer were already evident when she was a schoolgirl. She possessed the unusual ability to penetrate to the heart of a complex question, to draw the reader in, and to offer many vivid turns of phrase. The first three items in Part One—"The Macbeth of Shakespeare," "Bread Givers," and "Cassandra"—are samples of what is usual called "juvenalia." Because adult writers often find their adolescent writings embarrassing, they make a strenuous effort to obliterate all trace of such efforts. Not Jane Addams. She kept meticulous records of her many writings, and she found a continuous thread linking her early musings to her mature social thought.

Jane Addams was haunted by a number of philosophic and ethical questions: What is our purpose on earth? If we are called to duty, how do we recognize that duty? Once we have recognized our duty, what spheres of action are available to us to live out that ethic as best we can? What are the pitfalls and temptations along the way? Indeed, how are we formed, in the first place, in such a way that we not get bogged down in the Slough of Despond, but reach eventually the Celestial City (a reference to John Bunyan's *Pilgrim's Progress*, an inescapable text for schoolchildren in Addams's time and place).[1]

Early on, Addams recognized her own quest for power, one that compelled her to search for an expansive stage on which to enact her drama. But she feared egocentricity and hated self-pity, defining the latter throughout her life as the "lowest pit" into which a human being can sink. You have to own up to what you have done. You have to pay

1

the price of your words, thoughts, and deeds—a lesson she learned the hard way during her time in the civic wilderness in the World War I era when vituperation supplanted the kudos and testimonials to which she had become accustomed. One can see her toughening herself in her early writings. She was preparing to negotiate the rough terrain that might well lie ahead, particularly for a young woman of the nineteenth century determined to honor both the social and ethical expectations of the family claim as well as the growing legitimacy of the social claim— the call to wider service. Avenues were present for that social call. For young women, they were the mission fields, elementary and secondary school teaching, and nursing—professions into which women had flooded during the Civil War when so many men were called away to fight and to die, or, in the case of nursing, had been generated on a large scale to respond to the terrible needs of the battlefield.

Addams refused these options, although she was heavily lobbied for the mission field during her years at Rockford Seminary, later Rockford College (1877–1881). The redoubtable Anna Peck Sill, head of Rockford Seminary, evaluated her own success in that post in part by how many of her young wards took up mission work.[2] Jane Addams was to become her best-known failure in this regard. But other than rejecting missions, young Jane knew not where to turn. Her beloved father's death in 1881, the year of her graduation, threw her into a tailspin. She tells us that she was "all at sea." She took two extended tours of Europe. She experimented with the possibility of medical school. She was diagnosed with the social ailment of "neurasthenia."[3] She describes this period as "the snare of preparation" in a famous essay that forms the bulk of chapter 4 in her autobiography, *Twenty Years at Hull-House* (1910). She decided that young educated women of her own era were given over far too exclusively to cultivating things of beauty; they "had departed too suddenly from the active, emotional life led by their grandmothers and great-grandmothers"; in the process of being educated "they had lost that simple and almost automatic response to the human appeal."

But what form could such a response take? In the lives of grandmothers and great-grandmothers, domesticity was an all-consuming endeavor, as the home encompassed not only childrearing but production, home economics, education, tending to the ill, animal husbandry, and agriculture. Many of these tasks had been absorbed within the framework of other institutions with the dislocations and changes wrought by the industrial revolution and ever more complex differentiations of social institutions. The upshot was an ideal—at least for the middle class and relatively privileged young woman—that had become narrowly aesthetic. The ideal young matron-to-be of the mid–to-late nineteenth century should grace the hearth, practice the domestic arts (embroidery, piano-playing), and shine at social gatherings. Addams was frustrated to the point of paralysis by such a prospect. It wasn't until she witnessed ethical conviction in action in London's East End,[4] where the first settlement, Toynbee Hall, had been established, that she decided to go to Chicago to look for a "big house" in a congested immigrant quarter in which she and the friend she drew in on her scheme, Ellen Gates Starr, would "settle" and open the doors to their neighbors. Those doors were opened on September 18, 1889, and the rest, as they say, is history.

The writings in this section take us through the early years at Hull-House and offer examples of Addams's complex ruminations on both the subjective and the objective necessity and value of a social settlement. Her discussion of the "subtle problems" of charity alerts us to just how attuned she was to the complex role of the "charity worker" and how sensitive she was to the problem of intrusion of a stranger into the life of a home. Why, indeed, should such a person be trusted? It makes sense that the charity worker is often treated with wariness and even mistrusted. That is why she must be clear about her own strong and self-serving—hopefully not in a narrow way—motivation. This clarity will help to forestall a slide into a patronizing paternalism, as if she knows better than the persons she seeks to serve what it is they require, what it is they desire, and what it is they fear.[5]

Notes

1. As a religious nonconformist in mid-seventeenth-century England, Bunyan suffered persecution, spending twelve years in Bedford gaol for open preaching. It was during a second and much shorter imprisonment in 1672 that he finished the first part of *Pilgrim's Progress*. The book has gone through many editions over the years. It is now available in a Penguin paperback edition.

2. In *Twenty Years at Hull-House*, Addams describes the pressure she was put under: "Of course in such an atmosphere a girl like myself, of serious not

to say priggish tendency, did not escape a concerted pressure to push her into the 'missionary field.' During the four years it was inevitable that every sort of evangelical appeal should have been made to reach the comparatively few 'unconverted' girls in the school. We were the subject of prayer at daily chapel exercise and the weekly prayer meeting, attendance upon which was obligatory. I was singularly unresponsive to all these forms of emotional appeal" (p. 49).

3. Nowadays, no doubt, the condition would likely be diagnosed as a form of depression and the young person would be medicated. If Prozac had existed in the 1880s, would there have been a Hull-House?

4. One of the most famous passages in Jane Addams's writings details her visit to the impoverished East End of London. Decaying vegetables and fruits were sold at auction on the Mile End Road, where "ill-clad people" bid "for a vegetable held up by the auctioneer, which he at last scornfully flung, with a gibe for its cheapness, to the successful bidder. . . . In the momentary pause only one man detached himself from the groups. He had bidden in a cabbage, and when it struck his hand, he instantly sat down on the curb, tore it with his teeth, and hastily devoured it, unwashed and uncooked as it was. . . . They [the assembled crowd] were huddled into ill-fitting, cast-off clothing, the ragged finery which one sees only in East London. Their pale faces were dominated by that most unlovely of human expressions, the cunning and shrewdness of the bargain-hunter who starves if he cannot make a successful trade, and yet the final impressions was not of ragged, tawdry clothing nor of pinched and sallow faces, but of myriads of hands, empty, pathetic, nerveless and workworn, showing white in the uncertain light of the street, clutching forward for food which was already unfit to eat" (*Twenty Years at Hull-House*, pp. 67–68).

5. One of the reasons she rejected Marxism and socialism lay in the stated presumption that somehow *only* Marx, or those who subscribed to his doctrine, *really* understood those "laws of motion" that govern capitalist society and the bourgeois social order. They alone, then, had access to the truth. She also pokes fun at the utopian fantasies associated with Marxism and socialism, recalling an incident that took place during a discussion at the Working People's Social Science Club at Hull-House. One ardent fellow had proclaimed that in the future socialist society everybody with a toothache would be able to seek a cure. A second fellow, not to be outdone, declared that in the future socialist society there would be no need for dentists as there would be no toothache. Socialism would bring an end to all miseries—even dental ones!

1

⁕

"THE MACBETH OF SHAKESPEARE"

IN THE ELEVENTH CENTURY Duncan and Macbeth were two grandsons of the reigning king of Scotland. In the course of time the old king peacefully died and Duncan ascended the throne. He had but the shadow of a claim over his cousin, he was not as gifted a man, he probably made no greater effort toward the crown and yet he gained it. The divine right of kings was bestowed upon him while Macbeth was merely one of his subjects. We should take Duncan to be one of those men who some way have the material universe on their side, a "great vague backing" in all they do and undertake, the word "luck" somewhat expresses their success, things turn out just to suit them, and honors are easily granted them. Macbeth had no doubt observed this ever since he could remember, it seemed perfectly natural for Duncan to be king and gain that which he desires. Macbeth is not envious, but he continually thinks of these things, he is a nervous man and cannot think calmly.

Shakespeare leaves us to imagine all this. He does not present Macbeth until these thoughts have begun to pursue and control him; until his mind has gained that sort of exasperation which comes from using living muscle against some lifeless insurmountable resistance.

All the scenes of the play are laid at night, and we are hurried on with feverish rapidity—we do not know the Macbeth of the day time, how he appears in council or battle—we meet only the nervous high strung man at night, pursued by phantoms and ghosts, and ever poetically designing a murder.

Note: "The Macbeth of Shakespeare," *Rockford Seminary Magazine*, vol. 8 (January 1880).

Shakespeare presents the man's thoughts 'ere he presents the man himself, and in the very first scene the three witches frighten us before we know what they are to represent. As Macbeth enters they hail him with the three titles his heart most desires; he starts, who wouldn't? The thoughts he has been thinking and thinking, have suddenly embodied themselves, and stand before him on the bold bare heath; they have all at once grown into definite purposes, have spoken out before a third person, Banquo, and he knows that ever afterward he must acknowledge them, that they will pursue and harrass him. We have all had the experience—how we prepare ourselves for sudden deeds by the intuitive choice of good and evil, or, as our thoughts go forth never to be recalled, how they increase and gain enormous proportions until we lose all control of them. But Macbeth had this experience in a way that was simply frightful; his thought grew so powerful as to assume form and shape, as to be endowed with life and a distinct physical existence to baffle and confront him. His first impulse is one of fear and terror at the metaphysical confusion in which he is entangled. He is lost in a maze of his own thoughts, he known [sic] not what is real and what is fantastical, he is filled with horrible imaginings and doubts; but slowly from all this confusion there arises a phantom distinctly before him, it seems afar off, he detaches it from himself, and yet he knows it is his own creation. He says:

> "Why do I yield to that suggestion,
> "Whose horrid image doth unfix my hair"—

That image is murder, it takes a poetical man to call it an image, but Macbeth tries to deceive himself and keep his heart of hearts pure. Here he yields to that impulse of a sort of self-preservation, that shielding of his inner character, he wishes not to harm or shock himself; he would gain a deadly end, but without the illness that should attend it; with this purpose he reorganizes the witches and phantoms, and shifts upon them the entire moral responsibility of his future actions, he follows them mechanically and saves himself—it is a phantom that murders Duncan.

He discloses his purpose to Lady Macbeth, and thus gives to her the physical or material responsibility, she plans and contrives, does all cooly and calmly, for she is but murdering a man—avenging her father;

Macbeth meanwhile is struggling throughout with murder itself, invisible yet clinging and horrible the phantom pursues him until the last moment. Just before the final deed he soliloquizes:

"Now o'er the one half world
Nature seems dead, and withered murder
Alarmed by his sentinel the wolf
Moves like a ghost"—

'Tis "withered murder" that leads him on to destruction, and he follows it as something inevitable. Macbeth has slowly prepared a splendid defense for himself, it is utterly impossible for him, murdering Duncan, to receive any conscious harm or any violent shock to his inner self, and yet he is thwarted by his own ends. He kills Duncan and comes back to his wife horror-struck and frightened, not because of the bloody deed, but because he has murdered sleep, because he has heard a voice cry, "Sleep no more! Macbeth does murder sleep!" No matter how often we read it, it always produces the same thrilling effect; the idea of a man murdering sleep; think of being pursued by withered murder and a sleepless sleep.

This then is the result, by getting rid of his will and following merely the poetical idea, he kills not a man, but an imaginary, an invisible horrible being; it is the only possible retribution and it is frightful.

After the death of Duncan, the rest of the play is virtually a repetition. Macbeth is driven from murder to murder, ghosts and phantoms pursue him, he consults again the weird sisters, gains courage and is lost through his own daring—a poetical man doing the worst deeds in a poetical sense—the philosophy of murder.

2

∽◇∽

"BREAD GIVERS"

FRIENDS AND CITIZENS OF ROCKFORD:—The class of 1881 has invited you this evening to the First Junior Exhibition ever given within the walls of Rockford Seminary. The fact of its being the first, seems to us a significant one, for it undoubtedly points more or less directly to a movement which is gradually claiming the universal attention. We mean the change which has taken place during the last fifty years in the ambition and aspirations of woman; we see this change most markedly in her education. It has passed from accomplishments and the arts of pleasing, to the development of her intellectual force, and her capabilities for direct labor. She wishes not to be a man, nor like a man, but she claims the same right to independent thought and action. Whether this movement is tending toward the ballot-box, or will gain simply equal intellectual advantages, no one can predict, but certain it is that woman has gained a new confidence in her possibilities, and a fresher hope in her steady progress.

We then, the class of 1881, in giving this our Junior Exhibition, are not trying to imitate our brothers in college; we are not restless and anxious for things beyond us, we simply claim the highest privileges of our time and avail ourselves of its best opportunities.

But while on the one hand, as young women of the 19th century, we gladly claim these privileges, and proudly assert our independence, on the other hand we still retain the old ideal of womanhood—the Saxon lady whose mission it was to give bread unto her household. So we have planned to be "Bread-givers" throughout our lives; believing that

Note: "Bread Givers," Junior Class Oration, *Daily Register* (Rockford), April 21, 1880.

in labor alone is happiness, and that the only true and honorable life is one filled with good works and honest toil, we have planned to idealize our labor, and thus happily fulfil Woman's Noblest Mission. But if at any time we should falter in our trust, if under the burden of years, we should for the moment doubt the high culture which comes from giving, then may be the memory of this evening when we were young and strong, when we presented to our friends a portion of the work already accomplished, and told them of the further labor we had planned for the future, then, I say, the memory of our Junior Exhibition may come to us as an incentive to renewed effort. It may prove to us a vow by which we pledged ourselves unto our high calling; and if through some turn of fortune we should be confined to the literal meaning of our words, if our destiny throughout our lives should be to give good, sweet, wholesome bread unto our loved ones, then perchance we will do even that the better, with more of conscious energy and innate power for the memory of our Junior Exhibition.

3

"CASSANDRA"

UPON THE BROAD TROJAN PLAIN for ten years the mighty warriors of Greece and Troy fought hand to hand for honor and justice. Safe within the city walls the stately Trojan dames ever wove with golden threads the history of the conflict. To one of these beautiful women, to Cassandra, daughter of Priam, suddenly came the power of prophecy. Cassandra fearlessly received the power, with clear judgment and unerring instinct she predicted the victory of the Greeks and the destruction of her father's city. But the brave warriors laughed to scorn the beautiful prophetess and called her mad. The frail girl stood conscious of Truth but she had no logic to convince the impatient defeated warriors, and no facts to gain their confidence, she could only assert and proclaim until at last in sooth she becomes mad.

This was the tragic fate of Cassandra—always to be in the right, and always to be disbelieved and rejected. Three thousand years ago this Trojan woman represented pure intuition, powerful and God-given in itself but failing to accomplish. She, who might have changed the entire destiny of the ancient world, becomes only a curse and a thorn to her brethren. I would call this a feminine trait of mind—an accurate perception of Truth and Justice which rests contented in itself, and will make no effort to confirm itself, or to organize through existing knowledge. Permit me to repeat my subject; a mighty intuitive perception of Truth which yet counts nothing in the force of the world.

The nineteenth century is distinguished by the sudden acquisition of much physical knowledge. The nineteenth century has proclaimed the duty of labor and the bond of brotherhood. These acquisitions and

---

Note: "Cassandra," Valedictory, *Rockford Seminary Magazine* (July 1881).

high thoughts of the century have increased each man's responsibility, but as yet have added nothing to the vitality and spontaneous motives of mankind. With increasing demands the force of society tends to be mechanical and conscious, rather than vital. In other words, while men with hard research into science, with sturdy and unremitting toil, have shown the power and magnificence of knowledge, somewhere, some one has shirked to perform for intuition the same hard labor.

Knowledge is reverenced, and the old beautiful force which Plato taught is treated with contempt. Intuition is not telling on the world. Occasionally a weak woman, striving to use her high gift, will verge out into spiritualism and clairvoyance, others will become sentimentalists or those women who bear through life a high discontent, because of their very keen-sightedness, yet have not power to help those around them. The world looks upon such women with mingled pity and contempt; they continually reinact [sic] the fate of the fearless, unfortunate Cassandra, because they failed to make themselves intelligible; they have not gained what the ancients called *auethoritas* [sic], right of speaker to make themselves heard, and prove to the world that an intuition is a force in the universe, and a part of nature; that an intuitive perception committed to a woman's charge is not a prejudice or a fancy, but one of the holy means given to mankind in their search for truth.[1]

I will make one exception—there is one means which has hitherto saved this force from complete loss and contempt. The divine force of love which ever exalts talent and cultivates woman's insight. A loving woman believes in ministering spirits; the belief comes to her that her child's every footstep is tenderly protected by a guardian angel. Let her not sit and dreamily watch her child; let her work her way to a sentient idea that shall sway and ennoble those around her. All that subtile [sic], force among women which is now dreaming fancy, might be changed into creative genius.

There is a way opened, women of the nineteenth century, to convert this wasted force to the highest use, and under the feminine mind, firm and joyous in its intuitions; a way opened by the scientific ideal of culture; only by the accurate study of at least one branch of physical science can the intuitive mind gain that life which the strong passion of science and study, feeds and forms, more self-dependent than love, confident in errorless purpose. With eyes accustomed to the search for

Truth, she will readily detect all self-deceit and fancy in herself; she will test whether her intuition is genuine and a part of nature, or merely a belief of her own. She will learn silence and self-denial, to express herself not by dogmatism, but by quiet, progressive development. And besides this training, there is certainly a place in science reserved for this stamp of mind; there are discoveries to be made which cannot come by induction, only through perception, such as the mental laws which govern suggestion, or the place that rhythm [sic] holds in nature's movements. These laws have remained undiscovered for lack of the needed intuitive minds. Could an intuitive mind gain this scholarly training, or discover one of these laws, then she would attain her *auethoritas* [sic]. Men would see that while the searching for Truth, the patient adding one to one is the highest and noblest employment of the human faculties. Higher and nobler than even this, and infinitely more difficult, is the intuitive seeing of Truth, the quick recognition of the true and genuine wherever it appears.

Having gained accuracy, would woman bring this force to bear throughout morals and justice, then she must take the active, busy world as a test for the genuineness of her intuition. In active labor she will be ready to accept the promptings that come from growing insight, and when her sympathies are so enlarged that she can weep as easily over a famine in India as a pale child at her door, then she can face social ills and social problems as tenderly and as intuitively as she can now care for and understand a crippled factory child.

The actual Justice must be established in the world by trained intelligence; by broadened sympathies toward the individual man and woman who crosses one's path, only an intuitive mind has a grasp comprehensive enough to embrace the opposing facts and forces.

The opening of the ages has long been waiting for this type of womanhood. The Egyptians called her Neith; the Hebrews, Sophia, or Wisdom; the Greeks, Athene; the Romans, Justicia, holding in her hands the scale pans of the world; the Germans called her the Wise-woman, who was not all knowing, but had a power deeper and more primordial than knowledge. Now is the time for a faint realization of this type, with her faculties clear and acute, from the study of science, and with her hand upon the magnetic chain of humanity. Then the story of Cassandra will be forgotten, which now constantly meets and stirs us with its proud pathos.

Notes

1. On the right of a speaker to be heard, the ancient meaning of freedom of speech, see Peter Brown's brilliant essay on antique rhetoric, *Power and Persuasion in Late Antiquity: Towards a Christian Empire* (Madison: University of Wisconsin Press, 1992).

4

"THE SUBJECTIVE NECESSITY FOR SOCIAL SETTLEMENTS"

HULL HOUSE, WHICH WAS CHICAGO'S first Settlement, was established in September, 1889. It represented no association, but was opened by two women, backed by many friends, in the belief that the mere foothold of a house, easily accessible, ample in space, hospitable and tolerant in spirit, situated in the midst of the large foreign colonies which so easily isolate themselves in American cities, would be in itself a serviceable thing for Chicago. Hull House endeavors to make social intercourse express the growing sense of the economic unity of society. It is an effort to add the social function to democracy. It was opened on the theory that the dependence of classes on each other is reciprocal; and that as "the social relation is essentially a reciprocal relation, it gave a form of expression that has peculiar value."

This paper is an attempt to treat of the subjective necessity for Social Settlements, to analyze the motives which underlie a movement based not only upon conviction, but genuine emotion. Hull House of Chicago is used as an illustration, but so far as the analysis is faithful, it obtains wherever educated young people are seeking an outlet for that sentiment of universal brotherhood which the best spirit of our times is forcing from an emotion into a motive.

Note: "The Subjective Necessity for Social Settlements," in Henry C. Adams (ed.), *Philanthropy and Social Progress, Seven Essays by Miss Jane Addams, Robert A. Woods, Father J.O.S. Huntington, Professor Franklin H. Giddings and Bernard Bosanquet. Delivered before the School of Applied Ethics at Plymouth, Mass., during the Session of 1892* (New York: Thomas Y. Crowell, 1893).

I have divided the motives which constitute the subjective pressure toward Social Settlements into three great lines: the first contains the desire to make the entire social organism democratic, to extend democracy beyond its political expression; the second is the impulse to share the race life, and to bring as much as possible of social energy and the accumulation of civilization to those portions of the race which have little; the third springs from a certain *renaissance* of Christianity, a movement toward its early humanitarian aspects.

It is not difficult to see that although America is pledged to the democratic ideal, the view of democracy has been partial, and that its best achievement thus far has been pushed along the line of the franchise. Democracy has made little attempt to assert itself in social affairs. We have refused to move beyond the position of its eighteenth-century leaders, who believed that political equality alone would secure all good to all men. We conscientiously followed the gift of the ballot hard upon the gift of freedom to the negro, but we are quite unmoved by the fact that he lives among us in a practical social ostracism. We hasten to give the franchise to the immigrant from a sense of justice, from a tradition that he ought to have it, while we dub him with epithets deriding his past life or present occupation, and feel no duty to invite him to our houses. We are forced to acknowledge that it is only in our local and national politics that we try very hard for the ideal so dear to those who were enthusiasts when the century was young. We have almost given it up as our ideal in social intercourse. There are city wards in which many of the votes are sold for drinks and dollars; still there is a remote pretence, at least a fiction current, that a man's vote is his own. The judgment of the voter is consulted and an opportunity for remedy given. There is not even a theory in the social order, not a shadow answering to the polls in politics. The time may come when the politician who sells one by one to the highest bidder all the offices in his grasp, will not be considered more base in his code of morals, more hardened in his practice, than the woman who constantly invites to her receptions those alone who bring her an equal social return, who shares her beautiful surroundings only with those who minister to a liking she has for successful social events. In doing this is she not just as unmindful of the common weal, as unscrupulous in her use of power, as is any city "boss" who consults only the interests of the "ring"?

In politics "bossism" arouses a scandal. It goes on in society constantly and is only beginning to be challenged. Our consciences are becoming tender in regard to the lack of democracy in social affairs. We are perhaps entering upon the second phase of democracy, as the French philosophers entered upon the first, somewhat bewildered by its logical conclusions. The social organism has broken down through large districts of our great cities. Many of the people living there are very poor, the majority of them without leisure or energy for anything but the gain of subsistence. They move often from one wretched lodging to another. They live for the moment side by side, many of them without knowledge of each other, without fellowship, without local tradition or public spirit, without social organization of any kind. Practically nothing is done to remedy this. The people who might do it, who have the social tact and training, the large houses, and the traditions and custom of hospitality, live in other parts of the city. The club-houses, libraries, galleries, and semi-public conveniences for social life are also blocks away. We find working-men organized into armies of producers because men of executive ability and business sagacity have found it to their interests thus to organize them. But these working-men are not organized socially; although living in crowded tenement-houses, they are living without a corresponding social contact. The chaos is as great as it would be were they working in huge factories without foreman or superintendent. Their ideas and resources are cramped. The desire for higher social pleasure is extinct. They have no share in the traditions and social energy which make for progress. Too often their only place of meeting is a saloon, their only host a bartender; a local demagogue forms their public opinion. Men of ability and refinement, of social power and university cultivation, stay away from them. Personally, I believe the men who lose most are those who thus stay away. But the paradox is here: when cultivated people do stay away from a certain portion of the population, when all social advantages are persistently withheld, it may be for years, the result itself is pointed at as a reason, is used as an argument, for the continued withholding.

It is constantly said that because the masses have never had social advantages they do not want them, that they are heavy and dull, and that it will take political or philanthropic machinery to change them. This divides a city into rich and poor; into the favored, who express their sense of the social obligation by gifts of money, and into the unfavored, who express it by clamoring for a "share"—both of them actuated by a vague

sense of justice. This division of the city would be more justifiable, however, if the people who thus isolate themselves on certain streets and use
their social ability for each other gained enough thereby and added sufficient to the sum total of social progress to justify the withholding of the
pleasures and results of that progress from so many people who ought to
have them. But they cannot accomplish this. "The social spirit discharges
itself in many forms, and no one form is adequate to its total expression." We are all uncomfortable in regard to the sincerity of our best
phrases, because we hesitate to translate our philosophy into the deed.

It is inevitable that those who feel most keenly this insincerity and
partial living should be our young people, our so-called educated
young people who accomplish little toward the solution of this social
problem, and who bear the brunt of being cultivated into unnourished,
over-sensitive lives. They have been shut off from the common labor by
which they live and which is a great source of moral and physical
health. They feel a fatal want of harmony between their theory and
their lives, a lack of co-ordination between thought and action. I think
it is hard for us to realize how seriously many of them are taking to the
notion of human brotherhood, how eagerly they long to give tangible
expression to the democratic ideal. These young men and women, longing to socialize their democracy, are animated by certain hopes.

These hopes may be loosely formulated thus: that if in a democratic
country nothing can be permanently achieved save through the masses
of the people, it will be impossible to establish a higher political life
than the people themselves crave; that it is difficult to see how the notion of a higher civic life can be fostered save through common intercourse; that the blessings which we associate with a life of refinement
and cultivation can be made universal and must be made universal if
they are to be permanent; that the good we secure for ourselves is pre-
carious and uncertain, is floating in mid-air, until it is secured for all of
us and incorporated into our common life.

These hopes are responsible for results in various directions, pre-
eminently in the extension of educational advantages. We find that all
educational matters are more democratic in their political than in their
social aspects. The public schools in the poorest and most crowded
wards of the city are inadequate to the number of children, and many
of the teachers are ill-prepared and overworked; but in each ward there
is an effort to secure public education. The school-house itself stands as

a pledge that the city recognizes and endeavors to fulfil the duty of educating its children. But what becomes of these children when they are no longer in public schools? Many of them never come under the influence of a professional teacher nor a cultivated friend after they are twelve. Society at large does little for their intellectual development. The dream of transcendentalists that each New England village would be a university, that every child taken from the common school would be put into definite lines of study and mental development, had its unfulfilled beginning in the village lyceum and lecture courses, and has its feeble representative now in the multitude of clubs for study which are so sadly restricted to educators, to the leisure class, or only to the advanced and progressive wage-workers.[1]

The University Extension movement—certainly when it is closely identified with Settlements—would not confine learning to those who already want it, or to those who, by making an effort, can gain it, or to those among whom professional educators are already at work, but would take it to the tailors of East London and the dock-laborers of the Thames.[2] It requires tact and training, love of learning, and the conviction of the justice of its diffusion to give it to people whose intellectual faculties are untrained and disused. But men in England are found who do it successfully, and it is believed there are men and women in America who can do it. I also believe that the best work in University Extension can be done in Settlements, where the teaching will be further socialized, where the teacher will grapple his students, not only by formal lectures, but by every hook possible to the fuller intellectual life which he represents. This teaching requires distinct methods, for it is true of people who have been allowed to remain undeveloped and whose faculties are inert and sterile, that they cannot take their learning heavily. It has to be diffused in a social atmosphere. Information held in solution, a medium of fellowship and good-will can be assimilated by the dullest.

If education is, as Froebel defined it, "deliverance," deliverance of the forces of the body and mind, then the untrained must first be delivered from all constraint and rigidity before their faculties can be used. Possibly one of the most pitiful periods in the drama of the much-praised young American who attempts to rise in life is the time when his educational requirements seem to have locked him up and made him rigid. He fancies himself shut off from his uneducated family and misunderstood by his friends. He is bowed down by his mental accumulations and often gets no farther than to carry them through life as a great burden. Not once has he had a glimpse of the delights of knowledge. Intellectual life requires for its expansion and manifestation the influence and assimilation of the interests and affections of others. Mazzini, that greatest of all democrats, who broke his heart over the condition of the South European peasantry, said: "Education is not merely a necessity of true life by which the individual renews his vital force in the vital force of humanity; it is a Holy Communion with generations dead and living, by which he fecundates all his faculties. When he is withheld from this Communion for generations, as the Italian peasant has been, we point our finger at him and say, 'He is like a beast of the field; he must be controlled by force.'" Even to this it is sometimes added that it is absurd to educate him, immoral to disturb his content. We stupidly use again the effect as an argument for a continuance of the cause. It is needless to say that a Settlement is a protest against a restricted view of education, and makes it possible for every educated man or woman with a teaching faculty to find out those who are ready to be taught. The social and educational activities of a Settlement are but differing manifestations of the attempt to socialize democracy, as is the existence of the settlement itself.

I find it somewhat difficult to formulate the second line of motives which I believe to constitute the trend of the subjective pressure toward the Settlement. There is something primordial about these motives, but I am perhaps over-bold in designating them as a great desire to share the race life. We all bear traces of the starvation struggle which for so long made up the life of the race. Our very organism holds memories and glimpses of that long life of our ancestors which still goes on among so many of our contemporaries. Nothing so deadens the sympathies and shrivels the power of enjoyment as the persistent keeping away from the great opportunities for helpfulness and a continual ignoring of the starvation struggle which makes up the life of at least half the race. To shut one's self away from that half of the race life is to shut one's self away from the most vital part of it; it is to live out but half the humanity which we have been born heir to and to use but half our faculties. We have all had longings for a fuller life which should include the use of these faculties. These longings are the physical complement of the "Intimations of Immortality" on which no ode has yet been written. To portray these would be the work of a poet, and it is hazardous for any but a poet to attempt it.

You may remember the forlorn feeling which occasionally seizes you when you arrive early in the morning a stranger in a great city. The stream of laboring people goes past you as you gaze through the plate-glass window of your hotel. You see hard-working men lifting great burdens; you hear the driving and jostling of huge carts. Your heart sinks with a sudden sense of futility. The door opens behind you and you turn to the man who brings you in your breakfast with a quick sense of human fellowship. You find yourself praying that you may never lose your hold on it all. A more poetic prayer would be that the great mother breasts of our common humanity, with its labor and suffering and its homely comforts, may never be withheld from you. You turn helplessly to the waiter. You feel that it would be almost grotesque to claim from him the sympathy you crave. Civilization has placed you far apart, but you resent your position with a sudden sense of snobbery. Literature is full of portrayals of these glimpses. They come to shipwrecked men on rafts; they overcome the differences of an incongruous multitude when in the presence of a great danger or when moved by a common enthusiasm. They are not, however, confined to such moments, and if we were in the habit of telling them to each other, the recital would be as long as the tales of children are, when they sit down on the green grass and confide to each other how many times they have remembered that they lived once before. If these tales are the stirring of inherited impressions, just so surely is the other the striving of inherited powers.

"There is nothing after disease, indigence, and a sense of guilt so fatal to health and to life itself as the want of a proper outlet for active faculties." I have seen young girls suffer and grow sensibly lowered in vitality in the first years after they leave school. In our attempt then to give a girl pleasure and freedom from care we succeed, for the most part, in making her pitifully miserable. She finds "life" so different from what she expected it to be. She is besotted with innocent little ambitions, and does not understand this apparent waste of herself, this elaborate preparation, if no work is provided for her. There is a heritage of noble obligation which young people accept and long to perpetuate. The desire for action, the wish to right wrong and alleviate suffering, haunts them daily. Society smiles at it indulgently instead of making it of value to itself. The wrong to them begins even farther back, when we restrain the first childish desires for "doing good" and tell them that they must wait until they are older and better fitted. We intimate that social obligation begins at a fixed date, forgetting that it begins with birth itself. We treat them as children who, with strong-growing limbs, are allowed to use their legs but not their arms, or whose legs are daily carefully exercised that after awhile their arms may be put to high use. We do this in spite of the protest of the best educators, Locke and Pestalozzi. We are fortunate in the mean time if their unused members do not weaken and disappear. They do sometimes. There are a few girls who, by the time they are "educated," forget their old childish desires to help the world and to play with poor little girls "who haven't playthings." Parents are often inconsistent. They deliberately expose their daughters to knowledge of the distress in the world. They send them to hear missionary addresses on famines in India and China; they accompany them to lectures on the suffering in Siberia; they agitate together over the forgotten region of East London. In addition to this, from babyhood the altruistic tendencies of these daughters are persistently cultivated. They are taught to be self-forgetting and self-sacrificing, to consider the good of the Whole before the good of the Ego. But when all this information and culture show results, when the daughter comes back from college and begins to recognize her social claim to the "submerged tenth," and to evince a disposition to fulfil it, the family claim is strenuously asserted; she is told that she is unjustified, ill-advised in her efforts. If she persists the family too often are injured and unhappy, unless the efforts are called missionary, and the religious zeal of the family carry them over their sense of abuse. When this zeal does not exist the result is perplexing. It is a curious violation of what we would fain believe a fundamental law—that the final return of the Deed is upon the head of the Doer. The Deed is that of exclusiveness and caution, but the return instead of falling upon the head of the exclusive and cautious, falls upon a young head full of generous and unselfish plans. The girl loses something vital out of her life which she is entitled to. She is restricted and unhappy; her elders, meanwhile, are unconscious of the situation, and we have all the elements of a tragedy.

We have in America a fast-growing number of cultivated young people who have no recognized outlet for their active faculties. They hear constantly of the great social maladjustment, but no way is provided for them to change it, and their uselessness hangs about them heavily. Huxley declares that the sense of uselessness is the severest shock which the human system can sustain, and that, if persistently sustained, it results in atrophy of function. These young people have had advantages of college, of European travel and economic study, but they are sustaining this shock of inaction. They have pet phrases, and they tell you that the things that make us all alike are stronger than the things that make us different. They say that all men are united by needs and sympathies far more permanent and radical than anything that temporarily divides them and sets them in opposition to each other. If they affect art, they say that the decay in artistic expression is due to the decay in ethics, that art when shut away from the human interests and from the great mass of humanity is self-destructive. They tell their elders with all the bitterness of youth that if they expect success from them in business, or politics, or in whatever lines their ambition for them has run, they must let them consult all of humanity; that they must let them find out what the people want and how they want it. It is only the stronger young people, however, who formulate this. Many of them dissipate their energies in so-called enjoyment. Others, not content with that, go on studying and go back to college for their second degrees, not that they are especially fond of study, but because they want something definite to do, and their powers have been trained in the direction of mental accumulation. Many are buried beneath mere mental accumulation with lowered vitality and discontent. Walter Besant says they have had the vision that Peter had when he saw the great sheet let down from heaven, wherein was neither clean nor unclean.[3] He calls it the sense of humanity. It is not philanthropy nor benevolence. It is a thing fuller and wider than either of these. This young life, so sincere in its emotion and good phrases and yet so undirected, seems to me as pitiful as the other great mass of destitute lives. One is supplementary to the other, and some method of communication can surely be devised. Mr. Barnett, who urged the first Settlement,—Toynbee Hall, in East London,—recognized this need of outlet for the young men of Oxford and Cambridge, and hoped that the Settlement would supply the communication.[4] It is easy to see why the Settlement movement originated in England, where the years of education are more constrained and definite than they are here, where class distinctions are more rigid. The necessity of it was greater there, but we are fast feeling the pressure of the need and meeting the necessity for Settlements in America. Our young people feel nervously the need of putting theory into action, and respond quickly to the Settlement form of activity.

The third division of motives which I believe make toward the Settlement is the result of a certain *renaissance* going forward in Christianity.

The impulse to share the lives of the poor, the desire to make social service, irrespective of propaganda, express the spirit of Christ, is as old as Christianity itself. We have no proof from the records themselves that the early Roman Christians, who strained their simple art to the point of grotesqueness in their eagerness to record a "good news" on the walls of the catacombs, considered this "good news" a religion. Jesus had no set of truths labelled "Religious." On the contrary, his doctrine was that all truth is one, that the appropriation of it is freedom. His teaching had no dogma to mark it off from truth and action in general. He himself called it a revelation—a life. These early Roman Christians received the Gospel message, a command to love all men, with a certain joyous simplicity. The image of the Good Shepherd is blithe and gay beyond the gentlest shepherd of Greek mythology; the hart no longer pants, but rushes to the water brooks. The Christians looked for the continuous revelation, but believed what Jesus said, that this revelation to be held and made manifest must be put into terms of action; that action is the only medium man has for receiving and appropriating truth. "If any man will do His will, he shall know of the doctrine."

That Christianity has to be revealed and embodied in the line of social progress is a corollary to the simple proposition that man's action is found in his social relationships in the way in which he connects with his fellows, that his motives for action are the zeal and affection with which he regards his fellows. By this simple process was created a deep enthusiasm for humanity, which regarded man as at once the organ and object of revelation; and by this process came about that wonderful fellowship, that true democracy of the early Church, that so captivates the imagination. The early Christians were pre-eminently non-resistant. They believed in love as a cosmic force. There was no iconoclasm during the minor peace of the Church. They did not yet denounce, nor tear down temples, nor preach the end of the world. They grew to a mighty number, but it never occurred to them, either in their weakness or their strength, to regard other men for an instant as their foes or as aliens. The spectacle of the Christians loving all men was the most astounding Rome had ever seen. They were eager to sacrifice themselves for the weak, for children and the aged. They identified themselves with slaves and did not avoid the plague. They longed to share the common lot that they might receive the constant revelation. It was a new treasure which the early Christians added to the sum of all treasures, a joy hitherto unknown in the world—

the joy of finding the Christ which lieth in each man, but which no man can unfold save in fellowship. A happiness ranging from the heroic to the pastoral enveloped them. They were to possess a revelation as long as life had new meaning to unfold, new action to propose.

I believe that there is a distinct turning among many young men and women toward this simple acceptance of Christ's message. They resent the assumption that Christianity is a set of ideas which belong to the religious consciousness, whatever that may be, that it is a thing to be proclaimed and instituted apart from the social life of the community. They insist that it shall seek a simple and natural expression in the social organism itself. The Settlement movement is only one manifestation of that wider humanitarian movement which throughout Christendom, but pre-eminently in England, is endeavoring to embody itself, not in a sect, but in society itself. Tolstoï has reminded us all very forcibly of Christ's principle of non-resistance. His formulation has been startling and his expression has deviated from the general movement, but there is little doubt that he has many adherents, men and women who are philosophically convinced of the futility of opposition, who believe that evil can be overcome only with good and cannot be opposed. If love is the creative force of the universe, the principle which binds men together, and by their interdependence on each other makes them human, just so surely is anger and the spirit of opposition the destructive principle of the universe, that which tears down, thrusts men apart, and makes them isolated and brutal.

I cannot, of course, speak for other Settlements, but it would, I think, be unfair to Hull House not to emphasize the conviction with which the first residents went there, that it would simply be a foolish and an unwarrantable expenditure of force to oppose or to antagonize any individual or set of people in the neighborhood; that whatever of good the House had to offer should be put into positive terms; that its residents should live with opposition to no man, with recognition of the good in every man, even the meanest. I believe that this turning, this *renaissance* of the early Christian humanitarianism, is going on in America, in Chicago, if you please, without leaders who write or philosophize, without much speaking, but with a bent to express in social service, in terms of action, the spirit of Christ.[5] Certain it is that spiritual force is found in the Settlement movement, and it is also true that this force must be evoked and must be called into play before the success of any Settlement is assured. There must be the over-mastering belief that all that is noblest in life is common to men as men, in order to accentuate the likenesses and ignore the differences which are found among the people whom the Settlement constantly brings into juxtaposition. It may be true, as Frederic Harrison insists, that the very religious fervor of man can be turned into love for his race and his desire for a future life into content to live in the echo of his deeds. How far the Positivists' formula of the high ardor for humanity can carry the Settlement movement, Mrs. Humphry Ward's house in London may in course of time illustrate.[6] Paul's formula of seeking for the Christ which lieth in each man and founding our likenesses on him seems a simpler formula to many of us.

If you have heard a thousand voices singing in the Hallelujah Chorus in Handel's "Messiah," you have found that the leading voices could still be distinguished, but that the differences of training and cultivation between them and the voices of the chorus were lost in the unity of purpose and the fact that they were all human voices lifted by a high motive. This is a weak illustration of what a Settlement attempts to do. It aims, in a measure, to lead whatever of social life its neighborhood may afford, to focus and give form to that life, to bring to bear upon it the results of cultivation and training; but it receives in exchange for the music of isolated voices the volume and strength of the chorus. It is quite impossible for me to say in what proportion or degree the subjective necessity which led to the opening of Hull House combined the three trends: first the desire to interpret democracy in social terms; secondly, the impulse beating at the very source of our lives urging us to aid in the race progress; and, thirdly, the Christian movement toward Humanitarianism. It is difficult to analyze a living thing; the analysis is at best imperfect. Many more motives may blend with the three trends; possibly the desire for a new form of social success due to the nicety of imagination, which refuses worldly pleasures unmixed with the joys of self-sacrifice; possibly a love of approbation, so vast that it is not content with the treble clapping of delicate hands, but wishes also to hear the bass notes from toughened palms, may mingle with these.

The Settlement, then, is an experimental effort to aid in the solution of the social and industrial problems which are engendered by the modern conditions of life in a great city. It insists that these problems are not confined to any one portion of a city. It is an attempt to relieve, at the same time, the over-accumulation at one end of society and the destitution at the other; but it assumes that this over-accumulation and destitution is most sorely felt in the things that pertain to social and educational advantage. From its very nature it can stand for no political or social *propaganda.* It must, in a sense, give the warm welcome of an inn to all such *propaganda,* if perchance one of them be found an angel. The one thing to be dreaded in the Settlement is that it lose its flexibility, its power of quick adaptation, its readiness to change its methods as its environment may demand. It must be open to conviction and must have a deep and abiding sense of tolerance. It must be hospitable and ready for experiment. It should demand from its residents a scientific patience in the accumulation of facts and the steady holding of their sympathies as one of the best instruments for that accumulation. It must be grounded in a philosophy whose foundation is on the solidarity of the human race, a philosophy which will not waver when the race happens to be represented by a drunken woman or an idiot boy.[7] Its residents must be emptied of all conceit of opinion and all self-assertion, and ready to arouse and interpret the public opinion of their neighborhood. They must be content to live quietly side by side with their neighbors until they grow into a sense of relationship and mutual interests. Their neighbors are held apart by differences of race and language which the residents can more easily overcome. They are bound to see the needs of their neighborhood as a whole, to furnish data for legislation, and use their influence to secure it. In short, residents are pledged to devote themselves to the duties of good citizenship and to the arousing of the social energies which too largely lie dormant in every neighborhood given over to industrialism. They are bound to regard the entire life of their city as organic, to make an effort to unify it, and to protest against its over-differentiation.

Our philanthropies of all sorts are growing so expensive and institutional that it is to be hoped the Settlement movement will keep itself facile and unincumbered. From its very nature it needs no endowment, no roll of salaried officials. Many residents must always come in the attitude of students, assuming that the best teacher of life is life itself, and regarding the Settlement as a classroom. Hull House from the outside may appear to be a cumbrous plant of manifold industries, with its round of clubs and classes, its day nursery, diet kitchen, library, art exhibits, lectures, statistical work and polyglot demands for information, a thousand people coming and going in an average week. But viewed as a business enterprise it is not costly, for from this industry are eliminated two great items of expense—the cost of superintendence and the cost of distribution. All the management and teaching are voluntary and unpaid, and the consumers—to continue the commercial phraseology—are at the door and deliver the goods themselves. In the instance of Hull House, rent is also largely eliminated through the courtesy of the owner.

Life is manifold and Hull House attempts to respond to as many sides as possible. It does this fearlessly, feeling sure that among the able people of Chicago are those who will come to do the work when once the outline is indicated. It pursues much the same policy in regard to money. It seems to me an advantage—this obligation to appeal to business men for their judgment and their money, to the educated for their effort and enthusiasm, to the neighborhood for their response and cooperation. It tests the sanity of an idea, and we enter upon a new line of activity with a feeling of support and confidence. We have always been perfectly frank with our neighbors. I have never tried so earnestly to set forth the gist of the Settlement movement, to make clear its reciprocity, as I have to them. At first we were often asked why we came to live there when we could afford to live somewhere else. I remember one man who used to shake his head and say it was "the strangest thing he had met in his experience," but who was finally convinced that it was not strange but natural. I trust that now it seems natural to all of us that the Settlement should be there. If it is natural to feed the hungry and care for the sick, it is certainly natural to give pleasure to the young and to minister to the deep-seated craving for social intercourse that all men feel. Whoever does it is rewarded by something which, if not gratitude, is at least spontaneous and vital and lacks that irksome sense of obligation with which a substantial benefit is too often acknowledged. The man who looks back to the person who first put him in the way of good literature has no alloy in his gratitude.

I remember when the statement seemed to me very radical that the salvation of East London was the destruction of West London; but I believe now that there will be no wretched quarters in our cities at all when the conscience of each man is so touched that he prefers to live with the poorest of his brethren, and not with the richest of them that his income will allow. It is to be hoped that this moving and living will at length be universal and need no name. The Settlement movement is from its nature a provisional one. It is easy in writing a paper to make all philosophy point one particular moral and all history adorn one particular tale; but I hope you forgive me for reminding you that the best speculative philosophy sets forth the solidarity of the human race; that the highest moralists have taught that without the advance and improvement of the whole no man can hope for any lasting improvement in his own moral or material individual condition. The subjective necessity for Social Settlements is identical with that necessity which urges us on toward social and individual salvation.

Notes

1. The New England Transcendentalists were a philosophical movement that included many luminaries. One of these was Bronson Alcott, a famous educator and the father of Louisa May Alcott. Bronson Alcott's dates are 1799–1888. The Transcendentalists centered around Concord, Massachusetts, and also spearheaded an experiment in group living called Brook Farm.

2. The university extension movement aimed at bringing universities to the people. The general aim was to operate university extension branches throughout a country in order to promote new methods in industry and agriculture and, in general, to extend democracy by democratizing education.

3. Walter Besant (1836–1901), a British novelist and journalist who also contributed directly to philanthropic reform. Many of his novels are set in London's impoverished East End. It was the sight of the "submerged tenth" in the East End that helped to set Jane Addams on her course of reform.

4. Samuel Barnett (1844–1913) was one of the leaders of the settlement movement in England; Jane Addams looked to his efforts as an inspiration for her own.

5. Addams's reference point here is to the so-called social gospel movement of Christianity as a public and social force. Social gospelers emphasized the ethical message of Jesus of Nazareth as a call to social ministry. Salvation was deemphasized in favor of social change, itself construed as a form of earthly salvation.

6. Mrs. Humphry Ward (1851–1920), a prolific but now little-read English writer.

7. Addams's language here is not intended as derisory. "Idiot" was a clinical characterization during her day for those who were caught in the throes of profound mental disorientation or loss; drunkenness was thought of as a vice, not an illness. In other words, the cultural medicalization of various conditions had not yet taken place.

5

"THE OBJECTIVE VALUE OF A SOCIAL SETTLEMENT"

IN TREATING OF THE VALUE of the Social Settlement, I shall confine myself to Hull House, and what it has been able to do for its neighborhood, only because I am most familiar with that Settlement.

Hull House stands on South Halsted Street, next door to the corner of Polk. South Halsted Street is thirty-two miles long and one of the great thoroughfares of Chicago. Polk Street crosses Halsted midway between the stock-yards to the south and the ship-building yards on the north branch of the Chicago River. For the six miles between these two industries the street is lined with shops of butchers and grocers, with dingy and gorgeous saloons, and pretentious establishments for the sale of ready-made clothing. Polk Street, running west from Halsted Street, grows rapidly more respectable; running a mile east to State Street, it grows steadily worse, and crosses a net-work of gilded vice on the corners of Clark Street and Fourth Avenue.

Hull House is an ample old residence, well built and somewhat ornately decorated after the manner of its time, 1856. It has been used for many purposes, and although battered by its vicissitudes, is essentially sound and has responded kindly to repairs and careful furnishing. Its wide hall and open fires always insure it a gracious aspect. It once

Note: "The Objective Value of a Social Settlement," in Henry C. Adams (ed.), *Philanthropy and Social Progress, Seven Essays by Miss Jane Addams, Robert A. Woods, Father J.O.S. Huntington, Professor Franklin H. Giddings and Bernard Bosanquet. Delivered before the School of Applied Ethics at Plymouth, Mass., during the Session of 1892* (New York: Thomas Y. Crowell, 1893).

stood in the suburbs, but the city has steadily grown up around it and its site now has corners on three or four more or less distinct foreign colonies. Between Halsted Street and the river live about ten thousand Italians: Neapolitans, Sicilians, and Calabrians, with an occasional Lombard or Venetian. To the south on Twelfth Street are many Germans, and side streets are given over almost entirely to Polish and Russian Jews. Still farther south, these Jewish colonies merge into a huge Bohemian colony, so vast that Chicago ranks as the third Bohemian city in the world. To the northwest are many Canadian-French, clannish in spite of their long residence in America, and to the north are many Irish and first-generation Americans. On the streets directly west and farther north are well-to-do English-speaking families, many of whom own their houses and have lived in the neighborhood for years. I know one man who is still living in his old farm-house. This corner of Polk and Halsted Streets is in the fourteenth precinct of the nineteenth ward. This ward has a population of about fifty thousand, and at the last presidential election registered 7072 voters. It has had no unusual political scandal connected with it, but its aldermen are generally saloon-keepers and its political manipulations are those to be found in the crowded wards where the activities of the petty politician are unchecked.

The policy of the public authorities of never taking an initiative, and always waiting to be urged to do their duty, is fatal in a ward where there is no initiative among the citizens. The idea underlying our self-government breaks down in such a ward. The streets are inexpressibly dirty, the number of schools inadequate, factory legislation unenforced, the street-lighting bad, the paving miserable and altogether lacking in the alleys and smaller streets, and the stables defy all laws of sanitation. Hundreds of houses are unconnected with the street sewer. The older and richer inhabitants seem anxious to move away as rapidly as they can afford it. They make room for newly arrived immigrants who are densely ignorant of civic duties. This substitution of the older inhabitants is accomplished industrially also in the south and east quarters of the ward. The Hebrews and Italians do the finishing for the great clothing-manufacturers formerly done by Americans, Irish, and Germans, who refused to submit to the extremely low prices to which the sweating system has reduced their successors. As the design of the sweating system is the elimination of rent from the manufacture of clothing, the "outside work" is begun after the clothing leaves the cutter. An unscrupulous contractor regards no basement as too dark, no stable loft too foul, no rear shanty too provisional, no tenement room too small for his workroom, as these conditions imply low rental. Hence these shops abound in the worst of the foreign districts, where the sweater easily finds his cheap basement and his home finishers. There is a constant tendency to employ school-children, as much of the home and shop work can easily be done by children.

The houses of the ward, for the most part wooden, were originally built for one family and are now occupied by several. They are after the type of the inconvenient frame cottages found in the poorer suburbs twenty years ago. Many of them were built where they now stand; others were brought thither on rollers, because their previous site had been taken for a factory. The fewer brick tenement buildings which are three or four stories high are comparatively new. There are few huge and foul tenements. The little wooden houses have a temporary aspect, and for this reason, perhaps, the tenement-house legislation in Chicago is totally inadequate. Back tenements flourish; many houses have no water supply save the faucet in the back yard; there are no fire escapes; the garbage and ashes are placed in wooden boxes which are fastened to the street pavements. One of the most discouraging features about the present system of tenement houses is that many are owned by sordid and ignorant immigrants. The theory that wealth brings responsibility, that possession entails at length education and refinement, in these cases fails utterly. The children of an Italian immigrant owner do not go to school and are no improvement on their parents. His wife picks rags from the street gutter, and laboriously sorts them in a dingy court. Wealth may do something for her self-complacency and feeling of consequence; it certainly does nothing for her comfort or her children's improvement nor for the cleanliness of any one concerned. Another thing that prevents better houses in Chicago is the tentative attitude of the real-estate men. Many unsavory conditions are allowed to continue which would be regarded with horror if they were considered permanent. Meanwhile, the wretched conditions persist until at least two generations of children have been born and reared in them.

Our ward contains two hundred and fifty-five saloons; our own precinct boasts of eight, and the one directly north of us twenty. This allows one saloon to every twenty-eight voters, and there is no doubt that the saloon is the centre of the liveliest political and social life of the ward. The leases and fixtures of these saloons are, in the majority of cases, owned by the wholesale liquor houses, and the saloon-keeper himself is often a bankrupt.

There are seven churches and two missions in the ward. All of these are small and somewhat struggling, save the large Catholic church connected with the Jesuit College on the south boundary of the ward, and the French Catholic church on the west boundary. Out of these nine religious centres there are but three in which the service is habitually conducted in English. This enumeration of churches does not include the chevras found among the recently immigrated Jews of the Ashkenazite branch. The chevras combine the offices of public worship and the rites of mourning with the function of a sick benefit and mutual aid society. There are seven Catholic parochial schools in the ward, accommodating 6244 children; three Protestant schools care for 141 children. A fine manual-training school sustained by the Hebrews is found in the seventh ward just south of us. In the same ward is the receiving shelter for the Jewish refugees.

This site for a Settlement was selected in the first instance because of its diversity and the variety of activity for which it presented an opportunity. It has been the aim of the residents to respond to all sides of the neighborhood life: not to the poor people alone, nor to the well-to-do, nor to the young in contradistinction to the old, but to the neighborhood as a whole, "men, women, and children taken in families as the Lord mixes them." The activities of Hull House divide themselves into four, possibly more lines. They are not formally or consciously thus divided, but broadly separate according to the receptivity of the neighbors. They might be designated as the social, educational, and humanitarian, I have added civic—if indeed a Settlement of women can be said to perform civic duties. These activities spring from no preconceived notion of what a Social Settlement should be, but have increased gradually on demand. In describing these activities and their value to the neighborhood, I shall attempt to identify those people who respond to each form.

A Settlement which regards social intercourse as the terms of its expression logically brings to its aid all those adjuncts which have been found by experience to free social life. It casts aside nothing which the cultivated man regards as good and suggestive of participation in the best life of the past. It ignores none of the surroundings which one associates with a life of simple refinement. The amount of luxury which an individual indulges in is a thing which has to be determined by each for himself. It must always be a relative thing. The one test which the Settlement is bound to respect is that its particular amount of luxury shall tend to "free" the social expression of its neighbors, and not cumber that expression. The residents at Hull House find that the better in quality and taste their surroundings are, the more they contribute to the general enjoyment.

We have distinct advantages for Settlements in America. There are fewer poor people here than in England, there are fewer poor people who expect to remain poor, and they are less strictly confined to their own districts. It is an advantage that our cities are diversified by foreign colonies. We go to Europe and consider our view incomplete if we do not see something of the peasant life of the little villages with their quaint customs and suggestive habits. We can see the same thing here. There are Bohemians, Italians, Poles, Russians, Greeks, and Arabs in Chicago vainly trying to adjust their peasant life to the life of a large city, and coming in contact with only the most ignorant Americans in that city. The more of scholarship, the more of linguistic attainment, the more of beautiful surroundings a Settlement among them can command, the more it can do for them.

It is much easier to deal with the first generation of crowded city life than with the second or third, because it is more natural and cast in a simpler mould. The Italian and Bohemian peasants who live in Chicago still put on their bright holiday clothes on a Sunday and go to visit their cousins. They tramp along with at least a suggestion of having once walked over ploughed fields and breathed country air. The second generation of city poor have no holiday clothes and consider their cousins "a bad lot." I have heard a drunken man, in a maudlin stage, babble of his good country mother and imagine he was driving the cows home, and I knew that his little son, who laughed loud at him, would be drunk earlier in life, and would have no such pastoral interlude to his ravings. Hospitality still survives among foreigners, although it is buried under false pride among the poorest Americans. One thing seemed clear in regard to entertaining these foreigners: to preserve and keep for them whatever of value their past life contained and to bring them in contact with a better type of Americans. For two years, every

Saturday evening, our Italian neighbors were our guests; entire families came. These evenings were very popular during our first winter at Hull House. Many educated Italians helped us, and the house became known as a place where Italians were welcome and where national holidays were observed. They come to us with their petty lawsuits, sad relics of the *vendetta,* with their incorrigible boys, with their hospital cases, with their aspirations for American clothes, and with their needs for an interpreter.

Friday evening is devoted to Germans and is similar in purpose; but owing to the superior education of our Teutonic guests and the clever leading of a cultivated German woman, we can bring out the best of that cozy social intercourse which is found in its perfection in the "Fatherland." They sing a great deal in the tender minor of the German folksong or in the rousing spirit of the Rhine, and they are slowly but persistently pursuing a course in German history and literature. The relationship by no means ends with social civilities, and the acquaintance made there has brought about radical changes in the lives of many friendless families. I recall one peasant woman, straight from the fields of Germany. Her two years in America had been spent in patiently carrying water up and down two flights of stairs, and in washing the heavy flannel suits of iron-foundry workers. For this her pay had averaged thirty-five cents a day. Three of her daughters had fallen victims to the vice of the city. The mother was bewildered and distressed, but understood nothing. We were able to induce the betrayer of one daughter to marry her; the second, after a tedious lawsuit, supported his child; with the third we were able to do nothing. This woman is now living with her family in a little house seventeen miles from the city. She has made two payments on her land and is a lesson to all beholders as she pastures her cow up and down the railroad tracks and makes money from her ten acres. She did not need charity. She had an immense capacity for hard work, but she sadly needed "heading." She is our most shining example, but I think of many forlorn cases of German and Bohemian peasants in need of neighborly help.

Perhaps of more value than to the newly arrived peasant is the service of the Settlement to those foreigners who speak English fairly well, and who have been so successful in material affairs that they are totally absorbed by them. Their social life is too often reduced to a sense of comradeship. The lives of many Germans, for instance, are law-abiding, but inexpressibly dull. They have resigned poetry and romance with the other good things of the Fatherland. There is a strong family affection between them and their English-speaking children, but their pleasures are not in common and they seldom go out together. Perhaps the greatest value of the Settlement to them is in simply placing large and pleasant rooms with musical facilities at their disposal, and in reviving their almost forgotten enthusiasm for Körner and Schiller. I have seen sons and daughters stand in complete surprise as their mother's knitting-needles softly beat time to the song she was singing, or her worn face turned rosy under the hand-clapping as she made an old-fashioned courtesy at the end of a German poem. It was easy to fancy a growing touch of respect in her children's manner to her, and a rising enthusiasm for German literature and reminiscence on the part of all the family, an effort to bring together the old life and the new, a respect for the older cultivation, and not quite so much assurance that the new was the best. I think that we have a right to expect that our foreigners will do this for us: that they will project a little of the historic and romantic into the prosaic quarters of our American cities.

But our social evenings are by no means confined to foreigners. Our most successful clubs are entirely composed of English-speaking and American-born young people. Those over sixteen meet in two clubs, one for young men and one for girls, every Monday evening. Each club dispatches various literary programs before nine o'clock, when they meet together for an hour of social amusement before going home at ten. The members of the Tuesday evening clubs are from fourteen to sixteen years old; a few of them are still in school, but most of them are working. The boys who are known as the Young Citizen's Club are supposed to inform themselves on municipal affairs, as are the Hull House Columbian Guards who report alleys and streets for the Municipal Order League. We have various other clubs of young people that meet weekly; their numbers are limited only by the amount of room. We hold the dining-room, the reception-room, and the octagon with the art-exhibit-room and the studio each evening for the College Extension classes, and can reserve only the large drawing-room and gymnasium for the clubs and receptions. The gymnasium is a somewhat pretentious name for a building next door which was formerly a saloon, but which we rented last fall, repaired, and fitted up with good apparatus. A large and well-equipped gymnasium is at present being built for

Hull House. During the winter the old one sheltered some enthusiastic athletic classes. The evenings were equally divided between men and women. The children came in the afternoon. It is difficult to describe the social evenings, and there is much social life going on constantly which cannot be tabulated.

To turn to the educational effort, it will be perhaps better first to describe the people who respond to it. In every neighborhood where poorer people live, because rents are supposed to be cheaper there, is an element which, although uncertain in the individual, in the aggregate can be counted upon. It is composed of people of former education and opportunity who have cherished ambitions and prospects, but who are caricatures of what they meant to be—"hollow ghosts which blame the living men." There are times in many lives when there is a cessation of energy and loss of power. Men and women of education and refinement come to live in a cheaper neighborhood because they lack the power of making money, because of ill health, because of an unfortunate marriage, or for various other reasons which do not imply criminality or stupidity. Among them are those who, in spite of untoward circumstances, keep up some sort of an intellectual life, those who are "great for books" as their neighbors say. To such the Settlement is a genuine refuge. In addition to these there are many young women who teach in the public schools, young men who work at various occupations, but who are bent upon self-improvement and are preparing for professions. It is of these that the College Extension classes are composed. The majority of the two hundred students live within the radius of six blocks from the house, although a few of them come from other parts of the city. The educational effort of Hull House always has been held by the residents to be subordinate to its social life, and, as it were, a part of it. What is now known as the College Extension course, a series of lectures and classes held in the evening on the general plan of University Extension, had its origin in an informal club which, during the first winter, read "Romola" with the original residents.[1] During the last term thirty-five classes a week were in existence. The work is divided into terms of twelve weeks, and circulars are issued at the beginning of each term. Many students have taken studies in each of the seven terms of work offered.

The relation of students and faculty to each other and to the residents is that of guest and hostess, and those students who have been longest in relation to the Settlement feel the responsibility of old friends of the house to new guests. A good deal of tutoring is constantly going on among the students themselves in the rooms of Hull House. At the close of each term the residents give a reception to students and faculty, which is one of the chief social events of the season. Upon this comfortable social basis very good work has been done in the College Extension courses. Literature classes until recently have been the most popular. The last winter's Shakespeare class had a regular attendance of forty. The mathematical classes have always been large and flourishing. The faculty, consisting of college men and women, numbers thirty-five. Many of them have taught constantly at the house for two years, but their numbers are often re-enforced. During the last term a class in physics, preparatory for a class in electricity, was composed largely of workmen in the Western Electric Works, which are within a few blocks of Hull House. A fee of fifty cents is charged for each course of study. This defrays all incidental expenses and leaves on hand each term fifty or seventy dollars, with which to import distinguished lecturers.

During the last winter Hull House has been a successful "centre" for two University Extension courses in connection with the Chicago University. It has always been the policy of Hull House to co-operate as much as possible with public institutions. The Chicago Public Library has an almost unique system of branch reading-rooms and library stations. Five rooms are rented by the library in various parts of the city which are fitted up for reading-rooms, and in addition to magazines and papers they are supplied with several hundred books. There are also other stations where public-library cards can be left and to which books are delivered. Hull House was made one of these delivery stations during its second year, and when in June, 1891, the Butler Gallery was completed, we offered the lower floor free of rent as a branch reading-room. The City Library supplies English magazines and papers and two librarians who are in charge. There are papers in Italian, German, Bohemian, and French. The number of readers the first month was 1213; during the fifth month, 2454. The upper floor of the Butler Gallery is divided into an art exhibition room and a studio. Our first art exhibit was opened in June, 1891, by Mr. and Mrs. Barnett, of St. Jude's, Whitechapel. It is always pleasant to associate their hearty sympathy with that first exhibit. The pictures were some of the best that Chicago could afford, several by Corot, Watts, and Davis. European country scenes, sea views, and Dutch interiors bring forth many pleasant reminiscences, and the person who is in charge of the pictures to explain them is many times more edified than edifying. We have had five exhibits since the gallery was completed, two of oil-paintings, one of old engravings and etchings, one of water-colors, and one of pictures especially selected for use in the public schools. The average attendance at these exhibits has been three thousand. An exhibit is open from two in the afternoon until ten in the evening, and continues usually two weeks. The value of these exhibits to the neighborhood must, of course, be determined by the value one attaches to the sense of beauty and the pleasure which arises from its contemplation. Classes in free-hand drawing and clay modelling are held in the studio of the Butler Gallery. They have been very popular from the first, and some excellent work has been done.

Every Thursday evening for three years, save during the three summer months, we have had a lecture of some sort at Hull House. This has come to be an expected event in the neighborhood. These lectures are largely attended by the College Extension students, and the topics are supposed to connect with their studies; but many other people come to them and often join a class because of the interest a lecturer has awakened. This attraction is constantly in mind when these lectures are planned. For two years a summer school has been held at Rockford, Ill., in connection with the College Extension classes. From one-third to one-half the students have been able to attend it, paying their board for a month, and enjoying out-door study quite as much as the classes. I would recommend for imitation the very generous action on the part of the Rockford College trustees in placing at our disposal free of rent their entire educational apparatus, from the dining-room to the laboratories. On the border land between social and educational activity are our Sunday afternoon concerts, and the Plato Club which follows them.

The industrial education of Hull House has always been somewhat limited. From the beginning we have had large and enthusiastic cooking classes, first in the Hull House kitchen, and later in a tiny cottage across the yard which has been fitted up for the purpose. We have also always had sewing, mending, and embroidery classes. This leads me to speak of the children who meet weekly at Hull House, whose organization is between classes and clubs. There are three hundred of them who come on three days, not counting, of course, the children who come to the house merely as depositors in the Penny Provident Fund Savings Bank. A hundred Italian girls come on Monday. They sew and carry home a new garment, which becomes a pattern for the entire family. Tuesday afternoon has always been devoted to school-boys' clubs: they are practically story-telling clubs. The most popular stories are legends and tales of chivalry. The one hundred and fifty little girls on Friday afternoon are not very unlike the boys, although they want to sew while they are hearing their stories. The value of these clubs, I believe, lies almost entirely in their success in arousing the higher imagination. We have had a kindergarten at Hull House ever since we have lived there. Every morning miniature Italians, Hebrews, French, Irish, and Germans assemble in our drawing-room, and nothing seems to excite admiration in the neighborhood so much as the fact that we "put up with them."

In addition to the neighbors who respond to the receptions and classes are found those who are too battered and oppressed to care for them. To these, however, is left that susceptibility to the bare offices of humanity which raises such offices into a bond of fellowship. These claim humanitarian efforts. Perhaps the chief value of a Settlement to its neighborhood, certainly to the newly arrived foreigner, is its office as an information and interpretation bureau. It sometimes seems as if the business of the Settlement were that of a commission merchant. Without endowment and without capital itself, it constantly acts between the various institutions of the city and the people for whose benefit these institutions were erected. The hospitals, the county agencies, and State asylums, are often but vague rumors to the people who need them most. This commission work, as I take it, is of value not only to the recipient, but to the institutions themselves. Each institution, unlike a settlement, is obliged to determine upon the line of its activity, to accept its endowment for that end and do the best it can. But each time this is accomplished it is apt to lace itself up in certain formulas, is in danger of forgetting the mystery and complexity of life, of repressing the promptings that spring from growing insight.

The residents of a Social Settlement have an opportunity of seeing institutions from the recipient's standpoint, of catching the spirit of the original impulse which founded them. This experience ought to have a certain value and ultimately find expression in institutional management. One of the residents of Hull House received this winter an appointment from the Cook County agent as a county visitor. She reported at the agency each morning, and all the cases within a radius of several blocks from Hull House were given to her for investigation. This gave her a legitimate opportunity for knowing the poorest people in the neighborhood. In no cases were her recommendations refused or her judgments reversed by the men in charge of the office. From the very nature of our existence and purpose we are bound to keep on good terms with every beneficent institution in the city. Passing by our telephone last Sunday morning, I was struck with the list of numbers hung on the wall for easy reference. They were those of the Visiting Nurses' Association; Cook County Hospital; Women's and Children's Hospital; Maxwell Street Police Station for city ambulance; Health Department, City Hall; Cook County Agent, etc. We have been on very good terms with the Hebrew Relief and Aid Society, the Children's Aid, the Humane Society, the Municipal Order League, and with the various church and national relief associations. Every summer we send out dozens of children to the country on the "Daily News" Fresh Air Fund and to the Holiday Home at Lake Geneva. Our most complete co-operation has been with the Visiting Nurses' Association. One of the nurses lives at Hull House, pays her board as a resident, and does her work from there. Friends of the house are constantly in need of her ministrations, and her cases become friends of the house. Owing to the lack of a charity organization society in Chicago we have been obliged to keep a sum of money as a relief fund. Five bath-rooms in the rear of Hull House are open to the neighborhood and are constantly in use. The number of baths taken in July was nine hundred and eighty.

The more definite humanitarian effort of Hull House has taken shape in a day nursery, which was started during the second year of our residence on Halsted Street. A frame cottage of six rooms across our yard has been fitted up as a *crèche*. At present we receive from thirty to forty children daily. A young lady who has had kindergarten training is in charge; she has the assistance of an older woman, and a kindergarten by a professional teacher is held each morning in the play-room. This nursery is not merely a convenience in the neighborhood; it is, to a certain extent, a neighborhood affair. Similar in spirit is the Hull House Diet Kitchen, in a little cottage directly back of the nursery. Food is prepared for invalids and orders are taken from physicians and visiting nurses of the district. We have lately had an outfit of Mr. Atkinson's inventions, in which the women of the neighborhood have taken a most intelligent interest, especially the members of the Hull House Woman's Club. This club meets one afternoon a week. It is composed of the most able women of the neighborhood, who enjoy the formal addresses and many informal discussions. The economics of food and fuel are freely discussed. The Hull House household expenses are frankly compared with those of other households. There is little doubt that "friendly visiting," while of great value, to be complete should also include the "friendly visited." The residents at Hull House find in themselves a constantly increasing tendency to consult their neighbors on the advisability of each new undertaking. We have lately opened a boarding club for working girls near Hull House on the co-operative plan. I say advisedly that we have "opened" it; the running of it is quite in the hands of the girls themselves. The furniture, pictures, etc., belong to Hull House, and whatever experience we have is at their disposal; but it is in no sense a working-girls' "home," nor is it to be run from the outside. We hope a great deal from this little attempt at co-operative housekeeping. The club has been running three months on a self-supporting basis and has thirty-five members.

The Coffee House which is being built in connection with Hull House contains a large kitchen fitted on the New-England Kitchen plan. We hope by the sale of properly cooked foods, to make not only co-operative housekeeping but all the housekeeping of the neighborhood easier and more economical. The Coffee House itself, with its clubrooms, will be a less formal social centre than our drawing-room.

Helpful recourses from the neighborhood itself constantly develop, physicians benefit societies, ministers and priests are always ready to co-operate in any given case. Young girls from the neighborhood assist in the children's classes, mothers help in the nursery, young men teach in the gymnasium, or secure students for an experimental course of lectures. We constantly rely more and more on neighborhood assistance.

In summing up the objective value of Hull House, I am sorry we have not more to present in the line of civic activities. It was through the energy of a resident this spring that the fact that the public-school census recorded 6976 school-children in the nineteenth ward and that they were provided with only 2957 public-school sittings was made prominent just before the appropriations were voted for school buildings and sites. It was largely through her energy, and the energy of the people whom she interested in it, that the Board of Education was induced to purchase a site for a school building in our ward and to save and equip for immediate use a school-house about to be turned into a warehouse.

During two months of this summer the reports sent in from Hull House to the Municipal Order League, and through it to the Health Department, were one thousand and thirty-seven. The Department showed great readiness to co-operate with this volunteer inspection, and a marked improvement has taken place in the scavenger service and in the regulation of the small stables of the ward.

Hull House has had, I hope, a certain value to the women's trades unions of Chicago. It seems to me of great importance that as trades unions of women are being formed they should be kept, if possible, from falling into the self-same pits the men's unions have fallen into. Women possessing no votes, and therefore having little political value, will be both of advantage and disadvantage to their unions. Four women's unions have met regularly at Hull House: the book-binders', the shoe-makers', the shirtmakers', and the cloak-makers'. The last two were organized at Hull House. It has seemed to us that the sewing trades are most in need of help. They are thoroughly disorganized, Russian and Polish tailors competing against English-speaking tailors, young girls and Italian women competing against both. An efficient union which should combine all these elements seems very difficult, unless it grow strong enough to offer a label and receive unexpected aid from the manufacturers. In that case there would be the hope of co-operation on the part of the consumers, as the fear of contagion from ready-made clothing has at last seized the imagination of the public.

That the trades unions themselves care for what we have done for them, is shown by the fact that when the committee of investigation for the sweating system was appointed by the Trades and Labor Assembly, consisting of five delegates from the unions and five from other citizens, two of the latter were residents of Hull House. It is logical that a Settlement should have a certain value in labor complications, having from its very position sympathies entangled on both sides. Last May twenty girls from a knitting factory who struck because they were docked for loss of time when they were working by the piece, came directly from the factory to Hull House. They had heard that we "stood by working people." We were able to have the strike arbitrated, and although six girls lost their places, the unjust fines were remitted, and we had the satisfaction of putting on record one more case of arbitration in the slowly growing list. We were helped in this ease, as we have been in many others, by the Bureau of Justice. Its office is constantly crowded with working people who hope for redress from the law, but have no money with which to pay for it. There should be an office of this bureau in every ward; "down town" seems far away and inaccessible to the most ignorant. Hull House, in spite of itself, does a good deal of legal work. We have secured support for deserted women, insurance for bewildered widows, damages for injured operators, furniture from the clutches of the instalment store. One function of the Settlement to its neighborhood somewhat resembles that of the big brother whose mere presence on the play ground protects the little one from bullies. A resident at Hull House is at present collecting labor statistics in the neighborhood for the Illinois State Bureau of Labor. It is a matter of satisfaction that this work can be done from the Settlement, and the residents receive the benefit of the information collected.

It is difficult to classify the Working People's Social Science Club, which meets weekly at Hull House. It is social, educational, and civic in character, the latter chiefly because it strongly connects the House with the labor problems in their political and social aspects. This club was organized at Hull House in the spring of 1890 by an English working-man. It has met weekly since, save during the months of summer. At eight o'clock every Wednesday evening the secretary calls to order from forty to one hundred people. A chairman for the evening is elected, and a speaker is introduced who is allowed to talk until nine o'clock; his subject is then thrown open to discussion and a lively debate ensues until ten o'clock, at which hour the meeting is declared adjourned. The enthusiasm of this club seldom lags. Its zest for discussion is unceasing, and any attempt to turn it into a study or reading club always meets with the strong disapprobation of the members. Chicago is full of social theorists. It offers a cosmopolitan opportunity for discussion. The only possible danger from this commingling of many theories is incurred when there is an attempt at suppression; bottled up, there is danger of explosion; constantly uncorked, open to the deodorizing and freeing process of the air, all danger is averted. Nothing so disconcerts a social agitator as to find among his auditors men who have been through all that, and who are quite as radical as he in another direction.

The economic conferences which were held between business men and working-men, during the winter of 1888–89 and the two succeeding winters, doubtless did much toward relieving this state of effervescence. Many thoughtful men in Chicago are convinced that, if these conferences had been established earlier, the Haymarket riot and all its sensational results might have been avoided.[2] The Sunset Club is at present performing much the same function. There is still need, however, for many of these clubs where men who differ widely in their social theories can meet for discussion, where representatives of the various economic schools can modify each other, and at least learn tolerance and the futility of endeavering to convince all the world of the truth of one position. To meet in a social-science club is more educational than to meet in a single-tax club, or a socialistic chapter, or a personal-rights league, although the millennium may seem farther off after such a meeting. In addition to this modification of view there is doubtless a distinct modification of attitude. Last spring the Hull House Social Science Club heard a series of talks on municipal and county affairs by the heads of the various departments. During the discussion following the address on "The Chicago Police," a working-man had the pleasure of telling the chief of police that he had been arrested, obliged to pay two dollars and a half, and had lost three days' work, because he had come out of the wrong gate when he was working on the World's Fair grounds. The chief sighed, expressed his regret, and made no defence. The speaker sat down bewildered; evidently for the first time in his life he realized that blunders cut the heart of more than the victim.

Is it possible for men, however far apart in outward circumstances, for the capitalist and the working-man, to use the common phrase, to meet as individuals beneath a friendly roof, open their minds each to each, and not have their "class theories" insensibly modified by the kindly attrition of a personal acquaintance? In the light of our experience I should say not.

In describing Hull House and in referring so often to the "residents," I feel that I may have given a wrong impression. By far the larger amount of the teaching and formal club work is done by people living outside of the House. Between ninety and one hundred of these people meet an appointment regularly each week. Our strength lies largely in this element. The average number of people who come to the House during the week is one thousand.

I am always sorry to have Hull House regarded as philanthropy, although it doubtless has strong philanthropic tendencies, and has several distinct charitable departments which are conscientiously carried on. It is unfair, however, to apply the word philanthropic to the activities of the House as a whole. Charles Booth, in his brilliant chapter on "The Unemployed," expresses regret that the problems of the working class are so often confounded with the problems of the inefficient, the idle, and distressed. To confound thus two problems is to render the solution of both impossible. Hull House, while endeavoring to fulfil its obligations to neighbors of varying needs, will do great harm if it confounds distinct problems. Working people live in the same streets with those in need of charity, but they themselves, so long as they have health and good wages, require and want none of it. As one of their number has said, they require only that their aspirations be recognized and stimulated, and the means of attaining them put at their disposal. Hull House makes a constant effort to secure these means for its neighbors, but to call that effort philanthropy is to use the word unfairly and to underestimate the duties of good citizenship.

Notes

1. George Eliot's complex historic novel *Romola*, first published in 1864, is set in the Florence of Savanarola and was the text for the first reading club at Hull-House. Eliot was an Addams favorite. The novel's Italian setting made it attractive in the Nineteenth Ward given the presence of a vibrant Italian neighborhood, Hull-House's most immediate neighbors.

2. Chicago was roiled in 1886 by a riot in which policemen were killed by a homemade bomb. This led to widespread hysteria against all "anarchists." Jane Addams opposed violence as a method of social change, but she was equally vehement in her opposition to overreaction on the part of state authorities against anyone they suspected of harboring seditious tendencies, for it was all too easy to fail to distinguish between the method of public disputation and the method of incitement to riot.

6

"The Settlement as a Factor in the Labor Movement"

One man or group of men sometimes reveal to their contemporaries a higher conscience by simply incorporating into the deed what has been before but a philosophic proposition. By this deed the common code of ethics is stretched to a higher point.

Such an act of moral significance, for instance, was John Burns's loyalty to the dockers' strike of East London. "The injury to one" did at last actually "become the concern of all;" and henceforth the man who does not share that concern drops below the standard ethics of his day. The proposition which workingmen had long quoted was at last incarnated by a mechanic, who took his position so intelligently that he carried with him the best men in England, and set the public conscience. Other men became ashamed of a wrong to which before they had been easily indifferent.

When the social conscience, if one may use the expression, has been thus strikingly formulated, it is not so hard for others to follow. They do it weakly and stumblingly perhaps; but they yet see a glimmer of light of which the first man could not be sure, and they have a code of ethics upon which the first man was vague. They are also conscious of the backing of a large share of the community who before this expres-

---

Note: "The Settlement as a Factor in the Labor Movement," in *Hull-House Maps and Papers, by Residents of Hull-House, A Social Settlement, a Presentation of Nationalities and Wages in a Congested District of Chicago, Together with Comments and Essays on Problems Growing Out of Social Conditions* (New York: Thomas Y. Crowell, 1895).

sion knew not the compunction of their own hearts. A settlement accepts the ethics of its contemporaries that the sharing of the life of the poor is essential to the understanding and bettering of that life; but by its very existence it adopts this modern code somewhat formally. The social injury of the meanest man not only becomes its concern, but by virtue of its very locality it has put itself into a position to see, as no one but a neighbor can see, the stress and need of those who bear the brunt of the social injury. A settlement has not only taken a pledge towards those thus injured, but it is placed where the motive-power for the fulfilment of such a pledge is constantly renewed. Propinquity is an unceasing factor in its existence.

A review of the sewing-trades, as seen from a settlement, will be sufficient to illustrate this position.

Hull-House is situated in the midst of the sweaters' district of Chicago.[1] The residents came to the district with the general belief that organization for working-people was a necessity. They would doubtless have said that the discovery of the power to combine was the distinguishing discovery of our time; that we are using this force somewhat awkwardly, as men use that which is newly discovered. In social and political affairs the power to combine often works harm; but it is already operating to such an extent in commercial affairs, that the manufacturer who does not combine with others of his branch is in constant danger of failure; that a railroad cannot be successfully projected unless the interests of parallel roads are consulted; and that working-people likewise cannot be successful until they, too, learn skilfully to avail themselves of this power.

This was to the residents, as to many people, an accepted proposition, but not a working formula. It had not the driving force of a conviction. The residents have lived for five years in a neighborhood largely given over to the sewing-trades, which is an industry totally disorganized. Having observed the workers in this trade as compared to those in organized trades, they have gradually discovered that lack of organization in a trade tends to the industrial helplessness of the workers in that trade. If in all departments of social, political, and commercial life, isolation is a blunder, and results in dreariness and apathy, then in industrial affairs isolation is a social crime; for it there tends to extermination.

This process of extermination entails starvation and suffering, and the desperate moral disintegration which inevitably follows in their train, until the need of organization in industry gradually assumes a moral aspect. The conviction arrived at entails a social obligation.

No trades are so overcrowded as the sewing-trades; for the needle has ever been the refuge of the unskilled woman. The wages paid throughout the manufacture of clothing are less than those in any other trade. In order to meet the requirements of the workers, lack of skill and absence of orderly life, the work has been so subdivided that almost no skill is required after the garment leaves the cutter. It is given practically to the one who is at hand when it is ready, and who does it for the least money. This subdivision and low wage have gone so far, that the woman who does home finishing alone cannot possibly gain by it a living wage. The residents of Hull-House have carefully investigated many cases, and are ready to assert that the Italian widow who finishes the cheapest goods, although she sews from six in the morning until eleven at night, can only get enough to keep her children clothed and fed; while for her rent and fuel she must always depend upon charity or the hospitality of her countrymen. If the American sewing-woman, supporting herself alone, lives on bread and butter and tea, she finds a Bohemian woman next door whose diet of black bread and coffee enables her to undercut. She competes with a wife who is eager to have home finishing that she may add something to the family comfort; or with a daughter who takes it that she may buy a wedding outfit.

The Hebrew tailor, the man with a family to support, who, but for this competition of unskilled women and girls, might earn a wage upon which a family could subsist, is obliged, in order to support them at all, to put his little children at work as soon as they can sew on buttons.

It does not help his industrial situation that the woman and girl who have brought it about have accepted the lower wages in order to buy comforts for an invalid child, or to add to the earnings of an aged father. The mother who sews on a gross of buttons for seven cents, in order to buy a blue ribbon with which to tie up her little daughter's hair, or the mother who finishes a dozen vests for five cents, with which to buy her children a loaf of bread, commits unwittingly a crime against her fellow-workers, although our hearts may thrill with admiration for her heroism, and ache with pity over her misery.

The maternal instinct and family affection is woman's most holy attribute; but if she enters industrial life, that is not enough. She must supplement her family conscience by a social and an industrial conscience. She must widen her family affection to embrace the children of the community. She is working havoc in the sewing-trades, because with the meagre equipment, sufficient for family life she has entered industrial life.

Have we any right to place before untrained women the alternative of seeing their little children suffer, or of complicating the industrial condition until all the children of the community are suffering? We know of course what their decision would be. But the residents of a settlement are not put to this hard choice, although it is often difficult to urge organization when they are flying to the immediate relief of the underfed children in the neighborhood.

If the settlement, then, is convinced that in industrial affairs lack of organization tends to the helplessness of the isolated worker, and is a menace to the entire community, then it is bound to pledge itself to industrial organization, and to look about it for the lines upon which to work. And at this point the settlement enters into what is more technically known as the labor movement.

The labor movement may be called a concerted effort among the workers in all trades to obtain a more equitable distribution of the product, and to secure a more orderly existence for the laborers. How may the settlement be of value to this effort?

If the design of the settlement is not so much the initiation of new measures, but fraternal co-operation with all good which it finds in its neighborhood, then the most obvious line of action will be organization through the trades-unions, a movement already well established.

The trades-unions say to each workingman, "Associate yourself with the fellow-workers in your trade. Let your trade organization federate with the allied trades, and they, in turn, with the National and International Federation, until working-people become a solid body, ready for concerted action. It is the only possible way to prevent cuts in the rate of wages, and to regulate the hours of work. Capital is organized, and has influence with which to secure legislation in its behalf. We are scattered and feeble because we do not work together."

Trades-unionism, in spite of the many pits into which it has fallen, has the ring of altruism about it. It is clearly the duty of the settlement to keep it to its best ideal, and to bring into it something of the spirit which has of late characterized the unions in England. This keeping to the ideal is not so easy as the more practical work of increasing unions, although that is difficult enough. Of the two women's unions organized at Hull-House, and of the four which have regularly held their meetings there, as well as those that come to us during strikes at various times, I should venture to say of only one of them that it is filled with the new spirit, although they all have glimpses of it, and even during times of stress and disturbance strive for it.

It was perhaps natural, from the situation, that the unions organized at Hull-House should have been those in the sewing-trades. The shirt-makers were organized in the spring of 1891. The immediate cause was a cut in a large factory from twenty-five cents a dozen for the making of collars and cuffs to twelve cents. The factory was a model in regard to its sanitary arrangements, and the sole complaint of the girls was of the long hours and low rate of wages. The strike which followed the formation of the union was wholly unsuccessful; but the union formed then has thriven ever since, and has lately grown so strong that it has recently succeeded in securing the adoption of the national labels.

The cloakmakers were organized at Hull-House in the spring of 1892. Wages had been steadily falling, and there was great depression among the workers of the trade. The number of employees in the inside shops was being rapidly reduced, and the work of the entire trade handed over to the sweaters. The union among the men numbered two hundred; but the skilled workers were being rapidly supplanted by untrained women, who had no conscience in regard to the wages they accepted. The men had urged organization for several years, but were unable to secure it among the women. One apparently insurmountable obstacle had been the impossibility of securing any room, save one over a saloon, that was large enough and cheap enough for a general meeting. To a saloon hall the women had steadfastly refused to go, save once, when, under the pressure of a strike, the girls in a certain shop had met with the men from the same shop, over one of the more decent saloons, only to be up-braided by their families upon their return home. They of course refused ever to go again. The first meeting at Hull-House was composed of men and girls, and two or three of the residents. The meeting was a revelation to all present. The men, perhaps forty in number, were Russian-Jewish tailors, many of whom could command not even broken English. They were ill-dressed and grimy, suspicious that Hull-House was a spy in the service of the capitalists. They were skilled workers, easily superior to the girls when sewing on a cloak, but shamefaced and constrained in meeting with them. The American-Irish girls were well-dressed, and comparatively at ease. They felt chaperoned by the presence of the residents, and talked volubly among themselves. These two sets of people were held together only by the pressure upon their trade. They were separated by strong racial differences, by language, by nationality, by religion, by mode of life, by every possible social distinction. The interpreter stood between the two sides of the room, somewhat helpless. He was clear upon the economic necessity for combination; he realized the mutual interdependence; but he was baffled by the social aspect of the situation. The residents felt that between these men and girls was a deeper gulf than the much-talked of "chasm" between the favored and unfavored classes. The working-girls before them, who were being forced to cross such a gulf, had a positive advantage over the cultivated girl who consciously, and sometimes heroically, crosses the "chasm" to join hands with her working sisters.

There was much less difference of any sort between the residents and working-girls than between the men and girls of the same trade. It was a spectacle only to be found in an American city, under the latest conditions of trade-life. Working-people among themselves are being forced into a social democracy from the pressure of the economic situation. It presents an educating and broadening aspect of no small value.

The Woman's Cloakmakers' Union has never been large, but it always has been characterized by the spirit of generosity which marked its organization. It feels a strong sense of obligation toward the most ill-paid and ignorant of the sweaters' victims, and no working-people of Chicago have done more for abolition of the sweating-system than this handful of women.

But the labor movement is by no means so simple as trades-unionism. A settlement finds in the movement devoted men who feel keenly the need for better industrial organization, but who insist that industrial organization must be part of the general re-organization of society. The individualists, for instance, insist that we will never secure equal distribution until we have equality of opportunity; that all State and city franchises, all privilege of railroad, bank, and corporation, must be removed before competition will be absolutely free, and the man with his labor alone to offer will have a fair chance with the man who offers anything else; that the sole function of the State is to secure the freedom of each, guarded by the like freedom of all, and that each man free to work for his own existence and advantage will by this formula work out our industrial development. The individualist then works constantly for the recall of franchise and of special privilege, and for the untrammelled play of each man's force. There is much in our inheritance that responds to this, and he has followers among workingmen and among capitalists; those who fear to weaken the incentive to individual exertion, and those who believe that any interference would work injuriously. The residents of a settlement hear the individualist pleading in many trades assemblies. Opposite to him, springing up in discussion every time he speaks, is the socialist in all varieties. The scientific socialist reads his Karl Marx, and sees a gradual and inevitable absorption of all the means of production and of all capital by one entity, called the community. He makes out a strong case because he is usually a German or a Russian, with a turn for economic discussion, and widely read. He sees in the present tendency towards the concentration of capital, and in the growth of trusts and monopolies, an inevitable transition to the socialistic state. Every concentration of capital into fewer hands but increases the mass of those whose interests are opposed to the maintenance of its power, and vastly simplifies the final absorption. He contends that we have already had the transformation of scattered private property into capitalistic property, and that it is inevitable that it should be turned into collective property.[2] In the former cases we had the ex-propriation of the mass of the people by a few usurpers; in the latter we have the ex-propriation of a few usurpers by the mass of people. He points with pride to the strong tendency towards State regulation of the means of transportation, and of many industries, and he urges legislative check and control at every point.

Between these two divergent points of view we find many shades of opinion and many modifications of philosophy; but perhaps a presentation of these two, as heard many times from earnest workingmen, will illustrate how difficult a settlement finds it to be liberal in tone, and to decide what immediate measures are in the line of advantage to the labor movement and which ones are against it.

It has been said that the imagination in America has been seized in due turn by the minister, the soldier, and the lawyer, who have successively held the political appointments; but that it is now the turn of the economist; that the man who would secure votes and a leadership in politics is the one who has a line of action to propose which shall bring order out of the present industrial chaos. This may be illustrated by the marvellous growth of the single-tax movement, which offers a definite remedial measure. Is it not true that our knotty theological difficulties as matters for prolonged discussion are laid aside? Is it not true that the interpretation of the Constitution, and the standard of action for the law-abiding and upright citizen, are well determined in men's minds? But that the moral enterprise of each man, not by any means his morality, but his moral enterprise, has to be tested by his attitude toward the industrial problem? The crucial question of the time is, "In what attitude stand ye toward the present industrial system? Are you content that greed and the seizing upon disadvantage and the pushing of the weaker to the wall shall rule your business life, while in your family and social life you live so differently? Are you content that Christianity shall have no play in trade?" If these questions press upon all of us, then a settlement must surely face the industrial problem as a test of its sincerity, as a test of the unification of its interests with the absorbing interests of its neighbors. Must it, then, accept the creeds of one or the other of these schools of social thought, and work for a party; or is there some underlying principle upon which the settlement can stand, as in its Christianity it endeavors to stand on something more primitive than either Catholicism or Protestantism? Can it find the moral question involved? Is there a line of ethics which its action ought to follow? Is it possible to make the slow appeal to the nobler fibre in men, and to connect it with that tradition of what is just and right?

A glance at the labor movement shows that the preponderating force has been given to what may be called negative action. Unions use their power to frustrate the designs of the capitalist, to make trouble for corporations and the public, such as is involved, for instance, in a railroad strike. It has often seemed to be the only method of arresting attention to their demands; but in America, at least, they have come to trust it too far.

A movement cannot be carried on by negating other acts; it must have a positive force, a driving and self-sustaining motive-power. A moral revolution cannot be accomplished by men who are held together merely because they are all smarting under a sense of injury and injustice, although it may be begun by them.

Men thus animated may organize for resistance, they may struggle bravely together, and may destroy that which is injurious, but they cannot build up, associate, and unite. They have no common, collective faith. The labor movement in America bears this trace of its youth and immaturity. As the first social organizations of men were for purposes of war; as they combined to defend themselves, or to destroy their enemies, and only later they united for creative purposes and pacific undertakings, so the labor organizations first equip themselves for industrial war, and much later attempt to promote peaceful industrial progress. The older unions have already reached the higher development, but the unions among the less intelligent and less skilled workmen are still belligerent and organized on a military basis, and unfortunately give color to the entire movement.

It is doubtless true that men who work excessively certain weeks in the year, and bear enforced idleness, harassed by a fear of starvation, during certain other weeks, as the lumber-shovers and garment-workers do, are too far from that regulated life and sanity of mind in which the quiet inculcation of moral principle is possible. It is also doubtless true that a more uniform leisure and a calmer temper of mind will have to be secured before the sense of injury ceases to be an absorbing emotion. The labor movement is bound, therefore, to work for shorter hours and increased wages and regularity of work, that education and moral reform may come to the individual laborer; that association may be put upon larger principles, and assume the higher fraternal aspect. But it does not want to lose sight of the end in securing the means, nor assume success, nor even necessarily the beginnings of success, when these first aims are attained. It is easy to make this mistake. The workingman is born and reared in a certain discomfort which he is sure the rich man does not share with him. He feels constantly the restriction which comes from untrained power; he realizes that his best efforts are destined to go round and round in a circle circumscribed by his industrial opportunity, and it is inevitable that he should over-estimate the possession of wealth, of leisure, and of education. It is almost impossible for him to keep his sense of proportion.

The settlement may be of value if it can take a larger and steadier view than is always possible to the workingman, smarting under a sense of wrong; or to the capitalist, seeking only to "quiet down," without regard to the historic significance of the case, and insisting upon the inalienable right of "invested capital," to a return of at least four per cent, ignoring human passion. It is possible to recall them both to a sense of the larger development.

A century ago there was an irresistible impulse, an upward movement, among the mass of people to have their share in political life,—
hitherto the life of the privileged. The universal franchise was demanded, not only as a holy right, but as a means of entrance into the
sunshine of liberty and equality. There is a similar demand at the close
of this century on the part of working-people, but this time it is for a
share in the results of industry.

It is an impulse to come out into the sunshine of Prosperity [sic]. As
the leaders of political democracy over-estimated the possession of the
franchise, and believed it would obtain blessings for the working-
people which it has not done, so, doubtless, the leaders of the labor
movement are overestimating the possession of wealth and leisure.
Mazzini was the inspired prophet of the political democracy, preaching
duties and responsibilities rather than rights and franchises; and we
might call Arnold Toynbee the prophet of the second development
when we contend that the task of the labor movement is the interpretation of democracy into industrial affairs.[3] In that remarkable exposition called "Industry and Democracy," Toynbee sets forth the struggle
between the masters and men during the industrial revolution. Two
ideals in regard to the relationship between employer and employee
were then developed. Carlyle represented one, pleading passionately for
it.[4] He declared that the rich mill-owner's duty did not end with the
"cash nexus;" that after he had paid his men he should still cherish
them in sickness, protect them in misfortune, and not dismiss them
when trade was bad. In one word, he would have the rich govern and
protect the poor. But the workers themselves, the mass of the people,
had caught another ideal; they dreamed of a time when they should
have no need of protection, but when each workman should stand by
the side of his employer—the free citizen of a free state. Each working-
man demanded, not class protection, but political rights. He wished to
be a unit; not that he might be isolated, but that he might unite in a
fuller union, first with his fellow-workers, and then with the entire people. Toynbee asks who was right, Carlyle or the people. And replies
that the people were right—"The people who, sick with hunger and deformed with toil, dreamed that democracy would bring deliverance."
And democracy did save industry. It transformed disputes about wages
from social feuds into business bargains. It swept away the estranging
class elements of suspicion and arrogance. "It gradually did away with

the feudal notion among the masters that they would deal with their men one at a time, denying to them the advantages of association." It is singular that in America, where government is founded upon the principle of representation, the capitalist should have been so slow to accord this right to workingmen; that he should refuse so steadily to treat with a "walking delegate," and so long maintain that no "outsider" could represent the men in his shop.

We must learn to trust our democracy, giant-like and threatening as it may appear in its uncouth strength and untried applications. When the English people were demanding the charter, the English nobility predicted that the franchise would be used to inaugurate all sorts of wild measures, to overturn long-established customs, as the capitalist now sometimes assumes that higher wages will be spent only in the saloons. In both cases there is a failure to count the sobering effect of responsibility in the education and development which attend the entrance into a wider life.

The effort to keep the movement to some consciousness of its historic value in the race development is perhaps no more difficult than to keep before its view the larger ethical aims. There is doubtless a tendency among the working men who reach leadership in the movement to yield to individual ambition, as there is among capitalists to regard class interests, and yield only that which must be yielded. This tendency on one side to yield to ambition, and on the other to give in to threats, may be further illustrated.

The poor man has proverbially been the tyrant of poor men when he has become rich. But while such a man was yet poor, his heart was closed to his fellows, and his eyes were blinded to the exploitation of them and himself, because in his heart he hoped one day to be rich, and to do the exploiting; because he secretly approved the action of his master, and said, "I would do the same if I were he."

Workingmen say, sometimes, that the rich will not hear the complaint of the poor until it rises into a threat, and carries a suggestion of ruin with it; that they then throw the laborers a portion of the product, to save the remainder.

As the tendency to warfare shows the primitive state of the labor movement, so also this division on class lines reveals its present undeveloped condition. The organization of society into huge battalions with syndicates and corporations on the side of capital, and trades-unions and federations on the side of labor, is to divide the world into two hostile camps, and to turn us back into class warfare and class limitations. All our experience tells us that no question of civilization is so simple as that, nor can we any longer settle our perplexities by mere good fighting. One is reminded of one's childish conception of life—that Right and Wrong were drawn up in battle array into two distinct armies, and that to join the army of Right and fight bravely would be to settle all problems.

But life itself teaches us nothing more inevitable than that right and wrong are most confusedly mixed; that the blackest wrong is by our side and within our own motives; that right does not dazzle our eyes with its radiant shining, but has to be found by exerting patience, discrimination, and impartiality. We cease to listen for the bugle note of victory our childish imagination anticipated, and learn that our finest victories are attained in the midst of self-distrust, and that the waving banner of triumph is sooner or later trailed to the dust by the weight of self-righteousness. It may be that as the labor movement grows older and riper, it will cease to divide all men so sharply into capitalists and proletarians, into exploiter and exploited.

We may live to remind its leaders in later years, as George Eliot has so skilfully reminded us, that the path we all like when we first set out in our youth is the path of martyrdom and endurance, where the palm branches grow; but that later we learn to take the steep highway of tolerance, just allowance, and self-blame, where there are no leafy honors to be gathered and worn. As the labor movement grows older its leaders may catch the larger ethical view which genuine experience always gives; they may have a chance to act free from the pressure of threat or ambition. They should have nothing to gain or lose, save as they rise or fall with their fellows. In raising the mass, men could have a motive-power as much greater than the motive for individual success, as the force which sends the sun above the horizon is greater than the force engendered by the powder behind the rocket.

Is it too much to hope that as the better organized and older trades-unions are fast recognizing a solidarity of labor, and acting upon the literal notion of brotherhood, that they will later perceive the larger solidarity which includes labor and capital, and act upon the notion of universal kinship? That before this larger vision of life there can be no perception of "sides" and no "battle array"? In the light of the developed social conscience the "sympathetic strike" may be criticised, not because it is too broad, but because it is too narrow, and because the strike is but a wasteful and negative demonstration of ethical fellowship. In the summer of 1894 the Chicago unions of Russian-Jewish cloakmakers, German compositors, and Bohemian and Polish butchers, struck in sympathy with the cause of the American Railway Union, whom they believed to be standing for a principle. Does an event such as this, clumsy and unsatisfactory as its results are, prefigure the time when no factory child in Chicago can be overworked and underpaid without a protest from all good citizens, capitalist and proletarian? Such a protest would be founded upon an ethical sense so strong that it would easily override business interests and class prejudices.

Manifestations of the labor movement are erratic and ill-timed because of the very strength of its motive power. A settlement is not affrighted nor dismayed when it sees in labor-meetings, in caucuses, and turbulent gatherings, men who are—

"Groping for the right, with horny, calloused hands,
And staring round for God with bloodshot eyes,"

Although the clumsy hands may upset some heavy pieces of convention, as a strong blindman overturns furniture, and the bloodshot eyes may be wild and fanatical. The settlement is unworthy of its calling if it is too timid or dull to interpret this groping and staring. But the settlement should be affrighted, and bestir itself to action, when the groping is not for the right, but for the mere purpose of overturning; when the staring is not for God, but for Mammon—and there is a natural temptation towards both.

A settlement may well be dismayed when it sees workingmen apathetic to higher motives, and thinking only of stratagems by which to outwit the capitalists; or when workingmen justify themselves in the use of base measures, saying they have learned the lessons from the other side. Such an attitude at once turns the movement from a development into a struggle, and the sole judge left between the adversaries must in the end be force. Class interests become the governing and motive power, and the settlement can logically be of no value to either side. Its sympathies are naturally much entangled in such a struggle, but to be of value it must keep its judgment clear as to the final ethical outcome—and this requires both perceptions and training.

Fortunately, every action may be analyzed into its permanent and transient aspects. The transient aspect of the strike is the anger and opposition against the employer, and too often the chagrin of failure. The permanent is the binding together of the strikers in the ties of association and brotherhood, and the attainment of a more democratic relation to the employer; and it is because of a growing sense of brotherhood and of democracy in the labor movement that we see in it a growing ethical power.

Hence the duty of the settlement in keeping the movement from becoming in any sense a class warfare is clear. There is a temperamental bitterness among workingmen which is both inherited and fostered by the conditions of their life and trade; but they cannot afford to cherish a class bitterness if the labor movement is to be held to its highest possibilities. A class working for a class, and against another class, implies that within itself there should be trades working for trades, individuals working for individuals. The universal character of the movement is gone from the start, and cannot be caught until an all-embracing ideal is accepted.

A recent writer has called attention to the fact that the position of the power-holding classes—capitalists, as we call them just now—is being gradually undermined by the disintegrating influence of the immense fund of altruistic feeling with which society has become equipped; that it is within this fund of altruism that we find the motive force which is slowly enfranchising all classes and gradually insisting upon equality of condition and opportunity. If we can accept this explanation of the social and political movements of our time, then it is clear that the labor movement is at the bottom an ethical movement, and a manifestation of the orderly development of the race.

The settlement is pledged to insist upon the unity of life, to gather to itself the sense of righteousness to be found in its neighborhood, and as far as possible in its city; to work towards the betterment not of one kind of people or class of people, but for the common good. The settlement believes that just as men deprived of comradeship by circumstances or law go back to the brutality from which they came, so any class or set of men deprived of the companionship of the whole, become correspondingly decivilized and crippled. No part of society can afford to get along without the others.

The settlement, then, urges first, the organization of working people in order that as much leisure and orderly life as possible may be secured to them in which to carry out the higher aims of living; in the second place, it should make a constant effort to bring to bear upon the labor movement a consciousness of its historic development; and lastly, it accentuates the ultimate ethical aims of the movement.

The despair of the labor movement is, as Mazzini said in another cause long ago, that we have torn the great and beautiful ensign of Democracy. Each party has snatched a rag of it, and parades it as proudly as if it were the whole flag, repudiating and not deigning to look at the others.

It is this feeling of disdain to any class of men or kind of men in the community which is dangerous to the labor movement, which makes it a class-measure. It attacks its democratic character, and substitutes party enthusiasm for the irresistible force of human progress. The labor movement must include all men in its hopes. It must have the communion of universal fellowship. Any drop of gall within its cup is fatal. Any grudge treasured up against a capitalist, any desire to "get even" when the wealth has changed hands, are but the old experiences of human selfishness. All sense of injury must fall away and be absorbed in the consciousness of a common brotherhood. If to insist upon the universality of the best is the function of the settlement, nowhere is its influence more needed than in the labor movement, where there is constant temptation towards a class warfare.

Notes

1. Jane Addams's depictions of the horrors of the sweatshop system are among the most potent and poignant in her work. She helps the reader to see the scenes of misery as women, together with children as young as three years of age, sit hunched over cloth, pulling out basting threads or stitching hems in poorly ventilated, dark, dank rooms hour after hour, day after day.

2. Jane Addams's relationship to Marxism was one of critical engagement. In the Working Men's Social Science Club of Hull-House, varieties of socialism were hotly debated by immigrant partisans of one strain or another. She gently mocked the utopianism of those Marxists who believed the universe could be cured of all its ills, or would be, come the cataclysm of the final revolution. She also opposed the determinism in Marxism and the justifications of violence. She fought back when she was accused of repudiating Marxism because she had failed to understand it or because she was simply insufficiently bold to take up such a radical doctrine. For Addams, democratic social change re-

quired democratic methods. The ends and the means could not be separated by a chasm. Violent and autocratic methods brought violent and autocratic results.

3. Guiseppe Mazzini (1805–1872), great leader of the Italian *risorgimento*, or movement for Italian unification, and a prophet of national democracy, was one of Jane Addams's childhood heroes. She first learned of Mazzini as an opponent of "Hapsburg oppression" from her revered father, John Huy Addams, who saw a parallel between abolitionist efforts against slavery in the United States and Mazzini's struggle against Hapsburg domination in Italy. Arnold Toynbee (1852–1883) was a leader of British reform efforts, a settlement pioneer, and the author of major works on industrialization. Addams modeled Hull-House on Toynbee Hall in London's East End.

4. Thomas Carlyle, a prolific British writer (1795–1881), was associated with the "great man" theory of history. Carlyle's histories emphasized men of decision and action. Addams found his work stirring as a schoolgirl but depressing when she was felled by a nervous malaise called "neurasthenia." His call to willfulness and action profoundly depressed her, as she could not see a clear-cut way to connect abstract ideas to concrete action on behalf of social amelioration.

7

"THE SUBTLE PROBLEMS
OF CHARITY"

PROBABLY THERE IS NO RELATION in life which our democracy is changing more rapidly than the charitable relation—that relation which obtains between benefactor and beneficiary; at the same time, there is no point of contact in our modern experience which reveals more clearly the lack of that equality which democracy implies. We have reached the moment when democracy has made such inroads upon this relationship that the complacency of the old-fashioned charitable man is gone forever; while the very need and existence of charity deny us the consolation and freedom which democracy will at last give.

We find in ourselves the longing for a wider union than that of family or class, and we say that we have come to include all men in our hopes; but we fail to realize that all men are hoping; and are part of the same movement of which we are a part. Many of the difficulties in philanthropy come from an unconscious division of the world into the philanthropists and those to be helped. It is an assumption of two classes, and against this class assumption our democratic training revolts as soon as we begin to act upon it.

The trouble is that the ethics of none of us are clearly defined, and we are continually obliged to act in circles of habit based upon convictions which we no longer hold. Thus, our estimate of the effect of environment and social conditions has doubtless shifted faster than our methods of administering charity have changed. Formerly when it was be-

Note: "The Subtle Problems of Charity," *Atlantic Monthly*, vol. 83 (February 1899).

lieved that poverty was synonymous with vice and laziness, and that the prosperous man was the righteous man, charity was administered harshly with a good conscience; for the charitable agent really blamed the individual for his poverty, and the very fact of his own superior prosperity gave him a certain consciousness of superior morality. Since then we have learned to measure by other standards, and the money-earning capacity, while still rewarded out of all proportion to any other, is not respected as exclusively as it was; and its possession is by no means assumed to imply the possession of the highest moral qualities. We have learned to judge men in general by their social virtues as well as by their business capacity, by their devotion to intellectual and disinterested aims, and by their public spirit, and we naturally resent being obliged to judge certain individuals solely upon the industrial side for no other reason than that they are poor. Our democratic instinct constantly takes alarm at this consciousness of two standards.

Of the various struggles which a decade of residence in a settlement implies, none have made a more definite impression on my mind than the incredibly painful difficulties which involve both giver and recipient when one person asks charitable aid of another.

Another attempt is made in this paper to show what are some of the perplexities which harass the mind of the charity worker; to trace them to ethical survivals which are held not only by the benefactor, but by the recipients of charity as well; and to suggest wherein these very perplexities may possibly be prophetic.

It is easy to see that one of the root difficulties in the charitable relationship lies in the fact that the only families who apply for aid to the charitable agencies are those who have come to grief on the industrial side; it may be through sickness, through loss of work, or for other guiltless and inevitable reasons, but the fact remains that they are industrially ailing and must be bolstered and helped into industrial health. The charity visitor, let us assume, is a young college woman, well-bred and open-minded. When she visits the family assigned to her, she is embarrassed to find herself obliged to lay all the stress of her teaching and advice upon the industrial virtues, and to treat members of the family almost exclusively as factors in the industrial system. She insists that they must work and be self-supporting; that the most dangerous of all situations is idleness; that seeking one's own pleasure, while ignoring claims and responsibilities, is the most ignoble of actions. The members of her assigned family may have charms and virtues,—they may possibly be kind and affectionate and considerate of one another, generous to their friends; but it is her business to stick to the industrial side. As she daily holds up these standards, it often occurs to the mind of the sensitive visitor, whose conscience has been made tender by much talk of brotherhood and equality which she has heard at college, that she has no right to say these things; that she herself has never been self-supporting; that, whatever her virtues may be, they are not the industrial virtues; that her untrained hands are no more fitted to cope with actual conditions than are those of her broken-down family.

The grandmother of the charity visitor could have done the industrial preaching very well, because she did have industrial virtues; if not skillful in weaving and spinning, she was yet mistress of other housewifely accomplishments. In a generation our experiences have changed—our views with them; while we still keep on in the old methods, which could be applied when our consciences were in line with them, but which are daily becoming more difficult as we divide up into people who work with their hands and those who do not; and the charity visitor, belonging to the latter class, is perplexed by recognitions and suggestions which the situation forces upon her. Our democracy has taught us to apply our moral teaching all around, and the moralist is rapidly becoming so sensitive that when his life does not exemplify his ethical convictions, he finds it difficult to preach.

Add to this a consciousness in the mind of the visitor of a genuine misunderstanding of her motives by the recipients of her charity and by their neighborhoods. Let us take a neighborhood of poor people, and test their ethical standards by those of the charity visitor, who comes with the best desire in the world to help them out of their distresses. A most striking incongruity, at once apparent, is the difference between the emotional kindness with which relief is given by one poor neighbor to another poor neighbor, and the guarded care with which relief is given by a charity visitor to a charity recipient. The neighborhood mind is immediately confronted not only by the difference of method, but also by an absolute clashing of two ethical standards. . . .

The evolutionists tell us that the instinct to pity, the impulse to aid his fellows, served man at a very early period as a rude rule of right and wrong. There is no doubt that this rude rule still holds among many people with whom charitable agencies are brought into contact, and that their ideas of right and wrong are quite honestly outraged by the methods of these agencies. When they see the delay and caution with which relief is given, these do not appear to them conscientious scruples, but the cold and calculating action of the selfish man. This is not the aid that they are accustomed to receive from their neighbors, and they do not understand why the impulse which drives people to be good to the poor should be so severely supervised. They feel, remotely, that the charity visitor is moved by motives that are alien and unreal; they may be superior motives, but are "a'gin' nature." They cannot comprehend why a person whose intellectual perceptions are stronger than his natural impulses should go into charity work at all. The only man they are accustomed to see whose intellectual perceptions are stronger than his tenderness of heart is the selfish and avaricious man, who is frankly "on the make." If the charity visitor is such a person, why does she pretend to like the poor? Why does she not go into business at once? We may say, of course, that it is a primitive view of life which thus confuses intellectuality and business ability, but it is a view quite honestly held by many poor people who are obliged to receive charity from time to time. . . . In the minds of the poor success does not ordinarily go with charity and kind-heartedness, but rather with the opposite qualities. The rich landlord is he who collects with sternness; who accepts no excuse, and will have his own. There are moments of irritation and of real bitterness against him, but there is admiration because he is rich and successful. . . . The charity visitor, just because she is a person who concerns herself with the poor, receives a touch of. . . . good-natured and kindly contempt, sometimes real affection, but little genuine respect. The poor are accustomed to help one another, and to respond according to their kindliness; but when it comes to worldly judgment, they are still in that stage where they use industrial success as the sole standard. In the case of the charity visitor, they are deprived of both standards; she has neither natural kindness nor dazzling riches; and they find it of course utterly impossible to judge of the motive of organized charity.

Doubtless we all find something distasteful in the juxtaposition of the two words "organized" and "charity." The idea of organizing an emotion is in itself repelling, even to those of us who feel most sorely the need of more order in altruistic effort and see the end to be desired. We say in defense that we are striving to turn this emotion into a motive;

that pity is capricious, and not to be depended on; that we mean to give it the dignity of conscious duty. But at bottom we distrust a little a scheme which substitutes a theory of social conduct for the natural promptings of the heart, and we ourselves feel the complexity of the situation. The poor man who has fallen into distress, when he first asks aid, instinctively expects tenderness, consideration, and forgiveness. If it is the first time, it has taken him long to make up his mind to the step. He comes somewhat bruised and battered, and instead of being met by warmth of heart and sympathy he is at once chilled by an investigation and an intimation that he ought to work. He does not see that he is being dealt with as a child of defective will is cared for by a stern parent. There have been no years of previous intercourse and established relation, as between parents and children. He feels only the postponement or refusal, which he considers harsh. . . .

The state of mind which an investigation arouses on both sides is most unfortunate; but the perplexity and clashing of different standards, with the consequent misunderstandings, are not so bad as the moral deterioration which is almost sure to follow.

When the agent or visitor appears among the poor, and they discover that under certain conditions food and rent and medical aid are dispensed from some unknown source, every man, woman, and child is quick to learn what the conditions may be, and to follow them. Though in their eyes a glass of beer is quite right and proper when taken as any self-respecting man should take it; though they know that cleanliness is an expensive virtue which can be expected of the few; though they realize that saving is well-nigh impossible when but a few cents can be laid by at a time; though their feeling for the church may be something quite elusive of definition and quite apart from daily living,—to the visitor they gravely laud temperance and cleanliness and thrift and religious observance. The deception doubtless arises from a wondering inability to understand the ethical ideals which can require such impossible virtues, combined with a tradition that charity visitors do require them, and from an innocent desire to please. . . .

The most serious effect upon the individual comes when dependence upon the charitable society is substituted for the natural outgoing of human love and sympathy, which, happily, we all possess to some degree. The spontaneous impulse to sit up all night with a neighbor's sick child is turned into righteous indignation against the district nurse because she goes home at six o'clock. Or the kindness which would have prompted a quick purchase of much needed medicine is transformed into a voluble scoring of the dispensary, because it gives prescriptions, and not drugs; and "who can get well on a piece of paper?". . .

The neighborhood understands the selfish rich people who stay in their own part of town, where all their associates have shoes and other things. Such people do not bother themselves about the poor; they are like the rich landlords of the neighborhood experience. But this lady visitor, who pretends to be good to the poor, and certainly does talk as though she were kind-hearted, what does she come for, if she does not intend to give them things which so plainly are needed? The visitor says, sometimes, that in holding her poor family so hard to a standard of thrift she is really breaking down a rule of higher living which they formerly possessed; that saving, which seems quite commendable in a comfortable part of town, appears almost criminal in a poor quarter, where the next-door neighbor needs food, even if the children of the family do not. She feels the sordidness of constantly being obliged to urge the industrial view of life. The benevolent individual of fifty years ago honestly believed that industry and self-denial in youth would result in comfortable possessions for old age. It was, indeed, the method he had practiced in his own youth, and by which he had probably obtained whatever fortune he possessed. He therefore reproved the poor family for indulging their children, urged them to work long hours, and was utterly untouched by many scruples which afflict the contemporary charity visitor. . . .

. . . The [charity] visitor is continually surprised to find that the safest platitudes may be challenged. She refers quite naturally to the "horrors of the saloon," and discovers that the head of her visited family, who knows the saloons very well, does not connect them with "horrors" at all. He remembers all the kindnesses he has received there, the free lunch and treating which go on, even when a man is out of work and not able to pay up; the poor fellows who are allowed to sit in their warmth when every other door is closed to them; the loan of five dollars he got there, when the charity visitor was miles away, and he was threatened with eviction. He may listen politely to her references to horrors, but considers it only "temperance talk.". . .

The charity visitor may blame the women for lack of gentleness toward their children, for being hasty and rude to them, until she learns to reflect that the standard of breeding is not that of gentleness toward the children so much as the observance of certain conventions, such as the punctilious wearing of mourning garments after the death of a child. The standard of gentleness each mother has to work out largely by herself, assisted only by the occasional shamefaced remark of a neighbor, that "they do better when you are not too hard on them;" but the wearing of mourning garments is sustained by the definitely expressed sentiment of every woman in the street. The mother would have to bear social blame, a certain social ostracism, if she failed to comply with that requirement. It is not comfortable to outrage the conventions of those among whom we live, and if our social life be a narrow one, it is still more difficult. The visitor may choke a little when she sees the lessened supply of food and the scanty clothing provided for the remaining children, in order that one may be conventionally mourned. But she does not talk so strongly against it as she would have done during her first month of experience with the family since bereaved. . . .

The charity visitor is still more perplexed when she comes to consider such problems as those of early marriage and child labor; for she cannot deal with them according to economic theories, or according to the conventions which have regulated her own life. She finds both of these fairly upset by her intimate knowledge of the situation and her sympathy for those into whose lives she has gained a curious insight. She discovers how incorrigibly bourgeois her standards have been, and it takes but a little time to reach the conclusion that she cannot insist so strenuously upon the conventions of her own class, which fail to fit the bigger, more emotional, and freer lives of working people. The charity visitor holds well-grounded views upon the imprudence of early marriage; quite naturally, because she comes from a family and circle of professional and business people. A professional man is scarcely equipped and started in his profession before he is thirty; a business man, if he is on the road to success, is much nearer prosperity at thirty-five than at twenty-five, and it is therefore wise for these men not to marry in the twenties. But this does not apply to the workingman. In many trades he is laid upon the shelf at thirty-five, and in nearly all trades he receives the largest wages of his life between twenty and thirty. If the young workingman has all his wages too long to himself, he will probably establish habits of personal comfort which he cannot keep up when he has to divide with a family,—habits which, perhaps, he can never overcome. . . .

. . . He naturally regards his children as his savings-bank; he expects them to care for him when he gets old, and in some trades old age comes very early. A Jewish tailor was quite lately sent to the Cook County poorhouse, paralyzed beyond recovery at the age of thirty-five. Had his little boy of nine been a few years older, the father might have been spared this sorrow of public charity. He was, in fact, better able to support a family when he was twenty than when he was thirty-five, for his wages had steadily become less as the years went on. . . .

This economic pressure also accounts for the tendency to put children to work over-young, and thus cripple their chances for individual development and usefulness, and with the avaricious parent it often leads to exploitation. . . . It has long been a common error for the charity visitor, who is strongly urging her family toward self-support, to suggest, or at least connive, that the children be put to work early, although she has not the excuse that the parents have. It is so easy, after one has been taking the industrial view for a long time, to forget the larger and more social claim; to urge that the boy go to work and support his parents, who are receiving charitable aid. The visitor does not realize what a cruel advantage the person who distributes charity has, when she gives advice. The manager in a huge mercantile establishment employing many children was able to show, during a child-labor investigation, that the only children under fourteen years of age in his employ were proteges, urged upon him by philanthropic ladies, who were not only acquaintances of his, but valued patrons of the establishment. It is not that the charity visitor of an earlier day was less wise than other people, but she fixed her mind so long upon the industrial lameness of her family that she was eager to seize any crutch, however weak, which might enable them to get on. She failed to see that the boy who attempts prematurely to support his widowed mother may lower wages, add an illiterate member to the community, and arrest the development of a capable workingman. . . .

The struggle for existence, which is so much harsher among people near the edge of pauperism, sometimes leaves ugly marks on character, and the charity visitor finds the indirect results most mystifying. Parents who work hard and anticipate an old age when they can no longer earn, take care that their children shall expect to divide their wages with them from the very first. Such a parent, when successful, seizes the immature nervous system of the child and hypnotizes it, so to speak, into a habit of obedience, that the nerves and will may not depart from this control when the child is older. The charity visitor, whose family relation is lifted quite out of this, does not in the least understand the industrial foundation in this family despotism. . . .

There are an impressive number of children who uncomplainingly hand over their weekly wages to their parents, sometimes receiving back ten cents or a quarter for spending money, but quite as often nothing at all; and the writer knows one daughter of twenty-five who for six years has received two cents a week from the constantly falling wages which she earns in a large factory. Is it habit or virtue which holds her steady in this course? If love and tenderness had been substituted for parental despotism, would the mother have had enough affection, enough power of expression, to hold her daughter's sense of money obligation through all these years? This young woman, who spends her paltry two cents on chewing-gum, and goes plainly clad in clothes of her mother's choosing, while many of her friends spend their entire wages on clothes which factory girls love so well, must be held by some powerful force.

It is these subtle and elusive problems which, after all, the charity visitor finds most harassing. The head of a family she is visiting is a man who has become blacklisted in a strike. He is not a very good workman, and this, added to his reputation as an agitator, keeps him out of work for a long time. The fatal result of being long out of work follows. He becomes less and less eager for it, and "gets a job" less and less frequently. In order to keep up his self-respect, and still more to keep his wife's respect for him, he yields to the little self-deception that this prolonged idleness is due to his having been blacklisted, and he gradually becomes a martyr. Deep down in his heart, perhaps—But who knows what may be deep down in his heart? Whatever may be in his wife's, she does not show for an instant that she thinks he has grown lazy, and accustomed to see her earn, by sewing and cleaning, most of the scanty income for the family. The charity visitor does see this, and she also sees that the other men who were in the strike have gone back to work. She further knows, by inquiry and a little experience, that the man is not skillful. She cannot, however, call him lazy and good-for-nothing, and denounce him as worthless, because of certain intellectual conceptions at which she has arrived. She sees other workmen come to him for shrewd advice; she knows that he spends many more hours in the public library, reading good books, than the average workman has time to do. He has formed no bad habits, and has yielded only to those subtle temptations toward a life of leisure which come to the intellectual man. . . . The neighborhood women confide to the charity visitor their sympathy with his wife, because she has to work so hard, and because her husband does not "provide." Their remarks are sharpened by a certain resentment toward the superiority of the husband's education and gentle manners.

The charity visitor is ashamed to take this narrow point of view, for she knows that it is not altogether fair. . . . The charity visitor has been taught that her mission is to preserve the finest traits to be found in her visited family, and she shrinks from the thought of convincing the wife that her husband is worthless, and she suspects that she might turn all this beautiful devotion into complaining drudgery. To be sure, she could give up visiting the family altogether, but she has become much interested in the progress of the crippled child, who eagerly anticipates her visits, and she also suspects that she will never know many finer women than the mother. She is unwilling, therefore, to give up the friendship, and goes on, bearing her perplexities as best she may. . . .

A certain charity visitor is peculiarly appealed to by the weakness and pathos of forlorn old age. She is responsible for the well-being of perhaps a dozen old women, to whom she sustains a sincere and simple and almost filial relation. Some of them learn to take her benefactions quite as if they came from their own relatives, grumbling at all she does, and scolding her with a family freedom. One of these poor old women was injured in a fire years ago. She has but the fragment of a hand left, and is grievously crippled in her feet. Through years of pain she has become addicted to opium, and when she first came under the residents' care was held from the poorhouse only by the awful thought that there she would perish without her drug. Five years of tender care have done wonders for her. She lives in two neat little rooms, where with a thumb and two fingers she makes innumerable quilts, which she sells and gives away with the greatest delight. Her opium is regulated to a set amount each day, and she has been drawn away from much drinking. She is a voracious reader, and has her head full of strange tales made up from books and her own imagination. At one time it seemed impossible to do anything for her in Chicago, and she was kept for two years in a suburb where the family of the charity visitor lived, and where she was nursed through several hazardous illnesses. She now lives a better life than she did, but she is still far from being a model old woman. Her neighbors are constantly shocked by the fact that she is supported and comforted by "a charity lady," while at the same time she occasionally "rushes the growlers," scolding at the boys lest they jar her in her tottering walk. The care of her has broken through even that second standard, which the neighborhood had learned to recognize as the standard of charitable societies, that only the "worthy poor" are to be helped; that temperance and thrift are the virtues which receive the plums of benevolence. The old lady is conscious of this criticism. Indeed, irate neighbors tell her to her face that she does not in the least deserve what she gets. In order to disarm them, and at the same time to explain what would otherwise seem loving kindness so colossal as to be abnormal, she tells them that during her sojourn in the suburb she discovered an awful family secret, a horrible scandal connected with the long-suffering charity visitor; that it is in order to prevent the divulgence of this that the ministrations are continued. Some of her perplexed neighbors accept this explanation as simple and offering a solution of a vexed problem. Doubtless many of them have a glimpse of the real state of affairs, of the love and patience which minister to need irrespective of worth. But the standard is too high for most of them, and it sometimes seems unfortunate to break down the second standard, which holds that people who "rush the growler" are not worthy of charity, and that there is a certain justice attained when they go to the poor-house. It is doubtless dangerous to break down this sense of justice, unless the higher motive is made clear.

Just when our affection becomes large and real enough to care for the unworthy among the poor as we would care for the unworthy among our own kin, is a perplexing question. To say that it should never be so is a comment upon our democratic relations to them which few of us would be willing to make. . . .

We sometimes say that our charity is too scientific, but we should doubtless be much more correct in our estimate if we said that it is not scientific enough. We dislike the entire arrangement of cards alphabetically classified according to the streets and names of families, with the unrelated and meaningless details attached to them. Our feeling of revolt is, probably, not unlike that which afflicted the students of botany and geology in the early part of this century, when flowers were tabulated in alphabetical order, when geology was taught by colored charts and thin books. No doubt the students, wearied to death, many times said that it was all too scientific, and were much perplexed and worried when they found traces of structure and physiology which their so-called scientific principles were totally unable to account for. But all this happened before science had become evolutionary and scientific at all,—before it had a principle of life from within. . . . Collecting data in sociology may mean sorrow and perplexity and a pull upon one's sympathies, just as truly as collecting data in regard to the flora of the equatorial regions means heat and scratches and the test of one's endurance. Human motives have been so long a matter of dogmatism that to act upon the assumption that they are the result of growth, and to study their status with an open mind and a scientific conscience, seems well-nigh impossible to us. A man who would hesitate to pronounce an opinion upon the stones lying by the wayside because he has a suspicion that they are "geological specimens," and his veneration for science is such that he would not venture to state to which period they belonged, will, without a moment's hesitation, dogmatize about the delicate problems of human conduct, and will assert that one man is a scoundrel and another an honorable gentleman, without in the least considering the ethical epochs to which the two belong. He disregards the temptations and environment to which they have been subjected, and requires the same human development of an Italian peasant and a New England scholar.

Is this again a mark of our democracy or of our lack of science? We are singularly slow to apply the evolutionary principle to human affairs in general, although it is fast being applied to the education of children. We are at last learning to follow the development of the child; to expect certain traits under certain conditions; to adapt methods and matter to his growing mind. . . . But in our charitable efforts, we think much more of what a man ought to be than of what he is or of what he may become; and we ruthlessly force our conventions and standards upon him, with a sternness which we would consider stupid, indeed, did an educator use it in forcing his mature intellectual convictions upon an undeveloped mind. . . .

. . . There is no doubt that our development of charity methods has reached [this] pseudo-scientific and stilted stage. We have learned to condemn unthinking, ill-regulated kind-heartedness, and we take great pride in mere repression, much as the stern parent tells the visitor below how admirably he is rearing the child who is hysterically crying upstairs, and laying the foundation for future nervous disorders. The pseudo-scientific spirit, or rather the undeveloped stage of our philanthropy, is perhaps most clearly revealed in this tendency to lay stress on negative action. . . . We do not yet really believe that pity and sympathy, even, in point of fact quite as often precede the effort toward social amelioration as does the acceptance of a social dogma; we forget that the accumulation of knowledge and the holding of convictions must finally result in the application of that knowledge and those convictions to life itself, and that the course which begins by activity, and an appeal to the sympathies so severe that all the knowledge in the possession of the visitor is continually applied, has reasonably a greater chance for an ultimate comprehension.

For most of the years during a decade of residence in a settlement, my mind was sore and depressed over the difficulties of the charitable relationship. The incessant clashing of ethical standards, which had been honestly gained from widely varying industrial experience, the misunderstandings inevitable between people whose conventions and mode of life had been so totally unlike—made it seem reasonable to say that nothing could be done until industrial conditions were made absolutely democratic. The position of a settlement, which attempts at one and the same time to declare its belief in this eventual, industrial democracy, and to labor toward that end, to maintain a standard of living, and to deal humanely and simply with those in actual want, often seems utterly untenable and preposterous. Recently, however, there has come to my mind the suggestion of a principle, that while the painful condition of administering charity is the inevitable discomfort of a transition into a more democratic relation, the perplexing experiences of the actual administration have a genuine value of their own. . . . The social reformers who avoid the charitable relationship with any of their fellow men take a certain outside attitude toward this movement. They may analyze it and formulate it; they may be most valuable and necessary, but they are not essentially within it. The mass of men seldom move together without an emotional incentive, and the doctrinaire, in his effort to keep his mind free from the emotional quality, inevitably stands aside. He avoids the perplexity, and at the same time loses the vitality.

The Hebrew prophet made three requirements from those who would join the great forward-moving process led by Jehovah. "To love mercy," and at the same time "to do justly," is the difficult task. To fulfill the first requirement alone is to fall into the error of indiscriminate giving, with all its disastrous results; to fulfill the second exclusively is to obtain the stern policy of withholding, and it results in such a dreary lack of sympathy and understanding that the establishment of justice is impossible. It may be that the combination of the two can never be attained save as we fulfill still the third requirement, "to walk humbly with God," which may mean to walk for many dreary miles beside the lowliest of his creatures, not even in peace of mind, that the companionship of the humble is popularly supposed to give, but rather with the pangs and misgivings to which the poor human understanding is subjected whenever it attempts to comprehend the meaning of life.

8

"FILIAL RELATIONS"

THERE ARE MANY PEOPLE in every community who have not felt the "social compunction," who do not share the effort toward a higher social morality, who are even unable to sympathetically interpret it. Some of these have been shielded from the inevitable and salutary failures which the trial of new powers involve, because they are content to attain standards of virtue demanded by an easy public opinion, and others of them have exhausted their moral energy in attaining to the current standard of individual and family righteousness.

Such people, who form the bulk of contented society, demand that the radical, the reformer, shall be without stain or question in his personal and family relations, and judge most harshly any deviation from the established standards. There is a certain justice in this: it expresses the inherent conservatism of the mass of men, that none of the established virtues which have been so slowly and hardly acquired shall be sacrificed for the sake of making problematic advance; that the individual, in his attempt to develop and use the new and exalted virtue, shall not fall into the easy temptation of letting the ordinary ones slip through his fingers.

This instinct to conserve the old standards, combined with a distrust of the new standard, is a constant difficulty in the way of those experiments and advances depending upon the initiative of women, both because women are the more sensitive to the individual and family claims, and because their training has tended to make them content with the response to these claims alone.

Note: "Filial Relations," in *Democracy and Social Ethics* (New York: Macmillan, 1902; reissued by Belknap Press, Harvard University, 1964), chapter 3.

There is no doubt that, in the effort to sustain the moral energy necessary to work out a more satisfactory social relation, the individual often sacrifices the energy which should legitimately go into the fulfilment of personal and family claims, to what he considers the higher claim.

In considering the changes which our increasing democracy is constantly making upon various relationships, it is impossible to ignore the filial relation. This chapter deals with the relation between parents and their grown-up daughters, as affording an explicit illustration of the perplexity and mal-adjustment [sic] brought about by the various attempts of young women to secure a more active share in the community life. We constantly see parents very much disconcerted and perplexed in regard to their daughters when these daughters undertake work lying quite outside of traditional and family interests. These parents insist that the girl is carried away by a foolish enthusiasm, that she is in search of a career, that she is restless and does not know what she wants. They will give any reason, almost, rather than the recognition of a genuine and dignified claim. Possibly all this is due to the fact that for so many hundreds of years women have had no larger interests, no participation in the affairs lying quite outside personal and family claims. Any attempt that the individual woman formerly made to subordinate or renounce the family claim was inevitably construed to mean that she was setting up her own will against that of her family's for selfish ends. It was concluded that she could have no motive larger than a desire to serve her family, and her attempt to break away must therefore be willful [sic] and self-indulgent.

The family logically consented to give her up at her marriage, when she was enlarging the family tie by founding another family. It was easy to understand that they permitted and even promoted her going to college, travelling in Europe, or any other means of self-improvement, because these merely meant the development and cultivation of one of its own members. When, however, she responded to her impulse to fulfil the social or democratic claim, she violated every tradition.

The mind of each one of us reaches back to our first struggles as we emerged from self-willed childhood into a recognition of family obligations. We have all gradually learned to respond to them, and yet most of us have had at least fleeting glimpses of what it might be to disregard them and the elemental claim they make upon us. We have yielded at times to the temptation of ignoring them for selfish aims, of considering the individual and not the family convenience, and we remember with shame the self-pity which inevitably followed. But just as we have learned to adjust the personal and family claims, and to find an orderly development impossible without recognition of both, so perhaps we are called upon now to make a second adjustment between the family and the social claim, in which neither shall lose and both be ennobled.

The attempt to bring about a healing compromise in which the two shall be adjusted in proper relation is not an easy one. It is difficult to distinguish between the outward act of him who in following one legitimate claim has been led into the temporary violation of another, and the outward act of him who deliberately renounces a just claim and throws aside all obligation for the sake of his own selfish and individual development. The man, for instance, who deserts his family that he may cultivate an artistic sensibility, or acquire what he considers more fulness of life for himself, must always arouse our contempt. Breaking the marriage tie as Ibsen's "Nora" did, to obtain a larger self-development, or holding to it as George Eliot's "Romola" did, because of the larger claim of the state and society, must always remain two distinct paths.[1] The collision of interests, each of which has a real moral basis and a right to its own place in life, is bound to be more or less tragic. It is the struggle between two claims, the destruction of either of which would bring ruin to the ethical life. Curiously enough, it is almost exactly this contradiction which is the tragedy set forth by the Greek dramatist, who asserted that the gods who watch over the sanctity of the family bond must yield to the higher claims of the gods of the state. The failure to recognize the social claim as legitimate causes the trouble; the suspicion constantly remains that woman's public efforts are merely selfish and captious, and are not directed to the general good. This suspicion will never be dissipated until parents, as well as daughters, feel the democratic impulse and recognize the social claim.

Our democracy is making inroads upon the family, the oldest of human institutions, and a claim is being advanced which in a certain sense is larger than the family claim. The claim of the state in time of war has long been recognized, so that in its name the family has given up sons and husbands and even the fathers of little children. If we can once see the claims of society in any light, if its misery and need can be made clear and urged as an explicit claim, as the state urges its claims in the time of danger, then for the first time the daughter who desires to minister to that need will be recognized as acting conscientiously. This recognition may easily come first through the emotions, and may be admitted as a response to pity and mercy long before it is formulated and perceived by the intellect.

The family as well as the state we are all called upon to maintain as the highest institutions which the race has evolved for its safeguard and protection. But merely to preserve these institutions is not enough. There come periods of reconstruction, during which the task is laid upon a passing generation, to enlarge the function and carry forward the ideal of a long-established institution. There is no doubt that many women, consciously and unconsciously, are struggling with this task. The family, like every other element of human life, is susceptible of progress, and from epoch to epoch its tendencies and aspirations are enlarged, although its duties can never be abrogated and its obligations can never be cancelled. It is impossible to bring about the higher development by any self-assertion or breaking away of the individual will. The new growth in the plant swelling against the sheath, which at the same time imprisons and protects it, must still be the truest type of progress. The family in its entirety must be carried out into the larger life. Its various members together must recognize and acknowledge the validity of the social obligation. When this does not occur we have a most flagrant example of the ill-adjustment and misery arising when an ethical code is applied too rigorously and too conscientiously to conditions which are no longer the same as when the code was instituted, and for which it was never designed. We have all seen parental control and the family claim assert their authority in fields of effort which belong to the adult judgment of the child and such pertain to activity quite outside the family life. Probably the distinctively family tragedy of which we all catch glimpses now and then, is the assertion of this authority through all the entanglements of wounded affection and misunderstanding. We see parents and children acting from conscientious motives and with the tenderest affection, yet bringing about a misery which can scarcely be hidden.

Such glimpses remind us of that tragedy enacted centuries ago in Assisi, when the eager young noble cast his very clothing at his father's feet, dramatically renouncing his filial allegiance, and formally subjecting the narrow family claim to the wider and more universal duty.[2] All the conflict of tragedy ensued which might have been averted, had the father recognized the higher claim, and had he been willing to subordinate and adjust his own claim to it. The father considered his son disrespectful and hard-hearted, yet we know St. Francis to have been the most tender and loving of men, responsive to all possible ties, even to those of inanimate nature. We know that by his affections he freed the frozen life of his time. The elements of tragedy lay in the narrowness of the father's mind; in his lack of comprehension and his lack of sympathy with the power which was moving his son, and which was but part of the religious revival which swept Europe from end to end in the early part of the thirteenth century; the same power which built the cathedrals of the North, and produced the saints and sages of the South. But the father's situation was nevertheless genuine; he felt his heart sore and angry, and his dignity covered with disrespect. He could not, indeed, have felt otherwise, unless he had been touched by the fire of the same revival, and lifted out of and away from the contemplation of himself and his narrower claim. It is another proof that the notion of a larger obligation can only come through the response to an enlarged interest in life and in the social movements around us.

The grown-up son has so long been considered a citizen with well-defined duties and a need of "making his way in the world," that the family claim is urged much less strenuously in his case, and as a matter of authority, it ceases gradually to be made at all. In the case of the grown-up daughter, however, who is under no necessity of earning a living, and who has no strong artistic bent, taking her to Paris to study painting or to Germany to study music, the years immediately following her graduation from college are too often filled with a restlessness and unhappiness which might be avoided by a little clear thinking, and by an adaptation of our code of family ethics to modern conditions.

It is always difficult for the family to regard the daughter otherwise than as a family possession. From her babyhood she has been the charm and grace of the household, and it is hard to think of her as an integral part of the social order, hard to believe that she has duties outside of the family, to the state and to society in the larger sense. This assumption that the daughter is solely an inspiration and refinement to the family itself and its own immediate circle, that her delicacy and polish are but outward symbols of her father's protection and prosperity, worked very smoothly for the most part so long as her education was in line with it. When there was absolutely no recognition of the entity of woman's life beyond the family, when the outside claims upon her were still wholly unrecognized, the situation was simple, and the finishing school harmoniously and elegantly answered all requirements. She was fitted to grace the fireside and to add lustre to that social circle which her parents selected for her. But this family assumption has been notably broken into, and educational ideas no longer fit it. Modern education recognizes woman quite apart from family or society claims, and gives her the training which for many years has been deemed successful for highly developing a man's individuality and freeing his powers for independent action. Perplexities often occur when the daughter returns from college and finds that this recognition has been but partially accomplished. When she attempts to act upon the assumption of its accomplishment, she finds herself jarring upon ideals which are so entwined with filial piety, so rooted in the tenderest affections of which the human heart is capable, that both daughter and parents are shocked and startled when they discover what is happening, and they scarcely venture to analyze the situation. The ideal for the education of woman has changed under the pressure of a new claim. The family has responded to the extent of granting the education, but they are jealous of the new claim and assert the family claim as over against it.

The modern woman finds herself educated to recognize a stress of social obligation which her family did not in the least anticipate when they sent her to college. She finds herself, in addition, under an impulse to act her part as a citizen of the world. She accepts her family inheritance with loyalty and affection, but she has entered into a wider inheritance as well, which, for lack of a better phrase, we call the social claim. This claim has been recognized for four years in her training, but after her return from college the family claim is again exclusively and strenuously asserted. The situation has all the discomfort of transition and compromise. The daughter finds a constant and totally unnecessary conflict between the social and the family claims. In most cases the former is repressed and gives way to the family claim, because the latter is concrete and definitely asserted, while the social demand is vague and unformulated. In such instances the girl quietly submits, but she feels wronged whenever she allows her mind to dwell upon the situation. She either hides her hurt, and splendid reserves of enthusiasm and capacity go to waste, or her zeal and emotions are turned inward, and the result is an unhappy woman, whose heart is consumed by vain regrets and desires.

If the college woman is not thus quietly reabsorbed, she is even reproached for her discontent. She is told to be devoted to her family, inspiring and responsive to her social circle, and to give the rest of her time to further self-improvement and enjoyment. She expects to do this, and responds to these claims to the best of her ability even heroically sometimes. But where is the larger life of which she has dreamed so long? That life which surrounds and completes the individual and family life? She has been taught that it is her duty to share this life, and her highest privilege to extend it. This divergence between her self-centred existence and her best convictions becomes constantly more apparent. But the situation is not even so simple as a conflict between her affections and her intellectual convictions, although even that is tumultuous enough, also the emotional nature is divided against itself. The social claim is a demand upon the emotions as well as upon the intellect, and in ignoring it she represses not only her convictions but lowers her springs of vitality. Her life is full of contradictions. She looks out into the world, longing that some demand be made upon her powers, for they are too untrained to furnish an initiative. When her health gives way under this strain, as it often does, her physician invariably advises a rest. But to be put to bed and fed on milk is not what she requires. What she needs is simple, health-giving activity, which, involving the use of all her faculties, shall be a response to all the claims which she so keenly feels.

It is quite true that the family often resents her first attempts to be part of a life quite outside their own, because the college woman frequently makes these first attempts most awkwardly; her faculties have not been trained in the line of action. She lacks the ability to apply her knowledge and theories to life itself and to its complicated situations. This is largely the fault of her training and of the one-sidedness of educational methods. The colleges have long been full of the best ethical teaching, insisting that the good of the whole must ultimately be the measure of effort, and that the individual can only secure his own rights as he labors to secure those of others. But while the teaching has included an ever-broadening range of obligation and has insisted upon the recognition of the claims of human brotherhood, the training has been singularly individualistic; it has fostered ambitions for personal distinction, and has trained the faculties almost exclusively in the direction of intellectual accumulation. Doubtless, woman's education is at fault, in that it has failed to recognize certain needs, and has failed to cultivate and guide the larger desires of which all generous young hearts are full.

During the most formative years of life, it gives the young girl no contact with the feebleness of childhood, the pathos of suffering, or the needs of old age. It gathers together crude youth in contact only with each other and with mature men and women who are there for the purpose of their mental direction. The tenderest promptings are bidden to bide their time. This could only be justifiable if a definite outlet were provided when they leave college. Doubtless the need does not differ widely in men and women, but women not absorbed in professional or business life, in the years immediately following college, are baldly brought face to face with the deficiencies of their training. Apparently every obstacle is removed, and the college woman is at last free to begin the active life, for which, during so many years, she has been preparing. But during this so-called preparation, her faculties have been trained solely for accumulation, and she has learned to utterly distrust the finer impulses of her nature, which would naturally have connected her with human interests outside of her family and her own immediate social circle. All through school and college the young soul dreamed of self-sacrifice, of succor to the helpless and of tenderness to the unfortunate. We persistently distrust these desires, and, unless they follow well-defined lines, we repress them with every device of convention and caution.

One summer the writer went from a two weeks' residence in East London, where she had become sick and bewildered by the sights and sounds encountered there, directly to Switzerland. She found the beaten routes of travel filled with young English men and women who could walk many miles a day, and who could climb peaks so inaccessible that the feats received honorable mention in Alpine journals,—a result which filled their families with joy and pride. These young people knew to a nicety the proper diet and clothing which would best contribute toward endurance. Everything was very fine about them save their motive power. The writer does not refer to the hard-worked men and women who were taking a vacation, but to the leisured young people, to whom this period was the most serious of the year, and filled with the most strenuous exertion. They did not, of course, thoroughly enjoy it, for we are too complicated to be content with mere exercise. Civilization has bound us too closely with our brethren for any one of us to be long happy in the cultivation of mere individual force or in the accumulation of mere muscular energy.

With Whitechapel constantly in mind, it was difficult not to advise these young people to use some of this muscular energy of which they were so proud, in cleaning neglected alleys and paving soggy streets. Their stores of enthusiasm might stir to energy the listless men and women of East London and utilize latent social forces. The exercise would be quite as good, the need of endurance as great, the care for proper dress and food as important; but the motives for action would be turned from selfish ones into social ones. Such an appeal would doubtless be met with a certain response from the young people, but would never be countenanced by their families for an instant.

Fortunately a beginning has been made in another direction, and a few parents have already begun to consider even their little children in relation to society as well as to the family. The young mothers who attend "Child Study" classes have a larger notion of parenthood and expect given characteristics from their children, at certain ages and under certain conditions. They quite calmly watch the various attempts of a child to assert his individuality, which so often takes the form of opposition to the wishes of the family and to the rule of the house-hold. They recognize as acting under the same law of development the little child of three who persistently runs away and pretends not to hear his mother's voice, the boy of ten who violently, although temporarily, resents control of any sort, and the grown-up son who, by an individualized and trained personality, is drawn into pursuits and interests quite alien to those of his family.

This attempt to take the parental relation somewhat away from mere personal experience, as well as the increasing tendency of parents to share their children's pursuits and interests, will doubtless finally result in a better understanding of the social obligation. The understanding, which results from identity of interests, would seem to confirm the conviction that in the complicated life of to-day there is no education so admirable as that education which comes from participation in the constant trend of events. There is no doubt that most of the misunderstandings of life are due to partial intelligence, because our experiences have been so unlike that we cannot comprehend each other. The old difficulties incident to the clash of two codes of morals must drop away, as the experiences of various members of the family become larger and more identical.

At the present moment, however, many of those difficulties still exist and may be seen all about us. In order to illustrate the situation baldly, and at the same time to put it dramatically, it may be well to take an instance concerning which we have no personal feeling. The tragedy of King Lear has been selected, although we have been accustomed so long to give him our sympathy as the victim of the ingratitude of his two older daughters, and of the apparent coldness of Cordelia, that we have not sufficiently considered the weakness of his fatherhood, revealed by the fact that he should get himself into so entangled and unhappy a relation to all of his children. In our pity for Lear, we fail to analyze his character. The King on his throne exhibits utter lack of self-control. The King in the storm gives way to the same emotion, in repining over the wickedness of his children, which he formerly exhibited in his indulgent treatment of them.

It might be illuminating to discover wherein he had failed, and why his old age found him roofless in spite of the fact that he strenuously urged the family claim with his whole conscience. At the opening of the drama he sat upon his throne, ready for the enjoyment which an indulgent parent expects when he has given gifts to his children. From the two elder, the responses for the division of his lands were graceful and fitting, but he longed to hear what Cordelia, his youngest and best beloved child, would say. He looked toward her expectantly, but instead of delight and gratitude there was the first dawn of character. Cordelia made the awkward attempt of an untrained soul to be honest and scrupulously to express her inmost feeling. The king was baffled and distressed by this attempt at self-expression. It was new to him that his daughter should be moved by a principle obtained outside himself, which even his imagination could not follow; that she had caught the notion of an existence in which her relation as a daughter played but a part. She was transformed by a dignity which recast her speech and made it self-contained. She found herself in the sweep of a feeling so large that the immediate loss of a kingdom seemed of little consequence to her. Even an act which might be construed as disrespect to her father was justified in her eyes, because she was vainly striving to fill out this larger conception of duty. The test which comes sooner or later to many parents had come to Lear, to maintain the tenderness of the relation between father and child, after that relation had become one between adults, to be content with the responses made by the adult child to the family claim, while at the same time she responded to the claims of the rest of life. The mind of Lear was not big enough for this test; he failed to see anything but the personal slight involved, and the ingratitude alone reached him. It was impossible for him to calmly watch his child developing beyond the stretch of his own mind and sympathy.

That a man should be so absorbed in his own indignation as to fail to apprehend his child's thought, that he should lose his affection in his anger, simply reveals the fact that his own emotions are dearer to him than his sense of paternal obligation. Lear apparently also ignored the common ancestry of Cordelia and himself, and forgot her royal inheritance of magnanimity. He had thought of himself so long as a noble and indulgent father that he had lost the faculty by which he might perceive himself in the wrong. Even in the midst of the storm he declared himself more sinned against than sinning. He could believe any amount of kindness and goodness of himself, but could imagine no fidelity on the part of Cordelia unless she gave him the sign he demanded.

At length he suffered many hardships; his spirit was buffeted and broken; he lost his reason as well as his kingdom; but for the first time his experience was identical with the experience of the men around him, and he came to a larger conception of life. He put himself in the place of "the poor naked wretches," and unexpectedly found healing and comfort. He took poor Tim in his arms from a sheer desire for human contact and animal warmth, a primitive and genuine need, through which he suddenly had a view of the world which he had never had from his throne, and from this moment his heart began to turn toward Cordelia.

In reading the tragedy of King Lear, Cordelia receives a full share of our censure. Her first words are cold, and we are shocked by her lack of tenderness. Why should she ignore her father's need for indulgence, and be unwilling to give him what he so obviously craved? We see in the old king "the over-mastering desire of being beloved, selfish, and yet characteristic of the selfishness of a loving and kindly nature alone." His eagerness produces in us a strange pity for him, and we are impatient that his youngest and best-beloved child cannot feel this, even in the midst of her search for truth and her newly acquired sense of a higher duty. It seems to us a narrow conception that would break thus abruptly with the past and would assume that her father had no part in the new life. We want to remind her "that pity, memory, and faithfulness are natural ties," and surely as much to be prized as is the development of her own soul. We do not admire the Cordelia who through her self-absorption deserts her father, as we later admire the same woman who comes back from France that she may include her father in her happiness and freer life. The first had selfishly taken her salvation for herself alone, and it was not until her conscience had developed in her new life that she was driven back to her father, where she perished, drawn into the cruelty and wrath which had now become objective and tragic.

Historically considered, the relation of Lear to his children was archaic and barbaric, indicating merely the beginning of a family life since developed. His paternal expression was one of domination and indulgence, without the perception of the needs of his children, without any anticipation of their entrance into a wider life, or any belief that they could have a worthy life apart from him. If that rudimentary conception of family life ended in such violent disaster, the fact that we have learned to be more decorous in our conduct does not demonstrate that by following the same line of theory we may not reach a like misery.

Wounded affection there is sure to be, but this could be reduced to a modicum if we could preserve a sense of the relation of the individual to the family, and of the latter to society, and if we had been given a code of ethics dealing with these larger relationships, instead of a code designed to apply so exclusively to relationships obtaining only between individuals.

Doubtless the clashes and jars which we all feel most keenly are those which occur when two standards of morals, both honestly held and believed in, are brought sharply together. The awkwardness and constraint we experience when two standards of conventions and manners clash but feebly pre-figure this deeper difference.

Notes

1. Nora is the protagonist of Henrik Ibsen's (1828–1906) famous play *A Doll's House*. Addams contrasts Nora's angry repudiation of the family claim with Romola's faithfulness and her ability to transform that claim into an enduring vocation through her loyalty and integrity. Eliot is also the author of an essay on Sophocles' *Antigone*, "The Antigone and its Moral," published in 1856, in which she insists that there is truth to be found in the claims of both Antigone and her uncle Creon, king of Thebes. To give everything over either to the demands of family piety and duty or statescraft to the exclusion of the other is to invite imbalance and tragedy in domesticity and civic life alike.

2. Saint Francis of Assisi (1182–1226), one of the most beloved of saints and the father of the Franciscan order.

9

⟡

"THE INFLUENCE OF LINCOLN"

I SUPPOSE ALL THE CHILDREN who were born about the time of the Civil War have recollections quite unlike those of the children who are living now. Although I was but four and a half years old when Lincoln died, I distinctly remember the day when I found on our two white gate posts American flags companioned with black. I tumbled down on the harsh gravel walk in my eager rush into the house to inquire what they were "there for." To my amazement I found my father in tears, something that I had never seen before, having assumed, as all children do, that grown-up people never cried. The two flags, my father's tears and his impressive statement that the greatest man in the world had died, constituted my initiation, my baptism, as it were, into the thrilling and solemn interests of a world lying quite outside the two white gate posts. The great war touched children in many ways: I remember an engraved roster of names, headed by the words "Addams' Guard," and the whole surmounted by the insignia of the American eagle clutching many flags, which always hung in the family living-room. As children we used to read this list of names again and again. We could reach it only by dint of putting the family Bible on a chair and piling the dictionary on top of it; using the Bible to stand on was always accompanied by a little thrill of superstitious awe, although we carefully put the dictionary above that our profane feet might touch it alone. Having brought the roster within reach of our eager fingers,— fortunately it was glazed,—we would pick out the names of those who "had fallen on the field" from those who "had come back from the

Note: "The Influence of Lincoln," in *Twenty Years at Hull-House with Autobiographical Notes* (New York: Macmillan, 1910), chapter 2.

war," and from among the latter those whose children were our school-mates. When drives were planned, we would say, "Let us take this road," that we might pass the farm where a soldier had once lived; if flowers from the garden were to be given away, we would want them to go to the mother of one of those heroes whose names we knew from the "Addams' Guard." If a guest should become interested in the roster on the wall, he was at once led by the eager children to a small picture of Colonel Davis which hung next the opposite window, that he might see the brave Colonel of the Regiment. The introduction to the picture of the one-armed man seemed to us a very solemn ceremony, and long after the guest was tired of listening, we would tell each other all about the local hero, who at the head of his troops had suffered wounds unto death. We liked very much to talk to a gentle old lady who lived in a white farmhouse a mile north of the village. She was the mother of the village hero, Tommy, and used to tell us of her long anxiety during the spring of '62; how she waited day after day for the hospital to surren-der up her son, each morning airing the white homespun sheets and holding the little bedroom in immaculate readiness. It was after the bat-tle of Fort Donelson that Tommy was wounded and had been taken to the hospital at Springfield; his father went down to him and saw him getting worse each week, until it was clear that he was going to die; but there was so much red tape about the department, and affairs were so confused, that his discharge could not be procured. At last the hospital surgeon intimated to his father that he should quietly take him away; a man as sick as that, it would be all right; but when they told Tommy, weak as he was, his eyes flashed, and he said, "No, sir; I will go out of the front door or I'll die here." Of course after that every man in the hospital worked for it, and in two weeks he was honorably discharged. When he came home at last, his mother's heart was broken to see him so wan and changed. She would tell us of the long quiet days that fol-lowed his return, with the windows open that the dying eyes might look over the orchard slope to the meadow beyond where the younger brothers were mowing the early hay. She told us of those days when his school friends from the Academy flocked in to see him, their old ac-knowledged leader, and of the burning words of earnest patriotism spo-ken in the crowded little room, so that in three months the Academy was almost deserted and the new Company who marched away in the autumn took as drummer boy Tommy's third brother, who was only seventeen and too young for a regular. She remembered the still darker days that followed, when the bright drummer boy was in Andersonville prison, and little by little she learned to be reconciled that Tommy was safe in the peaceful home graveyard.

However much we were given to talk of war heroes, we always fell silent as we approached an isolated farmhouse in which two old people lived alone. Five of their sons had enlisted in the Civil War, and only the youngest had returned alive in the spring of 1865.[1] In the autumn of the same year, when he was hunting for wild ducks in a swamp on the rough little farm itself, he was accidentally shot and killed, and the old people were left alone to struggle with the half-cleared land as best they might. When we were driven past this forlorn little farm our childish voices always dropped into speculative whisperings as to how the accident could have happened to this remaining son out of all the men in the world, to him who had escaped so many chances of death! Our young hearts swelled in first rebellion against that which Walter Pater calls "the inexplicable shortcoming or misadventure on the part of life itself", we were over-whelmingly oppressed by that grief of things as they are, so much more mysterious and intolerable than those griefs which we think dimly to trace to man's own wrongdoing.[2]

It was well perhaps that life thus early gave me a hint of one of her most obstinate and insoluble riddles, for I have sorely needed the sense of universality thus imparted to that mysterious injustice, the burden of which we are all forced to bear and with which I have become only too familiar.

My childish admiration for Lincoln is closely associated with a visit made to the war eagle, Old Abe, who, as we children well knew, lived in the state capitol of Wisconsin, only sixty-five miles north of our house, really no farther than an eagle could easily fly! He had been carried by the Eighth Wisconsin Regiment through the entire war, and now dwelt an honored pensioner in the state building itself.

Many times, standing in the north end of our orchard, which was only twelve miles from that mysterious line which divided Illinois from Wisconsin, we anxiously scanned the deep sky, hoping to see Old Abe fly southward right over our apple trees, for it was clearly possible that he might at any moment escape from his keeper, who, although he had been a soldier and a sentinel, would have to sleep sometimes. We gazed with thrilled interest at one speck after another in the flawless sky, but although Old Abe never came to see us, a much more incredible thing happened, for we were at last taken to see him.

We started one golden summer's day, two happy children in the family carriage, with my father and mother and an older sister to whom, because she was just home from boarding school, we confidently appealed whenever we needed information. We were driven northward hour after hour, past harvest fields in which the stubble glinted from bronze to gold and the heavy-headed grain rested luxuriously in rounded shocks, until we reached that beautiful region of hills and lakes which surrounds the capital city of Wisconsin.

But although Old Abe, sitting sedately upon his high perch, was sufficiently like an uplifted ensign to remind us of a Roman eagle, and although his veteran keeper, clad in an old army coat, was ready to answer all our questions and to tell us of the thirty-six battles and skirmishes through which Old Abe had passed unscathed, the crowning moment of the impressive journey came to me later, illustrating once more that children are as quick to catch the meaning of a symbol as they are unaccountably slow to understand the real world about them.

The entire journey to the veteran war eagle had itself symbolized that search for the heroic and perfect which so persistently haunts the young; and I stood under the great white dome of Old Abe's stately home, for one brief moment the search was rewarded. I dimly caught a hint of what men have tried to say in their world-old effort to imprison a space in so divine a line that it shall hold only yearning devotion and high-hearted hopes. Certainly the utmost rim of my first dome was filled with the tumultuous impression of soldiers marching to death for freedom's sake, of pioneers streaming westward to establish self-government in yet another sovereign state. Only the great dome of St. Peter's itself has ever clutched my heart as did that modest curve which had sequestered from infinitude in a place small enough for my child's mind, the courage and endurance which I could not comprehend so long as it was lost in "the void of unresponsive space" under the vaulting sky itself. But through all my vivid sensations there persisted the image of the eagle in the corridor below and Lincoln himself as an epitome of all that was great and good. I dimly caught the notion of the martyred President as the standard bearer to the conscience of his countrymen, as the eagle had been the ensign of courage to the soldiers of the Wisconsin regiment.

Thirty-five years later, as I stood on the hill campus of the University of Wisconsin with a commanding view of the capitol building a mile directly across the city, I saw again the dome which had so uplifted my childish spirit. The University, which was celebrating its fiftieth anniversary, had honored me with a doctor's degree, and in the midst of the academic pomp and the rejoicing, the dome again appeared to me as a fitting symbol of a state's aspiration even in its high mission of universal education.

Thousands of children in the sixties and seventies, in the simplicity which is given to the understanding of a child, caught a notion of imperishable heroism when they were told that brave men had lost their lives that the slaves might be free. At any moment the conversation of our elders might turn upon these heroic events; there were red-letter days, when a certain general came to see my father, and again when Governor Oglesby, whom all Illinois children called "Uncle Dick," spent a Sunday under the pine trees in our front yard. We felt on those days a connection with the great world so much more heroic than the village world which surrounded us through all the other days. My father was a member of the state senate for the sixteen years between 1854 and 1870, and even as a little child I was dimly conscious of the grave march of public affairs in his comings and goings at the state capital.

He was much too occupied to allow time for reminiscence, but I remember overhearing a conversation between a visitor and himself concerning the stirring days before the war, when it was by no means certain that the Union men in the legislature would always have enough votes to keep Illinois from seceding. I heard with breathless interest my father's account of the trip a majority of the legislators had made one dark day to St. Louis, that there might not be enough men for a quorum, and so no vote could be taken on the momentous question until the Union men could rally their forces.

My father always spoke of the martyred President as Mr. Lincoln, and I never heard the great name without a thrill. I remember the day— it must have been one of comparative leisure, perhaps a Sunday—when at my request my father took out of his desk a thin packet marked "Mr. Lincoln's Letters," the shortest one of which bore unmistakable traces of that remarkable personality. These letters began, "My dear Double-D'ed Addams," and to the inquiry as to how the person thus addressed was about to vote on a certain measure then before the legislature, was added the assurance that he knew that this Addams "would vote according to his conscience," but he begged to know in which direction the same conscience "was pointing." As my father folded up the bits of paper I fairly held my breath in my desire that he should go on with the reminiscence of this wonderful man, whom he had known in his comparative obscurity, or better still, that he should be moved to tell some of the exciting incidents of the Lincoln-Douglas debates.[3] There were at least two pictures of Lincoln that always hung in my father's room, and one in our old-fashioned upstairs parlor, of Lincoln with little Tad. For one or all of these reasons I always tend to associate Lincoln with the tenderest thoughts of my father.

I recall a time of great perplexity in the summer of 1894, when Chicago was filled with federal troops sent there by the President of the United States, and their presence was resented by the governor of the state, that I walked the wearisome way from Hull-House to Lincoln Park—for no cars were running regularly at that moment of sympathetic strikes—in order to look at and gain magnanimous counsel, if I might, from the marvelous St. Gaudens statue which had been but recently placed at the entrance of the park.[4] Some of Lincoln's immortal words were cut into the stone at his feet, and never did a distracted town more sorely need the healing of "with charity towards all" than did Chicago at that moment, and the tolerance of the man who had won charity for those on both sides of "an irrepressible conflict."

Of the many things written of my father in that sad August in 1881, when he died, the one I cared for most was written by an old political friend of his who was then editor of a great Chicago daily. He wrote that while there were doubtless many members of the Illinois legislature who during the great contracts of the war time and the demoralizing reconstruction days that followed, had never accepted a bribe, he wished to bear testimony that he personally had known but this one man who had never been offered a bribe because bad men were instinctively afraid of him.

I feel now the hot chagrin with which I recalled this statement during those early efforts of Illinois in which Hull-House joined, to secure the passage of the first factory legislation. I was told by the representatives of an informal association of manufacturers that if the residents of Hull-House would drop this nonsense about a sweat shop bill, of which they knew nothing, certain business men would agree to give

fifty thousand dollars within two years to be used for any of the philanthropic activities of the Settlement. As the fact broke upon me that I
was being offered a bribe, the shame was enormously increased by the
memory of this statement. What had befallen the daughter of my father
that such a thing could happen to her? The salutary reflection that it
could not have occurred unless a weakness in myself had permitted it,
withheld me at least from an heroic display of indignation before the
two men making the offer, and I explained as gently as I could that we
had no ambition to make Hull-House "the largest institution on the
West Side," but that we were much concerned that our neighbors
should be protected from untoward conditions of work, and—so much
heroics, youth must permit itself—if to accomplish this the destruction
of Hull-House was necessary, that we would cheerfully sing a Te Deum
on its ruins. The good friend who had invited me to lunch at the Union
League Club to meet two of his friends who wanted to talk over the
sweat shop bill here kindly intervened, and we all hastened to cover
over the awkward situation by that scurrying away from ugly morality
which seems to be an obligation of social intercourse.

Of the many old friends of my father who kindly came to look up his
daughter in the first days of Hull-House, I recall none with more pleasure than Lyman Trumbull, whom we used to point out to the members
of the Young Citizens' Club as the man who had for days held in his
keeping the Proclamation of Emancipation until his friend President
Lincoln was ready to issue it. I remember the talk he gave at Hull-
House on one of our early celebrations of Lincoln's birthday, his assertion that Lincoln was no cheap popular hero, that the "common people" would have to make an effort if they would understand his
greatness, as Lincoln painstakingly made a long effort to understand
the greatness of the people. There was something in the admiration of
Lincoln's contemporaries, or at least of those men who had known him
personally, which was quite unlike even the best of the devotion and
reverent understanding which has developed since. In the first place,
they had so large a fund of common experience; they too had pioneered
in a western country, and had urged the development of canals and railroads in order that the raw prairie crops might be transported to market; they too had realized that if this last tremendous experiment in
self-government failed here, it would be the disappointment of the centuries and that upon their ability to organize self-government in state,

county and town depended the verdict of history. These men also knew, as Lincoln himself did, that if this tremendous experiment was to come to fruition, it must be brought about by the people themselves; that there was no other capital fund upon which to draw. I remember an incident occurring when I was about fifteen years old, in which the conviction was driven into my mind that the people themselves were the great resource of the country. My father had made a little address of reminiscence at a meeting of "the old settlers of Stephenson County," which was held every summer in the grove beside the mill, relating his experiences in inducing the farmers of the county to subscribe for stock in the Northwestern Railroad, which was the first to penetrate the county and to make a connection with the Great Lakes at Chicago. Many of the Pennsylvania German farmers doubted the value of "the whole new-fangled business," and had no use for any railroad, much less for one in which they were asked to risk their hard-earned savings. My father told of his despair in one farmers' community dominated by such prejudice which did not in the least give way under his argument, but finally melted under the enthusiasm of a high-spirited German matron who took a share to be paid for "out of butter and egg money." As he related his admiration of her, an old woman's piping voice in the audience called out: "I'm here to-day, Mr. Addams, and I'd do it again if you asked me." The old woman, bent and broken by her seventy years of toilsome life, was brought to the platform and I was much impressed by my father's grave presentation of her as "one of the public-spirited pioneers to whose heroic fortitude we are indebted for the development of this country." I remember that I was at that time reading with great enthusiasm Carlyle's "Heroes and Hero Worship," but on the evening of "Old Settlers' Day," to my surprise, I found it difficult to go on. Its sonorous sentences and exaltation of the man who "can" suddenly ceased to be convincing. I had already written down in my commonplace book a resolution to give at least twenty-five copies of this book each year to noble young people of my acquaintance. It is perhaps fitting to record in this chapter that the very first Christmas we spent at Hull-House, in spite of exigent demands upon my slender purse for candy and shoes, I gave to a club of boys twenty-five copies of the then new Carl Schurz's "Appreciation of Abraham Lincoln."

In our early effort at Hull-House to hand on to our neighbors whatever of help we had found for ourselves, we made much of Lincoln. We were often distressed by the children of immigrant parents who were ashamed of the pit whence they were digged, who repudiated the language and customs of their elders, and counted themselves successful as they were able to ignore the past. Whenever I held up Lincoln for their admiration as the greatest American, I invariably pointed out his marvelous power to retain and utilize past experiences; that he never forgot how the plain people in Sangamon County thought and felt when he himself had moved to town; that this habit was the foundation for his marvelous capacity for growth; that during those distracting years in Washington it enabled him to make clear beyond denial to the American people themselves, the goal towards which they were moving. I was sometimes bold enough to add that proficiency in the art of recognition and comprehension did not come without effort, and that certainly its attainment was necessary for any successful career in our conglomerate America.

An instance of the invigorating and clarifying power of Lincoln's influence came to me many years ago in England. I had spent two days in Oxford under the guidance of Arnold Toynbee's old friend Sidney Ball of St. John's College, who was closely associated with that group of scholars we all identify with the beginnings of the Settlement movement. It was easy to claim the philosophy of Thomas Hill Green, the road-building episode of Ruskin, the experimental living in the east end by Frederick Maurice, the London Workingmen's College of Edward Dennison, as foundations laid by university men for the establishment of Toynbee Hall.[5] I was naturally much interested in the beginnings of a movement whose slogan was "Back to the People," and which could doubtless claim the Settlement as one of its manifestations. Nevertheless the processes by which so simple a conclusion as residence among the poor in East London was reached, seemed to me very involved and roundabout. However inevitable these processes might be for class-conscious Englishmen, they could not but seem artificial to a western American who had been born in a rural community where the early pioneer life had made social distinctions impossible. Always on the alert lest American Settlements should become mere echoes and imitations of the English movement, I found myself assenting to what was shown me only with that part of my consciousness which had been formed by reading of English social movements, while at the same time the rustic American inside looked on in detached comment.

Why should an American be lost in admiration of a group of Oxford students because they went out to mend a disused road, inspired thereto by Ruskin's teaching for the bettering of the common life, when all the country roads in America were mended each spring by self-respecting citizens, who were thus carrying out the simple method devised by a democratic government for providing highways. No humor penetrated my high mood even as I somewhat uneasily recalled certain spring thaws when I had been mired in roads provided by the American citizen. I continued to fumble for a synthesis which I was unable to make until I developed that uncomfortable sense of play two rôles at once. It was therefore almost with a dual consciousness that I was ushered, during the last afternoon of my Oxford stay, into the drawing-room of the Master of Baliol. Edward Caird's "Evolution of Religion," which I had read but a year or two before, had been of unspeakable comfort to me in the labyrinth of differing ethical teachings and religious creeds which the many immigrant colonies of our neighborhood presented. I remember that I wanted very much to ask the author himself, how far it was reasonable to expect the same quality of virtue and a similar standard of conduct from these divers people. I was timidly trying to apply his method of study to those groups of homesick immigrants huddled together in strange tenement houses, among whom I seemed to detect the beginnings of a secular religion or at least of a wide humanitarianism evolved out of the various exigencies of the situation; somewhat as a household of children, whose mother is dead, out of their sudden necessity perform unaccustomed offices for each other and awkwardly exchange consolations, as children in happier households never dream of doing. Perhaps Mr. Caird could tell me whether there was any religious content in this

> *Faith to each other; this fidelity*
> *Of fellow wanderers in a desert place.*

But when tea was over and my opportunity came for a talk with my host, I suddenly remembered, to the exclusion of all other associations, only Mr. Caird's fine analysis of Abraham Lincoln, delivered in a lecture two years before.

The memory of Lincoln, the mention of his name, came like a refreshing breeze from off the prairie, blowing aside all the scholarly implications in which I had become so reluctantly involved, and as the philosopher spoke of the great American "who was content merely to dig the channels through which the moral life of his countrymen might flow," I was gradually able to make a natural connection between this intellectual penetration at Oxford and the moral perception which is always necessary for the discovery of new methods by which to minister to human needs. In the unceasing ebb and flow of justice and oppression we must all dig channels as best we may, that at the propitious moment somewhat of the swelling tide may be conducted to the barren places of life.

Gradually a healing sense of well-being enveloped me and a quick remorse for my blindness, as I realized that no one among his own countrymen had been able to interpret Lincoln's greatness more nobly than this Oxford scholar had done, and that vision and wisdom as well as high motives must lie behind every effective stroke in the continuous labor for human equality; I remembered that another Master of Baliol, Jowett himself, had said that it was fortunate for society that every age possessed at least a few minds which, like Arnold Toynbee's, were "perpetually disturbed over the apparent inequalities of mankind." Certainly both the English and American settlements could unite in confessing to that disturbance of mind.[6]

Traces of this Oxford visit are curiously reflected in a paper I wrote soon after my return at the request of the American Academy of Political and Social Science. It begins as follows:—

The word "settlement," which we have borrowed from London, is apt to grate a little upon American ears. It is not, after all, so long ago that Americans who settled were those who had adventured into a new country, where they were pioneers in the midst of difficult surroundings. The word still implies migrating from one condition of life to another totally unlike it, and against this implication the resident of an American settlement takes alarm.

We do not like to acknowledge that Americans are divided into two nations, as her prime minister once admitted of England. We are not willing, openly and professedly, to assume that American citizens are broken up into classes, even if we make that assumption the preface to a plea that the superior class has duties to the inferior. Our democracy is still our most precious possession, and we do well to resent any inroads upon it, even though they may be made in the name of philanthropy.

Is it not Abraham Lincoln who has cleared the title to our democracy? He made plain, once for all, that democratic government, associated as it is with all the mistakes and shortcomings of the common people, still remains the most valuable contribution America has made to the moral life of the world.

Notes

1. The destructiveness of the American Civil War nearly defies description: 558,052 men were killed; 417,175 were wounded, many grievously. Budgets of a number of Southern states after the war carried as a major line item prosthetic devices for amputees.

2. Walter Pater (1839–1934), a British essayist quoted frequently by Addams.

3. There were seven Lincoln-Douglas debates held between August 21 and October 15, 1858. One of these debates was in Freeport, Illinois, a short distance from the Addams home in Cedarville, Illinois, and it was attended by John Huy Addams, an acquaintance of Lincoln, an abolitionist and one of the leaders of the Illinois Republicans.

4. Her reference is to the events surrounding the Pullman Strike. The great sculptor Auguste St. Gaudens's dates are 1848–1907.

5. Thomas Hill Green (1836–1882), an English professor of moral philosophy. Green was a liberal who argued against British empiricism and whose work influenced John Dewey, among others. John Ruskin (1819–1900) is one of the inspirations of a communitarian ethos that linked together aesthetics and politics and experimented in various forms of communal living.

6. Benjamin Jowett was a master of Balliol College and a translator most famous for his translations of Plato.

10

"THE SNARE OF PREPARATION"

THE WINTER AFTER I LEFT SCHOOL was spent in the Woman's Medical College of Philadelphia, but the development of the spinal difficulty which had shadowed me from childhood forced me into Dr. Weir Mitchell's hospital for the late spring, and the next winter I was literally bound to a bed in my sister's house for six months.[1] In spite of its tedium, the long winter had its mitigations, for after the first few weeks I was able to read with a luxurious consciousness of leisure, and I remember opening the first volume of Carlyle's "Frederick the Great" with a lively sense of gratitude that it was not Gray's "Anatomy," having found, like many another, that general culture is a much easier undertaking than professional study.[2] The long illness inevitably put aside the immediate prosecution of a medical course, and although I had passed my examinations creditably enough in the required subjects for the first year, I was very glad to have a physician's sanction for giving up clinics and dissecting rooms and to follow his prescription of spending the next two years in Europe.

Before I returned to America I had discovered that there were other genuine reasons for living among the poor than that of practicing medicine upon them, and my brief foray into the profession was never resumed.

The long illness left me in a state of nervous exhaustion with which I struggled for years, traces of it remaining long after Hull-House was opened in 1889. At the best it allowed me but a limited amount of energy, so that doubtless there was much nervous depression at the foun-

---

Note: "The Snare of Preparation," in *Twenty Years at Hull-House with Autobiographical Notes* (New York: Macmillan, 1910), chapter 4.

dation of the spiritual struggles which this chapter is forced to record. However, it could not have been all due to my health, for as my wise little notebook sententiously remarked, "In his own way each man must struggle, lest the moral law become a far-off abstraction utterly separated from his active life."

It would, of course, be impossible to remember that some of these struggles ever took place at all, were it not for these selfsame notebooks, in which, however, I no longer wrote in moments of high resolve, but judging from the internal evidence afforded by the books themselves, only in moments of deep depression when overwhelmed by a sense of failure.

One of the most poignant of these experiences, which occurred during the first few months after our landing upon the other side of the Atlantic, was on a Saturday night, when I received an ineradicable impression of the wretchedness of East London, and also saw for the first time the over-crowded quarters of a great city at midnight. A small party of tourists were taken to the East End by a city missionary to witness the Saturday night sale of decaying vegetables and fruit, which, owing to the Sunday laws in London, could not be sold until Monday, and, as they were beyond safe keeping, were disposed of at auction as late as possible on Saturday night. On Mile End Road, from the top of an omnibus which paused at the end of a dingy street lighted by only occasional flares of gas, we saw two huge masses of ill-clad people clamoring around two hucksters' carts. They were bidding their farthings and ha'pennies for a vegetable held up by the auctioneer, which he at last scornfully flung, with a gibe for its cheapness, to the successful bidder. In the momentary pause only one man detached himself from the groups. He had bidden in a cabbage, and when it struck his hand, he instantly sat down on the curb, tore it with his teeth, and hastily devoured it, unwashed and uncooked as it was. He and his fellows were types of the "submerged tenth," as our missionary guide told us, with some little satisfaction in the then new phrase, and he further added that so many of them could scarcely be seen in one spot save at this Saturday night auction, the desire for cheap food being apparently the one thing which could move them simultaneously. They were huddled into ill-fitting, cast-off clothing, the ragged finery which one sees only in East London. Their pale faces were dominated by that most unlovely of human expressions, the cunning and shrewdness of the bargain-hunter who starves if he cannot make a successful trade, and yet the final impression was not of ragged, tawdry clothing nor of pinched and sallow faces, but of myriads of hands, empty, pathetic, nerveless and workworn, showing white in the uncertain light of the street, and clutching forward for food which was already unfit to eat.

Perhaps nothing is so fraught with significance as the human hand, this oldest tool with which man has dug his way from savagery, and with which he is constantly groping forward. I have never since been able to see a number of hands held upward, even when they are moving rhythmically in a calisthenic exercise, or when they belong to a class of chubby children who wave them in eager response to a teacher's query, without a certain revival of this memory, a clutching at the heart reminiscent of the despair and resentment which seized me then.

For the following weeks I went about London almost furtively, afraid to look down narrow streets and alleys lest they disclose again this hideous human need and suffering. I carried with me for days at a time that curious surprise we experience when we first come back into the streets after days given over to sorrow and death; we are bewildered that the world should be going on as usual and unable to determine which is real, the inner pang or the outward seeming. In time all huge London came to seem unreal save the poverty in its East End. During the following two years on the continent, while I was irresistibly drawn to the poorer quarters of each city, nothing among the beggars of South Italy nor among the saltminers of Austria carried with it the same conviction of human wretchedness which was conveyed by this momentary glimpse of an East London street. It was, of course, a most fragmentary and lurid view of the poverty of East London, and quite unfair. I should have been shown either less or more, for I went away with no notion of the hundreds of men and women who had gallantly identified their fortunes with these empty-handed people, and who, in church and chapel, "relief works," and charities, were at least making an effort towards its mitigation.

Our visit was made in November, 1883, the very year when the *Pall Mall Gazette* exposure started "The Bitter Cry of Outcast London," and the conscience of England was stirred as never before over this joyless city in the East End of its capital. Even then, vigorous and drastic plans were being discussed, and a splendid program of municipal reforms was already dimly outlined. Of all these, however, I had heard nothing but the vaguest rumor.

No comfort came to me then from any source, and the painful impression was increased because at the very moment of looking down the East London street from the top of the omnibus, I had been sharply and painfully reminded of "The Vision of Sudden Death" which had confronted De Quincey one summer's night as he was being driven through rural England on a high mail coach. Two absorbed lovers suddenly appear between the narrow, blossoming hedgerows in the direct path of the huge vehicle which is sure to crush them to their death.[3] De Quincey tries to send them a warning shout, but finds himself unable to make a sound because his mind is hopelessly entangled in an endeavor to recall the exact lines from the "Iliad" which describe the great cry with which Achilles alarmed all Asia militant. Only after his memory responds is his will released from its momentary paralysis, and he rides on through the fragrant night with the horror of the escaped calamity thick upon him, but he also bears with him the consciousness that he had given himself over so many years to classic learning—that when suddenly called upon for a quick decision in the world of life and death, he had been able to act only through a literary suggestion.

This is what we were all doing, lumbering our minds with literature that only served to cloud the really vital situation spread before our eyes. It seemed to me too preposterous that in my first view of the horror of East London I should have recalled De Quincey's literary description of the literary suggestion which had once paralyzed him. In my disgust it all appeared a hateful, vicious circle which even the apostles of culture themselves admitted, for had not one of the greatest among the moderns plainly said that "conduct, and not culture is three fourths of human life."

For two years in the midst of my distress over the poverty which, thus suddenly driven into my consciousness, had become to me the "Weltschmerz," there was mingled a sense of futility, of misdirected energy, the belief that the pursuit of cultivation would not in the end bring either solace or relief. I gradually reached a conviction that the first generation of college women had taken their learning too quickly, had departed too suddenly from the active, emotional life led by their grandmothers and great-grandmothers; that the contemporary education of young women had developed too exclusively the power of ac-

quiring knowledge and of merely receiving impressions; that somewhere in the process of "being educated" they had lost that simple and
almost automatic response to the human appeal, that old healthful reaction resulting in activity from the mere presence of suffering or of
helplessness; that they are so sheltered and pampered they have no
chance even to make "the great refusal."

In the German and French *pensions,* which twenty-five years ago
were crowded with American mothers and their daughters who had
crossed the seas in search of culture, one often found the mother making real connection with the life about her, using her inadequate German with great fluency, gayly measuring the enormous sheets or exchanging recipes with the German Hausfrau, visiting impartially the
nearest kindergarten and market, making an atmosphere of her own,
hearty and genuine as far as it went, in the house and on the street. On
the other hand, her daughter was critical and uncertain of her linguistic
acquirements, and only at ease when in the familiar receptive attitude
afforded by the art gallery and the opera house. In the latter she was
swayed and moved, appreciative of the power and charm of the music,
intelligent as to the legend and poetry of the plot, finding use for her
trained and developed powers as she sat "being cultivated" in the familiar atmosphere of the classroom which had, as it were, become sub-
limated and romanticized.

I remember a happy busy mother who, complacent with the knowledge that her daughter daily devoted four hours to her music, looked
up from her knitting to say, "If I had had your opportunities when I
was young, my dear, I should have been a very happy girl. I always had
musical talent, but such training as I had, foolish little songs and
waltzes and not time for half an hour's practice a day."

The mother did not dream of the sting her words left and that the
sensitive girl appreciated only too well that her opportunities were fine
and unusual, but she also knew that in spite of some facility and much
good teaching she had no genuine talent and never would fulfill the expectations of her friends. She looked back upon her mother's girlhood
with positive envy because it was so full of happy industry and extenu-
ating obstacles, with undisturbed opportunity to believe that her talents
were unusual. The girl looked wistfully at her mother, but had not the
courage to cry out what was in her heart: "I might believe I had unusual talent if I did not know what good music was; I might enjoy half

an hour's practice a day if I were busy and happy the rest of the time. You do not know what life means when all the difficulties are removed! I am simply smothered and sickened with advantages. It is like eating a sweet dessert the first thing in the morning."

This, then, was the difficulty, this sweet dessert in the morning and the assumption that the sheltered, educated girl has nothing to do with the bitter poverty and the social maladjustment which is all about her, and which, after all, cannot be concealed, for it breaks through poetry and literature in a burning tide which overwhelms her; it peers at her in the form of heavy-laden market women and underpaid street laborers, gibing her with a sense of her uselessness.

I recall one snowy morning in Saxe-Coburg, looking from the window of our little hotel upon the town square, that we saw crossing and recrossing it a single file of women with semicircular heavy wooden tanks fastened upon their backs. They were carrying in this primitive fashion to a remote cooling room these tanks filled with a hot brew incident to one stage of beer making. The women were bent forward, not only under the weight which they were bearing, but because the tanks were so high that it would have been impossible for them to have lifted their heads. Their faces and hands, reddened in the cold morning air, showed clearly the white scars where they had previously been scalded by the hot stuff which splashed if they stumbled ever so little on their way. Stung into action by one of those sudden indignations against cruel conditions which at times fill the young with unexpected energy, I found myself across the square, in company with mine host, interviewing the phlegmatic owner of the brewery who received us with exasperating indifference, or rather received me, for the innkeeper mysteriously slunk away as soon as the great magnate of the town began to speak. I went back to a breakfast for which I had lost my appetite, as I had for Gray's "Life of Prince Albert" and his wonderful tutor, Baron Stockmar, which I had been reading late the night before. The book had lost its fascination; how could a good man, feeling so keenly his obligation "to make princely the mind of his prince," ignore such conditions of life for the multitude of humble, hard-working folk. We were spending two months in Dresden that winter, given over to much reading of "The History of Art" and to much visiting of its art gallery and opera house, and after such an experience I would invariably suffer a moral revulsion against this feverish search after culture. It was doubtless in such moods that I founded my admiration for Albrecht Dürer, taking his wonderful pictures, however, in the most unorthodox manner, merely as human documents. I was chiefly appealed to by his unwillingness to lend himself to a smooth and cultivated view of life, by his determination to record its frustrations and even the hideous forms which darken the day for our human imagination and to ignore no human complications. I believed that his canvases intimated the coming religious and social changes of the Reformation and the peasants' wars, that they were surcharged with pity for the down-trodden, that his sad knights, gravely standing guard, were longing to avert that shedding of blood which is sure to occur when men forget how complicated life is and insist upon reducing it to logical dogmas.

The largest sum of money that I ever ventured to spend in Europe was for an engraving of his "St. Hubert," the background of which was said to be from an original Dürer plate.[4] There is nor doubt, I am afraid, that the background as well as the figures "were put in at a later date," but the purchase at least registered the high-water mark of my enthusiasm.

The wonder and beauty of Italy later brought healing and some relief to the paralyzing sense of the futility of all artistic and intellectual effort when disconnected from the ultimate test of the conduct it inspired. The serene and soothing touch of history also aroused old enthusiasms, although some of their manifestations were such as one smiles over more easily in retrospection than at the moment. I fancy that it was no smiling matter to several people of our party, whom I induced to walk for three miles in the hot sunshine beating down upon the Roman Campagna, that we might enter the Eternal City on foot through the Porta del Popolo, as pilgrims had done for centuries. To be sure, we had really entered Rome the night before, but the railroad station and the hotel might have been anywhere else, and we had been driven beyond the walls after breakfast and stranded at the very spot where the pilgrims always said "Ecce Roma" as they caught the first glimpse of St. Peter's dome. This melodramatic entrance into Rome, or rather pretended entrance, was the prelude to days of enchantment, and I returned to Europe two years later in order to spend a winter there and to carry out a great desire to systematically study the Catacombs. In spite of my distrust of "advantages" I was apparently not yet so cured but that I wanted more of them.

The two years which elapsed before I again found myself in Europe brought their inevitable changes. Family arrangements had so come about that I had spent three or four months of each of the intervening winters in Baltimore, where I seemed to have reached the nadir of my nervous depression and sense of maladjustment, in spite of my interest in the fascinating lectures given there by Lanciani of Rome, and a definite course of reading under the guidance of a Johns Hopkins lecturer upon the United Italy movement. In the latter I naturally encountered the influence of Mazzini, which was a source of great comfort to me, although perhaps I went too suddenly from a contemplation of his wonderful ethical and philosophical appeal to the workingmen of Italy, directly to the lecture rooms at Johns Hopkins University, for I was certainly much disillusioned at this time as to the effect of intellectual pursuits upon moral development.

The summers were spent in the old home in northern Illinois, and one Sunday morning I received the rite of baptism and became a member of the Presbyterian church in the village. At this time there was certainly no outside pressure pushing me towards such a decision, and at twenty-five one does not ordinarily take such a step from a mere desire to conform. While I was not conscious of any emotional "conversion," I took upon myself the outward expressions of the religious life with all humility and sincerity. It was doubtless true that I was

> *"Weary of myself and sick of asking*
> *What I am and what I ought to be,"*

and that various cherished safeguards and claims to self-dependence had been broken into by many piteous failures. But certainly I had been brought to the conclusion that "sincerely to give up one's conceit or hope of being good in one's own right is the only door to the Universe's deeper reaches." Perhaps the young clergyman recognized this as the test of the Christian temper, at any rate he required little assent to dogma or miracle, and assured me that while both the ministry and the officers of his church were obliged to subscribe to doctrines of well-known severity, the faith required of the laity was almost early Christian in its simplicity. I was conscious of no change from my childish acceptance of the teachings of the Gospels, but at this moment something persuasive within made me long for an outward symbol of fellowship, some bond of peace, some blessed spot where unity of spirit might claim right of way over all differences. There was also growing within me an almost passionate devotion to the ideals of democracy, and when in all history had these ideals been so thrillingly expressed as when the faith of the fisherman and the slave had been boldly opposed to the accepted moral belief that the well-being of a privileged few might justly be built upon the ignorance and sacrifice of the many? Who was I, with my dreams of universal fellowship, that I did not identify myself with the institutional statement of this belief, as it stood in the little village in which I was born, and without which testimony in each remote hamlet of Christendom it would be so easy for the world to slip back into the doctrines of selection and aristocracy?

In one of the intervening summers between these European journeys I visited a western state where I had formerly invested a sum of money in mortgages. I was much horrified by the wretched conditions among the farmers, which had resulted from a long period of drought, and one forlorn picture was fairly burned into my mind. A number of starved hogs—collateral for a promissory note—were huddled into an open pen. Their backs were humped in a curious, camel-like fashion, and they were devouring one of their own number, the latest victim of absolute starvation or possibly merely the one least able to defend himself against their voracious hunger. The farmer's wife looked on indifferently, a picture of despair as she stood in the door of the bare, crude house, and the two children behind her, whom she vainly tried to keep out of sight, continually thrust forward their faces almost covered by masses of coarse, sunburned hair, and their little bare feet so black, so hard, the great cracks so filled with dust that they looked like flattened hoofs. The children could not be compared to anything so joyous as satyrs, although they appeared but half-human. It seemed to me quite impossible to receive interest from mortgages placed upon farms which might at any season be reduced to such conditions, and with great inconvenience to my agent and doubtless with hardship to the farmers, as speedily as possible I withdrew all my investment. But something had to be done with the money, and in my reaction against unseen horrors I bought a farm near my native village and also a flock of innocent-looking sheep. My partner in the enterprise had not chosen the shepherd's lot as a permanent occupation, but hoped to speedily finish his college course upon half the proceeds of our venture. This pastoral enterprise still seems to me to have been essentially sound, both economically and morally, but perhaps one partner depended too much upon the impeccability of her motives and the other found himself too preoccupied with study to know that it is not a real kindness to bed a sheepfold with straw, for certainly the venture ended in a spectacle scarcely less harrowing than the memory it was designed to obliterate. At least the sight of two hundred sheep with four rotting hoofs each, was not reassuring to one whose conscience craved economic peace. A fortunate series of sales of mutton, wool, and farm enabled the partners to end the enterprise without loss, and they passed on, one to college and the other to Europe, if not wiser, certainly sadder for the experience.

It was during this second journey to Europe that I attended a meeting of the London match girls who were on strike and who met daily under the leadership of well-known labor men of London. The low wages that were reported at the meetings, the phossy jaw which was described and occasionally exhibited, the appearance of the girls themselves I did not, curiously enough, in any wise connect with what was called the labor movement, nor did I understand the efforts of the London trades-unionists, concerning whom I held the vaguest notions. But of course this impression of human misery was added to the others which were already making me so wretched. I think that up to this time I was still filled with the sense which Wells describes in one of his young characters, that somewhere in Church or State are a body of authoritative people who will put things to rights as soon as they really know what is wrong. Such a young person persistently believes that behind all suffering, behind sin and want, must lie redeeming magnanimity. He may imagine the world to be tragic and terrible, but it never for an instant occurs to him that it may be contemptible or squalid or self-seeking. Apparently I looked upon the efforts of the trades-unionists as I did upon those of Frederic Harrison and the Positivists whom I heard the next Sunday in Newton Hall, as a manifestation of "loyalty to humanity" and an attempt to aid in its progress. I was enormously interested in the Positivists during these European years; I imagined that their philosophical conception of man's religious development might include all expressions of that for which so many ages of men have struggled and aspired. I vaguely hoped for this universal comity when I stood in Stonehenge, on the Acropolis in Athens, or in the Sistine Chapel in the Vatican. But never did I so desire it as in the cathedrals of Winchester,

Notre Dame, Amiens. One winter's day I traveled from Munich to Ulm because I imagined from what the art books said that the cathedral horded a medieval statement of the Positivists' final synthesis, prefiguring their conception of a "Supreme Humanity."

In this I was not altogether disappointed. The religious history carved on the choir stalls at Ulm contained Greek philosophers as well as Hebrew prophets, and among the disciples and saints stood the discoverer of music and a builder of pagan temples. Even then I was startled, forgetting for the moment the religious revolutions of south Germany, to catch sight of a window showing Luther as he affixed his thesis on the door at Wittenberg, the picture shining clear in the midst of the older glass of saint and symbol.

My smug notebook states that all this was an admission that "the saints but embodied fine action," and it proceeds at some length to set forth my hope for a "cathedral of humanity," which should be "capacious enough to house a fellowship of common purpose," and which should be "beautiful enough to persuade men to hold fast to the vision of human solidarity." It is quite impossible for me to reproduce this experience at Ulm unless I quote pages more from the notebook in which I seem to have written half the night, in a fever of composition cast in ill-digested phrases from Comte. It doubtless reflected also something of the faith of the Old Catholics, a charming group of whom I had recently met in Stuttgart, and the same mood is easily traced in my early hopes for the Settlement that it should unite in the fellowship of the deed those of widely differing religious beliefs.

The beginning of 1887 found our little party of three in very picturesque lodgings in Rome, and settled into a certain student's routine. But my study of the Catacombs was brought to an abrupt end in a fortnight by a severe attack of sciatic rheumatism, which kept me in Rome with a trained nurse during many weeks, and later sent me to the Riviera to lead an invalid's life once more. Although my Catacomb lore thus remained hopelessly superficial, it seemed to me a sufficient basis for a course of six lectures which I timidly offered to a Deaconess's Training School during my first winter in Chicago, upon the simple ground that this early interpretation of Christianity is the one which should be presented to the poor, urging that the primitive church was composed of the poor and that it was they who took the wonderful news to the more prosperous Romans. The open-minded head of the school gladly accepted the lectures, arranging that the course should be given each spring to her graduating class of Home and Foreign Missionaries, and at the end of the third year she invited me to become one of the trustees of the school. I accepted and attended one meeting of the board, but never another, because some of the older members objected to my membership on the ground that "no religious instruction was given at Hull-House." I remember my sympathy for the embarrassment in which the head of the school was placed, but if I needed comfort, a bit of it came to me on my way home from the trustees' meeting when an Italian laborer paid my street car fare, according to the custom of our simpler neighbors. Upon my inquiry of the conductor as to whom I was indebted for the little courtesy, he replied roughly enough, "I cannot tell one dago from another when they are in a gang, but sure, any one of them would do it for you as quick as they would for the Sisters."

It is hard to tell just when the very simple plan which afterward developed into the Settlement began to form itself in my mind. It may have been even before I went to Europe for the second time, but I gradually became convinced that it would be a good thing to rent a house in a part of the city where many primitive and actual needs are found, in which young women who had been given over too exclusively to study, might restore a balance of activity along traditional lines and learn of life from life itself; where they might try out some of the things they had been taught and put truth to "the ultimate test of the conduct it dictates or inspires." I do not remember to have mentioned this plan to any one until we reached Madrid in April, 1888.

We had been to see a bull fight rendered in the most magnificent Spanish style, where greatly to my surprise and horror, I found that I had seen, with comparative indifference, five bulls and many more horses killed.[5] The sense that this was the last survival of all the glories of the amphitheater, the illusion that the riders on the caparisoned horses might have been knights of a tournament, or the matadore a slightly armed gladiator facing his martyrdom, and all the rest of the obscure yet vivid associations of an historic survival, had carried me beyond the endurance of any of the rest of the party. I finally met them in the foyer, stern and pale with disapproval of my brutal endurance, and but partially recovered from the faintness and disgust which the spectacle itself had produced upon them. I had no defense to offer to their reproaches save that I had not thought much about the bloodshed; but in the evening the natural and inevitable reaction came, and in deep chagrin I felt myself tried and condemned, not only by this disgusting experience but by the entire moral situation which it revealed. It was suddenly made quite clear to me that I was lulling my conscience by a dreamer's scheme, that a mere paper reform had become a defense for continued idleness, and that I was making it a *raison d'être* for going on indefinitely with study and travel. It is easy to become the dupe of a deferred purpose, of the promise the future can never keep, and I had fallen into the meanest type of self-deception in making myself believe that all this was in preparation for great things to come. Nothing less than the moral reaction following the experience at a bull fight had been able to reveal to me that so far from following in the wake of a chariot of philanthropic fire, I had been tied to the tail of the veriest oxcart of self-seeking.

I had made up my mind that next day, whatever happened, I would begin to carry out the plan, if only by talking about it. I can well recall the stumbling and uncertainty with which I finally set it forth to Miss Starr, my old-time school friend, who was one of our party. I even dared to hope that she might join in carrying out the plan, but nevertheless I told it in the fear of that disheartening experience which is so apt to afflict our most cherished plans when they are at last divulged, when we suddenly feel that there is nothing there to talk about, and as the golden dream slips through our fingers we are left to wonder at our own fatuous belief. But gradually the comfort of Miss Starr's companionship, the vigor and enthusiasm which she brought to bear upon it, told both in the growth of the plan and upon the sense of its validity, so that by the time we had reached the enchantment of the Alhambra, the scheme had become convincing and tangible although still most hazy in detail.

A month later we parted in Paris, Miss Starr to go back to Italy, and I to journey on to London to secure as many suggestions as possible from those wonderful places of which we had heard, Toynbee Hall and the People's Palace. So that it finally came about that in June, 1888, five years after my first visit in East London, I found myself at Toynbee Hall equipped not only with a letter of introduction from Canon Fremantle, but with high expectations and a certain belief that whatever perplexities and discouragement concerning the life of the poor were in store for me, I should at least know something at first hand and have the solace of daily activity. I had confidence that although life itself might contain many difficulties, the period of mere passive receptivity had come to an end, and I had at last finished with the everlasting "preparation for life," however ill-prepared I might be.

It was not until years afterward that I came upon Tolstoy's phrase "the snare of preparation," which he insists we spread before the feet of young people, hopelessly entangling them in a curious inactivity at the very period of life when they are longing to construct the world anew and to conform it to their own ideals.

Notes

1. Dr. S. Weir Mitchell (1829–1914), a famous physician of his time, was best known for his "rest cure" for young women suffering from the malaise called "neurasthenia"; nowadays, no doubt, it would be clinically labeled as depression. The irony of prescribing bedrest for those suffering from the effects of what Addams called "baulked disposition"—an inability to translate ideals into action—was not lost on Addams.

2. Henry Gray (1825–1861) is best known for his masterwork on anatomy, published in 1858.

3. Thomas de Quincey (1785–1859), British writer and essayist best remembered for his *Confessions of an Opium Eater*. This de Quincey text served as the inspiration for the famous opium experiment in Addams's *Twenty Years at Hull-House* in which she describes an attempt by she and four other "ardent girls" to go through a consciousness-transforming experiencing by ingesting opium powders, then readily available in drugstores. No reorientation occurred, she said; instead, the girls were wakeful and ill.

4. Albrecht Durer (1471–1528), great German artist noted for his brutal realism, his figures nearly grotesque in their creatureliness and carnality.

5. A controversy surrounds Addams's reaction to the Madrid bullfight, with the description in this text differing from her rather more staid reports in letters to home. Not very much hangs on the disparity, and it is, of course, a very common experience that past events are refracted differently when looked at from a distance and with a distinct purpose in mind.

Part Two

INTRODUCTION: JUSTICE AND AMELIORATION — FINDING DEMOCRACY'S MIDDLE WAY

FOR JANE ADDAMS, DEMOCRACY was a way to serve simultaneously authentic human needs and to attain distinctive, overlapping, and at times conflicting social and civic goods, for example, the good of human freedom and the good of community membership. These may, at times, conflict, but each is undeniably a cherished value. Addams detested violence, and the romanticization of violence, in the name of social change. She recognized, as many of her peers who turned to socialism did not, that violent social change aimed at overturning all that exists winds up putting the most ruthless and violent men in charge of things. The result is more likely to be horror than utopia. Addams also recognized that those who were weak or powerless in the overall structure of things, including women, are bound to lose in a movement for change that relies on violence. Her fight against what she called "militarism" was in part a fight against a narrow conception of social life that owed too much to older ways of doing things that democracy should ideally supplant. Democracy relies on moderation and amelioration. One fights injustice, yet one tries not to generate new injustices while fighting injustice. When extremism prevails, "bitter denunciation" supplants spirited debate. Because the social settlement is an instrument of mediation, it is bound to displease each side if a city is riven by a pitched battle between opposing camps: such is the theme of her 1908 essay "The Chicago Settlements and Social Unrest." For some, the settlement is seen as complicit with anarchy; for others, it is a tool of the oppressor.[1] Balance is not the trait one usually associates with ardent efforts, whether in the name of change or to forestall change, but that is precisely what Addams exemplified and aimed for.

Jane Addams possessed the rare ability to appreciate the "thirst for righteousness," the subject of chapter 6 of her lyrical tribute to youth, *The Spirit of Youth and the City Streets* (1909), her own favorite among her books, as well as the incomprehension of an industrial magnate who cannot figure out why "his" workers, living in the town he built for "them," are so ungrateful as to strike (here, see her complex, modulated analysis of the Pullman Strike in 1912's "A Modern Lear"). This latter essay strikes us as a paragon of moderation, but it was considered so incendiary by her peers that she couldn't get it published for years.[2]

Addams's ability to peer inside the complexity of a situation, when simple condemnation was the tack social reformers often took, is also on display in her appreciation of "Why the Ward Boss Rules" (1898). Addams and Hull-House opposed what was called the "boodling" system (we would just call it corruption today). Basically, it meant that those who were running things were on the take in the most brazen way, with "boodle" being exchanged between corrupt politicians, police officials, saloonkeepers, and even labor leaders. If there was one institution most conspicuous in immigrant Chicago, it was the saloon. There were far more saloons than churches, union halls, or schools. Addams was opposed to alcohol. She and other settlement workers saw the insidious destruction alcohol wrought on immigrant families, leading to penury, despair, domestic abuse, and criminality. Her most overwrought book, *A New Conscience and an Ancient Evil* (1912), of which chapter 4 is included here, is the closest Addams comes to denunciatory moralizing. But even so, and at the same time, she understood the attraction of the saloon. It was a social institution, a place where immigrant male factory workers and, increasingly, both their male and female working children, could unwind and, for a few hours, be happy, playful, even carefree. Sadly, they and their families paid a heavy price later, particularly as the saloon was also a place where the hard-earned pittances for hours of wage labor were literally consumed in drink and where the stranglehold of vice often ensnared young women who ran up debts for drink and sometimes fell into prostitution to pay off this indebtedness. Addams's characterization of this system is unsparing, but her appreciation of its attractions is remarkably evenhanded. Hull-House engaged in several pitched battles against the chief boodler in the Nineteenth Ward of Chicago, where Hull-House was situated on the corner of Polk and Halsted Streets, one Johnny Powers.[3] Hull-House lost in every direct electoral challenge to Powers. This led Addams to reflect on what the ward boss offers to those who give him loyal support.

In addition to her capacity for balance, Jane Addams also possessed a remarkable ability to anticipate social questions—for example, her prescient exploration of "The Home and the Special Child." She assays the many ways society induces a sense of shame in the parents of children with disabilities that may lead them to furtive attempts to hide such children or to bury them in awful institutions—generations removed from the Americans for Disabilities Act and the current emphasis on equal opportunity and access for persons with disabilities. Addams also foretells current debates over what is called "difference" in her treatment of "Americanization" (1919). She opposed what she called "dogmatic nationalism" even as she believed education in citizenship for the immigrant was a keen necessity. Here, once again, moderation is called for. As "a method of Americanizing the alien," the very worst course is "overzealous officialism" that breeds resentment. There is an important distinction between "blind patriotism" and "intelligent citizenship," whether for those who are born here or for those who immigrate. Addams asks her fellow countrymen and countrywomen to recognize that the "twenty-seven million people of foreign birth living among us are not only quite as diversified in their political opinions as those of us forming the remaining millions of the population." We should not fear such diversity even as we strive to make "more enclusive" our democracy. If difference becomes destructive division, that is a problem. If the search for commonality becomes forced unity, that, too, is a problem. Balance, once again, is the goal and that will help to put the brakes on a slide into an intemperate "national self-righteousness"—the theme of a 1933 essay included here that calls to mind her own bitter experiences during the World War I era.

The closest Jane Addams ever came to bitterness is on display in "If Men Were Seeking the Franchise" (1913), not nearly as well known as her famous justification of suffrage for women, "Why Women Should Vote" (1910), readily available to those interested in a number of collections and also online.[4] She ties women and the franchise not so much to any notion of inalienable political rights but instead to the responsibilities that women have to their families and their communities. These responsibilities now—for "untainted meat," say—require her to pay attention to what is happening in the social world. In order to care for her house and rear her children, "she will have to have some conscience in regard to public affairs lying quite outside of her immediate household." The complexities of the modern world demand this. In her treatment of the hypothetical—what if it were men, not women, denied access to the franchise—she imagines the arguments men would make to gain access and the counterarguments women would launch, in turn, to prevent men from gaining the vote. The fervor with which she presents this thought-experiment speaks to the indignity she associated with being denied access to the ballot.

Notes

1. It is hard for us to appreciate just how deep and wide was the fear and hostility toward anarchists, a tendency that manifested itself frequently as an attack on immigrants and immigration. This tendency is sometimes called "nativism." It had long been present in American life, but it reached a fever pitch during the World War I years and in their aftermath. Addams combatted throughout her life this nativist spirit and temperament and its many ugly manifestations, including imprisonment, deportation, the destruction of reading materials and printing presses, and even interfering with the U.S. mail.

2. The Pullman Strike roiled Chicago in May 1894. Jane Addams was named to a Citizens Arbitration Committee to try to negotiate a settlement. These efforts failed, and federal troops were sent to Chicago. The strike was broken and the situation embittered for years.

3. The contretemps with Johnny Powers is discussed in Jean Bethke Elshtain, *Jane Addams and the Dream of American Democracy* (New York: Basic Books, 2001), chapter 7.

4. "Why Women Should Vote" (1915), published as a pamphlet originally, was later incorporated into a multiauthor book on women's suffrage (available online at http:/douglass.speech.new.edu/adda-a03.htm). Throughout the essay Addams speaks of women's duties, not rights. Without the franchise women must fail "to discharge their duties to their own households," and she offers what she calls "many illustrations" of how and why this is so.

11

"WHY THE WARD BOSS RULES"

PRIMITIVE PEOPLE,[1] such as the South Italian peasants who live in the Nineteenth Ward, deep down in their hearts admire nothing so much as the good man. The successful candidate must be a good man according to the standards of his constituents. He must not attempt to hold up a morality beyond them, nor must he attempt to reform or change the standard. If he believes what they believe, and does what they are all cherishing a secret ambition to do, he will dazzle them by his success and win their confidence. Any one who has lived among poorer people cannot fail to be impressed with their constant kindness to each other; that unfailing response to the needs and distresses of their neighbors, even when in danger of bankruptcy themselves. This is their reward for living in the midst of poverty. They have constant opportunities for self-sacrifice and generosity, to which, as a rule, they respond. A man stands by his friend when he gets too drunk to take care of himself, when he loses his wife or child, when he is evicted for nonpayment of rent, when he is arrested for a petty crime. It seems to such a man entirely fitting that his Alderman should do the same thing on a larger scale—that he should help a constituent out of trouble just because he is in trouble, irrespective of the justice involved.

The Alderman, therefore, bails out his constituents when they are arrested, or says a good word to the police justice when they appear before him for trial; uses his "pull" with the magistrate when they are likely to be fined for a civil misdemeanor, or sees what he can do to "fix up matters" with the State's attorney when the charge is really a serious one.

Note: "Why the Ward Boss Rules," *Outlook*, vol. 57 (April 2, 1898).

Because of simple friendliness, the Alderman is expected to pay rent for the hard-pressed tenant when no rent is forthcoming, to find jobs when work is hard to get, to procure and divide among his constituents all the places which he can seize from the City Hall. The Alderman of the Nineteenth Ward at one time made the proud boast that he had two thousand six hundred people in his ward upon the public pay-roll. This, of course, included day-laborers, but each one felt under distinct obligations to him for getting the job.

If we recollect, further, that the franchise-seeking companies pay respectful heed to the applicants backed by the Alderman, the question of voting for the successful man becomes as much an industrial as a political one. An Italian laborer wants a job more than anything else, and quite simply votes for the man who promises him one.

The Alderman may himself be quite sincere in his acts of kindness. In certain stages of moral evolution, a man is incapable of unselfish action the results of which will not benefit some one of his acquaintances; still more, of conduct that does not aim to assist any individual whatsoever; and it is a long step in moral progress to appreciate the work done by the individual for the community.

The Alderman gives presents at weddings and christenings. He seizes these days of family festivities for making friends. It is easiest to reach people in the holiday mood of expansive good will, but on their side it seems natural and kindly that he should do it. The Alderman procures passes from the railroads when his constituents wish to visit friends or to attend the funerals of distant relatives; he buys tickets galore for benefit entertainments given for a widow or a consumptive in peculiar distress; he contributes to prizes which are awarded to the handsomest lady or the most popular man. At a church bazaar, for instance, the Alderman finds the stage all set for his dramatic performance. When others are spending pennies he is spending dollars. Where anxious relatives are canvassing to secure votes for the two most beautiful children who are being voted upon, he recklessly buys votes from both sides, and laughingly declines to say which one he likes the best, buying off the young lady who is persistently determined to find out, with five dollars for the flower bazaar, the posies, of course, to be sent to the sick of the parish. The moral atmosphere of a bazaar suits him exactly. He murmurs many times, "Never mind; the money all goes to the poor," or, "It is all straight enough if the church gets it."

There is something archaic in a community of simple people in their attitude towards death and burial. Nothing [is] so easy to collect money for as a funeral. If the Alderman seizes upon festivities for expressions of his good will, much more does he seize upon periods of sorrow. At a funeral he has the double advantage of ministering to a genuine craving for comfort and solace, and at the same time of assisting at an important social function.

In addition to this, there is among the poor, who have few social occasions, a great desire for a well-arranged funeral, the grade of which almost determines their social standing in the neighborhood. The Alderman saves the very poorest of his constituents from that awful horror of burial by the county; he provides carriages for the poor, who otherwise could not have them; for the more prosperous he sends extra carriages, so that they may invite more friends and have a longer procession; for the most prosperous of all there will be probably only a large "flower-piece." It may be too much to say that all the relatives and friends who ride in the carriages provided by the Alderman's bounty vote for him, but they are certainly influenced by his kindness, and talk of his virtues during the long hours of the ride back and forth from the suburban cemetery. A man who would ask at such a time where all this money comes from would be considered sinister. Many a man at such a time has formulated a lenient judgment of political corruption and has heard kindly speeches which he has remembered on election day. "Ah, well, he has a big Irish heart. He is good to the widow and the fatherless." "He knows the poor better than the big guns who are always about talking civil service and reform."

Indeed, what headway can the notion of civic purity, of honesty of administration make against this big manifestation of human friendliness, this stalking survival of village kindness? The notions of the civic reformer are negative and impotent before it. The reformers give themselves over largely to criticisms of the present state of affairs, to writing and talking of what the future must be; but their goodness is not dramatic; it is not even concrete and human.

Such an Alderman will keep a standing account with an undertaker, and telephone every week, and sometimes more than once, the kind of outfit he wishes provided for a bereaved constituent, until the sum may roll up into hundreds a year. Such a man understands what the people want, and ministers just as truly to a great human need as the musician or the artist does. I recall an attempt to substitute what we might call a later standard.

A delicate little child was deserted in the Hull House nursery. An investigation showed that it had been born ten days previously in the Cook County Hospital, but no trace could be found of the unfortunate mother. The little thing lived for several weeks, and then, in spite of every care, died. We decided to have it buried by the county, and the wagon was to arrive by eleven o'clock. About nine o'clock in the morning the rumor of this awful deed reached the neighbors. A half-dozen of them came, in a very excited state of mind, to protest. They took up a collection out of their poverty with which to defray a funeral. We were then comparatively new in the neighborhood. We did not realize that we were really shocking a genuine moral sentiment of the community. In our crudeness, we instanced the care and tenderness which had been expended upon the little creature while it was alive; that it had had every attention from a skilled physician and trained nurse; we even intimated that the excited members of the group had not taken part in this, and that it now lay with us to decide that the child should be buried, as it had been born, at the county's expense. It is doubtful whether Hull House has ever done anything which injured it so deeply in the minds of some of its neighbors. We were only forgiven by the most indulgent on the ground that we were spinsters and could not know a mother's heart. No one born and reared in the community could possibly have made a mistake like that. No one who had studied the ethical standards with any care could have bungled so completely.

Last Christmas our Alderman distributed six tons of turkeys, and four or more tons of ducks and geese; but each luckless biped was handed out either by himself or one of his friends with a "Merry Christmas." Inevitably, some families got three or four apiece, but what of that? He had none of the nagging rules of the charitable societies, nor was he ready to declare that, because a man wanted two turkeys for Christmas, he was a scoundrel, who should never be allowed to eat turkey again.

The Alderman's wisdom was again displayed in procuring from down-town friends the sum of three thousand dollars wherewith to uniform and equip a boys' temperance brigade which had been formed in the ward a few months before his campaign. Is it strange that the good leader, whose heart was filled with innocent pride as he looked upon these promising young scions of virtue, should decline to enter into a reform campaign?

The question does, of course, occur to many minds, Where does the money come from with which to dramatize so successfully? The more primitive people accept the truthful statement of its sources without any shock to their moral sense. To their simple minds he gets it "from the rich," and so long as he again gives it out to the poor, as a true Robin Hood, with open hand, they have no objections to offer. Their ethics are quite honestly those of the merry-making foresters. The next less primitive people of the vicinage are quite willing to admit that he leads "the gang" in the City Council, and sells out the city franchises; that he makes deals with the franchise-seeking companies; that he guarantees to steer dubious measures through the Council, for which he demands liberal pay; that he is, in short, a successful boodler. But when there is intellect enough to get this point of view, there is also enough to make the contention that this is universally done; that all the Aldermen do it more or less successfully, but that the Alderman of the Nineteenth Ward is unique in being so generous; that such a state of affairs is to be deplored, of course, but that that is the way business is run, and we are fortunate when a kind-hearted man who is close to the people gets a large share of the boodle; that he serves these franchised companies who employ men in the building and construction of their enterprises, and that they are bound in return to give jobs to his constituency. Even when they are intelligent enough to complete the circle, and to see that the money comes, not from the pockets of the companies' agents, but from the street-car fares of people like themselves, it almost seems as if they would rather pay two cents more each time they ride than give up the consciousness that they have a big, warm-hearted friend at court who will stand by them in an emergency. The sense of just dealing comes apparently much later than the desire for protection and kindness. The Alderman is really elected because he is a good friend and neighbor.

During a campaign a year and a half ago, when a reform league put up a candidate against our corrupt Alderman, and when Hull House worked hard to rally the moral sentiment of the ward in favor of the new man, we encountered another and unexpected difficulty. Finding that it was hard to secure enough local speakers of the moral tone which we desired, we imported orators from other parts of the town, from the "better element," so to speak. Suddenly we heard it rumored on all sides that, while the money and speakers for the reform candidate were coming from the swells, the money which was backing our corrupt Alderman also came from a swell source; it was rumored that the president of a street-car combination, for whom he performed constant offices in the City Council, was ready to back him to the extent of fifty thousand dollars; that he, too, was a good man, and sat in high places; that he had recently given a large sum of money to an educational institution, and was, therefore, as philanthropic, not to say good and upright, as any man in town; that our Alderman had the sanction of the highest authorities, and that the lecturers who were talking against corruption, and the selling and buying of franchises, were only the cranks, and not the solid business men who had developed and built up Chicago.

All parts of the community are bound together in ethical development. If the so-called more enlightened members of the community accept public gifts from the man who buys up the Council, and the so-called less enlightened members accept individual gifts from the man who sells out the Council, we surely must take our punishment together.

Another curious experience during that campaign was the difference of standards between the imported speakers and the audience. One man, high in the council of the "better element," one evening used as an example of the philanthropic politician an Alderman of the vicinity, recently dead, who was devotedly loved and mourned by his constituents. When the audience caught the familiar name in the midst of the platitudes, they brightened up wonderfully. But, as the speaker went on, they first looked puzzled, then astounded, and gradually their astonishment turned to indignation. The speaker, all unconscious of the situation, went on, imagining, perhaps, that he was addressing his usual audience, and totally unaware that he was perpetrating an outrage upon the finest feelings of the people who were sitting before him. He certainly succeeded in irrevocably injuring the chances of the candidate for whom he was speaking. The speaker's standard of ethics was upright dealing in positions of public trust. The standard of ethics held by his audience was, being good to the poor and speaking gently of the dead. If he considered them corrupt and illiterate voters, they quite honestly held him a blackguard.

If we would hold to our political democracy, some pains must be taken to keep on common ground in our human experiences, and to some solidarity in our ethical conceptions. And if we discover that men of low ideals and corrupt practice are forming popular political standards simply because such men stand by and for and with the people, then nothing remains but to obtain a like sense of identification before we can hope to modify ethical standards.

Notes

1. "Primitive" is now taken as a slur, but in Addams's day it was an anthropological and cultural category meaning "preindustrial," in some cases oral, often largely tribal or peasant cultures. For Addams, we must never lose contact with the goodness and simplicity of much that is associated with the primitive, not in a romantic sense but in a tough-minded recognition of the preemptory needs of bodies for food and shelter.

12

"THE WRECKED FOUNDATIONS OF DOMESTICITY"

"Sense with keenest edge unused
Yet unsteel'd by scathing fire:
Lovely feet as yet unbruised
On the ways of dark desire!"

THESE WORDS WRITTEN BY A POET to his young son express the longing which has at times seized all of us, to guard youth from the mass of difficulties which may be traced to the obscure manifestation of that fundamental susceptibility of which we are all slow to speak and concerning which we evade public responsibility, although it brings its scores of victims into the police courts every morning.

At the very outset we must bear in mind that the senses of youth are singularly acute, and ready to respond to every vivid appeal. We know that nature herself has sharpened the senses for her own purposes, and is deliberately establishing a connection between them and the newly awakened susceptibility of sex; for it is only through the outward senses that the selection of an individual mate is made and the instinct utilized for nature's purposes. It would seem, however, that nature was determined that the force and constancy of the instinct must make up for its lack of precision, and that she was totally unconcerned that this instinct ruthlessly seized the youth at the moment when he was least prepared to cope with it; not only because his

Note: "The Wrecked Foundations of Domesticity," in *The Spirit of Youth and the City Streets* (New York: Macmillan, 1909), chapter 2.

powers of self-control and discrimination are unequal to the task, but because his senses are helplessly wide open to the world. These early manifestations of the sex susceptibility are for the most part vague and formless, and are absolutely without definition to the youth himself. Sometimes months and years elapse before the individual mate is selected and determined upon, and during the time when the differentiation is not complete—and it often is not—there is of necessity a great deal of groping and waste.

This period of groping is complicated by the fact that the youth's power for appreciating is far ahead of his ability for expression. "The inner traffic fairly obstructs the outer current," and it is nothing short of cruelty to over-stimulate his senses as does the modern city. This period is difficult everywhere, but it seems at times as if a great city almost deliberately increased its perils. The newly awakened senses are appealed to by all that is gaudy and sensual, by the flippant street music, the highly colored theater posters, the trashy love stories, the feathered hats, the cheap heroics of the revolvers displayed in the pawn-shop windows.[1] This fundamental susceptibility is thus evoked without a corresponding stir of the higher imagination, and the result is as dangerous as possible. We are told upon good authority that "If the imagination is retarded, while the senses remain awake, we have a state of esthetic insensibility,"—in other words, the senses become sodden and cannot be lifted from the ground. It is this state of "esthetic insensibility" into which we allow the youth to fall which is so distressing and so unjustifiable. Sex impulse then becomes merely a dumb and powerful instinct without in the least awakening the imagination or the heart, nor does it overflow into neighboring fields of consciousness. Every city contains hundreds of degenerates who have been over-mastered and borne down by it; they fill the casual lodging houses and the infirmaries. In many instances it has pushed men of ability and promise to the bottom of the social scale. . . .

It is difficult to state how much evil and distress might be averted if the imagination were utilized in its higher capacities through the historic paths. An English moralist has lately asserted that "much of the evil of the time may be traced to outraged imagination. It is the strongest quality of the brain and it is starved. Children, from their earliest years, are hedged in with facts; they are not trained to use their minds on the unseen."

In failing to diffuse and utilize this fundamental instinct of sex through the imagination, we not only inadvertently foster vice and enervation, but we throw away one of the most precious implements for ministering to life's highest needs. There is no doubt that this ill adjusted function consumes quite unnecessarily vast stores of vital energy, even when we contemplate it in its immature manifestations which are infinitely more wholesome than the dumb swamping process. Every high school boy and girl knows the difference between the concentration and the diffusion of this impulse, although they would be hopelessly bewildered by the use of the terms. They will declare one of their companions to be "in love" if his fancy is occupied by the image of a single person about whom all the newly found values gather, and without whom his solitude is an eternal melancholy. But if the stimulus does not appear as a definite image, and the values evoked are dispensed over the world, the young person suddenly seems to have discovered a beauty and significance in many things—he responds to poetry, he becomes a lover of nature, he is filled with religious devotion or with philanthropic zeal. Experience, with young people, easily illustrates the possibility and value of diffusion.

It is neither a short nor an easy undertaking to substitute the love of beauty for mere desire, to place the mind above the senses; but is not this the sum of the immemorial obligation which rests upon the adults of each generation if they would nurture and restrain the youth, and has not the whole history of civilization been but one long effort to substitute psychic impulsion for the driving force of blind appetite?

Society has recognized the "imitative play" impulse of children and provides them with tiny bricks with which to "build a house," and dolls upon which they may lavish their tenderness. We exalt the love of the mother and the stability of the home, but in regard to those difficult years between childhood and maturity we beg the question and unless we repress, we do nothing. We are so timid and inconsistent that although we declare the home to be the foundation of society, we do nothing to direct the force upon which the continuity of the home depends. And yet to one who has lived for years in a crowded quarter where men, women and children constantly jostle each other and press upon every inch of space in shop, tenement and street, nothing is more impressive than the strength, the continuity, the varied and powerful manifestations, of family affection. It goes without saying that every tenement house contains women who for years spend their hurried days in preparing food and clothing and pass their sleepless nights in tending and nursing their exigent children, with never one thought for their own comfort or pleasure or development save as these may be connected with the future of their families. We all know as a matter of course that every shop is crowded with workingmen who year after year spend all of their wages upon the nurture and education of their children, reserving for themselves but the shabbiest clothing and a crowded place at the family table.

"Bad weather for you to be out in," you remark on a February evening, as you meet rheumatic Mr. S. hobbling home through the freezing sleet without an overcoat. "Yes, it is bad," he assents: "but I've walked to work all this last year. We've sent the oldest boy back to high school, you know," and he moves on with no thought that he is doing other than fulfilling the ordinary lot of the ordinary man.

These are the familiar and the constant manifestations of family affection which are so intimate a part of life that we scarcely observe them.

In addition to these we find peculiar manifestations of family devotion exemplifying that touching affection which rises to unusual sacrifice because it is close to pity and feebleness. "My cousin and his family had to go back to Italy. He got to Ellis Island with his wife and five children, but they wouldn't let in the feeble-minded boy, so of course they all went back with him. My cousin was fearful disappointed."

Or, "These are the five children of my brother. He and his wife, my father and mother, were all done for in the bad time at Kishinef.[2] It's up to me all right to take care of the kids, and I'd no more go back on them than I would on my own." Or, again: "Yes, I have seven children of my own. My husband died when Tim was born. The other three children belong to my sister, who died the year after my husband. I get on pretty well. I scrub in a factory every night from six to twelve, and I go out washing four days a week. So far the children have all gone through the eighth grade before they quit school," she concludes, beaming with pride and joy.

That wonderful devotion to the child seems at times, in the midst of our stupid social and industrial arrangements, all that keeps society human, the touch of nature which unites it, as it was that same devotion which first lifted it out of the swamp of bestiality. The devotion to the child is "the inevitable conclusion of the two premises of the practical syllogism, the devotion of man to woman." It is, of course, this tremendous force which makes possible the family, that bond which holds society together and blends the experience of generations into a continuous story. The family has been called "the fountain of morality," "the source of law," "the necessary prelude to the state" itself; but while it is continuous historically, this dual bond must be made anew a myriad times in each generation, and the forces upon which its formation depend must be powerful and unerring. It would be too great a risk to leave it to a force whose manifestations are intermittent and uncertain. The desired result is too grave and fundamental.

One Sunday evening an excited young man came to see me, saying that he must have advice; some one must tell him at once what to do, as his wife was in the state's prison serving a sentence for a crime which he himself had committed. He had seen her the day before, and though she had been there only a month he was convinced that she was developing consumption. She was "only seventeen, and couldn't stand the hard work and the 'low down' women" whom she had for companions. My remark that a girl of seventeen was too young to be in the state penitentiary brought out the whole wretched story.

He had been unsteady for many years and the despair of his thoroughly respectable family who had sent him West the year before. In Arkansas he had fallen in love with a girl of sixteen and married her. His mother was far from pleased, but had finally sent him money to bring his bride to Chicago, in the hope that he might settle there. *En route* they stopped at a small town for the naïve reason that he wanted to have an aching tooth pulled. But the tooth gave him an excellent opportunity to have a drink, and before he reached the office of the country practitioner he was intoxicated. As they passed through the vestibule he stole an overcoat hanging there, although the little wife piteously begged him to let it alone. Out of sheer bravado he carried it across his arm as they walked down the street, and was, of course, immediately arrested "with the goods upon him." In sheer terror of being separated from her husband, the wife insisted that she had been an accomplice, and together they were put into the county jail awaiting the action of the Grand Jury. At the end of the sixth week, on one of the rare occasions when they were permitted to talk to each other through the grating which separated the men's visiting quarters from the women's, the young wife told her husband that she made up her mind to swear that she had stolen the overcoat. What could she do if he were sent to prison and she were left free? She was afraid to go to his people and could not possibly go back to hers. In spite of his protest, that very night she sent for the state's attorney and made a full confession, giving her age as eighteen in the hope of making her testimony more valuable. From that time on they stuck to the lie through the indictment, the trial and her conviction. Apparently it had seemed to him only a well-arranged plot until he had visited the penitentiary the day before, and had really seen her piteous plight. Remorse had seized him at last, and he was ready to make every restitution. She, however, had no notion of giving up—on the contrary, as she realized more clearly what prison life meant, she was daily more determined to spare him the experience. Her letters, written in the unformed hand of a child—for her husband had himself taught her to read and write—were filled with a riot of self-abnegation, the martyr's joy as he feels the iron enter the flesh. Thus had an illiterate, neglected girl through sheer devotion to a worthless sort of young fellow inclined to drink, entered into that noble company of martyrs.

When girls "go wrong" what happens? How has this tremendous force, valuable and necessary for the foundation of the family, become misdirected? When its manifestations follow the legitimate channels of wedded life we call them praiseworthy; but there are other manifestations quite outside the legal and moral channels which yet compel our admiration.

A young woman of my acquaintance was married to a professional criminal named Joe. Three months after the wedding he was arrested and "sent up" for two years. Molly had always been accustomed to many lovers, but she remained faithful to her absent husband for a year. At the end of that time she obtained a divorce which the state law makes easy for the wife of a convict, and married a man who was "rich and respectable"—in fact, he owned the small manufacturing establishment in which her mother did the scrubbing. He moved his bride to another part of town six miles away, provided her with a "steam-heated flat," furniture upholstered in "cut velvet," and many other luxuries of which Molly heretofore had only dreamed. One day as she was wheeling a handsome baby carriage up and down the prosperous street, her brother, who was "Joe's pal," came to tell her that Joe was "out," had come to the old tenement and was "mighty sore" because "she had gone back on him." Without a moment's hesitation Molly turned the baby carriage in the direction of her old home and never stopped wheeling it until she had compassed the entire six miles. She and Joe rented the old room and went to housekeeping. The rich and respectable husband made every effort to persuade her to come back, and then another series of efforts to recover his child, before he set her free through a court proceeding. Joe, however, steadfastly refused to marry her, still "sore" because she had not "stood by." As he worked only intermittently, and was too closely supervised by the police to do much at his old occupation, Molly was obliged to support the humble ménage by scrubbing in a neighboring lodging house and by washing "the odd shirts" of the lodgers. For five years, during which time two children were born, when she was constantly subjected to the taunts of her neighbors, and when all the charitable agencies refused to give help to such an irregular household, Molly happily went on her course with no shade of regret or sorrow. "I'm all right as long as Joe keeps out of the jug," was her slogan of happiness, low in tone, perhaps, but genuine and "game." Her surroundings were as sordid as possible, consisting of a constantly changing series of cheap "furnished rooms" in which the battered baby carriage was the sole witness of better days. But Molly's heart was full of courage and happiness, and she was never desolate until her criminal lover was "sent up" again, this time on a really serious charge.

These irregular manifestations form a link between that world in which each one struggles to "live respectable," and that nether world in which are also found cases of devotion and of enduring affection arising out of the midst of the folly and the shame. The girl there who through all tribulation supports her recreant "lover," or the girl who overcomes her drink and opium habits, who renounces luxuries and goes back to uninteresting daily toil for the sake of the good opinion of a man who wishes her to "appear decent," although he never means to marry her, these are also impressive.

One of our earliest experiences at Hull-House had to do with a lover of this type and the charming young girl who had become fatally attached to him. I can see her now running for protection up the broad steps of the columned piazza then surrounding Hull-House. Her slender figure was trembling with fright, her tear-covered face swollen and bloodstained from the blows he had dealt her. "He is apt to abuse me when he is drunk," was the only explanation, and that given by way of apology, which could be extracted from her. When we discovered that there had been no marriage ceremony, that there were no living children, that she had twice narrowly escaped losing her life, it seemed a simple matter to insist that the relation should be broken off. She apathetically remained at Hull-House for a few weeks, but when her strength had somewhat returned, when her lover began to recover from his prolonged debauch of whiskey and opium, she insisted upon going home every day to prepare his meals and to see that the little tenement was clean and comfortable because "Pierre is always so sick and weak after one of those long ones." This of course meant that she was drifting back to him, and when she was at last restrained by that moral compulsion, by that overwhelming of another's will which is always so ruthlessly exerted by those who are conscious that virtue is struggling with vice, her mind gave way and she became utterly distraught.

A poor little Ophelia, I met her one night wandering in the hall half dressed in the tawdry pink gown "that Pierre liked best of all" and groping on the blank wall to find the door which might permit her to escape to her lover. In a few days it was obvious that hospital restraint was necessary, but when she finally recovered we were obliged to admit that there is no civic authority which can control the acts of a girl of eighteen. From the hospital she followed her heart directly back to Pierre, who had in the meantime moved out of the Hull-House neighborhood. We knew later that he had degraded the poor child still further by obliging her to earn money for his drugs by that last method resorted to by a degenerate man to whom a woman's devotion still clings.

It is inevitable that a force which is enduring enough to withstand the discouragements, the suffering and privation of daily living, strenuous enough to overcome and rectify the impulses which make for greed and self-indulgence, should be able, even under untoward conditions, to lift up and transfigure those who are really within its grasp and set them in marked contrast to those who are merely playing a game with it or using it for gain. But what has happened to these wretched girls? Why has this beneficent current cast them upon the shores of death and destruction when it should have carried them into the safe port of domesticity! Through whose fault has this basic emotion served merely to trick and deride them!

Older nations have taken a well defined line of action in regard to it.

Among the Hull-House neighbors are many of the Latin races who employ a careful chaperonage over their marriageable daughters and provide husbands for them at an early age. "My father will get a husband for me this winter," announces Angelina, whose father has brought her to a party at Hull-House, and she adds with a toss of her head, "I saw two already, but my father says they haven't saved enough money to marry me." She feels quite as content in her father's wisdom and ability to provide her with a husband as she does in his capacity to escort her home safely from the party. He does not permit her to cross the threshold after nightfall unaccompanied by himself, and unless the dowry and the husband are provided before she is eighteen he will consider himself derelict in his duty towards her. "Francesca can't even come to the Sodality meeting this winter. She lives only across from the church but her mother won't let her come because her father is out West working on a railroad," is a comment one often hears. The system works well only when it is carried logically through to the end of an early marriage with a properly provided husband.

Even with the Latin races, when the system is tried in America it often breaks down, and when the Anglo-Saxons anywhere imitate this régime it is usually utterly futile. They follow the first part of the program as far as repression is concerned, but they find it impossible to follow the second because all sorts of inherited notions deter them. The repressed girl, if she is not one of the languishing type, takes matters into her own hands, and finds her pleasures in illicit ways, without her parents' knowledge. "I had no idea my daughter was going to public dances. She always told me she was spending the night with her cousin on the South Side. I hadn't a suspicion of the truth," many a broken-hearted mother explains. An officer who has had a long experience in the Juvenile Court of Chicago, and has listened to hundreds of cases involving wayward girls, gives it as his deliberate impression that a large majority of cases are from families where the discipline had been rigid, where they had taken but half of the convention of the Old World and left the other half.[3]

Unless we mean to go back to these Old World customs which are already hopelessly broken, there would seem to be but one path open to us in America. That path implies freedom for the young people made safe only through their own self-control. This, in turn, must be based upon knowledge and habits of clean companionship. In point of fact no course between the two is safe in a modern city, and in the most crowded quarters the young people themselves are working out a protective code which reminds one of the instinctive protection that the free-ranging child in the country learns in regard to poisonous plants and "marshy places," or of the cautions and abilities that the mountain child develops in regard to ice and precipices. This statement, of course, does not hold good concerning a large number of children in every crowded city quarter who may be classed as degenerates, the children of careless or dissolute mothers who fall into all sorts of degenerate habits and associations before childhood is passed, who cannot be said to have "gone wrong" at any one moment because they have never been in the right path even of innocent childhood; but the statement is sound concerning thousands of girls who go to and from work every day with crowds of young men who meet them again and again in the occasional evening pleasures of the more decent dance halls or on a Sunday afternoon in the parks.

The mothers who are of most use to these normal city working girls are the mothers who develop a sense of companionship with the changing experiences of their daughters, who are willing to modify ill-fitting social conventions into rules of conduct which are of actual service to their children in their daily lives of factory work and of city amusements. Those mothers, through their sympathy and adaptability, substitute keen present interests and activity for solemn warnings and restraint, self-expression for repression. Their vigorous family life allies itself by a dozen bonds to the educational, the industrial and the recreational organizations of the modern city, and makes for intelligent understanding, industrial efficiency and sane social pleasures.

By all means let us preserve the safety of the home, but let us also make safe the street in which the majority of our young people find their recreation and form their permanent relationships. Let us not forget that the great processes of social life develop themselves through influences of which each participant is unconscious as he struggles alone and unaided in the strength of a current which seizes him and bears him along with myriads of others, a current which may so easily wreck the very foundations of domesticity.

Notes

1. Addams is prescient in her attunement to the dynamic economy of desire and pleasure. Her analysis is a sober social theory variant on Theodore Dreiser's at times overwrought but nonetheless powerful depiction of Carrie Meeber's journey into the maw of commodities and desire in *Sister Carrie,* published in 1900.

2. The reference is to a pogrom in Kishinev, located in Bessarabia, in which fifty Jews were killed, six hundred wounded. The massacre prompted an exodus of Russian Jews to the United States, and, Jane Addams notes, "hundreds of them settled in our neighborhood."

3. Among the many causes pioneered by Hull-House was that of the juvenile court. Addams and other Hull-House residents were distressed at the ways in which juvenile offenders, picked up frequently enough for truancy or general high jinks, wound up caught in the coils of the adult criminal justice system.

13

"THE THIRST FOR RIGHTEOUSNESS"

EVEN AS WE PASS BY THE JOY and beauty of youth on the streets without dreaming it is there, so we may hurry past the very presence of august things without recognition. We may easily fail to sense those spiritual realities, which, in every age, have haunted youth and called to him without ceasing. Historians tell us that the extraordinary advances in human progress have been made in those times when "the ideals of freedom and law, of youth and beauty, of knowledge and virtue, of humanity and religion, high things, the conflicts between which have caused most of the disruptions and despondences of human society, seem for a generation or two to lie in the same direction."

Are we perhaps at least twice in life's journey dimly conscious of the needlessness of this disruption and of the futility of the despondency! Do we feel it first when young ourselves we long to interrogate the "transfigured few" among our elders whom we believe to be carrying forward affairs of gravest import! Failing to accomplish this are we, for the second time, dogged by a sense of lost opportunity, of needless waste and perplexity, when we too, as adults, see again the dreams of youth in conflict with the efforts of our own contemporaries! We see idealistic endeavor on the one hand lost in ugly friction; the heat and burden of the day borne by mature men and women on the other hand, increased by their consciousness of youth's misunderstanding and high scorn. It may relieve the mind to break forth in moments of irritation against "the folly of the coming generation," but whoso pauses on his plodding way to call even his youngest and rashest brother a fool, ruins

---

Note: "The Thirst for Righteousness," in *The Spirit of Youth and the City Streets* (New York: Macmillan, 1909), chapter 6.

thereby the joy of his journey,—for youth is so vivid an element in life that unless it is cherished, all the rest is spoiled. The most praiseworthy journey grows dull and leaden unless companioned by youth's iridescent dreams. Not only that, but the mature of each generation run a grave risk of putting their efforts in a futile direction, in a blind alley as it were, unless they can keep in touch with the youth of their own day and know at least the trend in which eager dreams are driving them— those dreams that fairly buffet our faces as we walk the city streets.

At times every one possessed with a concern for social progress is discouraged by the form-less and unsubdued modern city, as he looks upon that complicated life which drives men almost without their own volition, that life of ingenuous enterprises, great ambitions, political jealousies, where men tend to become mere "slaves of possessions." Doubtless these striving men are full of weakness and sensitiveness even when they rend each other, and are but caught in the coils of circumstance; nevertheless, a serious attempt to ennoble and enrich the content of city life that it may really fill the ample space their ruthless wills have provided, means that we must call upon energies other than theirs. When we count over the resources which are at work "to make order out of casualty, beauty out of confusion, justice, kindliness and mercy out of cruelty and inconsiderate pressure," we find ourselves appealing to the confident spirit of youth. We know that it is crude and filled with conflicting hopes, some of them unworthy and most of them doomed to disappointment, yet these young people have the advantage of "morning in their hearts"; they have such power of direct action, such ability to stand free from fear, to break through life's trammelings, that in spite of ourselves we become convinced that

> *"They to the disappointed earth shall give*
> *The lives we meant to live."*

That this solace comes to us only in fugitive moments, and is easily misleading, may be urged as an excuse for our blindness and insensitiveness to the august moral resources which the youth of each city offers to those who are in the midst of the city's turmoil. A further excuse is afforded in the fact that the form of the dreams for beauty and righteousness change with each generation and that while it is always difficult for the fathers to understand the sons, at those periods when the demand of the young is one of social reconstruction, the misunderstanding easily grows into bitterness.

The old desire to achieve, to improve the world, seizes the ardent youth to-day with a stern command to bring about juster social conditions. Youth's divine impatience with the world's inheritance of wrong and injustice makes him scornful of "rose water for the plague" prescriptions, and he insists upon something strenuous and vital.

One can find innumerable illustrations of this idealistic impatience with existing conditions among the many Russian subjects found in the foreign quarters of every American city. The idealism of these young people might be utilized to a modification of our general culture and point of view, somewhat as the influence of the young Germans who came to America in the early fifties, bringing with them the hopes and aspirations embodied in the revolutions of 1848, made a profound impression upon the social and political institutions of America.[1] Long before they emigrated, thousands of Russian young people had been caught up into the excitements and hopes of the Russian revolution in Finland, in Poland, in the Russian cities, in the university towns. Life had become intensified by the consciousness of the suffering and starvation of millions of their fellow subjects. They had been living with a sense of discipline and of preparation for a coming struggle which, although grave in import, was vivid and adventurous. Their minds had been seized by the first crude forms of social theory and they had cherished a vague belief that they were the direct instruments of a final and ideal social reconstruction. When they come to America they sadly miss this sense of importance and participation in a great and glorious conflict against a recognized enemy. Life suddenly grows stale and unprofitable; the very spirit of tolerance which characterizes American cities is that which strikes most unbearably upon their ardent spirits. They look upon the indifference all about them with an amazement which rapidly changes to irritation. Some of them in a short time lose their ardor, others with incredible rapidity make the adaptation between American conditions and their store of enthusiasm, but hundreds of them remain restless and ill at ease. Their only consolation, almost their only real companionship, is when they meet in small groups for discussion or in larger groups to welcome a well known revolutionist who brings them direct news from the conflict, or when they arrange for a demonstration in memory of "The Red Sunday" or the death of Gershuni. Such demonstrations, however, are held in honor of men whose sense of justice was obliged to seek an expression quite outside the regular channels of established government. Knowing that Russia has forced thousands of her subjects into this position, one would imagine that patriotic teachers in America would be most desirous to turn into governmental channels all that insatiable desire for juster relations in industrial and political affairs. A distinct and well directed campaign is necessary if this gallant enthusiasm is ever to be made part of that old and still incomplete effort to embody in law—"the law that abides and falters not, ages long"—the highest aspirations for justice.

Unfortunately, we do little or nothing with this splendid store of youthful ardor and creative enthusiasm. Through its very isolation it tends to intensify and turn in upon itself, and no direct effort is made to moralize it, to discipline it, to make it operative upon the life of the city. And yet it is, perhaps, what American cities need above all else, for it is but too true that Democracy—"a people ruling"—the very name of which the Greeks considered so beautiful, no longer stirs the blood of the American youth, and that the real enthusiasm for self-government must be found among the groups of young immigrants who bring over with every ship a new cargo of democratic aspirations. That many of these young men look for a consummation of these aspirations to a social order of the future in which the industrial system as well as government shall embody democratic relations, simply shows that the doctrine of Democracy like any other of the living faiths of men, is so essentially mystical that it continually demands new formulation. To fail to recognize it in a new form, to call it hard names, to refuse to receive it, may mean to reject that which our fathers cherished and handed on as an inheritance not only to be preserved but also to be developed.

We allow a great deal of this precious stuff—this *Welt-Schmerz* of which each generation has need—not only to go unutilized, but to work havoc among the young people themselves.[2] One of the saddest illustrations of this, in my personal knowledge, was that of a young Russian girl who lived with a group of her compatriots on the west side of Chicago. She recently committed suicide at the same time that several others in the group tried it and failed. One of these latter, who afterwards talked freely of the motives which led her to this act, said that there were no great issues at stake in this country; that America was wholly commercial in its interests and absorbed in money making; that

Americans were not held together by any historic bonds nor great mutual hopes, and were totally ignorant of the stirring social and philosophic movements of Europe; that her life here had been a long, dreary, economic struggle, unrelieved by any of the higher interests; that she was tired of getting seventy-five cents for trimming a hat that sold for twelve dollars and was to be put upon the empty head of some one who had no concern for the welfare of the woman who made it. The statement doubtless reflected something of "The Sorrows of Werther," but the entire tone was nobler and more highly socialized.

It it difficult to illustrate what might be accomplished by reducing to action the ardor of those youths who so bitterly arraign our present industrial order. While no part of the social system can be changed rapidly, we would all admit that the present industrial arrangements in America might be vastly improved and that we are failing to meet the requirements of our industrial life with courage and success simply because we do not realize that unless we establish that humane legislation which has its roots in a consideration for human life, our industrialism itself will suffer from inbreeding, growing ever more unrestrained and ruthless. It would seem obvious that in order to secure relief in a community dominated by industrial ideals, an appeal must be made to the old spiritual sanctions for human conduct, that we must reach motives more substantial and enduring than the mere fleeting experiences of one phase of modern industry which vainly imagines that its growth would be curtailed if the welfare of its employees were guarded by the state. It would be an interesting attempt to turn that youthful enthusiasm to the aid of one of the most conservative of the present social efforts, the almost world-wide movement to secure protective legislation for women and children in industry, in which America is so behind the other nations. Fourteen of the great European powers protect women from all night work, from excessive labor by day, because paternalistic governments prize the strength of women for the bearing and rearing of healthy children to the state. And yet in a republic it is the citizens themselves who must be convinced of the need of this protection unless they would permit industry to maim the very mothers of the future.

In one year in the German Empire one hundred thousand children were cared for through money paid from the State Insurance fund to their widowed mothers or to their invalided fathers.[3] And yet in the American states it seems impossible to pass a most rudimentary employers' liability act, which would be but the first step towards that code of beneficent legislation which protects "the widow and fatherless" in Germany and England. Certainly we shall have to bestir ourselves if we would care for the victims of the industrial order as well as do other nations. We shall be obliged speedily to realize that in order to secure protective legislation from a governmental body in which the most powerful interests represented are those of the producers and transporters of manufactured goods, it will be necessary to exhort to a care for the defenseless from the religious point of view. To take even the non-commercial point of view would be to assert that evolutionary progress assumes that a sound physique is the only secure basis of life, and to guard the mothers of the race is simple sanity.

And yet from lack of preaching we do not unite for action because we are not stirred to act at all, and protective legislation in America is shamefully inadequate. Because it is always difficult to put the championship of the oppressed above the counsels of prudence, we say in despair sometimes that we are a people who hold such varied creeds that there are not enough of one religious faith to secure anything, but the truth is that it is easy to unite for action people whose hearts have once been filled by the fervor of that willing devotion which may easily be generated in the youthful breast. It is comparatively easy to enlarge a moral concept, but extremely difficult to give it to an adult for the first time. And yet when we attempt to appeal to the old sanctions for disinterested conduct, the conclusion is often forced upon us that they have not been engrained into character, that they cannot be relied upon when they are brought into contact with the arguments of industrialism, that the colors of the flag flying over the fort of our spiritual resources wash out and disappear when the storm actually breaks.

It is because the ardor of youth has not been attracted to the long effort to modify the ruthlessness of industry by humane enactments, that we sadly miss their resourceful enthusiasm and that at the same time groups of young people who hunger and thirst after social righteousness are breaking their hearts because the social reform is so long delayed and an unsympathetic and hardhearted society frustrates all their hopes. And yet these ardent young people who obscure the issue by their crying and striving and looking in the wrong place, might be of inestimable value if so-called political leaders were in any sense social philosophers. To permit these young people to separate themselves from the contemporaneous efforts of ameliorating society and to turn their vague hopes solely toward an ideal commonwealth of the future, is to withdraw from an experimental self-government founded in enthusiasm, the very stores of enthusiasm which are needed to sustain it.

The championship of the oppressed came to be a spiritual passion with the Hebrew prophets. They saw the promises of religion, not for individuals but in the broad reaches of national affairs and in the establishment of social justice. It is quite possible that such a spiritual passion is again to be found among the ardent young souls of our cities. They see a vision, not of a purified nation but of a regenerated and a reorganized society. Shall we throw all this into the future, into the futile prophecy of those who talk because they cannot achieve, or shall we commingle their ardor, their overmastering desire for social justice, with that more sober effort to modify existing conditions? Are we once more forced to appeal to the educators? Is it so difficult to utilize this ardor because educators have failed to apprehend the spiritual quality of their task?

It would seem a golden opportunity for those to whom is committed the task of spiritual instruction, for to preach and seek justice in human affairs is one of the oldest obligations of religion and morality. All that would be necessary would be to attach this teaching to the contemporary world in such wise that the eager youth might feel a tug upon his faculties, and a sense of participation in the moral life about him. To leave it unattached to actual social movements means that the moralist is speaking in incomprehensible terms. Without this connection, the religious teachers may have conscientiously carried out their traditional duties and yet have failed utterly to stir the fires of spiritual enthusiasm.

Each generation of moralists and educators find themselves facing an inevitable dilemma; first, to keep the young committed to their charge "unspotted from the world," and, second, to connect the young with the ruthless and materialistic world all about them in such wise that they may make it the arena for their spiritual endeavor. It is fortunate for these teachers that sometime during "The Golden Age" the most prosaic youth is seized by a new interest in remote and universal ends, and that if but given a clue by which he may connect his lofty aims with his daily living, he himself will drag the very heavens into the most sordid tenement. The perpetual difficulty consists in finding the clue for him and placing it in his hands, for, if the teaching is too detached from life, it does not result in any psychic impulsion at all. I remember as an illustration of the saving power of this definite connection, a tale told me by a distinguished labor leader in England. His affections had been starved, even as a child, for he knew nothing of his parents, his earliest memories being associated with a wretched old woman who took the most casual care of him. When he was nine years old he ran away to sea and for the next seven years led the rough life of a dock laborer, until he became much interested in a little crippled boy, who by the death of his father had been left solitary on a freight boat. My English friend promptly adopted the child as his own and all the questionings of life centered about his young protégé. He was constantly driven to attend evening meetings where he heard discussed those social conditions which bear so hard upon the weak and sick. The crippled boy lived until he was fifteen and by that time the regeneration of his foster father was complete, the young docker was committed for life to the bettering of social conditions. It is doubtful whether any abstract moral appeal could have reached such a roving nature. Certainly no attempt to incite his ambition would have succeeded. Only a pull upon his deepest sympathies and affections, his desire to protect and cherish a weaker thing, could possibly have stimulated him and connected him with the forces making for moral and social progress.

This, of course, has ever been the task of religion, to make the sense of obligation personal, to touch morality with enthusiasm, to bathe the world in affection—and on all sides we are challenging the teachers of religion to perform this task for the youth of the city.

For thousands of years definite religious instruction has been given by authorized agents to the youth of all nations, emphasized through tribal ceremonials, the assumption of the Roman toga, the Barmitzvah of the Jews, the First Communion of thousands of children in Catholic Europe, the Sunday Schools of even the least formal of the evangelical sects. It is as if men had always felt that this expanding period of human life must be seized upon for spiritual ends, that the tender tissue and newly awakened emotions must be made the repository for the historic ideals and dogmas which are, after all, the most precious possessions of the race. How has it come about that so many of the city youth are not given their share in our common inheritance of life's best goods? Why are their tender feet so often ensnared even when they are going about youth's legitimate business? One would suppose that in such an age as ours moral teachers would be put upon their mettle, that moral authority would be forced to speak with no uncertain sound if only to be heard above the din of machinery and the roar of industrialism; that it would have exerted itself as never before to convince the youth of the reality of the spiritual life. Affrighted as the moralists must be by the sudden new emphasis placed upon wealth, despairing of the older men and women who are already caught by its rewards, one would say that they would have seized upon the multitude of young people whose minds are busied with issues which lie beyond the portals of life, as the only resource which might save the city from the fate of those who perish through lack of vision.

Yet because this inheritance has not been attached to conduct, the youth of Jewish birth may have been taught that prophets and statesmen for three thousand years declared Jehovah to be a God of Justice who hated oppression and desired righteousness, but there is no real appeal to his spirit of moral adventure unless he is told that the most stirring attempts to translate justice into the modern social order have been inaugurated and carried forward by men of his own race, and that until he joins in the contemporary manifestations of that attempt he is recreant to his highest traditions and obligations.

The Christian youth may have been taught that man's heartbreaking adventure to find justice in the order of the universe moved the God of Heaven himself to send a Mediator in order that the justice man craves and the mercy by which alone he can endure his weakness might be reconciled, but he will not make the doctrine his own until he reduces it to action and tries to translate the spirit of his Master into social terms.

The youth who calls himself an "Evolutionist"—it is rather hard to find a name for this youth, but there are thousands of him and a fine fellow he often is—has read of that struggle beginning with the earliest tribal effort to establish just relations between man and man, but he still needs to be told that after all justice can only be worked out upon this earth by those who will not tolerate a wrong to the feeblest member of the community, and that it will become a social force only in proportion as men steadfastly strive to establish it.

If these young people who are subjected to varied religious instruction are also stirred to action, or rather, if the instruction is given validity because it is attached to conduct, then it may be comparatively easy to bring about certain social reforms so sorely needed in our industrial cities. We are at times obliged to admit, however, that both the school and the church have failed to perform this office, and are indicted by the young people themselves. Thousands of young people in every great city are either frankly hedonistic, or are vainly attempting to work out for themselves a satisfactory code of morals. They cast about in all directions for the clue which shall connect their loftiest hopes with their actual living.

Several years ago a committee of lads came to see me in order to complain of a certain high school principal because "He never talks to us about life." When urged to make a clearer statement, they added, "He never asks us what we are going to be; we can't get a word out of him, excepting lessons and keeping quiet in the halls."

Of the dozens of young women who have begged me to make a connection for them between their dreams of social usefulness and their actual living, I recall one of the many whom I had sent back to her clergyman, returning with this remark: "His only suggestion was that I should be responsible every Sunday for fresh flowers upon the altar. I did that when I was fifteen and liked it then, but when you have come back from college and are twenty-two years old, it doesn't quite fit in with the vigorous efforts you have been told are necessary in order to make our social relations more Christian."

All of us forget how very early we are in the experiment of founding self-government in this trying climate of America, and that we are making the experiment in the most materialistic period of all history, having as our court of last appeal against that materialism only the wonderful and inexplicable instinct for justice which resides in the hearts of men,—which is never so irresistible as when the heart is young. We may cultivate this most precious possession, or we may disregard it. We may listen to the young voices rising clear above the roar of industrialism and the prudent councils of commerce, or we may become hypnotized by the sudden new emphasis placed upon wealth and power, and forget the supremacy of spiritual forces in men's affairs. It is as if we ignored a wistful, over-confident creature who walked through our city streets calling out, "I am the spirit of Youth! With me, all things are possible!" We fail to understand what he wants or even to see his doings, although his acts are pregnant with meaning, and we may either translate them into a sordid chronicle of petty vice or turn them into a solemn school for civic righteousness.

We may either smother the divine fire of youth or we may feed it. We may either stand stupidly staring as it sinks into a murky fire of crime and flares into the intermittent blaze of folly or we may tend it into a lambent flame with power to make clean and bright our dingy city streets.

Notes

1. Addams refers to the "Springtime of the Peoples," when popular revolutions and uprisings broke out all over Europe with the aim of overturning autocracies and bringing in more popular and constitutional orders. The results were decidedly mixed, with advances made in some areas, the restoration of autocracy in others. These failed revolutions prompted a wave of emigration to the United States.

2. *Weltschmerz* is a German word meaning "world-weariness," signifying especially the torments of youth.

3. Of course, what Addams fails to note here is that the German welfare state was also very much a warfare state under the centralizing auspices of Chancellor Otto von Bismarck. Arguably, this potent fusion of warfare-welfare worked to cement and to solidify state control in Bismarck's Germany, a result at odds with the decentralized pluralism of Jane Addams's vision. But Addams had great admiration and affection for German literature, art, and culture, one of the many reasons World War I was such a horror for her, as she saw Germany and the Austro-Hungarian Empire demonized by the excesses and falsities of war propaganda (stories circulated concerning the hideous Huns bayoneting babies and the like).

14

"SURVIVALS OF MILITARISM IN CITY GOVERNMENT"

W E ARE ACCUSTOMED TO SAY that the machinery of government incorporated in the charters of the early American cities, as in the Federal and State constitutions, was worked out by men who were strongly under the influence of the historians and doctrinaires of the eighteenth century. The most significant representative of these men is Thomas Jefferson, and their most telling phrase, the familiar opening that "all men are created free and equal."

We are only now beginning to suspect that the present admitted failure in municipal administration, the so-called "shame of American cities," may be largely due to the inadequacy of those eighteenth-century ideals, with the breakdown of the machinery which they provided. We recognize the weakness inherent in the historic and doctrinaire method when it attempts to deal with growing and human institutions. While these men were strongly under the influence of peace ideals which were earnestly advocated, both in France and in America, even in the midst of their revolutionary periods, and while they read the burning poets and philosophers of their remarkable century, their idealism, after all, was largely founded upon theories concerning "the natural man," a creature of their sympathetic imaginations.

Because their idealism was of the type that is afraid of experience, these founders refused to look at the difficulties and blunders which a self-governing people were sure to encounter, and insisted that, if only

Note: "Survivals of Militarism in City Government," in *Newer Ideals of Peace* (New York: Macmillan, 1907), chapter 2.

the people had freedom, they would walk continuously in the paths of justice and righteousness.[1] It was inevitable, therefore, that they should have remained quite untouched by that worldly wisdom which counsels us to know life as it is, and by that very modern belief that if the world is ever to go right at all, it must go right in its own way.

A man of this generation easily discerns the crudeness of "that eighteenth-century conception of essentially unprogressive human nature in all the empty dignity of its 'inborn rights.'" Because he has grown familiar with a more passionate human creed, with the modern evolutionary conception of the slowly advancing race whose rights are not "inalienable," but hard-won in the tragic processes of experience, he realizes that these painfully acquired rights must be carefully cherished or they may at any moment slip out of our hands. We know better in America than anywhere else that civilization is not a broad road, with mile-stones indicating how far each nation has proceeded upon it, but a complex struggle forward, each race and nation contributing its quota; that the variety and continuity of this commingled life afford its charm and value. We would not, if we could, conform them to one standard. But this modern attitude, which may even now easily subside into negative tolerance, did not exist among the founders of the Republic, who, with all their fine talk of the "natural man" and what he would accomplish when he obtained freedom and equality, did not really trust the people after all.

They timidly took the English law as their prototype, "whose very root is in the relation between sovereign and subject, between lawmaker and those whom the law restrains," which has traditionally concerned itself more with the guarding of prerogative and with the rights of property than with the spontaneous life of the people. They serenely incorporated laws and survivals which registered the successful struggle of the barons against the aggressions of the sovereign, although the new country lacked both nobles and kings. Misled by the name of government, they founded their new government by an involuntary reference to a lower social state than that which they actually saw about them. They depended upon penalties, coercion, compulsion, remnants of military codes, to hold the community together; and it may be possible to trace much of the maladministration of our cities to these survivals, to the fact that our early democracy was a moral romanticism rather than a well-grounded belief in social capacity and in the efficiency of the popular will.

It has further happened that as the machinery, groaning under the pressure of new social demands put upon it, has broken down that from time to time, we have mended it by giving more power to administrative officers, because we still distrusted the will of the people. We are willing to cut off the dislocated part or to tighten the gearing, but are afraid to substitute a machine of newer invention and greater capacity. In the hour of danger we revert to the military and legal type although they become less and less appropriate to city life in proportion as the city grows more complex, more varied in resource and more highly organized, and is, therefore, in greater need of a more diffused local autonomy.

A little examination will easily show that in spite of the fine phrases of the founders, the Government became an entity by itself away from the daily life of the people. There was no intention to ignore them nor to oppress them. But simply because its machinery was so largely copied from the traditional European Governments which did distrust the people, the founders failed to provide the vehicle for a vital and genuinely organized expression of the popular will. The founders carefully defined what was germane to government and what was quite outside its realm, whereas the very crux of local self-government, as has been well said, is involved in the "right to locally determine the scope of the local government," in response to the needs as they arise.

They were anxious to keep the reins of government in the hands of the good and professedly public-spirited, because, having staked so much upon the people whom they really knew so little, they became eager that they should appear well, and should not be given enough power to enable them really to betray their weaknesses. This was done in the same spirit in which a kind lady permits herself to give a tramp five cents, believing that, although he may spend it for drink, he cannot get very drunk upon so small a sum. In spite of a vague desire to trust the people, the founders meant to fall back in every crisis upon the old restraints which government has traditionally enlisted in its behalf, and were, perhaps, inevitably influenced by the experiences of the Revolutionary War. Having looked to the sword for independence from oppressive governmental control, they came to regard the sword as an essential part of the government they had succeeded in establishing.

Regarded from the traditional standpoint, government has always needed this force of arms. The king, attempting to control the growing power of the barons as they wrested one privilege after another from him, was obliged to use it constantly; the barons later successfully established themselves in power only to be encroached upon by the growing strength and capital of the merchant class. These are now, in turn, calling upon the troops and militia for aid, as they are shorn of a pittance here and there by the rising power of the proletariat. The imperial, the feudal, the capitalistic forms of society each created by revolt against oppression from above, preserved their own forms of government only by carefully guarding their hardly won charters and constitutions. But in the very countries where these successive social forms have developed, full of survivals of the past, some beneficent and some detrimental, governments are becoming modified more rapidly than in this democracy where we ostensibly threw off traditional governmental oppression only to encase ourselves in a theory of virtuous revolt against oppressive government, which in many instances has proved more binding than the actual oppression itself.

Did the founders cling too hard to that which they had won through persecution, hardship, and finally through a war of revolution? Did these doctrines seem so precious to them that they were determined to tie men up to them as long as possible, and allow them no chance to go on to new devices of government, lest they slight these that had been so hardly won? Did they estimate, not too highly, but by too exclusive a valuation, that which they had secured through the shedding of blood?

Man has ever overestimated the spoils of war, and tended to lose his sense of proportion in regard to their value. He has ever surrounded them with a glamour beyond their deserts. This is quite harmless when the booty is an enemy's sword hung over a household fire, or a battered flag decorating a city hall, but when the spoil of war is an idea which is bound on the forehead of the victor until it cramps his growth, a theory which he cherishes in his bosom until it grows so large and near that it afflicts its possessor with a sort of disease of responsibility for its preservation, it may easily overshadow the very people for whose cause the warrior issued forth.

Was this overestimation of the founders the cause of our subsequent failures? or rather did not the fault lie with their successors, and does it not now rest with us, that we have wrapped our inheritance in a napkin and refused to add thereto? The founders fearlessly took the noblest word of their century and incorporated it into a public document. They ventured their fortunes and the future of their children upon its truth. We, with the belief of a progressive, developing human life, apparently accomplish less than they with their insistence upon rights and liberties which they so vigorously opposed to mediaeval restrictions and obligations. We are in that first period of conversion when we hold a creed which forecasts newer and larger possibilities for governmental development, without in the least understanding its spiritual implications. Although we have scrupulously extended the franchise to the varied immigrants among us, we have not yet admitted them into real political fellowship.

It is easy to demonstrate that we consider our social and political problems almost wholly in the light of one wise group whom we call native Americans, legislating for the members of humbler groups whom we call immigrants. The first embodies the attitude of contempt or, at best, the patronage of the successful towards those who have as yet failed to succeed. We may consider the so-called immigration situation as an illustration of our failure to treat our growing Republic in the spirit of a progressive and developing democracy.

The statement is made many times that we, as a nation, are rapidly reaching the limit of our powers of assimilation, that we receive further masses of immigrants at the risk of blurring those traits and characteristics which we are pleased to call American, with its corollary that the national standard of living is in danger of permanent debasement. Were we not in the midst of a certain intellectual dearth and apathy, of a skepticism in regard to the ideals of self-government which have ceased to charm men, we would see that we are testing our national life by a tradition too provincial and limited to meet its present motley and cosmopolitan character; that we lack mental energy, adequate knowledge, and a sense of the youth of the earth. The constant cry that American institutions are in danger betrays a spiritual waste, not due to our infidelity to national ideals, but arising from the fact that we fail to enlarge those ideals in accord with our faithful experience of life. Our political machinery, devised for quite other conditions, has not been readjusted and adapted to the successive changes resulting from our development. The clamor for the town meeting, for the colonial and early century ideals of government is in itself significant, for we are apt to cling to the past through a very paucity of ideas.

In a sense the enormous and unprecedented moving about over the face of the earth on the part of all nations is in itself the result of philosophic dogma of the eighteenth century—of the creed of individual liberty. The modern system of industry and commerce presupposes freedom of occupation, of travel, and residence; even more, it unhappily rests in a large measure upon the assumption of a body of the unemployed and the unskilled, ready to be absorbed or dropped according to the demands of production: but back of that, or certainly preceding its later developments, lies "the natural rights" doctrine of the eighteenth century. Even so late as 1892 an official treaty of the United States referred to the "inalienable rights of man to change his residence and religion." This dogma of the schoolmen, dramatized in France and penetrating under a thousand forms into the most backward European States, is still operating as an obscure force in sending emigrants to America and in our receiving them here. But in the second century of its existence it has become too barren and chilly to induce any really zealous or beneficent activity, on behalf of the immigrants after they arrive. On the other hand those things which we do believe—the convictions which might be formulated to the immeasurable benefit of the immigrants, and to the everlasting good of our national life, have not yet been satisfactorily stated, nor apparently apprehended by us, in relation to this field. We have no method by which to discover men, to spiritualize, to understand, to hold intercourse with aliens and to receive of what they bring. A century-old abstraction breaks down before this vigorous test of concrete cases and their demand for sympathetic interpretation. When we are confronted by the Italian lazzaroni, the peasants from the Carpathian foothills, and the proscribed traders from Galatia, we have no national ideality founded upon realism and tested by our growing experience with which to meet them, but only the platitudes of our crudest youth. The philosophers and statesmen of the eighteenth century believed that the universal franchise would cure all ills; that liberty and equality rested only upon constitutional rights and privileges; that to obtain these two and to throw off all governmental oppression constituted the full duty of the progressive patriot. We still keep to this formalization because the philosophers of this generation give us nothing newer. We ignore the fact that world-wide problems can no longer be solved by a political constitution assuring us against opposition, but that we must frankly face the proposition that the whole situation is more industrial than political. Did we apprehend this, we might then realize that the officers of the Government who are dealing with naturalization papers and testing the knowledge of the immigrants concerning the Constitution of the United States, are only playing with counters representing the beliefs of a century ago, while the real issues are being settled by the great industrial and commercial interests which are at once the products and the masters of our contemporary life. As children who are allowed to amuse themselves with poker chips pay no attention to the real game which their elders play with the genuine cards in their hands, so we shut our eyes to the exploitation and industrial debasement of the immigrant, and say, with placid contentment, that he has been given the rights of an American citizen, and that, therefore, all our obligations have been fulfilled. It is as if we should undertake to cure the contemporary political corruption founded upon a disregard of the Inter-State Commerce Acts, by requiring the recreant citizens to repeat the Constitution of the United States.

As yet no vigorous effort is made to discover how far our present system of naturalization, largely resting upon laws enacted in 1802, is inadequate, although it may have met the requirements of "the fathers." These processes were devised to test new citizens who had immigrated to the United States from political rather than from economic pressure, although these two have always been in a certain sense coextensive. Yet the early Irish came to America to seek an opportunity for self-government, denied them at home; the Germans and Italians started to come in largest numbers after the absorption of their smaller States into the larger nations; and the immigrants from Russia are the conquered Poles, Lithuanians, Finns, and Jews. On some such obscure notion the processes of naturalization were worked out, and, with a certain degree of logic, the first immigrants were presented with the Constitution of the United States as a type and epitome of that which they had come to seek. So far as they now come in search of political liberty, as many of them do every day, the test is still valid, but, in the meantime, we cannot ignore those significant figures which show emigration to rise with periods of depression in given countries, and immigration to be checked by periods of depression in America, and we refuse to see how largely the question has become an economic one.

At the present moment, as we know, the actual importing of immigrants is left largely to the energy of steamship companies and to those agents for contract labor who are keen enough to avoid the restrictive laws. The business man is here again in the saddle, as he so largely is in

American affairs. From the time that the immigrants first make the acquaintance of the steamship agent in their own villages, at least until a grandchild is born on the new soil, they are subjected to various processes of exploitation from purely commercial and self-seeking interests. It begins with the representatives of the transatlantic lines and their allies, who convert the peasant holdings into money, and provide the prospective emigrants with needless supplies, such as cartridge belts and bowie knives. The brokers in manufactured passports send their clients by successive stages for a thousand miles to a port suiting their purposes. On the way the emigrants' eyes are treated that they may pass the physical test; they are taught to read sufficiently well to meet the literacy test; they are lent enough money to escape the pauper test, and by the time they have reached America, they are so hopelessly in debt that it requires months of work to repay all they have received. During this time they are completely under the control of the last broker in the line, who has his dingy office in an American city. The exploitation continues under the employment agency whose operations verge into those of the politician, through the naturalization henchman, the petty lawyers who foment their quarrels and grievances by the statement that in a free country everybody "goes to law," by the liquor dealers who stimulate a lively trade among them, and, finally, by the lodging-house keepers and the landlords who are not obliged to give them the housing which the American tenant demands. It is a long dreary road, and the immigrant is successfully exploited at each turn. At moments one looking on is driven to quote the Titanic plaint of Walt Whitman:

"As I stand aloof and look, there is to me something profoundly affecting in large masses of men following the lead of those who do not believe in men."[2]

The sinister aspect of this exploitation lies in the fact that it is carried on by agents whose stock in trade are the counters and terms of citizenship. It is said that at the present moment there are more of these agents in Palermo than perhaps in any other European port, and that those politicians who have found it impossible to stay even in that corrupt city are engaged in the brokerage of naturalization papers in the United States. Certainly one effect of the stringent contract labor laws has been to make the padrones more powerful because "smuggled alien labor" has become more valuable to American corporations, and also to make simpler the delivery of immigrant votes according to the dictates of commercial interests. It becomes a veritable system of poisoning the notions of decent government; but because the entire process is carried on in political terms, because the poker chips are colored red, white, and blue, we are childishly indifferent to it. An elaborate avoidance of restrictions quickly adapts itself to changes either in legislation here or at the points of departure, because none of the legislation is founded upon a real analysis of the situation. For instance, a new type of broker in Russia during the Russian-Japanese War made use of the situation in the interests of young Russian Jews. If one of these men leaves the country ordinarily, his family is obliged to pay three hundred rubles to the Government, but if he first joins the army, his family is free from this obligation for he has passed into the keeping of his sergeant. Out of four hundred Russian Jews who, during three months, were drafted into the army at a given recruiting station, only ten reported, the rest having escaped through immigration. Of course the entire undertaking is much more hazardous, because the man is a deserter from the army in addition to his other disabilities; but the brokers merely put up the price of their services and continue their undertakings.

All these evasions of immigration laws and regulations are simply possible because the governmental tests do not belong to the current situation, and because our political ideas are inherited from governmental conditions not our own. In our refusal to face the situation, we have persistently ignored the political ideals of the Celtic, Germanic, Latin, and Slavic immigrants who have successively come to us; and in our overwhelming ambition to remain Anglo-Saxon, we have fallen into the Anglo-Saxon temptation of governing all peoples by one standard. We have failed to work out a democratic government which should include the experiences and hopes of all the varied peoples among us. We justify the situation by some such process as that employed by each English elector who casts a vote for seventy-five subjects besides himself. He indirectly determines—although he may be a narrow-minded tradesman or a country squire interested only in his hounds and horses—the colonial policy, which shall in turn control the destinies of the Egyptian child toiling in the cotton factory in Alexandria, and of the half-starved Parsee working the opium fields of North India. Yet he cannot, in the nature of the case, be informed of the needs of these far-away people and he would venture to attempt it only in regard to people whom he considered "inferior."

Pending a recent election, a Chicago reformer begged his hearers to throw away all selfish thoughts of themselves when they went to the polls and to vote in behalf of the poor and ignorant foreigners of the city. It would be difficult to suggest anything which would result in a more serious confusion than to have each man, without personal knowledge and experiences, consider the interests of the newly arrived immigrant. The voter would have to give himself over to a veritable debauch of altruism in order to persuade himself that his vote would be of the least value to those men of whom he knew so little, and whom he considered so remote and alien to himself. In truth the attitude of the advising reformer was in reality so contemptuous that he had never considered the immigrants really partakers and molders of the political life of his country.

This attitude of contempt, of provincialism, this survival of the spirit of the conqueror toward an inferior people, has many manifestations, but none so harmful as when it becomes absorbed and imitated and is finally evinced by the children of the foreigners toward their own parents.

We are constantly told of the increase of criminals in the second generation of immigrants, and, day after day, one sees lads of twelve and fourteen throwing off the restraint of family life and striking out for themselves. The break has come thus early, partly from the forced development of the child under city conditions, partly because the parents have had no chance of following, even remotely, this development, but largely because the Americanized child has copied the contemptuous attitude towards the foreigner which he sees all about him. The revolt has in it something of the city impatience of country standards, but much more of America against Poland or Italy. It is all wretchedly sordid with bitterness on the part of the parents, and hardhearted indifference and recklessness on the part of the boy. Only occasionally can the latter be appealed to by filial affection after the first break has once been thoroughly made; and yet, sometimes, even these lads see the pathos of the situation. A probation officer from Hull-House one day surprised three truants who were sitting by a bonfire which they had built near the river. Sheltered by an empty freight car, the officer was able to listen to their conversation. The Pole, the Italian, and the Bohemian boys who had broken the law by staying away from school, by building a fire in dangerous proximity to freight cars, and by "swiping" the potatoes which they were roasting, seemed to have settled down into an almost halcyon moment of gentleness and reminiscence. The Italian boy commiserated his parents because they hated the cold and the snow and "couldn't seem to get used to it;" the Pole said that his father missed seeing folks that he knew and was "sore on this country;" the Bohemian lad really grew quite tender about his old grandmother and the "stacks of relations" who came to see her every Sunday in the old country, where, in contrast to her loneliness here, she evidently had been a person of consequence. All of them felt the pathos of the situation, but the predominant note was the cheap contempt of the new American for foreigners, even though they are of his own blood. The weakening of the tie which connects one generation with another may be called the domestic results of the contemptuous attitude. But the social results of the contemptuous attitude are even more serious and nowhere so grave as in the modern city.

Men are there brought together by multitudes in response to the concentration of industry and commerce without bringing with them the natural social and family ties or the guild relationships which distinguished the mediaeval cities and held even so late as the eighteenth century, when the country people came to town in response to the normal and slowly formed ties of domestic service, family affection, and apprenticeship. Men who come to a modern city by immigration break all these older ties and the national bond in addition. There is all the more necessity to develop that cosmopolitan bond which forms their substitute. The immigrants will be ready to adapt themselves to a new and vigorous civic life founded upon the recognition of their needs if the Government which is at present administered in our cities will only admit that these needs are germane to its functions. The framers of the carefully prepared charters, upon which the cities are founded, did not foresee that after the universal franchise had once been granted, social needs and ideals were bound to enter in as legitimate objects of political action. Neither did these framers realize, on the other hand, that the only people in a democracy which can legitimately become the objects of repressive government, are those people who are too undeveloped to use their liberty or those who have forfeited their right to full citizenship. We have, therefore, a municipal administration in America which concerns itself only grudgingly with the social needs of the people, and is largely reduced to the administration of restrictive measures. The people who come most directly in contact with the executive officials, who are the legitimate objects of their control, are the vicious, who need to be repressed; and the semi-dependent poor, who appeal to them in their dire need; or, for quite the reverse reason, those who are trying to avoid an undue taxation, resenting the fact that they should be made to support a government which, from the nature of the case, is too barren to excite their real enthusiasm.

The instinctive protest against this mechanical method of civic control, with the lack of adjustment between the natural democratic impulse and the fixed external condition, inevitably produces the indifferent citizen, and the so-called "professional politician." The first, because he is not vicious, feels that the real processes of government do not concern him and wishes only to be let alone. The latter easily adapts himself to an illegal avoidance of the external fixed conditions by assuming that these conditions have been settled by doctrinaires who did not in the least understand the people, while he, the politician, makes his appeal beyond the conditions to the real desires of the people themselves. He is thus not only "the people's friend," but their interpreter. It is interesting to note how often simple people refer to "them," meaning the good and the great who govern but do not understand, and to "him," meaning the alderman, who represents them in these incomprehensible halls of State, as an ambassador to a foreign country to whose borders they themselves could not possibly penetrate, and whose language they do not speak.

In addition to this difficulty inherent in the difference between the traditional and actual situation, there is another, which constantly arises on the purely administrative side. The traditional governments which the founders had copied, in proceeding by fixed standards to separate the vicious from the good, and then to legislate against the vicious, had enforced these restrictive measures by trained officials, usually with a military background. In a democracy, however, the officers entrusted with the enforcement of this restrictive legislation, if not actually elected by the people themselves, are still the appointments of those thus elected and are, therefore, good-natured men who have made friends by their kindness and social qualities. This is only decreasingly true even in those cities where appointments are made by civil service examinations. The carrying out of repressive legislation, the remnant of a military state of society, in a democracy is at last put into the hands of men who have attained office because of political pull. The repressive measures must be enforced by those sympathizing with the people and belonging to those against whom the measures operate. This anomalous situation produces almost inevitably one result: that the police authorities themselves are turned into allies of vice and crime. This may be illustrated from almost any of the large American cities in the relation existing between the police force and the gambling and other illicit life. The officers are often flatly told that the enforcement of an ordinance which the better element of the city has insisted upon passing, is impossible; that they are expected to control only the robbery and crime that so often associate themselves with vice. As Mr. Wilcox[3] has recently pointed out, public sentiment itself assumes a certain hypocrisy, and in the end we have "the abnormal conditions which are created when vice is protected by the authorities," and in the very worst cases there develops a sort of municipal blackmail in which the administration itself profits by the violation of law. The very governmental agencies which were designed to protect the citizen from vice, foster and protect him in its pursuance because everybody involved is thoroughly confused by the human element in the situation. Further than this, the officer's very kindness and human understanding is that which leads to his downfall, for he is forced to uphold the remnant of a military discipline in a self-governing community. It is not remarkable, perhaps, that the police department, the most vigorous survival of militarism to be found in American cities, has always been responsible for the most exaggerated types of civic corruption. It is sad, however, that this corruption has largely been due to the kindliness of the officers and to their lack of military training. There is no doubt that keeping the saloons in lower New York open on Sunday appeared reasonable to the policemen of the East Side force long before it dawned upon the reform administration; and yet, that the policemen allowed themselves to connive at law-breaking was the beginning of their disgraceful downfall. Because kindness to an enemy may mean death or the annihilation of the army which he guards, all kindness is illicit on the part of the military sentinel on duty; but to bring that code over bodily into a peaceful social state is to break down the morals of both sides, of the enforcer of the ill-adapted law, as well as of those against whom it is so maladroitly directed.

In order to meet this situation, there is almost inevitably developed a politician of the corrupt type so familiar in American cities, the politician who has become successful because he has made friends with the vicious. The semi-criminal, who are constantly brought in contact with administrative government, are naturally much interested in its operations. Having much at stake, as a matter of course, they attend the primaries and all the other election processes which so quickly tire the good citizens whose interest in the government is a self-imposed duty. To illustrate: it is a matter of much moment to a gambler whether there is to be a "wide-open town" or not; it means the success or failure of his business; it involves, not only the pleasure, but the livelihood, of all his friends. He naturally attends to the election of the alderman, to the appointment and retention of the policeman. He is found at the caucus "every time," and would be much amused if he were praised for the performance of his civic duty; but, because he and the others who are concerned in semi-illicit business do attend the primaries, the corrupt politician is nominated over and over again.

As this type of politician is successful from his alliance with crime, there also inevitably arises from time to time a so-called reformer who is shocked to discover the state of affairs, the easy partnership between vice and administrative government. He dramatically uncovers the situation and arouses great indignation against it on the part of good citizens. If this indignation is enough, he creates a political fervor which is translated into a claim upon public gratitude. In portraying the evil he is fighting, he does not recognize, or at least does not make clear, all the human kindness upon which it has grown. In his speeches he inevitably offends a popular audience, who know that the evil of corruption exists in all degrees and forms of human weakness, but who also know that these evils are by no means always hideous, and sometimes even are lovable. They resent his over-drawn pictures of vice and of the life of the vicious; their sense of fair play, their deep-rooted desire for charity and justice, are all outraged.

To illustrate from a personal experience: Some years ago a famous New York reformer came to Chicago to tell us of his phenomenal success, his trenchant methods of dealing with the city "gambling-hells," as he chose to call them. He proceeded to describe the criminals of lower New York in terms and phrases which struck at least one of his auditors as sheer blasphemy against our common human nature. I thought of the criminals whom I knew, of the gambler for whom each Saturday I regularly collected his weekly wage of $24.00, keeping $18.00 for his wife and children and giving him $6.00 on Monday morning. His despairing statement, "the thing is growing on me, and I can never give it up," was certainly not the cry of a man living in hell, but of him who, through much tribulation had at least kept the loyal intention. I remembered the three girls who had come to me with a paltry sum of money collected from the pawn and sale of their tawdry finery in order that one of their number might be spared a death in the almshouse and that she might have the wretched comfort during the closing weeks of her life of knowing that, although she was an outcast, she was not a pauper. I recalled the first murderer whom I had ever known, a young man who was singing his baby to sleep and stopped to lay it in its cradle before he rushed downstairs into his father's saloon to scatter the gang of boys who were teasing the old man by giving him English orders. The old man could not understand English and the boys were refusing to pay for the drinks they had consumed, but technically had not ordered.

For one short moment I saw the situation from the point of view of humbler people, who sin often through weakness and passion, but seldom through hardness of heart, and I felt that in a democratic community such sweeping condemnations and conclusions as the speaker was pouring forth could never be accounted for righteousness.

As the policeman who makes terms with vice, and almost inevitably slides into making gain from vice, merely represents the type of politician who is living off the weakness of his fellows, so the over-zealous reformer who exaggerates vice until the public is scared and awestruck, represents the type of politician who is living off the timidity of his fellows. With the lack of civic machinery for simple democratic expression, for a direct dealing with human nature as it is, we seem doomed to one type or the other—corruptionists or anti-crime committees.

And one sort or the other we will continue to have so long as we distrust the very energy of existence, the craving for enjoyment, the pushing of vital forces, the very right of every citizen to be what he is without pretense or assumption of virtue. Too often he does not really admire these virtues, but he imagines them somewhere as a standard adopted by the virtuous whom he does not know. That old Frankenstein, the ideal man of the eighteenth century, is still haunting us, although he never existed save in the brain of the doctrinaire.

This dramatic and feverish triumph of the self-seeker, see-sawing with that of the interested reformer, does more than anything else, perhaps, to keep the American citizen away from the ideals of genuine evolutionary democracy. Whereas repressive government, from the nature of the case, has to do with the wicked who are happily always in a minority in the community, a normal democratic government would naturally have to do with the great majority of the population in their normal relations to each other.

After all, the so-called "slum politician" ventures his success upon an appeal to human sentiment and generosity. This venture often results in an alliance between the popular politician and the humblest citizens, quite as naturally as the reformer who stands for honest business administration usually becomes allied with the type of business man whose chief concern it is to guard his treasure and to prevent a rise in taxation. The community is again insensibly divided into two camps, the repressed, who is dimly conscious that he has no adequate outlet for his normal life and the repressive, represented by the cautious, careful citizen holding fast to his own,—once more the conqueror and his humble people.

Notes

1. Addams's critique of the Founding Fathers is remarkable, especially in light of the reverence with which her own hero, Abraham Lincoln, held the founders and that great document, the Declaration of Independence. Addams anticipates later critiques of, and debates about, "abstract rights" versus a more concrete and historicized way of talking about rights. Of course, in a sense, she looks back as well, here embracing, at least tacitly, Edmund Burke's critique of the abstract rights of man of the French Revolution, which ended in terror. For Burke, rights evolve historically out of concrete, local circumstances. In any case, Addams much preferred to talk about social responsibilities and duties rather than rights. Justice and equality were also key categories in her political vocabulary.

2. Walt Whitman is the great poet of American democracy as a lyrical, indeed a poetical, enterprise. Like Addams, he worshipped Abraham Lincoln. His dates are 1819–1892.

3. Addams here refers to Dr. Delos F. Wilcox, author of *The American City*.

15

"A Modern Lear"

THOSE OF US WHO LIVED IN CHICAGO during the summer of 1894 were confronted by a drama which epitomized and, at the same time, challenged the code of social ethics under which we live, for a quick series of unusual events had dispelled the good nature which in happier times envelops the ugliness of the industrial situation.[1] It sometimes seems as if the shocking experiences of that summer, the barbaric instinct to kill, roused on both sides, the sharp division into class lines, with the resultant distrust and bitterness, can only be endured if we learn from it all a great ethical lesson. To endure is all we can hope for. It is impossible to justify such a course of rage and riot in a civilized community to whom the methods of conciliation and control were open. Every public-spirited citizen in Chicago during that summer felt the stress and perplexity of the situation and asked himself, "How far am I responsible for this social disorder? What can be done to prevent such outrageous manifestations of ill-will?"

If the responsibility of tolerance lies with those of the widest vision, it behooves us to consider this great social disaster, not alone in its legal aspect nor in its sociological bearings, but from those deep human motives, which, after all, determine events.

During the discussions which followed the Pullman strike, the defenders of the situation were broadly divided between the people pleading for individual benevolence and those insisting upon social righteousness; between those who held that the philanthropy of the president of the Pullman company had been most ungratefully received and those who maintained that the situation was the in-

---

Note: "A Modern Lear," *Survey*, vol. 39 (November 2, 1912).

evitable outcome of the social consciousness developing among working people.

In the midst of these discussions the writer found her mind dwelling upon a comparison which modified and softened all her judgments. Her attention was caught by the similarity of ingratitude suffered by an indulgent employer and an indulgent parent. King Lear came often to her mind. We have all shared the family relationship and our code of ethics concerning it is somewhat settled. We also bear a part in the industrial relationship, but our ethics concerning that are still uncertain. A comparative study of these two relationships presents an advantage, in that it enables us to consider the situation from the known experience toward the unknown. The minds of all of us reach back to our early struggles, as we emerged from the state of self-willed childhood to a recognition of the family claim.

We have all had glimpses of what it might be to blaspheme against family ties; to ignore the elemental claim they make upon us, but on the whole we have recognized them, and it does not occur to us to throw them over. The industrial claim is so difficult; the ties are so intangible that we are constantly ignoring them and shirking the duties which they impose. It will probably be easier to treat of the tragedy of the Pullman strike as if it were already long past when we compare it to the family tragedy of Lear which has already become historic to our minds and which we discuss without personal feeling.

Historically considered, the relation of Lear to his children was archaic and barbaric, holding in it merely the beginnings of a family life, since developed. We may in later years learn to look back upon the industrial relationships in which we are now placed as quite as incomprehensible and selfish, quite as barbaric and undeveloped, as was the family relationship between Lear and his daughters. We may then take the relationship of this unusually generous employer at Pullman to his own townful of employes [sic] as at least a fair one, because so exceptionally liberal in many of its aspects. King Lear doubtless held the same notion of a father's duty that was held by the other fathers of his time; but he alone was a king and had kingdoms to bestow upon his children. He was unique, therefore, in the magnitude of his indulgence, and in the magnitude of the disaster which followed it. The sense of duty held by the president of the Pullman company doubtless represents the ideal in the minds of the best of the present employers as to their obligations toward their employes, but he projected this ideal more magnificently than the others. He alone gave his men so model a town, such perfect surroundings. The magnitude of his indulgence and failure corresponded and we are forced to challenge the ideal itself: the same deal [sic] which, more or less clearly defined, is floating in the minds of all philanthropic employers.

This older tragedy implied mal-adjustment [sic] between individuals; the forces of the tragedy were personal and passionate. This modern tragedy in its inception is a mal-adjustment between two large bodies of men, an employing company and a mass of employes. It deals not with personal relationships, but with industrial relationships.

Owing, however, to the unusual part played in it by the will of one man, we find that it closely approaches Lear in motif. The relation of the British King to his family is very like the relation of the president of the Pullman company to his town; the denouement of a daughter's break with her father suggests the break of the employes [sic] with their benefactor. If we call one an example of the domestic tragedy, the other of the industrial tragedy, it is possible to make them illuminate each other.

It is easy to discover striking points of similarity in the tragedies of the royal father and the philanthropic president of the Pullman company. The like quality of ingratitude they both suffered is at once apparent. It may be said that the ingratitude which Lear received was poignant and bitter to him in proportion as he recalled the extraordinary benefits he had heaped upon his daughters, and that he found his fate harder to bear because he had so far exceeded the measure of a father's duty, as he himself says. What, then, would be the bitterness of a man who had heaped extraordinary benefits upon those toward whom he had no duty recognized by common consent; who had not only exceeded the righteousness of the employer, but who had worked out original and striking methods for lavishing goodness and generosity? More than that, the president had been almost persecuted for this goodness by the more utilitarian members of his company and had at one time imperilled his business reputation for the sake of the benefactions to his town, and he had thus reached the height of sacrifice for it. This model town embodied not only his hopes and ambitions, but stood for the peculiar effort which a man makes for that which is misunderstood.[2]

It is easy to see that although the heart of Lear was cut by ingratitude and by misfortune, it was cut deepest of all by the public pity of his people, in that they should remember him no longer as a king and benefactor, but as a defeated man who had blundered through over-softness. So the heart of the Chicago man was cut by the unparalleled publicity which brought him to the minds of thousands as a type of oppression and injustice, and to many others as an example of the evil of an irregulated sympathy for the "lower classes." He who had been dined and feted throughout Europe as the creator of a model town, as the friend and benefactor of workingmen, was new execrated by workingmen throughout the entire country. He had not only been good to those who were now basely ungrateful to him, but he felt himself deserted by the admiration of his people.

In shops such as those at Pullman, indeed, in all manufacturing affairs since the industrial revolution, industry is organized into a vast social operation. The shops are managed, however, not for the development of the workman thus socialized, but for the interests of the company owning the capital. The divergence between the social form and the individual aim becomes greater as the employes [sic] are more highly socialized and dependent, just as the clash in a family is more vital in proportion to the development and closeness of the family tie. The president of the Pullman company went further than the usual employer does. He socialized not only the factory but the form in which his workmen were living. He built and, in a great measure, regulated an entire town. This again might have worked out into a successful associated effort, if he had had in view the sole good of the inhabitants thus socialized, if he had called upon them for self-expression and had made the town a growth and manifestation of their wants and needs. But, unfortunately, the end to be obtained became ultimately commercial and not social, having in view the payment to the company of at least 4 per cent on the money invested, so that with this rigid requirement there could be no adaptation of rent to wages, much less to needs. The rents became statical [sic] and the wages competitive, shifting inevitably with the demands of trade. The president assumed that he himself knew the needs of his men, and so far from wishing them to express their needs he denied to them the simple rights of trade organization, which would have been, of course, the merest preliminary to an attempt at associated expression. If we may take the dictatorial relation of Lear to Cordelia as a typical and most dramatic example of the distinctively family tragedy, one will asserting its authority through all the entanglement of wounded affection, and insisting upon its selfish ends at all costs, may we not consider the absolute authority of this employer over his town as a typical and dramatic example of the industrial tragedy? One will directing the energies of many others, without regard to their desires, and having in view in the last analysis only commercial results?

It shocks our ideal of family life that a man should fail to know his daughter's heart because she awkwardly expressed her love, that he should refuse to comfort and advise her through all difference of opinion and clashing of will. That a man should be so absorbed in his own indignation as to fail to apprehend his child's thought; that he should lose his affection in his anger, is really no more unnatural than that the man who spent a million of dollars on a swamp to make it sanitary for his employes, should refuse to speak to them for ten minutes, whether they were in the right or wrong; or that a man who had given them his time and thought for twenty years should withdraw from them his guidance when he believed them misled by ill-advisers and wandering in a mental fog; or that he should grow hard and angry when they needed tenderness and help.

Lear ignored the common ancestry of Cordelia and himself. He forgot her royal inheritance of magnanimity, and also the power of obstinacy which he shared with her. So long had he thought of himself as the noble and indulgent father that he had lost the faculty by which he might perceive himself in the wrong. Even when his spirit was broken by the storm he declared himself more sinned against than sinning. He could believe any amount of kindness and goodness of himself, but could imagine no fidelity on the part of Cordelia unless she gave him the sign he demanded.

The president of the Pullman company doubtless began to build his town from an honest desire to give his employes the best surroundings. As it developed it became a source of pride and an exponent of power, that he cared most for when it gave him a glow of benevolence. Gradually, what the outside world thought of it became of importance to him and he ceased to measure its usefulness by the standard of the men's needs. The theater was complete in equipment and beautiful in design, but too costly for a troupe who depended upon the patronage of mechanics, as the church was too expensive to be rented continuously. We can imagine the founder of the town slowly darkening his glints of memory and forgetting the common stock of experience which he held with his men. He cultivated the great and noble impulses of the benefactor, until the power of attaining a simple human relationship with his employes, [sic] that of frank equality with them, was gone from him. He, too, lost the faculty of affectionate interpretation, and demanded a sign. He and his employes [sic] had no mutual interest in a common cause.

Was not the grotesque situation of the royal father and the philanthropic employer to perform so many good deeds that they lost the power of recognizing good in beneficiaries? Were not both so absorbed in carrying out a personal plan of improvement that they failed to catch the great moral lesson which their times offered them? This is the crucial point of the tragedies and may be further elucidated.

Lear had doubtless swung a bauble before Cordelia's baby eyes that he might have the pleasure of seeing the little pink and tender hands stretched for it. A few years later he had given jewels to the young princess, and felt an exquisite pleasure when she stood before him, delighted with her gaud and grateful to her father. He demanded the same kind of response for his gift of the kingdom, but the gratitude must be larger and more carefully expressed, as befitted such a gift. At the opening of the drama he sat upon his throne ready for this enjoyment, but instead of delight and gratitude he found the first dawn of character. His daughter made the awkward attempt of an untrained soul to be honest, to be scrupulous in the expressions of its feelings. It was new to him that his child should be moved by a principle outside of himself, which even his imagination could not follow; that she had caught the notion of an existence so vast that her relationship as a daughter was but part of it.

Perhaps her suitors, the King of France or the Duke of Burgundy, had first hinted to the young Cordelia that there was a fuller life beyond the seas. Certain it is that someone had shaken her from the quiet measure of her insular existence and that she had at last felt the thrill of the world's life. She was transformed by a dignity which recast her speech and made it self-contained, as is becoming a citizen of the world. She found herself in the sweep of a notion of justice so large that the immediate loss of a kingdom seemed of little consequence to her. Even an act which might be construed as disrespect to her father was justified in her eyes because she was vainly striving to fill out this larger conception of duty.

The test which comes sooner or later to many parents had come to Lear, to maintain the tenderness of the relation between father and child after that relation had become one between adults; to be contented with the responses which this adult made to the family claim, while at the same time, she felt the tug upon her emotions and faculties of the larger life, the life which surrounds and completes the individual and family life, and which shares and widens her attention. He was not sufficiently wise to see that only that child can fulfill the family claim in its sweetness and strength who also fulfills the larger claim, that the adjustment of the lesser and larger implies no conflict. The mind of Lear was not big enough for this test. He failed to see anything but the personal slight involved, the ingratitude alone reached him. It was impossible for him to calmly watch his child developing beyond the strength of his own mind and sympathy.

Without pressing the analogy too hard may we not compare the indulgent relation of this employer to his town to the relation which existed between Lear and Cordelia? He fostered his employes for many years, gave them sanitary houses and beautiful parks, but in their extreme need, when they were struggling with the most difficult question which the times could present to them, when, if ever, they required the assistance of a trained mind and a comprehensive outlook, he lost his touch and had nothing wherewith to help them. He did not see the situation. He had been ignorant of their gropings toward justice. His conception of goodness for them had been cleanliness, decency of living, and above all, thrift and temperance. He had provided them means for all this; had gone further, and given them opportunities for enjoyment and comradeship. But he suddenly found his town in the sweep of a world-wide moral impulse. A movement had been going on about him and through the souls of his workingmen of which he had been unconscious. He had only heard of this movement by rumor. The men who consorted with him at his club and in his business had spoken but little of it, and when they had discussed it had contemptuously called it the "Labor Movement," headed by deadbeats and agitators. Of the force and power of this movement, of all the vitality within it, of that conception of duty which induces men to go without food and to see their wives and children suffer for the sake of securing better wages for fellow-workmen whom they have never seen, this president had dreamed absolutely nothing. But his town had at last become swept into this larger movement, so that the giving up of comfortable homes, of beautiful surroundings, seemed as naught to the men within its grasp.

Outside the ken of this philanthropist, the proletariat had learned to say in many languages that "the injury of one is the concern of all." Their watchwords were brotherhood, sacrifice, the subordination of individual and trade interests to the good of the working class; and their persistent strivings were toward the ultimate freedom of that class from the conditions under which they now labor.

Compared to these watchwords the old ones which the philanthropic employer had given his town were negative and inadequate.

When this movement finally swept in his own town, or, to speak more fairly, when in their distress and perplexity his own employes appealed to the organized manifestation of this movement, they were quite sure that simply because they were workmen in distress they would not be deserted by it. This loyalty on the part of a widely ramified and well organized union toward the workmen in a "scab shop," who had contributed nothing to its cause, was certainly a manifestation of moral power.

That the movement was ill-directed, that it was ill-timed and disastrous in results, that it stirred up and became confused in the minds of the public with the elements of riot and blood-shed, can never touch the fact that it started from an unselfish impulse.

In none of his utterances or correspondence did the president of the company for an instant recognize this touch of nobility, although one would imagine that he would gladly point out this bit of virtue, in what he must have considered the moral ruin about him. He stood throughout pleading for the individual virtues, those which had distinguished the model workman of his youth, those which had enabled him and so many of his contemporaries to rise in life, when "rising in life" was urged upon every promising boy as the goal of his efforts. Of the new code of ethics he had caught absolutely nothing. The morals he had taught his men did not fail them in their hour of confusion. They were self-controlled and destroyed no property.[3] They were sober and exhibited no drunkenness, even though obliged to hold their meetings in the saloon hall of a neighboring town. They repaid their employer in kind, but he had given them no rule for the higher fellowship and life of association into which they were plunged.

The virtues of one generation are not sufficient for the next, any more than the accumulations of knowledge possessed by one age are adequate to the needs of another.

Of the virtues received from our fathers we can afford to lose none. We accept as a precious trust those principles and precepts which the race has worked out for its highest safeguard and protection. But merely to preserve those is not enough. A task is laid upon each generation to enlarge their application, to ennoble their conception, and, above all, to apply and adapt them to the peculiar problems presented to it for solution.

The president of this company desired that his employes should possess the individual and family virtues, but did nothing to cherish in them those social virtues which his own age demanded. He rather substituted for that sense of responsibility to the community, a feeling of gratitude to himself, who had provided them with public buildings, and had laid out for them a simulacrum of public life.

Is it strange that when the genuine feeling of the age struck his town this belated and almost feudal virtue of personal gratitude fell before it?

Day after day during that horrible suspense, when the wires constantly reported the same message, "The president of the company holds that there is nothing to arbitrate," one longed to find out what was in the mind of this man, to unfold his ultimate motive. One concludes that he must have been sustained by the consciousness of being in the right. Only that could have held him against the great desire for fair play which swept over the country. Only the training which an arbitrary will receives by years of consulting first its own personal and commercial ends could have made it strong enough to withstand the demands for social adjustment. He felt himself right from the *commercial* standpoint, and could not see the situation from the *social* standpoint. For years he had gradually accustomed himself to the thought that his motive was beyond reproach; that his attitude to his town was always righteous and philanthropic. Habit held him persistent in this view of the case through all the changing conditions.

The diffused and subtle notion of dignity held by the modern philanthropist bears a curious analogy to the personal barbaric notion of dignity held by Lear. The man who persistently paced the seashore, while the interior of his country was racked with a strife which he alone might have arbitrated, lived out within himself the tragedy of King Lear. The shock of disaster upon egotism is apt to produce self-pity. It is possible that his self-pity and loneliness may have been so great and absorbing as to completely shut out from his mind a compunction of derelict duty. He may have been unconscious that men were charging him with a shirking of the issue.

Lack of perception is the besetting danger of the egoist, from whatever cause his egoism arises and envelopes him. But, doubtless, philanthropists are more exposed to this danger than any other class of people within the community. Partly because their efforts are overestimated, as no standard of attainment has yet been established, and partly because they are the exponents of a large amount of altruistic feeling with which the community has become equipped and which has not yet found adequate expression, they are therefore easily idealized.

Long ago Hawthorne called our attention to the fact that "philanthropy ruins, or is fearfully apt to ruin, the heart, the rich juices of which God never meant should be pressed violently out, and distilled into alcoholic liquor by an unnatural process; but it should render life sweet, bland and gently beneficent."

One might add to this observation that the muscles of this same heart may be stretched and strained until they lose the rhythm of the common heart-beat of the rest of the world.

Modern philanthropists need to remind themselves of the old definition of greatness: that it consists in the possession of the largest share of the common human qualities and experiences, not in the acquirements of peculiarities and excessive virtues. Popular opinion calls him the greatest of Americans who gathered to himself the largest amount of American experience, and who never forgot when he was in Washington how the "crackers" in Kentucky and the pioneers of Illinois thought and felt, striving to retain their thoughts and feelings, and to embody only the mighty will of the "common people." The danger of professionally attaining to the power of the righteous man, of yielding to the ambition "for doing good," compared to which the ambitions for political position, learning, or wealth are vulgar and commonplace, ramifies throughout our modern life, and is a constant and settled danger in philanthropy.

In so far as philanthropists are cut off from the influence of the *Zeit-Geist*,[4] from the code of ethics which rule the body of men, from the great moral life springing from our common experiences, so long as they are "good to people," rather than "with them," they are bound to accomplish a large amount of harm. They are outside of the influence of that great faith which perennially springs up in the hearts of the people, and re-creates the world.

In spite of the danger of overloading the tragedies with moral reflections, a point ought to be made on the other side. It is the weakness in the relation of the employes to the employer, the fatal lack of generosity in the attitude of workmen toward the company under whose exactions they feel themselves wronged.

In reading the tragedy of King Lear, Cordelia does not escape our censure. Her first words are cold, and we are shocked by her lack of tenderness. Why should she ignore her father's need for indulgence, and be so unwilling to give him what he so obviously craved? We see in the old king "the overmastering desire of being beloved, which is selfish, and yet characteristic of the selfishness of a loving and kindly nature alone." His eagerness produces in us a strange pity for him, and we are impatient that his youngest and best-beloved child cannot feel this, even in the midst of her search for truth and her newly acquired sense of a higher duty. It seems to us a narrow conception that would break thus abruptly with the past, and would assume that her father had no part in her new life. We want to remind her that "pity, memory and faithfulness are natural ties," and surely as much to be prized as is the development of her own soul. We do not admire the Cordelia "who loves according to her bond" as we later admire the same Cordelia who comes back from France that she may include in her happiness and freer life the father whom she had deserted through her self-absorption. She is aroused to her affection through her pity, but when the floodgates are once open she acknowledges all. It sometimes seems as if only hardship and sorrow could arouse our tenderness, whether in our personal or social relations; that the king, the prosperous man, was the last to receive the justice which can come only through affectionate interpretation. We feel less pity for Lear on his throne than in the storm, although he is the same man, bound up in the same self-righteousness, and exhibiting the same lack of self-control.

As the vision of the life of Europe caught the sight and quickened the pulses of Cordelia, so a vision of the wider life has caught the sight of workingmen. After the vision has once been seen it is impossible to do aught but to press toward its fulfillment. We have all seen it. We are all practically agreed that the social passion of the age is directed toward the emancipation of the wage-worker; that a great accumulation of moral force is overmastering men and making for this emancipation as in another time it has made for the emancipation of the slave; that nothing will satisfy the aroused conscience of men short of the complete participation of the working classes in the spiritual, intellectual and material inheritance of the human race. But just as Cordelia failed to include her father in the scope of her salvation and selfishly took it for herself alone, so workingmen in the dawn of the vision are inclined to claim it for themselves, putting out of their thoughts the old relationships; and just as surely as Cordelia's conscience developed in the new life and later drove her back to her father, where she perished, drawn into the cruelty and wrath which had now become objective and tragic, so the emancipation of working people will have to be inclusive of the employer from the first or it will encounter many failures, cruelties and reactions. It will result not in the position of the repentant Cordelia but in that of King Lear's two older daughters.

If the workingmen's narrow conception of emancipation was fully acted upon, they would hold much the same relationship to their expropriated employer that the two elder daughters held to their abdicated father. When the kingdom was given to them they received it as altogether their own, and were dominated by a sense of possession; "it is ours not yours" was never absent from their consciousness. When Lear ruled the kingdom he had never been without this sense of possession, although he expressed it in indulgence and condescending kindness. His older daughters expressed it in cruelty, but the motive of father and children was not unlike. They did not wish to be reminded by the state and retinue of the old King that he had been the former possessor. Finally, his mere presence alone reminded them too much of that and they banished him from the palace. That a newly acquired sense of possession should result in the barbaric, the incredible scenes of bitterness and murder, which were King Lear's portion, is not without a reminder of the barbaric scenes in our political and industrial relationships, when the sense of possession, to obtain and to hold, is aroused on both sides. The scenes in Paris during the political revolution or the more familiar scenes at the mouths of the mines and the terminals of railways occur to all of us.

The doctrine of emancipation preached to the wage-workers alone runs an awful risk of being accepted for what it offers them, for the sake of the fleshpots, rather than for the human affection and social justice which it involves. This doctrine must be strong enough in its fusing power to touch those who think they lose, as well as those who think they gain. Only thus can it become the doctrine of a universal movement.

The new claim on the part of the toiling multitude, the new sense of responsibility on the part of the well-to-do, arise in reality from the same source. They are in fact the same "social compunction," and, in spite of their widely varying manifestations, logically converge into the same movement. Mazzini once preached, "the consent of men and your own conscience are two wings given you whereby you may rise to God." It is so easy for the good and powerful to think that they can rise by following the dictates of conscience by pursuing their own ideals, leaving those ideals unconnected with the consent of their fellow-men. The president of the Pullman company thought out within his own mind a beautiful town. He had power with which to build this town, but he did not appeal to nor obtain the consent of the men who were living in it. The most unambitious reform, recognizing the necessity for this consent, makes for slow but sane and strenuous progress, while the most ambitious of social plans and experiments, ignoring this, is prone to the failure of the model town of Pullman.

The man who insists upon consent, who moves with the people, is bound to consult the feasible right as well as the absolute right. He is often obliged to attain only Mr. Lincoln's "best possible," and often have the sickening sense of compromising with his best convictions. He has to move along with those whom he rules toward a goal that neither he nor they see very clearly till they come to it. He has to discover what people really want, and then "provide the channels in which the growing moral force of their lives shall flow." What he does attain, however, is not the result of his individual striving, as a solitary mountain climber beyond the sight of the valley multitude, but it is underpinned and upheld by the sentiments and aspirations of many others. Progress has been slower perpendicularly, but incomparably greater because lateral.

He has not taught his contemporaries to climb mountains, but he has persuaded the villagers to move up a few feet higher. It is doubtful if personal ambition, whatever may have been its commercial results, has ever been of any value as a motive power in social reform. But whatever it may have done in the past, it is certainly too archaic to accomplish anything now. Our thoughts, at least for this generation, cannot be too much directed from mutual relationships and responsibilities.

They will be warped, unless we look all men in the face, as if a community of interests lay between, unless we hold the mind open, to take strength and cheer from a hundred connections.

To touch to vibrating response the noble fibre in each man, to pull these many fibres, fragile, impalpable and constantly breaking, as they are, into one impulse, to develop that mere impulse through its feeble and tentative stages into action, is no easy task, but lateral progress is impossible without it.

If only a few families of the English speaking race had profited by the dramatic failure of Lear, much heart-breaking and domestic friction might have been spared. Is it too much to hope that some of us will carefully consider this modern tragedy, if perchance it may contain a warning for the troublous times in which we live? By considering the dramatic failure of the liberal employer's plans for his employes we may possibly be spared useless industrial tragedies in the uncertain future which lies ahead of us.

Notes

1. Addams's reference is to the upheavals of the Pullman Strike, which roiled Chicago for months and led, when arbitration events failed, to federal intervention and the breaking of the strike.

2. While the town of Pullman was in the process of construction, the Pullman stock was sometimes called out on the New York Exchange—"How much for flowerbeds and fountains?"—to which the company naturally objected.

3. The bill presented to the city of Chicago by the Pullman Company for damages received during the strike was $20—the result only of petty accidents.

4. A German word meaning "spirit of the time" or "spirit of the age."

16

"MORAL EDUCATION AND LEGAL PROTECTION OF CHILDREN"

No GREAT WRONG HAS EVER ARISEN more clearly to the social consciousness of a generation than has that of commercialized vice in the consciousness of ours, and that we are so slow to act is simply another evidence that human nature has a curious power of callous indifference towards evils which have been so entrenched that they seem part of that which has always been. Educators of course share this attitude; at moments they seem to intensify it, although at last an educational movement in the direction of sex hygiene is beginning in the schools and colleges. Primary schools strive to satisfy the child's first questionings regarding the beginnings of human life and approach the subject through simple biological instruction which at least places this knowledge on a par with other natural acts. Such teaching is an enormous advance for the children whose curiosity would otherwise have been satisfied from poisonous sources and who would have learned of simple physiological matters from such secret undercurrents of corrupt knowledge as to have forever perverted their minds. Yet this first direct step towards an adequate educational approach to this subject has been surprisingly difficult owing to the self-consciousness of grown-up people; for while the children receive the teaching quite simply, their parents often take alarm. Doubtless cooperation with parents will be necessary before the subject can fall into its proper place in the schools. In Chicago, the largest women's club in the city has established normal

---

Note: "Moral Education and Legal Protection of Children," in *A New Conscience and an Ancient Evil* (New York: Macmillan, 1912), chapter 4.

courses in sex hygiene attended both by teachers and mothers, the National and State Federations of Women's Clubs are gradually preparing thousands of women throughout America for fuller co-operation with the schools in this difficult matter. In this, as in so many other educational movements, Germany has led the way. Two publications are issued monthly in Berlin, which promote not only more effective legislation but more adequate instruction in the schools on this basic subject. These journals are supported by men and women anxious for light for the sake of their children. Some of them were first stirred to action by Wedekind's powerful drama "The Awakening of Spring," which, with Teutonic grimness, thrusts over the footlights the lesson that death and degradation may be the fate of a group of gifted school-children, because of the cowardly reticence of their parents.

A year ago the Bishop of London gathered together a number of influential people and laid before them his convictions that the root of the social evil lay in so-called "parental modesty," and that in the quickening of the parental conscience lay the hope for the "lifting up of England's moral tone which has for so long been the despair of England's foremost men."

In America the eighth year-book of the National Society for the Scientific Study of Education treats of this important subject with great ability, massing the agencies and methods in impressive array. Many other educational journals and organized societies could be cited as expressing a new conscience in regard to this world-old evil. The expert educational opinion which they represent is practically agreed that for older children the instruction should not be confined to biology and hygiene, but may come quite naturally in history and literature, which record and portray the havoc wrought by the sexual instinct when uncontrolled, and also show that, when directed and spiritualized, it has become an inspiration to the loftiest devotions and sacrifices. The youth thus taught sees this primal instinct not only as an essential to the continuance of the race, but also, when it is transmuted to the highest ends, as a fundamental factor in social progress. The entire subject is broadened out in his mind as he learns that his own struggle is a common experience. He is able to make his own interpretations and to combat the crude inferences of his patronizing companions. After all, no young person will be able to control his impulses and to save himself from the grosser temptations, unless he has been put under the sway of nobler influences. Perhaps we have yet to learn that the inhibitions of character as well as its reinforcements come most readily through idealistic motives.

Certainly all the great religions of the world have recognized youth's need of spiritual help during the trying years of adolescence. The ceremonies of the earliest religions deal with this instinct almost to the exclusion of others, and all later religions attempt to provide the youth with shadowy weapons for the struggle which lies ahead of him, for the wise men in every age have known that only the power of the spirit can overcome the lusts of the flesh. In spite of this educational advance, courses of study in many public and private schools are still prepared exactly as if educators had never known that at fifteen or sixteen years of age, the will power being still weak, the bodily desires are keen and insistent. The head master of Eton, Mr. Lyttleton, who has given much thought to this gap in the education of youth says, "The certain result of leaving an enormous majority of boys unguided and uninstructed in a matter where their strongest passions are concerned, is that they grow up to judge of all questions connected with it, from a purely selfish point of view." He contends that this selfishness is due to the fact that any single suggestion or hint which boys receive on the subject comes from other boys or young men who are under the same potent influences of ignorance, curiosity and the claims of self. No wholesome counter-balance of knowledge is given, no attempt is made to invest the subject with dignity or to place it in relation to the welfare of others and to universal law. Mr. Lyttleton contends that this alone can explain the peculiarly brutal attitude towards "outcast" women which is a sustained cruelty to be discerned in no other relation of English life. To quote him again: "But when the victims of man's cruelty are not birds or beasts but our own country-women, doomed by the hundred thousand to a life of unutterable shame and hopeless misery, then and then only the general average tone of young men becomes hard and brutally callous or frivolous with a kind of coarse frivolity not exhibited in relation to any other form of human suffering." At the present moment thousands of young people in our great cities possess no other knowledge of this grave social evil which may at any moment become a dangerous personal menace, save what is imparted to them in this brutal flippant spirit. It has been said that the child growing up in the midst of civilization receives from its parents and teachers something of the accumulated experience of the world on all other subjects save upon that of sex. On this one subject alone each generation learns little from its predecessors.

An educator has lately pointed out that it is an old lure of vice to pretend that it alone deals with manliness and reality, and he complains that it is always difficult to convince youth that the higher planes of life contain anything but chilly sentiments. He contends that young people are therefore prone to receive moralizing and admonitions with polite attention, but when it comes to action, they carefully observe the life about them in order to conduct themselves in such wise as to be part of the really desirable world inhabited by men of affairs. Owing to this attitude, many young people living in our cities at the present moment have failed to apprehend the admonitions of religion and have never responded to its inner control. It is as if the impact of the world had stunned their spiritual natures, and as if this had occurred at the very time that a most dangerous experiment is being tried. The public gaieties formerly allowed in Catholic countries where young people were restrained by the confessional, are now permitted in cities where this restraint is altogether unknown to thousands of young people, and only faintly and traditionally operative upon thousands of others. The puritanical history of American cities assumes that these gaieties are forbidden, and that the streets are sober and decorous for conscientious young men and women who need no external protection. This ungrounded assumption, united to the fact that no adult has the confidence of these young people, who are constantly subjected to a multitude of imaginative impressions, is almost certain to result disastrously.

The social relationships in a modern city are so hastily made and often so superficial, that the old human restraints of public opinion, long sustained in smaller communities, have also broken down. Thousands of young men and women in every great city have received none of the lessons in self-control which even savage tribes imparted to their children when they taught them to master their appetites as well as their emotions. These young people are perhaps further from all community restraint and genuine social control than the youth of the community have ever been in the long history of civilization. Certainly only the modern city has offered at one and the same time every possible stimulation for the lower nature and every opportunity for secret vice. Educators apparently forget that this unrestrained stimulation of young people, so characteristic of our cities, although developing very rapidly, is of recent origin, and that we have not yet seen the outcome. The present education of the average young man has given him only the most unreal protection against the temptations of the city. Schoolboys are subjected to many lures from without just at the moment when they are filled with an inner tumult which utterly bewilders them and concerning which no one has instructed them save in terms of empty precept and unintelligible warning.

We are authoritatively told that the physical difficulties are enormously increased by uncontrolled or perverted imaginations, and all sound advice to young men in regard to this subject emphasizes a clean mind, exhorts an imagination kept free from sensuality and insists upon days filled with wholesome athletic interests. We allow this régime to be exactly reversed for thousands of young people living in the most crowded and most unwholesome parts of the city. Not only does the stage in its advertisements exhibit all the allurements of sex to such an extent that a play without a "love interest" is considered foredoomed to failure, but the novels which form the sole reading of thousands of young men and girls deal only with the course of true or simulated love, resulting in a rose-colored marriage, or in variegated misfortunes.

Often the only recreation possible for young men and young women together is dancing, in which it is always easy to transgress the proprieties. In many public dance halls, however, improprieties are deliberately fostered. The waltzes and two-steps are purposely slow, the couples leaning heavily on each other barely move across the floor, all the jollity and bracing exercise of the peasant dance is eliminated, as is all the careful decorum of the formal dance. The efforts to obtain pleasure or to feed the imagination are thus converged upon the senses which it is already difficult for young people to understand and to control. It is therefore not remarkable that in certain parts of the city groups of idle young men are found whose evil imaginations have actually inhibited their power for normal living. On the streets or in the poolrooms where they congregate their conversation, their tales of adventure, their remarks upon women who pass by, all reveal that they have been caught in the toils of an instinct so powerful and primal that when left without direction it can easily overwhelm its possessor and swamp his faculties. These young men, who do no regular work who expect to be supported by their mothers and sisters and to get money for the shows and the-atres by any sort of disreputable undertaking, are in excellent training for the life of the procurer, and it is from such groups that they are re-cruited. There is almost a system of apprenticeship, for boys when very small act as "look-outs" and are later utilized to make acquaintances with girls in order to introduce them to professionals. From this they gradually learn the method of procuring girls and at last do an indepen-dent business. If one boy is successful in such a life, throughout his ac-quaintance runs the rumor that a girl is an asset that will bring a larger return than can possibly be earned in hard-working ways. Could the imaginations of these young men have been controlled and cultivated, could the desire for adventure have been directed into wholesome chan-nels, could these idle boys have been taught that, so far from being manly they were losing all virility, could higher interests have been aroused and standards given them in relation to this one aspect of life, the entire situation of commercialized vice would be a different thing.

The girls with a desire for adventure seem confined to this one dubi-ous outlet even more than the boys, although there are only one-eighth as many delinquent girls as boys brought into the juvenile court in Chicago, the charge against the girls in almost every instance involves a loss of chastity. One of them who was vainly endeavoring to formulate the causes of her downfall, concentrated them all in the single state-ment that she wanted the other girls to know that she too was a "good Indian." Such a girl, while she is not an actual member of a gang of boys, is often attached to one by so many loyalties and friendships that she will seldom testify against a member, even when she has been in-jured by him. She also depends upon the gang when she requires bail in the police court or the protection that comes from political influence, and she is often very proud of her quasi-membership. The little girls brought into the juvenile court are usually daughters of those poorest immigrant families living in the worst type of city tenements, who are frequently forced to take boarders in order to pay rent. A surprising number of little girls have first become involved in wrong-doing through the men of their own household. A recent inquiry among 130 girls living in a sordid red light district disclosed the fact that a majority of them had thus been victimized and the wrong had come to them so early that they had been despoiled at an average age of eight years. Looking upon the forlorn little creatures, who are often brought into the Chicago juvenile court to testify against their own relatives, one is seized with that curious compunction Goethe expressed in the now hackneyed line from "Mignon:"

"Was hat Man dir, du armes Kind, gethan?"

One is also inclined to reproach educators for neglecting to give children instruction in play when one sees the unregulated amusement parks which are apparently so dangerous to little girls twelve or fourteen years old. Because they are childishly eager for amusement and totally unable to pay for a ride on the scenic railway or for a ticket to an entertainment, these disappointed children easily accept many favors from the young men who are standing near the entrances for the express purpose of ruining them. The hideous reward which is demanded from them later in the evening, after they have enjoyed the many "treats" which the amusement park offers, apparently seems of little moment. Their childish minds are filled with the memory of the lurid pleasures to the oblivion of the later experience, and they eagerly tell their companions of this possibility "of getting in to all the shows." These poor little girls pass unnoticed amidst a crowd of honest people seeking recreation after a long day's work, groups of older girls walking and talking gaily with young men of their acquaintance, and happy children holding their parents' hands. This cruel exploitation of the childish eagerness for pleasure is, of course, possible only among a certain type of forlorn city children who are totally without standards and into whose colorless lives a visit to the amusement park brings the acme of delirious excitement. It is possible that these children are the inevitable product of city life; in Paris, little girls at local fêtes wishing to ride on the hobby horse frequently buy the privilege at a fearful price from the man directing the machinery, and a physician connected with the New York Society for the Prevention of Cruelty to Children writes: "It is horribly pathetic to learn how far a nickel or a quarter will go towards purchasing the virtue of these children."

The home environment of such children has been similar to that of many others who come to grief through the five-cent theatres. These eager little people, to whom life has offered few pleasures, crowd around the door hoping to be taken in by some kind soul and, when they have been disappointed over and over again and the last performance is about to begin, a little girl may be induced unthinkingly to barter her chastity for an entrance fee.

Many children are also found who have been decoyed into their first wrong-doing through the temptation of the saloon, in spite of the fact that one of the earliest regulations in American cities for the protection of children was the prohibition of the sale of liquor to minors. That children may be easily demoralized by the influence of a disorderly saloon was demonstrated recently in Chicago; one of these saloons was so situtated that the pupils of a public school were obliged to pass it and from the windows of the schoolhouse itself could see much of what was passing within the place. An effort was made by the Juvenile Protective Association to have it closed by the chief of police, but although he did so, it was opened again the following day. The Association then took up the matter with the mayor, who refused to interfere, insisting that the objectionable features had been eliminated. Through months of effort, during which time the practices of the place remained quite unchanged, one group after another of public-spirited citizens endeavored to suppress what had become a public scandal, only to find that the place was protected by brewery interests which were more powerful, both financially and politically, than themselves. At last, after a peculiarly flagrant case involving a little girl, the mothers of the neighborhood arranged a mass meeting in the schoolhouse itself, inviting local officials to be present. The mothers then produced a mass of testimony which demonstrated that dozens and hundreds of children had been directly or indirectly affected by the place whose removal they demanded. A meeting so full of genuine anxiety and righteous indignation could not well be disregarded, and the compulsory education department was at last able to obtain a revocation of the license. The many people who had so long tried to do away with this avowedly disreputable saloon received a fresh impression of the menace to children who became sophisticated by daily familiarity with vice. Yet many mothers, hard pressed by poverty, are obliged to rent houses next to vicious neighborhoods and their children very early become familiar with all the outer aspects of vice. Among them are the children of widows who make friends with their dubious neighbors during the long days while their mothers are at work. I recall two sisters in one family whose mother had moved her household to the borders of a Chicago segregated district, apparently without knowing the character of the neighborhood. The little sisters, twelve and eight years old, accepted many invitations from a kind neighbor to come into her house to see her pretty things.

The older girl was delighted to be "made up" with powder and paint and to try on long dresses, while the little one who sang very prettily was taught some new songs, happily without understanding their import. The tired mother knew nothing of what the children did during her absence, until an honest neighbor who had seen the little girls going in and out of the district, interfered on their behalf. The frightened mother moved back to her old neighborhood which she had left in search of cheaper rent, her pious soul stirred to its depths that the children for whom she patiently worked day by day had so narrowly escaped destruction.

Who cannot recall at least one of these desperate mothers, overworked and harried through a long day, prolonged by the family washing and cooking into the evening, followed by a night of foreboding and misgiving because the very children for whom her life is sacrificed are slowly slipping away from her control and affection? Such a spectacle forces one into an agreement with Wells, that it is a "monstrous absurdity" that women who are "discharging their supreme social function, that of rearing children, should do it in their spare time, as it were, while they 'earn their living' by contributing some half-mechanical element to some trivial industrial product." Nevertheless, such a woman whose wages are fixed on the basis of individual subsistence, who is quite unable to earn a family wage, is still held by a legal obligation to support her children with the desperate penalty of forfeiture if she fail.

I can recall a very intelligent woman who long brought her children to the Hull House day nursery with this result at the end of ten years of devotion: the little girl is almost totally deaf owing to neglect following a case of measles, because her mother could not stop work in order to care for her; the youngest boy has lost a leg flipping cars; the oldest boy has twice been arrested for petty larceny; the twin boys, in spite of prolonged sojourns in the parental school, have been such habitual truants that their natural intelligence has secured little aid from education. Of the five children three are now in semi-penal institutions, supported by the state. It would not therefore have been so uneconomical to have boarded them with their own mother, requiring a standard of nutrition and school attendance at least up to that national standard of nurture which the more advanced European governments are establishing.

The recent Illinois law, providing that the children of widows may be supported by public funds paid to the mother upon order of the juvenile court, will eventually restore a mother's care to these poor children; but in the meantime, even the poor mother who is receiving such aid, in her forced search for cheap rent may be continually led nearer to the notoriously evil districts. Many appeals made to landlords of disreputable houses in Chicago on behalf of the children living adjacent to such property have never secured a favorable response. It is apparently difficult for the average property owner to resist the high rents which houses in certain districts of the city can command if rented for purposes of vice. I recall two small frame houses identical in type and value standing side by side. One which belonged to a citizen without scruples was rented for $30.00 a month, the other belonging to a conscientious man was rented for $9.00 a month. The supposedly respectable landlords defend themselves behind the old sophistry: "If I did not rent my house for such a purpose, someone else would," and the more hardened ones say that "It is all in the line of business." Both of them are enormously helped by the secrecy surrounding the ownership of such houses, although it is hoped that the laws requiring the name of the owner and the agent of every multiple house to be posted in the public hallway will at length break through this protection, and the discovered landlords will then be obliged to pay the fine to which the law specifically states they have made themselves liable. In the meantime, women forced to find cheap rents are subjected to one more handicap in addition to the many others poverty places upon them. Such experiences may explain the fact that English figures show a very large proportion of widows and deserted women among the prostitutes in those large towns which maintain segregated districts.

The deprivation of a mother's care is most frequently experienced by the children of the poorest colored families who are often forced to live in disreputable neighborhoods because they literally cannot rent houses anywhere else. Both because rents are always high for colored people and because the colored mothers are obliged to support their children, seven times as many of them, in proportion to their entire number, as of the white mothers, the actual number of colored children neglected in the midst of temptation is abnormally large. So closely is child life founded upon the imitation of what it sees that the child who knows all evil is almost sure in the end to share it. Colored children seldom roam far from their own neighborhoods: in the public playgrounds, which are theoretically open to them, they are made so uncomfortable by the slights of other children that they learn to stay away, and, shut out from legitimate recreation, are all the more tempted by the careless, luxurious life of a vicious neighborhood. In addition to the colored girls who have thus from childhood grown familiar with the outer aspects of vice, are others who are sent into the district in the capacity of domestic servants by unscrupulous employment agencies who would not venture to thus treat a white girl. The community forces the very people who have confessedly the shortest history of social restraint, into a dangerous proximity with the vice districts of the city. This results, as might easily be predicted, in a very large number of colored girls entering a disreputable life. The negroes themselves believe that the basic cause for the high percentage of colored prostitutes is the recent enslavement of their race with its attendant unstable marriage and parental status, and point to thousands of slave sales that but two generations ago disrupted the negroes' attempts at family life.[1] Knowing this as we do, it seems all the more unjustifiable that the nation which is responsible for the broken foundations of this family life should carelessly permit the negroes, making their first struggle towards a higher standard of domesticity, to be subjected to the most flagrant temptations which our civilization tolerates.

The imaginations of even very young children may easily be forced into sensual channels. A little girl, twelve years old, was one day brought to the psychopathic clinic connected with the Chicago juvenile court. She had been detained under police surveillance for more than a week, while baffled detectives had in vain tried to verify the statements she had made to her Sunday-school teacher in great detail of certain horrible experiences which had befallen her. For at least a week no one concerned had the remotest idea that the child was fabricating. The police thought that she had merely grown confused as to the places to which she had been "carried unconscious." The mother gave the first clue when she insisted that the child had never been away from her long enough to have had these experiences, but came directly home from school every afternoon for her tea, of which she habitually drank ten or twelve cups. The skilful questionings at the clinic, while clearly establishing the fact of a disordered mind, disclosed an astonishing knowledge of the habits of the underworld.

Even children who live in respectable neighborhoods and are guarded by careful parents so that their imaginations are not perverted, but only starved, constantly conduct a search for the magical and impossible which leads them into moral dangers. An astonishing number of them consult palmists, soothsayers, and fortune tellers. These dealers in futurity, who sell only love and riches, the latter often dependent upon the first, are sometimes in collusion with disreputable houses, and at the best make the path of normal living more difficult for their eager young patrons. There is something very pathetic in the sheepish, yet radiant, faces of the boy and girl, often together, who come out on the street from a dingy doorway which bears the palmist's sign of the spread-out hand. This remnant of primitive magic is all they can find with which to feed their eager imaginations, although the city offers libraries and galleries, crowned with man's later imaginative achievements. One hard-working girl of my acquaintance, told by a palmist that "diamonds were coming to her soon," afterwards accepted without a moment's hesitation a so-called diamond ring from a man whose improper attentions she had hitherto withstood.

In addition to these heedless young people, pulled into a sordid and vicious life through their very search for romance, are many little children ensnared by means of the most innocent playthings and pleasures of childhood. Perhaps one of the saddest aspects of the social evil as it exists to-day in the modern city, is the procuring of little girls who are too young to have received adequate instruction of any sort and whose natural safeguard of modesty and reserve has been broken down by the overcrowding of tenement house life. Any educator who has made a careful study of the children from the crowded districts is impressed with the numbers of them whose moral natures are apparently unawakened. While there are comparatively few of these nonmoral children in any one neighborhood, in the entire city their number is far from negligible. Such children are used by disreputable people to invite their more normal playmates to house parties, which they attend again and again, lured by candy and fruit, until they gradually learn to trust the vicious hostess. The head of one such house, recently sent to the penitentiary upon charges brought against her by the Juvenile Protective Association, founded her large and successful business upon the activities of three or four little girls who, although they had gradually come to understand her purpose, were apparently so chained to her by the goodies and favors which they received, that they were quite indifferent to the fate of their little friends. Such children, when brought to the psychopathic clinic attached to the Chicago juvenile court, are sometimes found to have incipient epilepsy or other physical disabilities from which their conduct may be at least partially accounted for. Sometimes they come from respectable families, but more often from families where they have been mistreated and where dissolute parents have given them neither affection nor protection. Many of these children whose relatives have obviously contributed to their delinquency are helped by the enforcement of the adult delinquency law.

One looks upon these hardened little people with a sense of apology that educational forces have not been able to break into their first ignorance of life before it becomes toughened into insensibility, and one knows that, whatever may be done for them later, because of this early neglect, they will probably always remain impervious to the gentler aspects of life, as if vice seared their tender minds with red-hot irons. Our public-school education is so nearly universal, that if the entire body of the teachers seriously undertook to instruct all American youth in regard to this most important aspect of life, why should they not in time train their pupils to continence and self-direction, as they already discipline their minds with knowledge in regard to many other matters? Certainly the extreme youth of the victims of the white slave traffic, both boys and girls, places a great responsibility upon the educational forces of the community.

The state which supports the public school is also coming to the rescue of children through protective legislation. This is another illustration that the beginnings of social advance have often resulted from the efforts to defend the weakest and least-sheltered members of the community. The widespread movement which would protect children from premature labor, also prohibits them from engaging in occupations in which they are subjected to moral dangers. Several American cities have of late become much concerned over the temptations to which messenger boys, delivery boys, and newsboys are constantly subjected when their business takes them into vicious districts. The Chicago vice commission makes a plea for these "children of the night" that they shall be protected by law from those temptations which they are too young and too untrained to withstand. New York and Wisconsin are the only states which have raised the legal age of messenger boys employed late at night to twenty-one years. Under the inadequate sixteen-year limit, which regulates night work for children in Illinois, boys constantly come to grief through their familiarity with the social evil. One of these, a delicate boy of seventeen, had been put into the messenger service by his parents when their family doctor had recommended out-of-door work. Because he was well-bred and good-looking, he became especially popular with the inmates of disreputable houses. They gave him tips of a dollar and more when he returned from the errands which he had executed for them, such as buying candy, cocaine or morphine. He was inevitably flattered by their attentions and pleased with his own popularity. Although his mother knew that his duties as a messenger boy occasionally took him to disreputable houses, she fervently hoped his early training might keep him straight, but in the end realized the foolhardiness of subjecting an immature youth to these temptations. The vice commission report gives various detailed instances of similar experiences on the part of other lads, one of them being a high-school boy who was merely earning extra money as a messenger boy during the rush of Christmas week.

The regulations in Boston, New York, Cincinnati, Milwaukee and St. Louis for the safe-guarding of these children may be but a forecast of the care which the city will at last learn to devise for youth under special temptations. Because the various efforts made in Chicago to obtain adequate legislation for the protection of street-trading children have not succeeded, incidents like the following have not only occurred once, but are constantly repeated: a pretty little girl, the only child of a widowed mother, sold newspapers after school hours from the time she was seven years old. Because her home was near a vicious neighborhood and because the people in the disreputable hotels seldom asked for change when they bought a paper and good-naturedly gave her many little presents, her mother permitted her to gain a clientele within the district on the ground that she was too young to understand what she might see. This continued familiarity, in spite of her mother's admonitions, not to talk to her customers, inevitably resulted in so vitiating the standard of the growing girl, that at the age of fourteen she became an inmate of one of the houses. A similar instance concerns three little girls who habitually sold gum in one of the segregated districts. Because they had repeatedly been turned away by kind-hearted policemen who felt that they ought not to be in such a neighborhood, each one of these children had obtained a special permit from the mayor of the city in order to protect herself from "police interference." While the mayor had no actual authority to issue such permits, naturally the piece of paper bearing his name, when displayed by a child, checked the activity of the police officer. The incident was but one more example of the old conflict between mistaken kindness to the individual child in need of money, and the enforcement of those regulations which may seem to work a temporary hardship upon one child, but save a hundred others from entering occupations which can only lead into blind alleys. Because such occupations inevitably result in increasing the number of unemployables, the educational system itself must be challenged.

A royal commission has recently recommended to the English Parliament that "the legally permissible hours for the employment of boys be shortened, that they be required to spend the hours so set free, in physical and technological training, that the manufacturing of the unemployable may cease." Certainly we are justified in demanding from our educational system, that the interest and capacity of each child leaving school to enter industry, shall have been studied with reference to the type of work he is about to undertake. When vocational bureaus are properly connected with all the public schools, a girl will have an intelligent point of departure into her working life, and a place to which she may turn in time of need, for help and advice through those long and dangerous periods of unemployment which are now so inimical to her character.

This same British commission divided all of the unemployed, the under-employed, and the unemployable as the results of three types of trades: first, the subsidized labor trades, wherein women and children are paid wages insufficient to maintain them at the required standard of health and industrial efficiency, so that their wages must be supplemented by relatives or charity; second, labor deteriorating trades, which have sapped the energy, the capacity, the character, of workers; third, bare subsistence trades, where the worker is forced to such a low level in his standard of life that he continually falls below self-support. We have many trades of these three types in America, all of them demanding the work of young and untrained girls. Yet, in spite of the obvious dangers surrounding every girl who enters one of them, little is done to guide the multitude of children who leave school prematurely each year into reasonable occupations.

Unquestionably the average American child has received a more expensive education than has yet been accorded to the child of any other nation. The girls working in department stores have been in the public schools on an average of eight years, while even the factory girls, who so often leave school from the lower grades, have yet averaged six and two-tenths years of education at the public expense, before they enter industrial life. Certainly the community that has accomplished so much could afford them help and oversight for six and a half years longer, which is the average length of time that a working girl is employed. The state might well undertake this, if only to secure its former investment and to save that investment from utter loss.

Our generation, said to have developed a new enthusiasm for the possibilities of child life, and to have put fresh meaning into the phrase "children's rights," may at last have the courage to insist upon a child's right to be well born and to start in life with its tiny body free from disease. Certainly allied to this new understanding of child life and a part of the same movement is the new science of eugenics with its recently appointed university professors.[2] Its organized societies publish an ever-increasing mass of information as to that which constitutes the inheritance of well-born children. When this new science makes clear to the public that those diseases which are a direct outcome of the social evil are clearly responsible for race deterioration, effective indignation may at last be aroused, both against the preventable infant mortality for which these diseases are responsible, and against the ghastly fact that the survivors among these afflicted children infect their contemporaries and hand on the evil heritage to another generation. Public societies for the prevention of blindness are continually distributing information on the care of new-born children and may at length answer that old, confusing question "Did this man sin or his parents, that he was born blind?" Such knowledge is becoming more widespread every day and the rising interest in infant welfare must in time re-act upon the very existence of the social evil itself.

This new public concern for the welfare of little children in certain American cities has resulted in a municipal milk supply; in many German cities, in free hospitals and nurseries. New York, Chicago, Boston and other large towns, employ hundreds of nurses each summer to instruct tenement-house mothers upon the care of little children. Doubtless all of this enthusiasm for the nurture of children will at last arouse public opinion in regard to the transmission of that one type of disease which thousands of them annually inherit, and which is directly traceable to the vicious living of their parents or grand-parents. This slaughter of the innocents, this infliction of suffering upon the new-born, is so gratuitous and so unfair, that it is only a question of time until an outraged sense of justice shall be aroused on behalf of these children. But even before help comes through chivalric sentiments, governmental and municipal agencies will decline to spend the tax-payers' money for the relief of suffering infants, when by the exertion of the same authority they could easily provide against the possibility of the birth of a child so afflicted. It is obvious that the average tax-payer would be moved to demand the extermination of that form of vice which has been declared illegal, although it still flourishes by official connivance, did he once clearly apprehend that it is responsible for the existence of these diseases which cost him so dear. It is only his ignorance which makes him remain inert until each victim of the white slave traffic shall be avenged unto the third and fourth generation of them that bought her. It is quite possible that the tax-payer will himself contend that, as the state does not legalize a marriage without a license officially recorded, that the status of children may be clearly defined, so the state would need to go but one step further in the same direction, to insist upon health certificates from the applicant for a marriage license, that the health of future children might in a certain measure, be guaranteed. Whether or not this step may be predicted, the mere discussion of this matter in itself, is an indication of the changing public opinion, as is the fact that such legislation has already been enacted in two states, which are only now putting into action the recommendation made centuries ago by such social philosophers as Plato and Sir Thomas More. A sense of justice outraged by the wanton destruction of new-born children, may in time unite with that ardent tide of rising enthusiasm for the nurture of the young, until the old barriers of silence and inaction, behind which the social evil has so long intrenched itself, shall at last give way.

Certainly it will soon be found that the sentiment of pity, so recently aroused throughout the country on behalf of the victims of the white slave traffic, will be totally unable to afford them protection unless it becomes incorporated in government. It is possible that we are on the eve of a series of legislative enactments similar to those which resulted from the attempts to regulate child labor. Through the entire course of the last century, in that anticipation of coming changes which does so much to bring changes about, the friends of the children were steadily engaged in making a new state, from the first child labor law passed in the English parliament in 1803 to the final passage of the so-called children's charter in 1909. During the long century of transforming pity into political action there was created that social sympathy which has become one of the greatest forces in modern legislation, and to which we may confidently appeal in this new crusade against the social evil.

Another point of similarity to the child labor movement is obvious, for the friends of the children early found that they needed much statistical information and that the great problem of the would-be reformer is not so much overcoming actual opposition—the passing of time gradually does that for him—as obtaining and formulating accurate knowledge and fitting that knowledge into the trend of his time. From this point of view and upon the basis of what has already been accomplished for "the protection of minors," the many recent investigations which have revealed the extreme youth of the victims of the white slave traffic, should make legislation on their behalf all the more feasible. Certainly no reformer could ever more legitimately make an emotional appeal to the higher sensibility of the public.

In the rescue homes recently opened in Chicago by the White Slave Traffic Committee of the League of Cook County Clubs, the tender ages of the little girls who were brought there horrified the good clubwomen more than any other aspect of the situation. A number of the little inmates in the home wanted to play with dolls and several of them brought dolls of their own, which they had kept with them through all their vicissitudes. There is something literally heart-breaking in the thought of these little children who are ensnared and debauched when they are still young enough to have every right to protection and care. Quite recently I visited a home for semi-delinquent girls against each one of whom stood a grave charge involving the loss of her chastity. Upon each of the little white beds or on one of the stiff chairs standing by its side was a doll belonging to a delinquent owner still young enough to love and cherish this supreme toy of childhood. I had come to the home prepared to "lecture to the inmates." I remained to dress dolls with a handful of little girls who eagerly asked questions about the dolls I had once possessed in a childhood which seemed to them so remote. Looking at the little victims who supply the white slave trade, one is reminded of the burning words of Dr. Howard Kelly uttered in response to the demand that the social evil be legalized and its victims licensed. He says: "Where shall we look to recruit the ever-failing ranks of these poor creatures as they die yearly by the tens of thousands? Which of the little girls of our land shall we designate for this traffic? Mark their sweet innocence to-day as they run about in our streets and parks prattling and playing, ever busy about nothing; which of them shall we snatch as they approach maturity, to supply this foul mart?"

It is incomprehensible that a nation whose chief boast is its free public education, that a people always ready to respond to any moral or financial appeal made in the name of children, should permit this infamy against childhood to continue! Only the protection of all children from the menacing temptations which their youth is unable to withstand, will prevent some of them from falling victims to the white slave traffic; only when moral education is made effective and universal will there be hope for the actual abolition of commercialized vice. These are illustrations perhaps of that curious solidarity of which society is so rapidly becoming conscious.

Notes

1. Jane Addams here anticipates later scholarly discussions of the black family and the continuing effects of the shock of genealogical discontinuity brought about, in many instances, by the slave system.

2. Unfortunately, Jane Addams appears to have picked up on some of the enthusiasm for eugenics that was rife in the first three decades of the twentieth century. Progressive opinion seemed particularly susceptible to the claims of eugenicists that they might perfect the race genetically, no doubt because they could tie this in to an overarching, general theory of progress. One of the most notorious reminders of that era is the U.S. Supreme Court decision *Buck v. Bell* (1927), which sanctioned sterilization without consent of the feeble-minded. This case has become notorious in part because it includes Justice Oliver Wendell Holmes's infamous sentence: "Three generations of imbeciles are enough." The full horrors of state-sponsored eugenics enterprises came into view during World War II, and, following the war, eugenics got associated with the biological politics of German national socialism; however, under the rubric of "positive genetic enhancement," eugenics is once again a force to be reckoned with. It needs to be said that eugenics was, for Addams, a minor point, touched on glancingly, and it did not lie at the heart of her democratic vision.

17

⌒∞⌒

"RELIGIOUS EDUCATION AND CONTEMPORARY SOCIAL CONDITIONS"

IN A RECENT ARTICLE IN AN educational journal upon the vexed subject of Sex Hygiene the writer complains that it is always difficult to convince the youth that reality reaches upward as well as outward, and that the higher planes of life contain anything but chilly sentiments. He further finds that youth is so insatiably eager for experience, that one lure of vice itself is its constant pretension that it represents the reality of human existence, and that the educator who would make war upon vice must put his message as part of that worldly wisdom which substantial men everywhere have accepted.

Something of the same difficulty constantly confronts the religious educator who finds that the young people under his charge receive his moralizings and admonitions with polite attention, but when it comes to action that they carefully imitate the life about them in order to conduct themselves in such wise as to be part of the really desirable world.

The religious educator is further handicapped by the fact that much of the final curricula which he uses is left over from the days when education was carefully designed for men who had withdrawn from the world, and that of necessity it does not avail with the youth who is fretting with impatience to throw himself into the stream of life and to become a part of its fast flowing current.

Note: "Religious Education and Contemporary Social Conditions," in *Journal of the Religious Education Association*, vol. 6 (June 1911).

This divergence between the unreality of religious education and the demands of stirring religious experiences never became more apparent than it did in England and America during the last decade of the past century. The religious educator lost hundreds of young men and women who by training and temperament should have gone into the ministry or the missionary field, simply because his statements appeared to them as magnificent pieces of self-assertion totally unrelated to the world.

This failure to make religious teaching appear valid was due to many causes; the times were ripe for such divergence, and there are several reasons why life at this moment should have seemed more real outside of that which we call the religious world, than it did within it. In the first place modern economists had taught that man was abjectly dependent upon the material world about him, and had demonstrated as never before the iron clamp which industry imposes upon life; they had moreover gravely asserted that man's very freedom, morality and progress may be overwhelmed by the material conditions which surround him.

Secondly, the situation was further complicated by the fact that at this very same time the doctrine of evolution having made clear man's intimate connection with the entire external world, was establishing itself in ethics and social philosophy. Students of the social order in the spirit of the scientist became content merely to collect data, and to arrange it in orderly sequence. The social field still contains hundreds of them devotedly considering the reactions of economic forces upon human life, who have for the most part disregarded all theological considerations, as they have long since lightly renounced the theological explanations of a final cause.

Thirdly, during these decades hundreds of young people were drawn into the congested quarters of the modern city by sheer humanitarianism, by the impulse at least to know the worst. In their reaction against materialism they would warm their affections and renew their beliefs in those places where humanity appeared most pitiable and infirm, somewhat in the spirit of Carlyle who impatiently bade his contemporaries to worship and admire the hero if they could no longer worship and admire the saint. It is as if various types of young people ardently desiring reality above all else had said to the religious teachers, "we wish to know truth for ourselves, we care not how logical your theological tenets may be unless we can make them valid."

It was therefore inevitable that these lines of development should shift the center of the difficulties in religious education to the most crowded industrial districts where materialism holds undisputed sway.

The Failure of the Church.

And yet it was during these same decades that the churches, as if appalled by the industrial situation, failed to hold their own in these very districts. The church apparently felt no lure in the hideously uncouth factories in which men sometimes worked twelve hours a day for seven days in the week until they were utterly brutalized by fatigue; nor in the insanitary tenements so crowded that the mere decencies of life were often impossible; nor in the raw towns of newly arrived immigrants where the standard of life was pushed below that of their European poverty unmitigated either by natural beauty or social resources.

And yet it was into these very regions that the young people whom the church lost were most often attracted, and it was no unworthy lure which drew them into the thick of that industrial misery into which the church had not only failed to proceed them, but for so long a time failed to follow them.

Did the religious educator at the present moment but enter into this industrial inferno he would find many ardent young people, possibly not his own pupils, but those who would gladly unite with him in asserting the reality of spiritual forces, could he but share their experiences, and reach conclusions by a method they could comprehend. Among these young people he would find those who might have brought enthusiasm and ability to his own profession had it but seemed to them valid and dealing with realities. His experience would indeed be similar to that of Dante when he hesitated to enter the Inferno dreading above all else his loneliness there, although when he boldly proceeded step by step he found it peopled with old friends and comrades, speaking the beautiful language of Florence and cherishing the same great hopes as his own.

This adventurous educator would find traces of a new religious expression, although with marked scientific and humanitarian aspects as befitting its period. Even as the Humanism which grew out of the Renaissance was a reaction against grotesque Ecclesiasticalism he would discover in the beginning of this Humanitarianism a reaction against Materialism arising in the very midst of it.

He would find the economists groping their way from the 19th century darkness which considered the nation as an agglomeration of selfish men each moved by self-interest, forgetful of the women and children, to a conception of a state maintained to develop and nurture the highest type of human life, and testing its success by the care afforded to the most defenceless women and children within its borders. One of these economists whom we used to call "hard headed" has actually made out a program to protect wage-earners from what he calls the five great misfortunes to which they are exposed:

Industrial accidents, preventable illness, premature death, unemployment, neglected old age.

The Economic Motive Modified.

Such a program, however, cannot be enunciated by a scientist who merely studies life as conditioned by economic forces, for when he ventures to suggest that these forces should be controlled, he at once assumes the permanent dignity and value of human life, one of the tenets of all the great ethnic religions. It is as if the men most exclusively devoted to the analysis of physical conditions had been driven to contemplate them from the standpoint of their ultimate purposes.

When the economist also insists that this program of social reform is to be inaugurated by legislative enactment under a democratic government, he practically asserts that the chief end of man is realizable only through an unfolding of his own being and that he must have an efficacious share in the regulation of his own life. He is forced to give attention to the aim of human existence, and whether he formulates it in the language of science, sympathy, or experience, he finds himself back to an expression of the teleological aim, to an assertion of the ethical primacy of human life.

The religious educator venturing into the industrial inferno would be much startled by the discovery of the anomaly that the most enthusiastic believers in economic determinism are at the present moment giving us the most inspiring demonstration of religious enthusiasm; that the socialist party is drawing to itself thousands of ardent young people simply because it holds up an ideal and demands sacrifices on its behalf. It is as if the socialists had picked up the banner inscribed with the promises of a future life, which had slipped from the hands of the ecclesiastic, as if they had changed the promise of salvation from individual to social, had substituted the word earth for heaven and had then raised the banner aloft once more.[1] To the crowd of young people who follow this banner is happening that which always happens to those who are held together in a mutual purpose; certain readjustments take place as they realize that their own future is dependent upon the consummation of their ideal, and as they demand that the whole world unite in a common effort for its realization. There are thirty million of these socialists in the world with a definite political program in every civilized nation. The religious teacher may well long to claim this enthusiastic host for his own, and to turn these myriad idealists into a living church.

The religious educator as he proceeded would also find those humbler investigators of social conditions living either singly or in groups in the thick of untoward industrial conditions. At moments these find their own carefully collected data gathered into statistical tables and monographs almost as discouraging and overwhelming in its bulk as in the dreary-conditions it discloses. They are beginning to mutter darkly concerning degeneracy and to assert that evolutionary processes are not always upward, or ethogenic as they prefer to say. They realize that the possession of accurate information, moving and stirring as it is, does not by itself arouse a social energy sufficiently enterprising to cope with the situation. Masses of men are moved but slowly by mere knowledge and their information even when fused together by indignation and presented through our beloved popular magazines, which have so strikingly become the leaders of our moral purposes, bring about social changes very slowly.

Such investigators feel that their efforts should be supplemented by the religious teachers through a vigorous appeal to the public conscience and to the higher affections. They claim that as social development is an essentially continuing process, it is the business of morality to share its growth, not only to modify its harshness and brutality, but to actually direct it; and they also are thus again brought close to the religious purpose.

Neighborly Sympathy.

Then there are those groups found in all our large cities who are neither investigators nor students in the technical sense, but who have deliberately put themselves in vital touch, or rather in living relationship with the distressing aspects of industrial surroundings. The large colonies of immigrants, each one with its own history and conscious ambition emphasizing the enormous variability of the conditions of human life, constantly drive such a group to a study of the "normative" in contrast to the practical sciences. For just as the social worker has come to demand a form of housing or a standard of living, so they are sorely in need of a form of ethics. The common sense, the household tradition, the inherited customs, the desultory reading by which so much life is directed, is constantly breaking down in the face of these larger problems and the social workers demand help in regard to the final end and ideals of life. The social relationships in a modern city are so hastily made and often so superficial that it is not to be wondered at that the old human restraints long sustained in smaller communities by public opinion should have broken down and that large areas of city life seem to be dominated by the more primitative instincts. The members of such a group who spend their days in efforts to alleviate the conditions of poverty, would not for the world use the religious phrases of comforting the sorrowful or binding up the wounds of the broken hearted, but in spite of themselves there are moments when they experience the most intimate sanctions and comforts of religion. When they see a man so beaten down by his daily toil that their pity overflows into indignation, it is largely because human life itself is outraged; the sight of an ill-nourished child, not only fills them with sorrow for the object before them, but with a desolating sense of futility and waste of the most precious stuff the world contains. Is it not the office of religion to lift a man from personal pity into a sense of the universal compassion, from petty wrath to comprehension? A contemporary play depicts a strolling minstrel who refuses to surrender a stolen child to his mother although she pleads with him in the broken phrases of one stricken unto death. This same stroller, half man half faun, yields later to the silent reproaches of a figure of Christ stationed at the crossways, overcome as it were by the universal pity of "the lonely Man" who for so many centuries has plead with the passerby to be loving and compassionate. Who shall say that these poignant human experiences are not without religious significance and may not in the end require the expression represented by the religious forms which have survived through many generations.

Would not these beginnings of a new religious expression among the economists, the investigators, and the humanitarians, point to a moment in which the religious teacher might avail himself of a great opportunity? Could he but make the old formulas express the scruples, the painful sense of difference between rich and poor which haunt these dwellers in industrial quarters day by day; could he but transmute the comradeship of mutual suffering into a religious communion he would find them ready to walk into the old paths.

After all the business of religion is not only to comfort and conserve, but to prophecy and to fortify men for coming social changes. He who in a moment of transition boldly formulates his hidden scruples, does so not only for himself but for many others, and finds himself surrounded by a multitude of followers. For many years Count Tolstoy formulated these newer scruples for thousands of his contemporaries, and when the familiar pain drove him forth at the very end and he lay dying in the forlorn little station house, he was surrounded by the representatives of the Greek church eager to receive a word or even a gesture of assent as evidence that he had returned into the fold of orthodoxy.[2] Why were they so eager to have him back but that the church wished to claim as its own the religious teaching and leadership of one who had expressed the longing of a great nation; the church felt that it was its own function and its vested prerogative to have expressed that longing for a higher type of living, and to have prophesied juster social conditions.

Again and again during its history the church has been obliged to leave the temples and the schools in order to cast in its lot with the poor, and to minister without ceremony or ritual, directly to the needs of the sinner and the outcast.

A Religious Mission.

Is it not possible that such a moment has come now, that the religious teacher must go forth into the midst of modern materialism if only effectually to insist upon the eternal antithesis between the material and the spiritual, and to prove that religious enthusiasm is all-enduring when founded upon the realities of life?

A noted English publicist once told me that twenty-five years ago at every public meeting in the industrial quarters of London, whatever the subject of discussion, some working men always arose and in fiery terms agitated the disestablishment of the English Church, but that during the last decade such a speech was seldom heard owing entirely to the efforts of certain high-church clergymen who had gone to live throughout the industrial districts of London, and had their [sic] identified themselves with all the leading movements of social reform until the working men had become convinced that the church wanted the thing that they wanted, and that they and the clergymen were working towards a common end.

Thus to convince thousands of young people of the validity and reality of religion, the church must go out to meet them both willing to take their point of view, and to understand social methods. Could the religious teacher unite in the deed with the social reformers, could he formulate for many others a course of action which would relieve their consciences in regard to social maladjustments, he would discover that he had become part of a new fellowship, while at the same time his teaching was attaining a new sense of reality.

No one in considering this subject could for a moment ignore the great social awakening at present going forward in the churches. The federal organization of thirty-four Protestant Denominations with its social department; the Y. M. C. A. with its well directed social work in a dozen departments; the church committees to improve the conditions of labor, and the departments of sociology in all the theological seminaries would all indicate a new emphasis which the church is placing upon social welfare. Perhaps after all the difference is not so profound. A story is told of a country clergyman who was not a great scholar, but who had had much experience with church choirs. A parishioner in all seriousness asked him one day what was the difference between the Cherubim and the Seraphim; the poor clergyman hesitated a moment, and somewhat confusedly replied that he believed that there had once been a difference, but that now all was amicably adjusted.

Could the differences between progressive churchmen and the social reformer be amicably adjusted, I venture to predict that we should find ourselves united in a new religious fellowship and living in the sense of a religious revival.

Notes

1. Addams here describes socialist millenarianism, or the tendency to assume one can bring heaven down to earth and create something akin to an earthly paradise in which no injustice, no alienation, and no misery exist. She appreci-

ated that such a totalistic perspective often breeds desperate and dangerous actions and invites disillusionment as social change is slow, hard work.

2. Jane Addams made a pilgrimage to the home of the great Leo Tolstoy (1828–1910), but it proved somewhat frustrating, as Tolstoy urged her to do her own "bread labor"; Addams, back in Chicago, determined that the time she spent in personally baking bread could be more usefully spent elsewhere. But Addams was drawn throughout her life to Tolstoy's message of Christian love and pacifism.

18

"THE CHICAGO SETTLEMENTS AND SOCIAL UNREST"

WHATEVER OTHER SERVICES THE settlement may have endeavored to perform for its community, there is no doubt that it has come to regard that of interpreting foreign colonies to the rest of the city in the light of a professional obligation. This settlement interpretation may be right or wrong, but it is at least based upon years of first hand information and upon an opportunity for free intercourse with the foreign people themselves.

The city as a whole is ready to listen to this interpretation in times of peace, but when an event implying "anarchy" occurs such as the Averbuch incident in Chicago or the Silverstein bomb throwing in New York, it is apparently impossible for the over-wrought community to distinguish between the excitement the settlements are endeavoring to understand and to allay and the attitude of the settlement itself.[1] At such times fervid denunciation is held to be the duty of every good citizen, and if the settlement chooses to use its efforts to interpret rather than denounce the sentiments of the foreign colony, its attitude is at once taken to imply a championship of anarchy itself.

The public mind at such a moment falls into the old mediaeval confusion—he who feeds or shelters a heretic is upon *prima facie* evidence a heretic himself—he who knows intimately people among whom anarchists arise is therefore an anarchist.

Note: "The Chicago Settlements and Social Unrest," *Charities and The Commons*, vol. 20 (May 2, 1908).

Certainly the settlements do not wish to pose as martyrs because of these inevitable misunderstandings, but we may perhaps be permitted to utilize the occasion to explain the settlement position, and to assert that it is difficult to ascribe any real social value to settlements at all, if they are not ready in times of public panic to stake the sober results of their experience and their mature convictions against the hasty public opinion of the moment, and to do this irrespective of the result upon themselves.

In fact the more excited and irrational public opinion is, the more recklessly newspapers state mere surmises as facts and upon these surmises arouse unsubstantiated prejudices against certain immigrants, the more necessary it is that some body of people should be ready to put forward the spiritual and intellectual conditions of the foreign colony which is thus being made the subject of inaccurate surmises and unjust suspicion.

We might possibly be permitted to go a step further and to assert that quite as settlements have a unique opportunity for seeing and understanding the state of mind into which a foreign colony is thrown by such an untoward event, so it might be assumed that settlements have exceptional opportunities for suggesting the best method for meeting the situation, or at least for treating it in a way which will not destroy confidence in the American institutions which are so adored by the refugees from foreign governmental oppression.

Every settlement has classes in citizenship in which the principles of American institutions are expounded and of these the community as a whole, approves. But the settlements know better than anyone else that while these classes and lectures are useful, nothing can possibly give lessons in citizenship so effectively and make so clear the constitutional basis of a self-governing community as the current event itself. The treatment at a given moment of that foreign colony which feels itself outraged and misunderstood, either makes its constitutional rights clear to it, or forever confuses it, on the subject.

Because my first American ancestor bought his land of William Penn in 1684, and because Olga Averbuch has been in America for two years, does not make the least difference in our constitutional rights. It does, however, put me under an obligation to interpret to her and her kindred, the spirit and intent of American institutions as they are understood by those who have inherited them, so to speak; it may cause me to reflect that unless their protection shall be extended equally to all, they are slipping from our grasp.

It sometimes seems that each set of immigrants goes through much the same political development, and that the present arrivals, quite as our own ancestors did, care most passionately of all for "freedom." The phrases one hears most often among the Russian Jewish immigrants are "free speech," "freedom of assemblage" and a "free press," doubtless the same words which were most often repeated in broad Oxfordshire dialect by those early founders of the Pennsylvania colony.

This paper is an attempt to state some of the reactions of the Averbuch affair upon the Russian Jewish colony of which the young man was a newly arrived member, and to put down some of the reflections to which these reactions have given rise. It makes not the slightest effort to go into the facts of the case, nor to give judgment upon the guilt or innocence of Averbuch, but to state a position which seems to us a just one, whether or not the police theory should be substantiated.

One realizes of course the inevitable sense of horror with which the community regards an attack upon an official as such. It adds the horror of anarchy to assassination and is the essence of that which distinguishes anarchy from assassination. The crime against government itself compels an instinctive recoil from all law-abiding citizens and both the horror and recoil have their roots deep down in human experience. The earliest forms of government implied a group which offered competent resistance to invasion or attack from outsiders, but assumed that no protection was necessary between any two of its own members. When, therefore, one member, who in all good faith had been taken into the privileges of the group, turned against another member, the offence was regarded as one of unpardonable treason promptly punishable with death. This prompt dealing with the traitor still continues in military organizations, where treason is so fraught with immediate danger that even insolence to a superior officer, which may be the first symptom of insubordination, is not tolerated for an instant. The anarchist corresponds in civil society to the traitor in military circles, and is the modern representative of the long line of creatures, despised always, reaching back to the tribe itself. When an anarchistic attack is made against an official representative of law and order we have the baldest possible situation and an accredited basis, as it were, for unreasoning hatred and for prompt punishment. There is, too, no doubt that in the present instance there is added to this old horror the sense of being betrayed by a newcomer, by one who has been kindly received and who is undermining the government which others have painstakingly built up. It becomes almost a mark of patriotism in the first excitement to fulminate against the "foreign anarchist."

But because such a deed is colossal in its reaction upon a law-abiding community, it is well to remember that the very horror and dread which it produces naturally extends to the entire colony of newly immigrated foreigners with whom the idea of anarchy thus becomes associated. Because of the consciousness of this, the Russian Jewish colony on the west side of Chicago was thrown into a state of intense excitement as soon as the nationality of the young man who went to the house of the chief of police became known.

During the hours of uncertainty as to the young man's identity, the time between the first and last editions of the evening papers, the members of both the Italian and Russian colony were filled with dark forebodings, with a swift prescience of what it would mean to either of them were the odium of anarchy rightly or wrongly attached to one of their members.

An Italian in my hearing cried out,

> ... We can endure no more. We have an uphill fight as it is with the American prejudice against 'dagoes'. . .

An ambitious Russian Jew who thought himself quite free from the faith of his orthodox fathers, the same afternoon said, with white lips:

> That picture in the *News* looks like a Russian Jew; we can't have it so. All our radicals are socialists, not anarchists. We are not such fools as to pursue the method of terrorism in a country where there is free speech and an opportunity for agitation. We fill up the night schools, we learn English faster than anyone else; no one tries so hard as we do, to be Americans. To attach anarchy to us means persecution, plain Jewbaiting and nothing else.

For the next few weeks at least his worst fears in this direction were realized. Every member in the colony in varying degrees immediately felt the result of the public panic. A large tract of land near Paris, Ill., [sic] which had been negotiated for that an agricultural colony of Russian

Jews might be established, was withdrawn by the seller on the ground that the people of the vicinity were not willing to have anarchists settle there, although the land was practically sold and only the final arrangements remained to be completed. The society having the matter in charge was forced to give up the entire affair. School children were hooted and stoned upon the streets. Inoffensive young people returning from their work upon the street cars were treated with the utmost contempt. One young man was obliged to leave a dental college because of the persecution of his fellow students, and similar instances might be cited by the hundred. The old anti-Semitic feeling held sway, encouraged and sustained by the sense that to indulge it was "to put down anarchy."

The inevitable resentment engendered by this treatment first expressed itself against the "Americans" that they so readily took the hasty newspaper conclusions that the man was an anarchist. The Russians themselves give this version of the incident, which I may be permitted to repeat as from them: that the chief of police saw a young man with an envelope in his hand enter his door; that according to the chief's own statement he was at once convinced that the man was an Italian anarchist sent to assassinate him in the furtherance of an anarchistic plot, of which he had been warned. The Russian colony says that it has been clearly ascertained since, that the chief was mistaken as to the man's nationality; a searching inquiry failed to establish the fact that the man was an anarchist, and it is certainly within the range of human possibilities that the man's intent was also misinterpreted. Nothing could have been further apart than this certainly possible version and the one spread over the front pages of the leading Chicago dailies. A sense of injustice, of a lack of fair play, rankled through all those first experiences of persecution.

It seemed to the Russian colony that none of the Americans took the position that because a man has been attacked in his official capacity, an obligation is implied to go into the matter with that decorum and gravity which is inevitably attached to governmental affairs. It is certainly true that just because anarchy is so hideous an affront upon society, upon the most precious of its inherited institutions, the most elemental sense of justice demands that before its stigma is attached to an entire colony of immigrants, not only the facts themselves should be carefully ascertained, but the method of dealing with such a situation should be soberly considered. It may also be maintained that the pursuance of an unintelligent policy may easily result in increasing the very tendencies which it is desired to suppress.

A most superficial analysis shows the advocates of the violent overthrow of government, whether or not they justify their action by anarchistic doctrines, are inevitably produced in countries such as Russia, where the government is interpreted to them by a series of unjust and repressive measures. In these countries the officials are concerned only to assert their paramount authority, no constitutional rights are guaranteed, and such untoward events as the massacre at Kishinev are readily suspected of sinister direction by the government itself. The only sane, the only possible cure for such a state of mind, the only method by which a reasonable and loyal conception of government may be substituted for the one formed upon such an experience, is that the actual experience of the refugees with government in America shall gradually demonstrate what a very different thing government means here. Such an event as the Averbuch affair affords an unprecedented opportunity to make clear this difference and to demonstrate beyond the possibility of misunderstanding that the guarantee of constitutional rights implies that officialism shall be restrained and guarded at every point, that the official represents not the will of a small administrative body but the will of the entire people, and that methods therefore have been constituted by which official aggression may be restrained. The opportunity comes to demonstrate this to that very body of people who need it most; to those who have had experience in Russia where autocratic officers represent autocratic power and where government is officialism.

It is deeply to be regretted that instead of using this opportunity to present to the Russian Jewish colony the sharp contrast between the two forms of government, the republican government right on its own ground and in the hands of its friends should have fallen into the Russian method of dealing with a similar incident, and that because the community was in a state of panic it should have connived at and apparently approved of these very drastic methods on the part of the police.

It is a common saying among Russians of all classes that the real ruler of a Russian city is the chief of police, doubtless because the police, backed many times by the Cossack soldiery, are the final executors and interpreters of autocracy. The fact, therefore, that it was the Russian colony to which the Chicago police repaired immediately after Averbuch had been identified made the action of the police all the more deplorable and caused feeling to run very high. The Averbuch family was not the only one which had been subjected to persecution and threatened with massacre in "the old country." The Russian Jewish colony was largely made up of such families, only too familiar with the methods of the Russian police. Therefore, when the Chicago police ransacked all the printing offices they could locate in the colony, when they raided a restaurant which they regarded as suspicious because it had been supplying food at cost to the unemployed, when they searched through private houses for papers and photographs of revolutionaries, when they seized the library of the Edelstadt group and carried the books away to the city hall, when they arrested two friends of young Averbuch and kept them in the police station forty-eight hours after the police themselves acknowledged their acquaintance with the young man had been most casual; when they mercilessly "sweated" the sister, Olga, and led her up between two officers to the half naked body of her brother, that she might be startled into a confession; when they so persistently told her that her brother had killed three men, so that she could scarcely be made to believe that this was a mistake when she was released on the fourth day and returned to her friends;—all these things so poignantly reminded them of Russian methods that indignation, fed both by old memory and bitter disappointment in America, swept over the entire colony.[2] The older men asked whether constitutional rights gave no guarantee against such violent aggression of police power, and the hot-headed ones cried out at once that the only way to deal with the police was to defy them: that that was true of the police the world over.

The younger and more radical members of the Russian Jewish colony were determined to protest against the action of the police, which they considered brutal, by the only method possible in Russia, that of a procession and public demonstration so large that the police should not suppress it. It was planned to make this demonstration at the reburial of the body of Averbuch. This time was selected partly because it was a dramatic moment and partly because great resentment had been aroused in the Jewish colony by the needless indignity heaped upon the body, Jewish sentiment being most sensitive upon such a matter. They did not so much resent the fact that the body was placed in the potter's field as they resented all the needless suffering of the sister, Olga, that she had been brutally told that no Jewish cemetery would receive the body of an anarchist and that, of course, no Christian cemetery would, "that traces of anarchy had been found in the brain," as if the words were written across the front lobes. It seemed to the older and more conservative members of the Russian Jewish colony, as it did indeed to the residents of the two settlements with whom they were in constant communication, that such a demonstration was most unwise, and should be prevented if possible. A procession at such a time, a possible collision with the police, might result disastrously.

The only method of accomplishing this was to keep the time of the re-burial a secret. This was most difficult because in order to remove the body legally it was necessary to obtain permits not only from the burial division of the city Health Department but from the coroner who held jurisdiction over the body until a report of the inquest should have been made, and from the president of the County Board of Commissioners, because the potter's field in which the body had temporarily been buried belonged to the county. If the reburial was to be carried through without a demonstration, it was necessary to procure these three permissions si-multaneously upon the opening of the offices in the morning and to pro-ceed at once before the noon edition of the newspapers informed the public that the permits had been issued. The young radicals had sta-tioned two men in the corridor of the burial department of the Board of Health that they might notify their comrades whenever a burial permit should be granted, which they anticipated would be given to a Hebrew burial society. Everything was arranged to give the signal quickly to those young comrades throughout the colony, who were only too eager to march and to show their contempt for the police. Through the friendly co-operation of the physician in charge of this department the permits were given without their knowledge. As these various permits were ob-tained from city and county—and the one from the coroner's office was not obtained without almost insuperable difficulties—they were assem-bled at the down town office of an attorney who was interested in the af-fair on the same basis as many of us were.

Armed with all this red tape, the body was disinterred, a second au-topsy was held by a distinguished pathologist who fortunately cared for fair play as much as he did for medical etiquette, the reburial took place with appropriate Jewish rites, and a hostile demonstration was avoided.

The settlement people were able to carry through this delicate and extremely difficult affair more easily perhaps than the members of the Russian Jewish colony could have done; at least the latter themselves eagerly insisted upon this settlement help, and came to the house in the moment of their perplexity and distress with no notion that help and counsel would be denied them. They—the settlement people—did not, however, by this win encomiums from the radical portion of the colony, who felt that their demonstration had been unwarrantably interfered with and that an excellent opportunity for propaganda had been lost. It was indeed a somewhat ironic situation, a leading newspaper calling the settlement people "socialists" and "disturbers of the peace" at the very moment when they were being denounced by the socialists themselves as "cowards" and "bourgeoisie."

This attitude toward the police on the part of the young Russian revolutionaries is in itself a new development. Their normal attitude has been that in America the policeman is pursuing his natural function of preserving peace and has not been turned into the spy of a suspicious government or the executive officer of "a pogrom." But the Russian colony now says that if the police are to use these drastic measures, the Russian method is preferable to the American one, for in Russia it has been carefully worked out and is at least guarded at certain points; that the Russian police have a list of books marked illegal, but that the excited men acting for the Chicago police department carried away all of the books belonging to the Edelstadt group including a full set of Shakespeare and a full set of Spencer. The Russian colony also insists that the Russian government has many agents in this country whose business it is to do everything possible to stop the flow of money sent from America to support the Russian revolutionists; that such agents are always trying to break up meetings held by Russian Jews in which they discuss the Russian revolutionary movement, and that if the American police can be persuaded that all such meetings are dangerous and anarchistic, if they can receive orders to break them up on sight wherever found, it will do more than any other one thing to prevent the collection of funds for the Russian revolution. The Russian colony believes that these agents of the Russian government are constantly seeking to influence public opinion. If Americans say that the police will have to be stringent with these anarchists who threaten officials and throw bombs, and that it is easy to understand how the Russian government has been driven into restrictive and strong-handed measures, a great point will have been made. . . . It is quite possible that the young Russians are most unjustly suspicious in this regard, but certain it is that so soon as the matter is discussed by one of them dark hints are thrown out concerning governmental agents who may have induced a young man of eighteen [Averbuch], fumbling in the midst of bewildering hopes and reactions, to go to the chief of police at the moment when public panic and excitement on the subject of anarchy was at its height, because of the Denver affair. Such a boy would inevitably expose himself to a suspicion of evil intent, and it is of course further intimated that these same agents may have prepared the mind of the chief by tales of anarchistic plots and upset his nerves by mysterious messages.

There are many hundreds of adherents in the colony to the theory that the boy was obscurely induced to go to the chief's house by a man in the employ of the Russian government. Certainly nothing could happen which would so well serve the purpose of the Russian government and the American public is taking it in exactly the way which makes it most valuable to the Russians.

Would it not provoke to ironic laughter that very Nemesis which presides over the destinies of nations, if the most autocratic government yet remaining in civilization should succeed in pulling back into its own autocratic methods the youngest and most daring experiment in democratic government which the world has ever seen? Stranger results have followed a course of stupidity and injustice resulting from blindness and panic! The only way to meet such a suspicion is of course by perfect frankness and by inviting a full and searching inquiry into the entire situation. To the reply that the coroner's inquest invited such a searching examination they make the rejoinder that the attorney who appeared there on behalf of the sister, Olga, did so at the cost of public opprobrium, that an attempt made to testify as to the good character of Averbuch was put down in the most high-handed fashion. The following instance is indeed well authenticated: A young man, a friend of Averbuch, who had earlier figured in the newspapers as a mysterious "curly headed" person, went to Captain O'Brien's office at nine o'clock on the morning of the inquest offering to appear as a witness as to the good character of Averbuch. He was promptly arrested and detained until four o'clock the same afternoon and so was prevented from giving favorable testimony.

They maintain that not a scintilla of evidence was produced at the inquest to prove the charge of anarchy, and yet that the same newspapers which had so assiduously spread the police charge of anarchy did nothing whatever to rectify the mistake when the coroner's inquest not only failed to establish such a charge, but when their silence confirmed a lack of material upon which they were willing to make such a charge. They, the Russian Jewish colony, further assert that the Americans throughout the community were brutally indifferent to the fact that the odium of this unsubstantiated charge should remain upon thousands of their fellow citizens of Russian Jewish birth.

. . . It registered a conviction that in a moment of panic a republican government cared no more for justice and fair play than an autocratic government did; that in America as in Russia the statement of an official was without question taken as over against the statements of the obscure members of the community. It was said many times that those who are without influence and protection in a strange country fare exactly as hard as do the poor in Europe; that all the talk of guaranteed protection through political institutions is nonsense.

It seemed to those who lived in the settlements nearest the Russian Jewish colony that it was an obvious piece of public spirit to at least try out all the legal value involved, to insist that American institutions were stout enough not to break down in times of stress and public panic. In fact, there was no other group of Americans available to whom the Russian Jewish colony might reasonably appeal. The political parties were much too timid to take upon themselves the odium of anarchy and they were furthermore only too eager to use the hue and cry of anarchy to their own political advantage, posing as defenders of vested interests. While some of the churches spoke out later, at the time, of course, there was no way of knowing which clergymen would do so, and naturally the Russian Jewish colony had no personal acquaintance with them. For the first few days at least the churches were silent. Indeed the settlements have always cherished a secret apprehension lest they might in a given crisis act as so many of the churches do,—keep quiet and do nothing at all until the immediate crisis is past and public opinion set, thus leaving the unknown members of the community who are anxiously seeking help in the formation of their opinions, moral guidance as it were, utterly at sea. It is curious that at the moment the settlements themselves thought the first help might come from *Collier's Weekly* or the *American Magazine,* thus corroborating the words of Professor William James in regard to higher institutions in general, although he spoke solely in relation to colleges and universities:

It would be a pity if any future historian would have to write words like these: "By the middle of the twentieth century the higher institutions of learning had lost all influence over public opinion in the United States. But the mission of raising the tone of democracy, which they had proved themselves so lamentably unfitted to exert, was assumed with rare enthusiasm and prosecuted with extraordinary skill and success by a new educational power; and for the clarification of their human sympathies and elevation of their human preferences, the people at large had acquired the habit of resorting exclusively to the guidance of certain private literary adventures, commonly designated in the market by the affectionate name of ten-cent magazines."

The settlement might of course have waited until one of these beloved ten-cent magazines should have sent an intelligent man from New York to investigate the situation. Perhaps they would have added a detective, as McClure's previously had sent one to San Francisco to investigate its "graft" for it.

I am quite willing to predict that if this had been done the settlements would have given uniform testimony that anarchy as a philosophy is dying down, not only in Chicago but everywhere; that their leading organs have discontinued publication and that their most eminent men in America have deserted them; that even those groups which have continued to meet are dividing, and the major half in almost every instance calls itself socialist-anarchists, an apparent contradiction of terms, whose members insist that the socialistic organization of society must be the next stage of social development and must be gone through with, so to speak, before the ideal state of society can be reached, so nearly begging the question that many orthodox socialists are willing to join them; that anarchists have never had an elaborate organization, signs, or passwords, as the newspapers state, because the very philosophy of individualism prevents it.

If I personally had been consulted by this harbinger of justice, representing a ten-cent magazine, and if he were a gentle soul who would have indulged me in a little sermon on a pet topic of non-resistance, I should have pointed out to him that to my mind the danger from the American colonies of Russian refugees lies not in the philosophies they may hold but in the moral twist which comes to him who, because he has been hard driven, has justified terrorism; that this menace comes equally from the terrorist refugees and from the agents of the Russian government which itself has instituted the terrorism of the four hundred. Perhaps he would have permitted me to expatiate at some length, in which case I should have said that when the sense of justice seeks to express itself quite outside the regular channels of established government it is set forth on a dangerous journey inevitably ending in disaster, and that this is true in spite of the fact that the adventure may have been inspired by noble motives. In the course of a recent argument with a Russian revolutionist, he once repeated to me the speech he had made to the court which sentenced him to Siberia. As representing the government against which he had rebelled, he told the court that he might in time be able to forgive all of their outrages and injustices save one, but that hundreds of men like himself, who were vegetarians because they were not willing to participate in the destruction of living creatures, who had never struck a child even in punishment because it was against their principles, who were consumed with tenderness for the outcast and oppressed and had lived for weeks among starving peasants only that they might cheer and solace them, that these men should have been driven into terrorism, and should feel impelled to "execute", as they call it, assassinate the Anglo-Saxon would term it, public officials, was something for which he would never forgive the Russian government. It was perhaps the heat of the argument, as much as conviction, which led me to reply that it would be equally difficult for society to forgive these very revolutionists for one thing they had done, and that was that they had re-instituted this use of force in such wise that it would inevitably be imitated by men of less scruple and restraint; that to have revived such a method in civilization, to have justified it by their disinterestedness of purpose and nobility of character, was perhaps the gravest responsibility that any group of men could assume. That the methods of terrorism have become justified in the minds of thousands of young Russian revolutionaries who have reacted against the outrages of the autocracy and who contend that it must be appealed to as a last resort induces them to justify this position to Americans with the statement that the number of violent executions in Russia do not in a given six months or a year equal the number of lynchings in America; that it is only a question of provocation before men will resort to it.

These two points of lawlessness justified by elaborate argument—one in Russia and one in America—seem to me matters of grave concern. All this I should have ventured to say to a hypothetical representative; but of course a little talk like this could only be made to an organ which appeals to the entire people, a less inclusive audience would be sure to misunderstand.

After all, are the settlements not somewhat impertinent? In trying to state that facts of the case, is [it] not true, as Professor Small said in the Chicago *Evening Post* of March 14, "that the settlements are doing that which the whole city should have done." To quote from him further "All that they desire is that nothing should remain hidden which may throw light on the affair. They wish to see that every means of getting information is exhausted before a final opinion is formed."

That the settlements feel a responsibility for this more sharply than the rest of the community does, is doubtless the result of propinquity. . . .

At the end of twenty years it seems absurd that the Chicago settlements should be explaining their position to the public upon these grave matters. They have received much generous support from Chicago; in many respects they have been overestimated, but in a moment of great public excitement it is possible that they themselves are realizing for the first time that they have attained a professional standard of conduct and may perhaps begin to clear themselves of the charge of being amateur. This standard may demand that the newly arrived immigrant shall have his defense and his chance, in so far as the settlements can obtain it.

Some years ago when the mayor of Chicago was brutally assassinated and in the moment of excitement the first trial was considered hasty and inadequate, leading attorneys of this city insisted that the trial should be re-opened; that the case should be taken up to a higher court, not because there was any doubt that the condemned prisoner killed the mayor, but because the standards of the legal profession demanded that the case should be adequately and properly cared for. When the assassin of President McKinley was brought to trial in Buffalo, the legal profession there insisted that one of their number should defend him, because the professional ethics demanded that this should be done. The fact that it was a distasteful undertaking to the chosen representative had nothing whatever to do with it.

Quite as the legal profession feels its obligations in these matters, as a medical man would care for a wounded assassin as scientifically and as carefully as for a "leading citizen," so possibly the settlements are coming to a professional standard of conduct in regard to matters pertaining to foreign colonies and the interpretation of American institutions to them.

Certain books written by settlement residents are used in the department of social ethics in several American universities. Any value such books may have arises from the fact that they present a first hand study of social and ethical conditions in the immigrant quarters and represent convictions upon which settlement residents are willing to act. That these convictions lead them to advise a different treatment for "anarchy" from that pursued by the Chicago police department may possibly mean that they are advocating an effective treatment instead of a stupid treatment.

In the first place the Chicago police department made utterly contradictory statements as to the number of anarchists which the town contains. Several days before the attack they declared that they had definite information as to a well laid anarchistic plot which would probably consummate in an assassination. So sure were they of this information that the chief himself, seeing a dark young man with a letter in his hand standing in his doorway at an unusual hour, concluded that he was an Italian anarchist about to carry out his part in this definite anarchistic plot. And yet when the police are put to it to give information, they are utterly unable to locate any such plot either among Italians or Russians, and are forced to the conclusion that whatever young Averbuch had in his mind, it was a solitary effort, "sporadic" anarchy, if anarchy at all. . . . There is no method by which any community can be guarded against sporadic efforts on the part of half-crazed, discouraged men, save by a sense of community right and security which will include each one.

One is driven at last to the Christian assertion that society is not safe unless it includes "the least of these," and that this inclusion must be world wide with compassionate understanding for the outcast of every land, drawing him in to the reassurance and warmth of a fellow-ship against which he could not strive if he would. I suppose that all of our religious teaching has to be translated into experience before we really believe it. But this conviction that a sense of fellowship is the only implement which will break into the locked purpose of a half-crazed creature bent upon destruction in the name of justice, certainly came to me through an experience, curiously enough, recited to me by an old anarchist.

He was a German cobbler who, through all the changes in the manufacturing of shoes, had steadily clung to his little shop on a Chicago
thoroughfare, partly as an expression of his individualism and partly because he preferred bitter poverty in a place of his own to good wages
under a disciplinary foreman. The assassin of President McKinley on his
way through Chicago only a few days before he committed his dastardly
deed, had visited all the anarchists whom he could find in the city, asking them for "the pass-word," as he called it. They, of course, possessed
no such thing, and had turned him away, some with disgust and all with
a certain degree of impatience, as a type of the ill-balanced man who, as
they put it, was always "hanging around the movement without the
slightest conception of its meaning." Among other people, he visited the
German cobbler, who treated him much as the others had done, but
who, after the event had made clear the identity of his visitor, was filled
with the most bitter remorse that he had failed to utilize his chance
meeting with the assassin to deter him from his purpose. He knew, as
well as any psychologist who has read the solitary history of such men,
that the only possible way to break down such a persistent and secretive
purpose was by the kindliness which might have induced confession,
which might have restored him into fellowship with normal men.

In the midst of his remorse, the cobbler told me a tale of his own
youth; that years before, when an ardent young fellow in Germany,
newly converted to the philosophy of anarchism, as he called it, he had
made up his mind that the church, as much as the state, was responsible for human oppression, and that this fact could best be set forth "in
the deed" by the public destruction of a clergyman or priest; that he
had carried firearms for a year with this purpose in mind, but that one
pleasant summer evening, in a moment of weakness, he had confided
his intention to a friend, and that from that moment he not only lost all
desire to carry it out, but it seemed to him the most preposterous thing
imaginable. In concluding the story, he also said: "That poor fellow sat
just beside me on my bench,—if I had only put my hand on his shoul-
der and said: 'Now, look here brother, what is on your mind? What
makes you talk such nonsense? Tell me. I have seen much of life, and
understand all kinds of men. I have been young and hot-headed and
foolish myself.' If he had told me of his purpose then and there, he
would never have carried it out. The whole nation would have been
spared this horror." He would always shake his gray head and sigh as if

the whole incident were more than he could bear. One of those terrible sins of omission; one of the things he "ought to have done," the memory of which is the hardest to endure.

The far reaching consequences of this incident must be my excuse for this long paper. For many years differences of opinion have existed between public spirited citizens on the subject of restricting immigration and upon the treatment of refugees who have broken police or military regulations in order to escape from oppressive governmental conditions. If immigration laws are enacted which make it infinitely more difficult for Russian Jews to come to America, we shall close up the last loophole of escape for thousands of people who are living under an oppression and a persecution which are simply intolerable.

The statement has gone throughout the country that young Averbuch intended to kill the chief of police of Chicago because he represented a society of anarchists who advocated the killing of police as such. Even so eminent a man as Senator Lodge of Massachusetts, in a public address delivered in Boston before the City Club on March 20, said: "Within the last few weeks we have seen a murderous assault by an alien immigrant upon the chief of police of a great city, not to avenge a personal wrong but because he represented law and order."[3] Senator Lodge made this a plea for further restrictive measures in our immigration laws. It is difficult to estimate the effect upon minds all over the country, most of them presumably less careful than that possessed by the senior senator of Massachusetts, and it is difficult to estimate the result upon immigration legislation.

Because of its effect upon immigration laws, if for no other reson, it is most essential, first and foremost, to ascertain just what did happen, and what the social implications of the event mean. As we allow our public officials to act in this instance, so the American policy will be largely determined; so free speech, "freedom of assemblage," and all other stirring words in the bill of rights will become interpreted; so may "our charter be torn," to use the pregnant phrase of Abraham Lincoln.

Let us review the situation as the police themselves state it. The police in New York beat a man over the head because he is talking about socialism on the street. The man has always been told that "free speech" is guaranteed in America and he is enraged beyond bounds by this treatment. Then he hears that the unemployed have been forbidden a permit to assemble in Union Square in order to state their case and to discuss

measures of relief. This seems to him an invasion of the American guarantee to the right of "free assemblage" and he, therefore, from directions
in the encyclopedia, prepares a bomb to throw at the police as a protest
against their invasion of American rights as he conceives them. The police in Chicago prevent a parade of the unemployed, and threaten to
break up a meeting in Brand's Hall if it shall be addressed by Emma
Goldman.[4] These two acts of the Chicago police worked upon the mind
of the young Russian revolutionary named Averbuch and are the only
psychological clue the police themselves give in support of their theory
that he went to the house of the chief with the intent of assassination.

But with the curious logic of the policeman, the police of New York
and Chicago both cite these two acts of violence which they themselves
say were indirectly resultant from oppressive measures, as a justification for further repressive measures, and insist that unless further repressive measures are used, such acts will constantly occur.

When I first came to Chicago, in 1889, the events of the Haymarket
riot were already two years old, but during that time Chicago had apparently gone through the first period of repressive measures, and during the winter of 1889–1890, by the advice and with the active participation of its leading citizens, had reached the conclusion that the only
cure for the acts of anarchy was free speech and an open discussion of
the ills of which the opponents of government complained.

As many of you doubtless remember, great open meetings were held
every Sunday evening in the recital hall of the then new Auditorium,
which were presided over by such representative citizens as Lyman
Gage, and where every possible shade of opinion was freely expressed.
A man who spoke constantly at these meetings used to be pointed out
to the visiting stranger as one who had been involved with the group of
convicted anarchists, and as one who doubtless would have been arrested and tried but for the accident of his having been in Milwaukee
when the explosion occurred.

One cannot imagine such meetings being held in Chicago to-day, nor
that such a man should be allowed to raise his voice in a public assemblage presided over by a leading banker. What has happened to
Chicago in the meantime? What change has come over our philosophy?

If the under dog were always right, one might quite easily try to defend him. The trouble is that very often he is but obscurely right, sometimes only partially right, and often quite wrong, but perhaps he is

never so altogether, wrong and pig-headed and utterly reprehensible as he is represented to be by those who add the possession of prejudice to the other almost insuperable difficulties in understanding him.

As for those who attempt to interpret him, when he is apparently in his worst temper, they may perhaps be cheered by a phrase often quoted by Matthew Arnold:

"Conscience and the present constitution of things are not corresponding terms. It is conscience and the issue of things which go together."

Notes

1. Addams refers to two incidents involving anarchists, or alleged anarchists, that ended disastrously. In the Chicago case, an apparently disoriented young man, Lazerus Averbuch, made his way to the home of Chicago's police chief, entered, and attempted to hand something to the chief. This was construed as menacing and Averbuch was shot dead. A roundup of anarchists (or alleged anarchists) followed. Averbuch's sister was taken into custody and "sweated." There was a conflict surrounding surrender of the body to the family for burial. Hull-House found itself in the thick of things, attempting to allay hysteria in the Russian-Jewish immigrant community and in the wider Chicago community, where fear of anarchists was widespread. She insisted that in dealing with those who mistrust the law it is especially important that the law be even-handed and punctilious. All this took place in 1908.

2. The Edelstadt was one of dozens of small, rather vaguely defined anarchist or quasianarchist groups, this one named after Yiddish poet, David Edelstadt (1866–1892), who started the group.

3. The first of two Senators Lodge of Massachusetts, he served during the Wilson era, from 1893 to 1924.

4. Emma Goldman (1869–1940), anarchist and all-around protestor. She was for sexual liberation and anarchy and was profoundly hostile toward those she considered tame, tepid "bourgeois" feminists.

19

"THE HOME AND THE SPECIAL CHILD"

IN DISCUSSING THE PROBLEM of the special child it is, of course, necessary to consider it from the point of view of the child who is somewhat mentally deficient, and of the child who is what we now call incorrigible or delinquent.

Mr. Barnes [a fellow panelist] is doubtless right when he says that it is difficult for a parent to make a clear judgment in regard to his own child, especially in respect to the child's mental or moral capacities. But, if parental affection clouds the power of diagnosis, at the same time, after the diagnosis has been made by the trained mind, parental affection enormously increases the power of devotion which is necessary to carry out the regimen which the trained mind has laid down. To convince the parent that by following a certain line of action his child will be enormously benefited [sic] is simply to turn affection into a scientifically prepared channel.

When deficient children are discovered in their homes, are taken care of by trained teachers, after they have been diagnosed by child-study departments, and when all the apparatus of public education is turned on, the parent is convinced that his child is not an exception. When the parent is besought to aid in this process of special education, then he first loses his peculiar sensitiveness in regard to his child. The reaction of this change of attitude upon the entire family is something astounding. I think it was Father Huntington who once said that the essence of

---

Note: "The Home and the Special Child," in National Education Association, *Journal of Proceedings and Addresses* (1908), pp. 99–102.

immorality is to make an exception of one's self, and certainly the essence of self-pity is the conviction that one is so isolated. Comradeship dispels self-pity as the sun dries up dampness. You think you have a child unlike other children; you are anxious that your neighbor shall not find it out; it makes you secretive; it makes you singularly sensitive; it places you and the normal children in the family in a curious relation to the rest of the community; but if you find out that there are many other such children in your city and in other cities throughout [sic] the United States, and that a whole concourse of people are studying to help these children, considering them not at all queer and outrageous, but simply a type of child which occurs from time to time and which can be enormously helped, you come out of that peculiarly sensitive attitude and the whole family is lifted with you into a surprising degree of hopefulness and normality. I could illustrate this with many tales. I remember one case where a family consisted of a widow, two self-supporting children, and three younger children, the eldest of whom was feeble-minded. The entire family had lived a perfectly abnormal life. In the first place, they always rented a rear tenement, because it was thus made easier to conceal the boy from public view. The four other children were never permitted, under any circumstances, to bring companions to the house. The boy was treated with tenderness and care, but with the utmost secrecy. The mother's attitude was gradually changed after days of patient talk and many visits on the part, first, of a trained nurse, and later of a person who was especially interested in the care of backward children. The day finally came when the boy was put in the omnibus for crippled children—for it was one of those cases where mental abnormality is combined with deformity—and taken to the public school openly and boldly, with the omnibus standing in the street, and the child carried out in the arms of a policeman. From that day there was a world-wide difference in the status of the family to the entire neighborhood. Of course such a change could not be brought about until the mother was freed from her sense of isolation, until she discovered that there were many other people who had children of that sort who were not thereby disgraced, that the community recognized such children and provided for them, demanding her coöperation.

That, it may be, is the most valuable result which the recognition of the duty of the state to these children is bringing about. But not even second to this is the opportunity of unlocking their affection, this peculiar care and solicitude which parents have for the abnormal child, whether he is abnormal thru [sic] his deficiencies or thru his moral development; thus pouring into public education almost a new force. Froebel used to believe that if he could unlock the love for little children which is manifested by their mothers, if he could pour into the educational system the gaiety of the mother, her delight in her child, her spontaneous desire to play with it, it would bring into education a new and transforming element. At the same time, of course, his kindergarten systematized its manifestations, as the educator of the deficient child would have to train and use scientifically this mysterious tender affection.

There is just one thing more which I would like to emphasize which is being worked out in Chicago. We have a child-study department where any child whom a teacher is confused about and worried about and considers backward may be sent and examined—perhaps to be excluded from the system, but more likely to be put into a special room. We have a school for crippled children—very much such an one as Mr. Barnes has described, and some of us believe that from these points of special education Chicago may secure the best suggestions for educational advance. To illustrate from another great educator—Pestalozzi.[1] He made his discoveries because he had a little handful of orphan children whom he was obliged to care for in a primitive way—to wash and dress and feed. He was obliged to appeal to the children for help; to follow their lead. Of course he was put into the very best possible attitude for making educational discoveries. Perhaps in time educators who are assisted by the devoted parents may come to recognize these children as possible contributors toward the solution of the public-school problems. Educators may face them simply and fairly in a change of attitude to which the parents have brought them.

This reaction of the schools for special children upon the home may bring back into the school some of that early devotion to them which we are in danger of losing. I might illustrate from a family whom I knew very well, who had a mentally deficient child. The family became quite prosperous and moved away from our neighborhood into a suburb, which was a step up for them both in the economic and social scale. They stayed in their suburb only two months however, because the little girl was too far away from a school containing a room for special children. They moved back again so that she might be within the old district, and when the teacher of this special room was put into another district, they moved again into another crowded neighbor-hood, renting their little house in the suburbs, sacrificing their only pleasure and the advancement of the normal children because they cared so much that the one "special child" should be in contact with the particular person who would teach the mother how to treat her day after day. The mother felt the need of the coöperation, of the renewal of her courage. She wanted the sense of companionship which her connection with this particular teacher gave her, and which no one in the suburb with its tidy streets and its "swell people," as she called them, was able to afford to her. In this combination of pedagogical training and parental devotion, it would of course be necessary to keep a standard of achievement; because the child has gone beyond that which you thought he might reasonably attain, it is not going to help him when he is thrown out into the world where he will be subject to the normal standard, if you have assumed that everything is lovely, when it is indeed only partially lovely. Not to distinguish between optimism and confusion of standard often leads to disaster, and never more surely so than when we over-estimate the capacity of these special children. It is much better to teach such a child to do one thing well and then to place him *hors de combat* as to the rest of life.

I have seen an Italian family change their entire attitude toward a crippled child who was taught to carve wood with his one hand so well that he earned a very fair wage in a furniture factory; but they did not ask him to wash windows although that was the occupation of the father. And altho [sic] it may take half of the seventy years of which Mr. Barnes spoke to recognize the capacity of the defective child, that recognition must, in the end, react upon the home most marvelously. To bring the home and the school into closer connection thru these special children affords a glorious educational opportunity, and the results may react upon the schools in a way we can, as yet, scarcely estimate.

I could illustrate the same psychological process—the reaction on the home by the delinquent boy—in other ways. Take the boy who is arrested and brought into the Juvenile Court in Chicago. Such a child is examined very carefully by a physician—all of the things which Dr. Barnes has been advocating for the ordinary school children are being showered upon incorrigible children while they are waiting for trial. During the period of detention every child is subject to the medical treatment which he specially needs; he is put into a school and given a chance to do all of this advance handwork which has been so much emphasized in this meeting. The results are simply amazing. Sometimes one actually fails to recognize a boy after he has been in this school a short time, such is the result of good food, of baths and all the rest of the things. . . . After he had been subjected to this treatment for a month or six weeks his own parents subtly change in their attitude to him. The mother recognizes that which she always knew was there, altho she had no power to bring it out; and the father, who was said not to be fond of him, suddenly swells with a new sense of pride. The onlooker wonders why this hasn't been done before the child was arrested, before he had to be brought to this preliminary disgrace. Here again I think it is the open acknowledgment which frees the situation, the moral effect when the community is not hostile, nor suspicious, nor watching to see how bad your boy is and to whisper that opinion to the next door neighbor. The coöperating community versus the hostile community enables the parents to lift up their heads and march along once more. I could easily illustrate this, but I am sure illustrations occur to many of you and I am not going to take your time for them, but with your permission I will very hastily resume the three points which I tried to make: First, the changed attitude of the family when the mother understands that her child is one of many similar children, that she is not having a burden unlike any one else which she has been specially selected by an unfair Providence to bear, but that a large group of people are considering the best methods of dealing with children such as hers, and that she may be of great help to them as well as to her child. Second, the advance that may be made in education when we are forced to the special education, and the many suggestions that will result. Third, the care which may be given to them, at the same time keeping parallel the old tenderness and old standard of educational achievement and educational advancement. These, I should say, were three things which we might well bear in mind in relation to the training of the special child and the home.

Notes

1. Johann Heinrich Pestalozzi (1746–1827), famous pedagogue and pedagogical theorist.

20

⌒∞⌒

"IF MEN WERE SEEKING

THE FRANCHISE"

LET US IMAGINE THROUGHOUT this article, if we can sustain an absurd hypothesis so long, the result upon society if the matriarchal period had held its own; if the development of the State had closely followed that of the Family until the chief care of the former, as that of the latter, had come to be the nurture and education of children and the protection of the weak, sick and aged. In short let us imagine a hypothetical society organized upon the belief that "there is no wealth but life." With this Ruskinian foundation let us assume that the political machinery of such a society, the franchise and the rest of it, were in the hands of women because they had always best exercised those functions. Let us further imagine a given moment when these women, who in this hypothetical society had possessed political power from the very beginnings of the State, were being appealed to by the voteless men that men might be associated with women in the responsibilities of citizenship.

Plagiarizing somewhat upon recent suffrage speeches let us consider various replies which these citizen women might reasonably make to the men who were seeking the franchise; the men insisting that only through the use of the ballot could they share the duties of the State.

First, could not the women say: "Our most valid objection to extending the franchise to you is that you are so fond of fighting—you always have been since you were little boys. You'd very likely forget that the real object of the State is to nurture and protect life, and out of sheer

---

Note: "If Men Were Seeking the Franchise," *Ladies Home Journal*, vol. 30 (June 1913).

vainglory you would be voting away huge sums of money for battle-ships, not one of which could last more than a few years, and yet each would cost ten million dollars; more money than all the buildings of Harvard University represent, although it is the richest educational institution in America. Every time a gun is fired in a battleship it expends, or rather explodes, seventeen hundred dollars, as much as a college education costs many a country boy, and yet you would be firing off these guns as mere salutes, with no enemy within three thousand miles, simply because you so enjoy the sound of shooting.

"Our educational needs are too great and serious to run any such risk. Democratic government itself is perilous unless the electorate is educated; our industries are suffering for lack of skilled workmen; more than half a million immigrants a year must be taught the underlying principles of republican government. Can we, the responsible voters, take the risk of wasting our taxes by extending the vote to those who have always been so ready to lose their heads over mere military display?"

Second, would not the hypothetical women, who would have been responsible for the advance of industry during these later centuries, as women actually were during the earlier centuries when they dragged home the game and transformed the pelts into shelter and clothing, say further to these disenfranchised men: "We have carefully built up a code of factory legislation for the protection of the workers in modern industry; we know that you men have always been careless about the house, perfectly indifferent to the necessity for sweeping and cleaning; if you were made responsible for factory legislation it is quite probable that you would let the workers in the textile mills contract tuberculosis through needlessly breathing the fluff, or the workers in machine shops through inhaling metal filings, both of which are now carried off by an excellent suction system which we women have insisted upon, but which it is almost impossible to have installed in a man-made State because the men think so little of dust and its evil effects. In many Nations in which political power is confined to men, and this is notably true in the United States of America, there is no protection even for the workers in white lead, although hundreds of them are yearly incapacitated from lead poisoning, and others actually die.

"We have also heard that in certain States, in order to save the paltry price of a guard which would protect a dangerous machine, men legislators allow careless boys and girls to lose their fingers and sometimes their hands, thereby crippling their entire futures. These male legislators do not make guarded machinery obligatory, although they know that when the heads of families are injured at these unprotected machines the State must care for them in hospitals, and when they are killed, that if necessary the State must provide for their widows and children in poorhouses."

These wise women, governing the State with the same care they had always put into the management of their families, would further place against these men seeking the franchise the charge that men do not really know how tender and delicate children are, and might therefore put them to work in factories, as indeed they have done in man-made States during the entire period of factory production. We can imagine these women saying: "We have been told that in certain States children are taken from their beds in the early morning before it is light and carried into cotton mills, where they are made to run back and forth tending the spinning frames until their immature little bodies are so bent and strained that they never regain their normal shapes; that little children are allowed to work in canneries for fifteen and seventeen hours until, utterly exhausted, they fall asleep among the debris of shells and husks."

Would not these responsible women voters gravely shake their heads and say that as long as men exalt business profit above human life it would be sheer folly to give them the franchise; that, of course, they would be slow to make such matters the subject of legislation?

Would not the enfranchised women furthermore say to these voteless men: "You have always been so eager to make money; what assurance have we that in your desire to get the largest amount of coal out of the ground in the shortest possible time you would not permit the mine supports to decay and mine damp to accumulate, until the percentage of accidents among miners would be simply heartbreaking? Then you are so reckless. Business seems to you a mere game with big prizes, and we have heard that in America, where the women have no vote, the loss of life in the huge steel mills is appalling; and that the number of young brakemen, fine young fellows, every one of them the pride of some mother, killed every year is beyond belief; that the average loss of life among the structural-iron workers who erect the huge office buildings and bridges is as disastrous in percentages as was the loss of life in the

Battle of Bull Run. When the returns of this battle were reported to President Lincoln he burst into tears of sorrow and chagrin; but we have never heard of any President, Governor or Mayor weeping over the reports of this daily loss of life, although such reports have been presented to them by Governmental investigators; and this loss of life might easily be reduced by protective legislation."

Having thus worked themselves into a fine state of irritation, analogous to that ever-recurrent uneasiness of men in the presence of insurgent women who would interfere in the management of the State, would not these voting women add: "The trouble is that men have no imagination, or rather what they have is so prone to run in the historic direction of the glory of the battlefield, that you cannot trust them with industrial affairs. Because a crew in a battle-ship was once lost under circumstances which suggested perfidy the male representatives of two great Nations voted to go to war; yet in any day of the year in one of these Nations alone—the United States of America—as many men are killed through industrial accidents as this crew contained. These accidents occur under circumstances which, if not perfidious, are at least so criminally indifferent to human life as to merit Kipling's characterization that the situation is impious."[1]

Certainly these irritated women would designate such indifference to human life as unpatriotic and unjustifiable, only to be accounted for because men have not yet learned to connect patriotism with industrial affairs.

These conscientious women responsible for the State in which life was considered of more value than wealth would furthermore say: "Then, too, you men exhibit such curious survivals of the mere savage instinct of punishment and revenge. The United States alone spends every year five hundred million dollars more on its policemen, courts and prisons than upon all its works of religion, charity and education. The price of one trial expended on a criminal early in life might save the State thousands of dollars and the man untold horrors. And yet with all this vast expenditure little is done to reduce crime. Men are kept in jails and penitentiaries where there is not even the semblance of education or reformatory measure; young men are returned over and over again to the same institution until they have grown old and gray, and in all of that time they have not once been taught a trade, nor have they been in any wise prepared to withstand the temptations of life.

"A homeless young girl looking for a lodging may be arrested for soliciting on the streets, and sent to prison for six months, although there is no proof against her save the impression of the policeman. A young girl under such suspicion may be obliged to answer the most harassing questions put to her by the city attorney, with no woman near to protect her from insult; she may be subjected to the most trying examination conducted by a physician in the presence of a policeman, and no matron to whom to appeal. At least these things happen constantly in the United States—in Chicago, for instance—but possibly not in the Scandinavian countries where juries of women sit upon such cases, women whose patience has been many times tested by wayward girls and who know the untold moral harm which may result from such a physical and psychic shock."

Then these same women would go further, and, because they had lived in a real world and had administered large affairs and were therefore not prudish and affected, would say: "Worse than anything which we have mentioned is the fact that in every man-ruled city the world over a great army of women are so set aside as outcasts that it is considered a shame to speak the mere name which designates them. Because their very existence is illegal they may be arrested whenever any police captain chooses; they may be brought before a magistrate, fined and imprisoned. The men whose money sustains their houses, supplies their tawdry clothing and provides them with intoxicating drinks and drugs, are never arrested, nor indeed are they even considered lawbreakers."

Would not these fearless women, whose concern for the morals of the family had always been able to express itself through State laws, have meted out equal punishment to men as well as to women, when they had equally transgressed the statute law?

Did the enfranchised women evoked by our imagination speak thus to the disenfranchised men, the latter would at least respect their scruples and their hesitation in regard to an extension of the obligation of citizenship. But what would be the temper of the masculine mind if the voting women representing the existing State should present to them only the following half-dozen objections, which are unhappily so familiar to many of us: If the women should say, first, that men would find politics corrupting; second, that they would doubtless vote as their wives and mothers did; third, that men's suffrage would only double the vote without changing results; fourth, that men's suffrage would diminish the respect for men; fifth, that most men do not want to vote; sixth, that the best men would not vote?

I do no believe that women broadened by life and its manifold experiences would actually present these six objections to men as real reasons for withholding the franchise from them, unless indeed they had long formed the habit of regarding men not as comrades and fellow-citizens, but as a class by themselves, in essential matters really inferior although always held sentimentally very much above them.

Certainly no such talk would be indulged in between men and women who had together embodied in political institutions the old affairs of life which had normally and historically belonged to both of them. If woman had adjusted herself to the changing demands of the State as she did to the historic mutations of her own house-hold she might naturally and without challenge have held the place in the State which she now holds in the family.

When Plato once related his dream of an ideal Republic he begged his fellow-citizens not to ridicule him because he considered the cooperation of women necessary for its fulfillment. He contended that so far as the guardianship of the State is concerned there is no distinction between the powers of men and women save those which custom has made.

Notes

1. Rudyard Kipling (1865–1926), one of the most popular British writers of his era and a defender of a "correct" form of Western imperialism.

21

"THE PUBLIC SCHOOL AND THE IMMIGRANT CHILD"

I AM ALWAYS DIFFIDENT WHEN I come before a professional body of teachers, realizing as I do that it is very easy for those of us who look on to bring indictments against results; and realizing also that one of the most difficult situations you have to meet is the care and instruction of the immigrant child, especially as he is found where I see him, in the midst of crowded city conditions.

And yet in spite of the fact that the public school is the great savior of the immigrant district, and the one agency which inducts the children into the changed conditions of American life, there is a certain indictment which may justly be brought, in that the public school too often separates the child from his parents and widens that old gulf between fathers and sons which is never so cruel and so wide as it is between the immigrants who come to this country and their children who have gone to the public school and feel that they have there learned it all. The parents are thereafter subjected to certain judgment, the judgment of the young which is always harsh and in this instance founded upon the most superficial standard of Americanism. And yet there is a notion of culture which we would define as a knowledge of those things which have been long cherished by men, the things which men have loved because thru [sic] generations they have softened and interpreted life, and have endowed it with value and meaning. Could this standard have been given rather than the things which they see about them as the test

---

Note: "The Public School and the Immigrant Child," in National Education Association, *Journal of Proceedings and Addresses* (1908).

of so-called success, then we might feel that the public school has given at least the beginnings of culture which the child ought to have. At present the Italian child goes back to its Italian home more or less disturbed and distracted by the contrast between the school and the home. If he throws off the control of the home because it does not represent the things which he has been taught to value he takes the first step toward the Juvenile Court and all the other operations of the law, because he has prematurely asserted himself long before he is ready to take care of his own affairs.

We find in the carefully prepared figures which Mr. Commons and other sociologists have published that while the number of arrests of immigrants is smaller than the arrests of native born Americans, the number of arrests among children of immigrants is twice as large as the number of arrests among the children of native born Americans. It would seem that in spite of the enormous advantages which the public school gives to these children it in some way loosens them from the authority and control of their parents, and tends to send them, without a sufficient rudder and power of self-direction, into the perilous business of living. Can we not say, perhaps, that the schools ought to do more to connect these children with the best things of the past, to make them realize something of the beauty and charm of the language, the history, and the traditions which their parents represent. It is easy to cut them loose from their parents, it requires cultivation to tie them up in sympathy and understanding. The ignorant teacher cuts them off because he himself cannot understand the situation, the cultivated teacher fastens them because his own mind is open to the charm and beauty of that old-country life. In short, it is the business of the school to give to each child the beginnings of a culture so wide and deep and universal that he can interpret his own parents and countrymen by a standard which is world-wide and not provincial.

The second indictment which may be brought is the failure to place the children into proper relation toward the industry which they will later enter. . . . I believe that the figures of the United States census show the term to be something like six years for the women in industry as over against twenty-four years for men, in regard to continuity of service. Yet you cannot disregard the six years of the girls nor the twenty-four years of the boys, because they are the immediate occupation into which they enter after they leave the school—even the girls are bound to go thru that period—that is, the average immigrant girls are—before they enter the second serious business of life and maintain homes of their own. Therefore, if they enter industry unintelligently, without some notion of what it means, they find themselves totally unprepared for their first experience with American life, they are thrown out without the proper guide or clue which the public school might and ought to have given to them. Our industry has become so international, that it ought to be easy to use the materials it offers for immigrant children. The very processes and general principles which industry represents give a chance to prepare these immigrant children in a way which the most elaborated curriculum could not present. Ordinary material does not give the same international suggestion as industrial material does.

Third, I do not believe that the children who have been cut off from their own parents are going to be those who, when they become parents themselves, will know how to hold the family together and to connect it with the state. I should begin to teach the girls to be good mothers by teaching them to be good daughters. Take a girl whose mother has come from South Italy. The mother cannot adjust herself to the changed condition of housekeeping, does not know how to wash and bake here, and do the other things which she has always done well in Italy, because she has suddenly been transported from a village to a tenement house. If that girl studies these household conditions in relation to the past and to the present needs of the family, she is under-taking the very best possible preparation for her future obligations to a household of her own. And to my mind she can undertake it in no better way. Her own children are mythical and far away, but the little brothers and sisters pull upon her affections and her loyalty, and she longs to have their needs recognized in the school so that the school may give her some help. Her mother complains that the baby is sick in America because she cannot milk her own goat; she insists if she had her own goat's milk the baby would be quite well and flourishing, as the children were in Italy. If that girl can be taught that the milk makes the baby ill because it is not clean and be provided with a simple test that she may know when milk is clean, it may take her into the study not only of the milk within the four walls of the tenement house, but into the inspection of the milk of her district. The milk, however, remains good educational material, it makes even more concrete the connection which you would be glad to use between the household and the affairs of the American city. Let her not follow the mother's example of complaining about changed conditions; let her rather make the adjustment for her mother's entire household. We cannot tell what adjustments the girl herself will be called upon to make ten years from now; but we can give her the clue and the aptitude to adjust the family with which she is identified to the constantly changing conditions of city life. Many of us feel that, splendid as the public schools are in their relation to the immigrant child, they do not understand all of the difficulties which surround that child—all of the moral and emotional perplexities which constantly harass him. The children long that the school teacher should know something about the lives their parents lead and should be able to reprove the hooting children who make fun of the Italian mother because she wears a kerchief on her head, not only because they are rude but also because they are stupid. We send young people to Europe to see Italy, but we do not utilize Italy when it lies about the schoolhouse. If the body of teachers in our great cities could take hold of the immigrant colonies, could bring out of them their handicrafts and occupations, their traditions, their folk songs and folk lore, the beautiful stories which every immigrant colony is ready to tell and translate; could get the children to bring these things into school as the material from which culture is made and the material upon which culture is based, they would discover that by comparison that which they give them now is a poor meretricious and vulgar thing. Give these children a chance to utilize the historic and industrial material which they see about them and they will begin to have a sense of ease in America, a first consciousness of being at home. I believe if these people are welcomed upon the basis of the resources which they represent and the contributions which they bring, it may come to pass that these schools which deal with immigrants will find that they have a wealth of cultural and industrial material which will make the schools in other neighborhoods positively envious. A girl living in a tenement household, helping along this tremendous adjustment, healing over this great moral upheaval which the parents have suffered and which leaves them bleeding and sensitive—such a girl has a richer experience and a finer material than any girl from a more fortunate household can have at the present moment.

I wish I had the power to place before you what it seems to me is the opportunity that the immigrant colonies present to the public school: the most endearing occupation of leading the little child, who will in turn lead his family, and bring them with him into the brotherhood for which they are longing. The immigrant child cannot make this demand upon the school because he does not know how to formulate it; it is for the teacher both to perceive it and to fulfil it.

22

"AMERICANIZATION"

THE WORD "AMERICANIZATION" has recently become such a widespread slogan among us and so much a test of an alien's patriotism that, as most germane to my subject, may I ask you to consider for a few moments the marked change in the concept of nationalism which has taken place during the last quarter of a century? May I do this by contrasting the impressions I received in Europe last summer with those I received thirty-five years before?

At the earlier moment, in all political matters the great popular word was "unity": a coming together into new national systems of little states which had long been separated. New Italy was vociferously jubilant from the toe to the heel, for Venice had been so recently rescued from Austria that she still wore wreaths of welcome in honor of her home-coming, and Victor Emanuel was the most popular king in Europe.

The first kaiser and Bismarck ruled over a newly made German Empire, represented by an imperial parliament in which it was said that a homogeneous people, long estranged, had at last been united. It rather smacked of learning, in those days, to use the words slavophile and pan-slavic, but we knew that the words stood for a movement toward unity in the remoter parts of Europe where Bohemia was the most vocal, although she then talked less of a republic of her own than of her desire to unite with her fellow-Slavs. The very striking characteristic of all these nationalistic movements was their buring [sic] humanitarianism, a sense that the new groupings were but a preparation for a wider

---

Note: "Americanization," in American Sociological Society, *Publications*, vol. 14 (1919).

synthesis, that a federation of at least the European states was a possibility in the near future.

The words of Mazzini, who had died scarcely a decade before, were constantly on the lips of ardent young orators, who stressed his statement that it was impossible to unite men into stable nations unless such efforts were founded upon a recognition of the higher claims and obligations of humanity. And, inevitably, one still heard mid-Victorian phrases concerning the Parliament of Man. Certainly the desire to unite, to overcome differences, to accentuate likenesses, was everywhere a ruling influence in political affairs.

All this was, of course, in marked contrast to the impressions I received in the summer of 1919. Nationalism was still the great word, but with quite another content. Whereas I had formerly seen nationalistic fervor stressing likenesses and pulling scattered people together, it now seemed equally dogmatic and effective in pushing apart those who had once been combined—a whole ring of states was pulling out of mother-Russia, Bavaria was organizing her own government, and Italy in the name of nationalism was separating a line of coast from its Slavic hinterland, to mention but a few instances.

Had nationalism become overgrown and over-reached itself, or was it merely for the moment so self-assertive that the creative impulse was submerged into the possessive instinct? To be sure, there was the old type found in Poland gathering together her scattered people, although it was constantly explained that the new Poland was a valuable barrier and that the guaranty to defend France from attack extended to her outposts as well; apparently the motives were so inextricably mixed that it was impossible to make a fair statement. Then there was much disconcerting talk about coal and iron deposits in regard to all the new boundaries. Of course, the formation of Czecho-Slovakia had much about it of the old ideas. Cavour as well as Masurek had sent an army to fight in a cause not his own in order to secure recognition for his newly formed state, but on the other hand there was nothing corresponding to the solemn pride of the young Italians, thirty-five years before, that if Nice had to be given up, it had been relinquished as the result of a plebiscite and not of conquest.[1]

Had the notion of nationalism become institutionalized and dogmatized during thirty-five years, or was it only that now, older and disillusioned, I had been talking too much with other older and disillusioned people? Certainly not all the people with whom I talked had been disillusioned. In Paris one day I had been received by Venizelos, out of respect for my many Greek neighbors; he at least had seemed at ease and sure of his nationalism. He said that, thanks to the glorious traditions of Greece, she need put forth no claims because the people of Hellenic temper and aspirations were themselves asking to join their fortunes to hers. That sounded like the old talk, and it would have been a great comfort if I had not heard a Bulgarian later say that the Bulgarians of Thrace who were to be handed over to Greece could not understand why they had been given no opportunity to decide their own fate, and had become most restive and threatening. Signor Orlando, when he had received our committee on resolutions, had grown eloquent over Italia Irredenta and in sonorous phrases had set forth Italy's historic claim to the east coast of the Adriatic, her expanding commercial needs, and the military necessity for defensive ports. This was in contrast to the statement of an Albanian official I had met who was much worried over the surrender to Italy of the port of Avalona, which after all was little compared to the fate now awaiting Albania—a possible division between Greece and Servia.

In yet another contrast I recalled several Roumanians we had seen, who were proud of their Latin speech, so pleased that the Entente was ready to enforce their claims, that there was no Bolshevism within their borders; but later, in Holland, we were told of the Unitarians, the Calvinists, the Roman Catholics, the Lutherans, and Jews, long living in Transylvania, who were now all to be brought under the rule of the Greek church of Roumania. A distinguished Unitarian clergyman had just been released from prison but was still interned; the sectarian schools and seminaries had been closed that the children and young people might all be instructed by orthodox teachers of the national church. The whole situation was apparently still more complicated where the religious test yet remained as part of the national concept and imposed itself under the name of patriotism.

Was that perhaps the clue? Had nationalism become dogmatic, like the Greek church itself? Had it hardened in thirty-five years? It was as if I had left a group of early Christians and come back into a flourishing medieval church holding great possessions and equipped with well-tried methods of propaganda. Had the early spontaneity now changed into an authoritative imposition of power? Certainly one receives the impression every-where, in this moment when nationalism has been so tremendously stressed, that the nation demands worship and devotion for its own sake, as if it existed irrespective of the tests of reality. It requires unqualified obedience, denounces all who differ as heretics, insists that it alone has the truth, and exhibits all the well-known signs of dogmatism. It sends out its missionaries, and in Germany at least its state universities were analogous to the theological schools in which propagandists were carefully prepared.

This utter inability to see the "other side," to apply impartially the ordinary standards of just dealing, is a well-known characteristic of the dogmatic mind, as is a habit of considering ordinary standards inapplicable to a certain line of conduct because the motives inspiring it are above reproach.

Although dogmatic nationalism was curiously exaggerated in Germany, there was a similar manifestation of it last summer in the dealings of the Entente with their heretics, so to speak. We saw arriving in Rotterdam, from the German colonies in Africa, many families fleeing from their pioneer homes; in the railroad stations were posted directions for the fugitives coming from Posen, from Alsace, from Czecho-Slovakia, and from the Dantzig corridor. They told of prohibition of language, of the forced sale of real estate, of the confiscation of business, of the expulsion from university faculties, and the alienation of old friends. There was something about it all that was curiously anachronistic, like the expulsion of the Jews from Spain, of Cromwell's drive through Ireland, of the banishment of the Huguenots from France. It was as if nationalism had fallen back into an earlier psychology, exhibiting a blind intolerance which does not properly belong to these later centuries, as if it had become purely creedal. In fact, the very existence of these widespread nationalistic dogmas suggests one of those great historic myths which "large bodies of men are prone to make for themselves when they unite in a common purpose requiring for its consummation the thorough and efficient output of moral energy." It is said that the making and unmaking of these myths always accompanies a period of great moral awakening. Such myths are almost certain to outlast their social utility, and they frequently outlive their originators; as the myth of the Second Coming—evolved by the early Christians when only Heaven itself could contain their hopes—endured for a thousand years.

Upon my return to the United States last August I seemed to encounter a similar situation, affording the sharpest possible contrast to what had existed in the late eighties and throughout the nineties in the century of our youth.

In that remote decade the young men's movements in the church, in politics, in labor, in reform, in philanthropies as diverse as the Settlement and the Salvation Army, were all characterized by a desire to get back to the people, to be identified with the common lot; each of them magnified the obligation inherent in human relationships as such.

Americanism was then regarded as a great cultural task and we eagerly sought to invent new instruments and methods with which to undertake it. We believed that America could be best understood by the immigrants if we ourselves, Americans, made some sort of a connection with their past history and experiences. We extolled free association and the discussion of common problems as the basis of self-government and constantly instanced the New England town meeting. We especially urged upon the immigrant that he talk out his preconceived theories and untoward experiences. We believed that widespread discussion might gradually rid the country of the compulsions and inhibitions, the traditions and dogmatisms, under which newly arrived immigrants suffered. This method was not without its success.

We are, in fact, thirty years later, able to point to thousands of instances in which the radical young man, who most earnestly arraigned unjust conditions, has become the typical prosperous and bourgeois citizen, sometimes so complacent that one is moved to repeat the English statement that if a man is not too liberal when he is young, he becomes too reactionary when he is old.

The early settlements practically staked their future upon an identification with the alien and considered his interpretation their main business. We stuck to this at some cost, for we believed that especially in times of crisis it was our mission to interpret American institutions to those who were bewildered concerning them; although it was often apparently impossible for the overwrought community to distinguish between the public incident which the settlements were trying to understand and the attitude of the settlement itself.

At one such moment of public panic which had to do with a Russian immigrant twelve years ago, I wrote as follows:

> Every settlement has classes in citizenship in which the principles of American institutions are expounded, and of these the community,

as a whole, approves. But the settlements know better than anyone else that while these classes and lectures are useful, nothing can possibly give lessons in citizenship so effectively and make so clear the constitutional basis of a self-governing community as the current event itself. The treatment at a given moment of that foreign colony which feels itself outraged and misunderstood either makes its constitutional rights clear to it or forever confuses it on the subject.

The only method by which a reasonable and loyal conception of the government may be substituted for the one formed upon Russian experiences is that the actual experience of refugees with government in America shall gradually demonstrate what a very different thing government means here. Such an event as the Averbuch affair affords an unprecedented opportunity to make clear this difference and to demonstrate beyond the possibility of misunderstanding that the guaranty of constitutional rights implies that officialism shall be restrained and guarded at every point, that the official represents, not the will of a small representative body, but the will of the entire people, and that methods have therefore been constituted by which official aggression may be restrained.

These words written so recently already have a remote sound—to advocate the restraint of overzealous officialism as a method of Americanizing the alien would indeed be considered strange doctrine, for there is no doubt that at the present moment one finds in the United States the same manifestation of the world-wide tendency toward national dogmatism, the exaltation of blind patriotism above intelligent citizenship, as that evinced elsewhere.

Many of the liberties supposedly inherent in a system of self-government were doubtless necessarily cancelled during the war, but it is as if we were now wilfully prohibiting their normal and natural restoration.

Is it that the odium and animosity lavished upon the central Powers during the war has not yet spent itself and that, connected as it is with an intense nationalistic feeling, it is at present being turned upon the alien because he is perforce outside the national life? Because the emotions aroused by the war are not yet fully discharged do we see in the suspicion of the alien, the mania to hold him responsible for every strike and for every heresy, only a case of "balked disposition" so familiar to the psychologist?

To ticket bodies of men by a collective name, and to regard the men as we believe the principles deserve to be regarded, is an egregious blunder similar to that made by the dull schoolboy who obtains "his answer" in apples and pears because he has confused them with dollars and cents. When we confound doctrines with people, it shows that we understand neither one nor the other. Many men, not otherwise stupid, when they consider a doctrine detestable, failing to understand that changes can be made only by enlightening people, feel that they suppress the doctrine itself when they denounce and punish its adherents. They really are as confused as the aforementioned schoolboy.

The application of a collective judgment in regard to aliens in the United States is particularly stupid. The twenty-seven million people of foreign birth living among us are not only quite as diversified in their political opinions as those of us forming the remaining millions of the population, but they are in fact more highly differentiated from each other by race, tradition, religion, and European background than the rest of us can possibly be even though we are as diverse as "the cracker" in Georgia and the Yankee in Maine.

The task before us is to utilize properly the enthusiastic patriotism engendered by the war by making it more inclusive. The slogan, "To make the world safe for democracy," which transcended the nationalistic point of view, secured an unhesitating response and resulted in a great output of self-denying and heroic action upon an international scale. "To Americanize every alien in America" might become a compelling slogan, but it could be consummated only if our enthusiasm ran in wider channels and after the conception of nationalism has been transformed from a dogma of the eighteenth century to the evolutionary conception of the twentieth century.

Would it not be possible for students of the social order, such as are gathered here, to reassure a panic-stricken public? Could our fellow-citizens not be told how gradually social changes come about if free opportunity for modification is guaranteed? Quite as the capitalistic system so incompletely superseded the feudal system that great tracts of the feudal régime are still extant not only in European countries but in democratic England itself, doubtless the capitalistic system in turn will yield to a more socialized form of society so gradually and incompletely that the processes of change, as such, will be much more normal than a static condition, a standing still, could possible be.

It is certainly most important that Americans should not make a problem for themselves by placing an unfair emphasis upon differences which are inevitable in a country such as ours; that we should not get into the habit of arresting aliens for holding meetings of a type which have been held for many years without disorder and free from espionage. The altered equilibriums and distributions brought about by war opened avenues for a tremendously increased activity along the lines of teaching English and of classes in preparation for securing first and second citizenship papers. These are most praiseworthy, but we might discover many opportunities for mutual effort with the alien population and thus establish a new center and perspective. It is possible, for instance, to collect funds for starving Poland, Armenia, Roumania, indeed for almost any part of underfed Europe, in cooperation with bodies of citizens whose affections and interests are centered in those starving countries. As we undertake a mutual task of this sort "how our convulsive insistencies, how our antipathies and dreads of each other" would soften down; what tolerance and good humor, what willingness to live and let live, would inevitably emerge.

William James was constantly urging us to look at each other *sub specie aeternitatis;* perhaps that advice was never so needed as now.

Notes

1. Tomas Masurek (more properly, Masaryk; 1850–1937) was first president of the Czechoslovakian Republic created by the peace settlements that ended World War I. Masaryk had visited Chicago and toured Hull-House.

Part Three

INTRODUCTION: "WOMAN'S REMEMBERING HEART": BREAD-GIVING, PEACE-MAKING, AND SYMPATHY AS POLITICAL FORCES

TODAY JANE ADDAMS MIGHT BE called a "difference feminist," one who stresses the unique or particular features of what she takes to be women's nature, or women's way of being in the world, or women's ways of thinking and knowing. But this does not capture adequately Jane Addams's views on women and what they bring to the human story. In her own context, she embodies a strand called "social feminism." Social feminists saw great strengths in women's traditional, historic roles and contributions. Addams was deeply versed in some of the most important anthropological currents of her time that stressed the primordial nature of women's tasks—as mothers, agriculturists, weavers, healers, artisans, toolmakers, and builders of communities. She insisted that that history, and the knowledge and sociality and insight derived from it, could and should be brought to bear upon current social life and social problems. To compel women to occupy the precise molds carved out by and for men would do violence to all of us, as the gifts that women have to offer to the wider social world would never be accepted or appreciated.

For the most part, the traits Addams stressed involved women as first and foremost the nurturers of vulnerable human life and the primary force behind compelling settled social abodes so that they might more safely care for their children. Women precipitated the shift from hunting-gathering to agricultural ways of life. Women continue to labor under an overwhelming impulse to sustain human life, Addams believed, and this is

248

what makes war such a horror and a waste. Addams would have an explanation for why women tended to predominate in antiwar and pacifist organizations and efforts. Far more difficult for her was accounting for the many women—the majority, in fact—who supported the wars of their respective countries and fell into the same nationalist fervor that overtook their male compatriots. [1] For this she had no satisfactory explanation save for the general human tendency not to want to stand out from the rest and not to want, thereby, to brave public censure and opprobrium.

Women as the primary keepers of a tradition of "social amelioration" as the way to push for both national and international change is a view from which Addams never wavered. From her school days at Rockford Seminary to her last years, Addams saw women as the "bread-givers"— those destined to give bread to their households.[2] What changed over the years was the meaning and scope of "households." Addams was convinced that the household in her time had become so expansive as to cross international borders and to become a problem and impetus of global scope. What happens "over there" affects families "here."

The writings in this section speak to Addams's understanding of what women's social movements should embody; what women can and should do to forestall war; and, if war should be embarked upon, those ethical imperatives that should guide women's words and deeds during the course of a conflict. Most important among the latter is to try to prevent the worst damage from being done—to feed the hungry, to bind up the wounded, to heal broken bodies and spirits insofar as one can. Her activities before, during, and in the aftermath of World War I are remarkable. She struggled to prevent American entry into the war, not on behalf of the narrow isolationism embraced by many of those who spoke out against American participation but in the name of a new internationalism. Pacifism for her was not withdrawal but engagement: One was obliged to try to put one's ethical convictions into action to create international institutions that would generate and sustain alternative ways of dealing with enmity, hostility, and open conflict between nations. Her arguments presage the emergence into full view in our own era of international nongovernmental organizations that readily cross borders in the name of human rights, medical treatment, offering asylum, and preventing persecution.

Once the war broke out, and the United States under President Woodrow Wilson mistakenly, in Addams's view, committed itself to the conflict, she called upon women to revert to an undertaking based on "primitive and compelling motives"—those of feeding children; see "A Review of Bread Rations and Woman's Traditions," from her remarkable work *Peace and Bread in Time of War* (1922). Perhaps, she hoped against hope, an international ethic might arise from the "humble beginnings" of the woman feeding her tribe. She saw that ethic at work among the poor in the immigrant city as well and held out hope that the ways in which diverse immigrant communities found to cooperate with one another might serve as a model for a new ethic of international cooperation. It is easy enough to criticize this hope as naïve, presuming too smooth a transition from an urban city within the framework of a constitutional order to relations between sovereign nation-states. But Addams's essays are instructive because they remind us that earlier generations of Americans struggled with how to promote peace that wasn't what Addams called the "goody-goody" variety but was institutionally based and tougher-minded.

It was certainly her tough-mindedness and commitment to truth-telling that got her into enormous trouble and led to her denunciation as a traitor. In July 1915, she returned from an international congress of women held at The Hague. This conference brought together women from the warring nations as well as neutrals—the United States had not yet entered the war at this point—and led to a call for continuous mediation and arbitration of the dispute even as the war was going on. Addams gained remarkable access to the highest policymakers in the belligerent nations. She was part of one of two delegations from the Hague Conference that fanned out to capitals—London, Berlin, Budapest, Paris, Rome, and others—to make the case for arbitration.[3] Addams also had the opportunity to talk to combatants themselves. She observed something extraordinary that pointed, or so she concluded, to moral progress and was therefore a source of hope. What she had observed was that it was not easy for young men who had not grown up in warrior cultures to kill other human beings. She noted—in what became her "bayonet charge" speech delivered at Carnegie Hall, New York, on July 9, 1915— that soldiers knew when they were going to mount an offensive ("go over the top" and charge "the enemy") because alcoholic stimulants were distributed to the troops: rum, absinthe, some kind of "dope."[4] She added: "Well, now, think of that"—this from "Address of Miss Addams at Carnegie Hall" (1915), included here. The vast majority of her countrymen and women didn't want to "think of that" at all. Addams was denounced as calling soldiers cowards. But that hadn't been her point. Her point was the need to overcome collective inhibition at the thought of disemboweling another human being. Addams took this as a good sign about our human nature: We cavil when it comes to killing one another. But the damage to her public reputation had been done. Eventually she gave up trying to explain herself, for she knew the media, in her time newspapers, were determined simply to repeat the charges against her in order to maintain at fever pitch the incessant drumbeat of war. The loneliness of the pacifist during wartime, the pain at being separated from one's fellow citizens who are united by those bonds of fellowship Lincoln so eloquently limned in his Second Inaugural Address, were at times almost more than she could bear. She nearly fell into the stance she loathed: self-pity. But what kept her going were her continuing efforts on behalf of Hull-House, international peace efforts, and feeding the hungry in war-torn Europe both during and especially after the war, when the effects of the allied blockade of Germany led to widespread malnutrition and even starvation. Also helping to sustain her were her friendships, celebrated in her posthumously published book, *My Friend, Julia Lathrop* (1935). The war taxed Addams's well-developed capacity for raising moral and ethical questions without sliding into narrow moralisms. Her modulated stance is on display in a telling essay, "The Sheltered Woman and the Magdalen" (1913), a meditation on the social evil of prostitution. She assaults that evil, hating the sin, in the old formulation, even as she would love and not ostracize the sinner.

Notes

1. My book *Women and War* (New York: Basic Books, 1987; 2nd ed., University of Chicago Press, 1994) details the historic story of women, men, and war and the complex positions each has identified in the Western war story.

2. See her "Bread Givers," Junior Class Oration at Rockford Seminar, 1880, in Part One of this reader.

3. It is very difficult to imagine a group of amateur women gaining that sort of access today, especially in the very thick of things as a war is being fought. Addams's reputation was worldwide, and the knowledge that she was on personal terms with the U.S. president no doubt helps to account for her access to heads of foreign ministries.

4. On the pervasive, routine use of alcohol in battle situations, see John Keegan's classic *The Face of Battle* (New York: Penguin Books, 1983).

23

"WOMEN'S CONSCIENCE AND SOCIAL AMELIORATION"

WE HAVE BEEN ACCUSTOMED for many generations to think of woman's place as being entirely within the walls of her own household, and it is indeed impossible to imagine the time when her duty there shall be ended or to forecast any social change which shall ever release her from that paramount obligation. There is no doubt, however, that many women to-day are failing properly to discharge their duties to their own families and households simply because they fail to see that as society grows more complicated it is necessary that women shall extend her sense of responsibility to many things outside of her own home, if only in order to preserve the home in its entirety.

One could illustrate in many ways. A woman's simplest duty, one would say, is to keep her house clean and wholesome and to feed her children properly. Yet, if she lives in a tenement house, as so many of my neighbors do, she can not [sic] fulfill these simple obligations by her own efforts because she is utterly dependent upon the city administration for the conditions which render decent living possible. Her basement will not be dry, her stairways will not be fireproof, her house will not be provided with sufficient windows to give her light and air, nor will it be equipped with sanitary plumbing unless the Public Works Department shall send inspectors who constantly insist that these elementary decencies be provided. These same women who now live in tene-

---

Note: "Women's Conscience and Social Amelioration," in Charles Stelzle et al., *Social Application of Religion*, Merrick Lectures, Ohio Wesleyan University (Cincinnatti: Jennings and Graham, 1908).

252

ments, when they lived in the country, swept their own dooryards and either fed the refuse of the table to a flock of chickens or allowed it innocently to decay in the open air and sunshine; now, however, if the street is not cleaned by the city authorities, no amount of private sweeping will keep the tenant free from grime; if the garbage is not properly collected and destroyed, she may see her children sicken and die of diseases from which she alone is powerless to shield them, although her tenderness and devotion are unbounded; she can not even secure clean milk for her children, she can not provide them with fruit, which is untainted, unless the milk has been properly taken care of by the City Health Department, and the decayed fruit, which is so often placed upon sale in the tenement districts, shall have been promptly destroyed in the interest of public health. In short, if woman would keep on with her old business of caring for her house and rearing her children, she will have to have some conscience in regard to public affairs lying quite outside of her immediate household. The individual conscience and devaluation are no longer effective. In the tenement quarters of Chicago, I am sorry to say that last spring we had a spreading contagion of scarlet fever just at the time that the school nurses had been discontinued, because it was supposed that they were no longer necessary. If the women who sent their children to these schools had been sufficiently public-spirited they would have insisted that the schools be supplied with nurses in order that their own children might be protected from contagion. So I could go on with a dozen other illustrations. Women are pushed outside of the home in order that they may preserve the home. If they would affectively continue their old avocations, they must take part in the movements looking toward social amelioration.

On the other hand, this contention may be equally well illustrated by women who take no part in public affairs in order that they may give themselves exclusively to their own families, sometimes going so far as to despise their neighbors and their ways, and even to take a certain pride in being separate from them. Our own neighborhood was at one time suffering from a typhoid epidemic. Although the Nineteenth Ward had but one thirty-sixth of the population of Chicago, it had one-sixth of all the deaths in the city occurring from typhoid. A careful investigation was made by which we were able to establish a very close connection between the typhoid and a mode of plumbing which made it most probable that the infection had been carried by flies. Among the people who had been exposed to the infection was a widow who had lived in the ward for a number of years, in a comfortable little house which she owned. Although the Italian immigrants were closing in all around her, she was not willing to sell her property and to move away until she had finished the education of her children, because she considered that her paramount duty. In the meantime she held herself quite aloof from her Italian neighbors and their affairs. Her two daughters were sent to an Eastern college; one had graduated, the other had still two years before she took her degree, when they came home to the spotless little house and to their self-sacrificing mother for the summer's holiday. They both fell ill,—not because their own home was not clean, not because their mother was not devoted, but because next door to them and also in the rear were wretched tenements and because the mother's utmost efforts could not keep the infection out of her own house. One daughter died; and one recovered, but was an invalid for two years following. This is, perhaps, a fair illustration of the futility of the individual conscience when woman insists upon isolating her family from the rest of the community and its interests. The result is sure to be a pitiful failure.

In the process of socialization of their affairs, women might have received many suggestions from the changes in the organization of industry which have been going on for the last century. Ever since steam power has been applied to the processes of spinning and weaving, woman's old traditional work has been slowly but inevitably slipping out of the household into the factory. The clothing is not only spun and woven but largely sewed by machinery; the household linen, the preparation of grains, the butter and cheese have also passed into the factory, and, necessarily, a certain number of women have been obliged to follow their work there, although it is doubtful, in spite of the large number of factory girls, whether women now are doing as large a proportion of the world's work as they used to do. If we contemplate the many thousands of them who enter industry and who are working in factories and shops, we at once recognize the great necessity there is that older women should feel interested in the conditions of industry. According to the census reports, there are in the United States more than five million self-supporting women. Most of them are between the ages of sixteen and twenty-four, so that when we say working-women we really mean working-girls. It is the first time in history that such numbers of young girls have been permitted to walk unattended on city streets and to work under alien roofs. The very fact that these girls are not going to remain in industry permanently makes it more important that some one should see to it that they shall not be incapacitated for their future family life because they work for exhausting hours and under unsanitary conditions. One would imagine that as our grandmothers guarded the health and morals of the young women who spun and wove and sewed in their household, so the women of to-day would feel equally responsible for the young girls who are doing the same work under changed conditions. This would be true if women's sense of obligation had modified and enlarged as the social conditions changed, so that she might naturally and almost imperceptibly have inaugurated the movements for social amelioration in the line of factory legislation and shop sanitation. That she has not done so is doubtless due to the fact that her conscience is slow to recognize any obligation outside of her own family circle and because she was so absorbed in her own affairs that she failed to see what the conditions outside actually were. As one industry after another has slipped from the household; as the education of her children has been more and more transferred to the school, so that now children of four years old begin to go to the kindergarten, the woman has been left in a household of constantly narrowing interests.

Possibly the first step towards restoration is publicity as to industrial affairs, for we are all able to see only those things to which we bring the "informing mind." Perhaps you will permit me to illustrate from a group of home-keeping women who became interested in the problem of child labor. I was at one time a member of the Industrial Committee of the General Federation of Women's Clubs, which is, as you know, an association of women's clubs from all parts of the United States. We were very much interested in finding out how much child labor prevailed in the various States in which no legislation had been passed for the protection of children. We sent out questionnaires to all the women's clubs, and among others we received a very interesting reply from a woman's club in Florida. We had asked that the club members count all of the children under fourteen who were at work in the factories and mills in the club vicinities. The Florida women sent back the reply that they had found three thousand children in the sugar factories, and they added that they were very sorry that we had not asked them about child labor earlier, because their Legislature would not convene for two years and there would be no chance until then to secure protective legislation. They evidently thought that it was very remiss on the part of the committee that they had not earlier called their attention to child labor conditions. The whole incident is a good illustration of the point we would make. These women had lived in the same place for years. The children had doubtless gone to work back and forth right under their windows, but they had never looked in order to count them and did not even know they were there. The Industrial Committee sent out a questionnaire which said, in effect, "Please look out of your windows and count the working-children." The club women suddenly waked up and bestirred themselves to protect the children they had thus discovered. Something of that sort goes on in every community. We see those things to which our attention has been drawn, we feel responsibility for those things which are brought to us as matters of responsibility. In what direction, then, should women at the present moment look towards a more effective amelioration for the many social ills which are all about us?

If they follow only the lines of their traditional activities, there are certainly three primary duties which we would all admit belong to even the most conservative women and which no one woman or group of women can adequately discharge, unless they join the more general movements looking toward social amelioration.

The first of these is a responsibility for the members of her own household, that they may be properly fed and clothed and surrounded by hygienic conditions.

The second is responsibility for the education of children, that they may be provided with good schools, or kept free from vicious influences on the streets, and as a natural result of this concern, that when they first go to work that they shall be protected from dangerous machinery and from exhausting hours.

The third is responsibility for the social standards of the community, implying some comprehension of the difficulties and perplexities of the newly arrived immigrant, and adequate provision for the cultivation of music and other art sources which the commonality may contain.

We have already touched upon the first line of obligation and the difficulty of securing pure food without the help of pure food laws on the part of State and federal authorities and the impossibility of keeping the tenement family in sanitary surroundings without the constant regulation on the part of city officials. If the public authorities are indifferent to wretched conditions, as they often are, the only effective way to secure their reform is by a concerted effort on the part of the women who are responsible for the households. Perhaps you will permit me to illustrate from the Hull House Woman's Club: One summer, fifteen years ago, we discovered the death rate in our ward for children under five years of age was far above the average, rating second highest of any ward in town. An investigation disclosed that, among other things, the refuse was not properly collected. The woman's club divided the ward into sections, and three times every week certain women went through each section in order to find out what could be done to make the territory clean. Of course it is not very pleasant to go up and down the alleys and get into trouble with people about garbage conditions; it takes a good deal of moral vigor and civic determination to do it effectively. Yet the members of the club did this day after day until they were able to gather sufficient material to dismiss three inspectors from office and finally to secure the appointment of a competent inspector. When the ward became cleaner, when the death rate fell month by month, and each health bulletin was read in the Woman's Club, all the members listened with breathless interest. I shall never forget the day, three years later, when the club broke into applause because the death rate of our ward had fallen to the average. They felt that they had been responsible in securing this result, that the neighborhood had been brought into a reasonable condition through their initiative and concerted effort. Of course, the household of each woman profited by the result, but it could not have been secured through the unaided effort of any one household. One might use, by way of illustration, the impossibility of knowing the sanitary conditions under which clothing is produced, unless women join together into an association like the Consumers' League, which supports officers whose business it is to inform the members of the league as to garments which are made in sweatshops and to indicate by a label those which are produced under sanitary conditions. Country doctors testify as to the outbreak of scarlet fever in remote neighborhoods each autumn, after the children have begun to wear the winter cloaks and overcoats which have been sent from infected city sweatshops. That their mothers mend their stockings and guard them from "taking cold" is not a sufficient protection when the tailoring of the family is done in a distant city under conditions which the mother can not possibly control. Sweatshop legislation and the organization of consumers' leagues are the most obvious lines of amelioration of those glaring social evils which directly affect family life.

The duty of the mother towards schools which her children attend is so obvious that it is not necessary to dwell upon it, but even this simple obligation can not be effectively carried out without some form of social organization, as the mothers' school clubs and mothers' congresses testify. But women are also beginning to realize that children need attention outside of school hours; that much of the petty vice in cities is merely the love of pleasure gone wrong, the over-restrained boy or girl seeking improper recreation and excitement. In Chicago a map has recently been made demonstrating that juvenile crime is decreasing in the territory surrounding the finely equipped playgrounds and athletic fields which the South Park Board three years ago placed in thirteen small parks. We know in Chicago, from ten years' experience in a juvenile court, that many boys are arrested from sheer excess of animal spirits, because they do not know what to do with themselves after school. The most daring thing the leader of a gang of boys can do is to break into an empty house, steal the plumbing fixtures and sell them for money with which to treat the gang. Of course that sort of thing gets a boy into very serious trouble, and is almost sure to land him in the reform school. It is obvious that a little collective study of the needs of the boys, a sympathetic understanding of the conditions under which they go astray, might save hundreds of them. Women traditionally have had an opportunity to observe the plays of children and the needs of growing boys, and yet they have done singularly little in this vexed problem of juvenile delinquency until they helped to inaugurate the juvenile court movement a dozen years ago; since then they have done valiant service, and they are at last trying to minimize some of the dangers of city life which boys and girls encounter; they are beginning to see the relation between public recreation and social morality. The women of Chicago are studying the effect of these recreational centers provided by the South Park Committee upon the social life of the older people who use them. One thing they have done is enormously to decrease the patronage of the neighboring saloons. Before we had these park houses, the saloon hall was hired for weddings and christenings, or any sort of an event which in the foreign mind is associated with general feasting, because the only places for hire were the public halls attached to the saloons. As you know, the saloon hall is rented free, with the understanding that a certain amount of money be paid across the bar; that is, the rent must be made up in other ways. The park hall, of course, is under no such temptation and, therefore, drinking has almost ceased at the parties held in the parks. If a man must go two or three blocks to get an alcoholic drink, and can step down-stairs to secure other refreshments, it goes without saying that in most cases he does the latter. The park halls close promptly at eleven o'clock. The city is, therefore, approaching the temperance problem from the point of view of substitution, which appears to some of us more reasonable than the solely restrictive method. Many of the larger movements towards social amelioration in which women are active have taken their rise from the interest the women felt in the affairs of the juvenile court, and yet this does not mean that collective effort minimizes individual concern. On the other hand, we often see a woman stirred to individual effort only after she has been brought into contact with the general movement. I recall a woman in the Hull House neighborhood who, although she had a large family of her own, took charge every evening of a boy whose mother scrubbed offices down-town every day from five o'clock in the afternoon until eleven at night. This kindly woman gave the boy his supper with her own children, saw that he got into no difficulty during the evening, and allowed him to sleep on the lounge in her sitting-room until his mother came by in the evening and took him home. After she had been doing this for about six months, I spoke to her about it one day and congratulated her on her success with the boy, who had formerly been a ward of the juvenile court. She replied that she had undertaken to help the boy because the juvenile court officer had spoken to her about him and had said that he thought she might be willing to help because he had observed her interest in juvenile court matters. Although the boy's mother was a neighbor of hers, she had not apparently seen her obligation to the lad until it had been brought home to her in this somewhat remote way. It is another illustration of our inability to see the duty "next to hand" until we have become alert through our knowledge of conditions in connection with the larger duties. We would all agree that social amelioration must come about through the efforts of many people who are moved thereto by the compunction and stirring of the individual conscience, but we are only beginning to understand that the individual conscience will respond to the special challenge and will heed the call largely in proportion as the individual is able to see the social conditions and intelligently to under-stand the larger need. Therefore, careful investigation and mutual dis-cussion is perhaps the first step in securing the legal enactment and civic amelioration of obvious social ills.

The third line of effort which every community needs to have carried on if it would obtain a social life in any real sense. I may perhaps illus-trate from experiments at Hull House, not because they have been es-pecially successful, but because an attempt has there been made to de-velop the social resources of an immigrant community.

If an historian, one hundred years from now, should write the social history of America, he would probably say that one of the marked characteristics of our time was the arrival of immigrants at the rate of a million a year and the fact that the American people had little social connection with them. If the historian a hundred years hence used the same phrases which the psychologists now use—perhaps they will get over them by that time—he would say that our minds seem to be "in-hibited" by certain mental concepts which apparently prevented us from forming social relations with immigrants. What are these mental concepts, this state of mind which keeps us apart from the immigrant populations? The difference in language, in religion, in history and tra-dition always makes social intercourse difficult, and yet every year peo-ple go to Europe for the very purpose of overcoming that difference and of seeing the life of other nations. They discover that people may differ in language and education and still possess similar interests. We would say that a person who went to Europe and returned without that point of view had made rather a failure of his trip. In the midst of American cities there are various colonies of immigrants who represent European life and conditions, and that we who stay at home know so little about them is only because we do not make the adequate effort. We have in the neighborhood of Hull House a colony of about five thousand Greeks, who once produced in the Hull House theater the classic play of "Ajax," written by Sophocles. The Greeks were very much surprised when the professors came from the various universities in order to follow the play in the Greek text from books which they brought with them. The Greeks were surprised, because they did not know there were so many people in Chicago who cared for ancient Greece. The professors in turn were astonished to know that the mod-ern Greeks were able to give such a charming interpretation of Sophocles. It was a mutual revelation on both sides. On one side the Greeks felt more nearly a part of America, and on the other side the professors felt that perhaps the traditions had not been so wholly broken in the case of Greece as they had been led to believe. It would have been difficult for the Greeks to have made for themselves all the preliminary arrangements for this play; they needed some people to act as ambassador, as it were, and yet they themselves possessed this tradition, the historic background, this beauty of classic form, which our American cities so sadly need and which they were able to supply.

We may illustrate from Italy, if you please, the very word which charms us so completely when we hear it on the other side of the Atlantic, and yet it means so little to us in our own country. These colonies of Italians might yield to our American life something very valuable if their resources were intelligently studied and developed. They have all sorts of artistic susceptibility, and even trained craftsmanship, which is never recovered for use here. I tell the story sometimes of an Italian who was threatened with arrest by his landlord because he had ornamented the doorpost of his tenement with a piece of beautiful wood carving. The Italian was very much astonished at this result of his attempt to make his home more beautiful. He could not understand why his landlord did not like it; he said that he had carved a reredos in a church in Naples, which Americans came to look at and which they thought was very beautiful; the man was naturally bewildered by the contrast between the appreciation of his work in Naples and Chicago. And yet we need nothing more in America than that same tendency to make beautiful the surroundings of our common life. The man's skill was a very precious thing, and ought to have been conserved and utilized in our American life. The Italians in our neighborhood occasionally agitate for the erection of a public wash-house. They do not like to wash in their own tenements; they have never seen a washing tub until they came to America, and find it very difficult to use it in the restricted space of their little kitchens and to hang the clothes within the house to dry. They say that in Italy washing clothes is a pleasant task. In the villages the women all go to the stream together; in the towns, to the public wash-house, and washing, instead of being lonely and disagreeable, is made pleasant by cheerful conversation. It is asking a great deal of these women to change suddenly all their habits of living, and their contention that the tenement house kitchen is too small for laundry work is well taken. If women in Chicago knew the needs of the Italian colony and were conversant with their living in Italy, they, too, would agitate for the erection of public wash-houses for the use of Italian women. Anything that would bring cleanliness and fresh clothing into the Italian households would be a very sensible and hygienic measure. It is, perhaps, asking a great deal that the members of the city council should understand this, but surely a comprehension of the needs of these women and efforts towards ameliorating their lot might be regarded as a matter of conscientious duty on the part of American women.

One constantly sees also, in the Italian colony, that sad break between the customs of the older people and their children, who, because they have learned English and certain American ways, come to be half ashamed of their parents. It does not make for good Americans that the children should thus cut themselves away from the European past. If the reverse could be brought about; if the children, by some understanding of the past, could assist their parents in making the transition to American habits and customs, it would be most valuable from both points of view. An Italian girl who has gone to the public school and has had lessons in cooking and the household arts, will help her mother much more and connect the entire family with American foods and household habits more easily, if she understands her mother's Italian experiences. That the mother has never baked bread in Italy—only mixed it in her own house, and then taken it out to the village oven— makes it all the more necessary that her daughter should understand the complication of a cooking stove and introduce her to its mysteries. At the same time, the daughter and her American teacher could get something of the historic sense and background in the long line of woman's household work by knowing this primitive woman and learning from her some of the old recipes and methods which have been preserved among the simplest people because of their worth. Take the girl who learns to sew in the public school, whose Italian mother is able to spin with the old stick spindle, reaching back to the period of Homer and David; who knows how to weave and to make her own loom; such a girl's mother could bring a most valuable background into a schoolroom over-filled with machine-made products, often shoddy and meaningless. As the old crafts may be recovered from a foreign colony and used for the edification of our newer cities, so it is possible to recover something of the arts. We have in Hull House a music school in which some of the foreign-born children have been pupils for twelve years. These children often discover in the neighboring foreign colonies old folk songs which have never been reduced to writing. The music school reproduces these songs and invites the older people to hear them; their pleasure at such a concert is quite touching as they hear the familiar melodies connecting them with their earliest experiences, reminiscent perhaps of their parents and grandparents.

After all, what is the function of art but to preserve in permanent and beautiful form those emotions and solaces which cheer life, make it kindlier and more comprehensible, lift the mind of the worker from the harshness of his task, and, by connecting him with what has gone before, free him from a sense of isolation and hardship. Many American women of education are beginning to feel a sense of obligation for work of this sort. If women have been responsible in any sense for that gentler side of life which softens and blurs some of the conditions of life, then certainly they have a duty to perform in the large foreign colonies which make up so large a part of the American cities. I am sure illustrations occur to all of you as to what might be done in this third line of responsibility, for, whatever we think as to a woman's fitness to secure betterment through legal enactment, we must agree that responsibility for social standards has always been hers.

In closing, may I recapitulate that if woman would fulfill her traditional responsibility to her own children; if she would educate and protect from danger the children in the community, who now work in factories although they formerly worked in households; if she would in any sense meet the difficulties which modern immigration has brought us; then she must be concerned to push her conscience into the general movements for social amelioration.

24

"THE SHELTERED WOMAN AND THE MAGDALEN"

A GREAT ENGLISH PREACHER HAS SAID that life holds for every man one searching test of the sincerity of his religious life, and that, although this test is often absurdly trivial, to encounter it is to "fall from grace." We all know these tests: a given relative or familiar friend has an irritating power of goading us into anger or self-pity; a certain public movement inevitably hardens us into a contemptuous mood of all uncharitableness; one particular type of sinner fills us with an unholy sense of superior virtue.

If we may assume that society itself is subject to one such test—if it, too, possesses a touchstone which reveals its inmost weakness and ultimate uncharitableness—may we not say that its supreme test is the existence of the social evil, and that the sorry results of that test are registered in the hypocrisy and hardness of heart of the average good citizen toward the so-called "fallen woman"? May we not claim that in consequence of this attitude the social evil has come to be regarded as a vice which cannot be eradicated, as a sin which cannot be forgiven? . . .

This attitude has become so established in our political affairs that any probe made by a grand jury or a special commission into the vice conditions of a city uniformly discovers that the social evil is the root source of political corruption. Although laws declaring it illegal have been placed upon the statute books, and even the hardiest politician dares not repeal them, nevertheless, backed by a universal cynicism, the

Note: "The Sheltered Woman and the Magdalen," *Ladies Home Journal*, vol. 30 (November 1913).

politicians openly consider the laws too impracticable to be enforced, and not only deliberately decide not to enforce them, but also actually define the conditions under which law-breaking is permitted.

To permit such license in one particular is, of course, utterly to demoralize the entire police service. This police connivance at the social evil inevitably creates a necessity for both graft and blackmail; the graft is easy because the owner of an illicit business expects to pay for it, and every politician to the tiptop of the administration receives his share of the illicit fund. In connection with this a municipal blackmail is also established which just escapes legal recognition. The social evil, protected by a thick hedge of secrecy, imperceptibly renewing itself through changing administrations, is the one fixed point of maladministration— the unbreakable bank to which every corrupt politician may repair when in need of funds. The corruption spreads under the trio of the brothel, the saloon and the gambling hall. . . . The men who consider the segregated distinct as a legitimate source of revenue in a thousand ways fleece the decent taxpayers who contemptuously refuse to think of these disagreeable matters, and the very existence of the social evil, through one administration to another, frustrates and overthrows all genuine movements for civic reform. . . .

While this contempt of the fallen woman is registered in the lax administration of good laws it also finds expression in the laws of the land which accord her scant justice or redress and furthermore becomes registered in the ethical code of contemporary society held by good women as well as men. Women, kindly toward all other human creatures, become hard and hostile to young girls who, in evil houses, are literally beaten and starved by the dissolute men whom they support. Kind-hearted women could not brook these things; their hearts would break had they not been trained to believe that virtue itself demanded from them first ignorance and then harshness. This contempt of good women for their erring sister, this desire to keep their own family free from contamination regardless of any wrong to the outcast, has become the base of a caste system in morality which has the narrowness and prejudice of all caste distinctions. Women have yet to learn that virtue cannot be preserved by merely asserting its superiority to vice, and that the supreme test of a good woman may come to be her willingness to lift up those who have been relegated to the very bottom of society.

At the Congress of Religions which was held during the World's Fair in Chicago a man from India told the following story: A woman, after death, found herself at the very bottom of that pit which in almost every religion in the world is reserved for the wicked. When, after many years, she felt that she could endure it no longer she sent up to the throne in Heaven one petition after another, begging that she might be released from her fearful punishment. The story goes on to relate that at last a message came down from the high throne saying that her petition would be considered if she could think of one unselfish act which she had ever done and would send up the record of that act.

The woman thought and thought a very long time before she could remember one unselfish deed, but she finally recalled that one day when she had been getting some carrots ready for dinner a beggar had come by asking for good and she had given him a defective carrot. She sent up the pitiful record of her one unselfish deed with some fear and misgiving, realizing that she had given the carrot to the beggar because she did not want it herself. Nevertheless she was told that she would be given a chance, and it came in the shape of a carrot tied to a string, which was lowered until it reached the bottom of the pit. She was told to take hold of it and that it might be the good deed would pull her up. She seized hold of the carrot, the string began to wind and she began to rise. All was going well until she looked back and saw some one else clinging to her, and so on all the way down until a large group of people were being pulled up with her. Much alarmed she called out. "This is my carrot; let go at once; it is not strong enough for so many, and it will surely break if you all take hold." Of course as soon as she had uttered the words the carrot did break and they all went down together.

This old tale from India may illustrate the responsibility we all have for the wicked, and that no one is good enough to rise to Heaven unless she is concerned to carry with her those who are the very bottom of the lowest pit. The definition of unselfishness is enlarged to include the outcast—that she is not to be despised and put away as an enemy to society, but, on the contrary, that she is to be understood and helped, and wherever possible brought back into a normal life.

Contemporary women, as well as men, ought to find it much easier at the present moment to meet this supreme test of religion than it has ever been before in the long history of civilization. A new publicity in regard to the social evil is a striking characteristic of the last decade. This publicity has disclosed the fact that thousands of these so-called "fallen" women are piteously young, and that thousands of others lost their chastity when they were helpless, unthinking little girls, many of them through members of their own households in that crowing which life in a large tenement postulates.

Not long ago a young girl of sixteen was sent by her mother to Chicago to a white-slave trader who arranged to meet her at a given place in one of the large railroad stations. She came into the city by train, although she had been brought across the state line in an automobile, to avoid the Interstate Pandering laws which imply the use of a common carrier. The careful plot failed somewhere, and when the man did not appear she came directly to Hull-House because in the house kept by her mother the girls had been in the habit of pretending that they were related to people whose names they had seen in the newspapers, and as I had figured as a hypothetical relative she knew by name and that I lived in the Settlement. The girl's story—which she gave most reluctantly—was corroborated by officials, and revealed the fact that for four years she had been subjected to unspeakable experiences although she scarcely knew what they all meant. She at once responded to an opportunity for education, and the two years since, which she has spent in a convent school, shows that she is gentle and refined and possessed of unusual ability.

Such a girl may be an exception, but her very existence indicates that girls of this type are found in the life, and that a number of women have entered against their own volition. . . .

In connection with this new publicity, there has been disclosed the existence of a widespread commerce organized for business profits. The man who owns the house, the one who procures the girl, the one styled her "protector," the agent who supplies her clothing—all exploit her, each for his personal gain. Even the women in charge of the houses, who from the days of Babylon have reaped large profits, are now becoming merely the paid agents of an organized business, much as a saloon-keeper is engaged by a brewery.

The girl upon whom all this activity rests, young for the most part, stands in the middle of a complex system which she does not understand. Having invested so much money in the enterprise commercial organizations are obliged continually to trump up business in order to secure enough men to make their business profitable, and they deliberately lure them through alcohol and other vicious devices.

The success of the business, which in Chicago pays its promoters fifteen million dollars a year, is founded upon the hypocrisy and self-righteousness of the decent citizen, and it continues to capture girls, to ruin young men, to spread disease, and to corrupt city politics, because good citizens do not consider it part of their religious obligation to face it openly and to undertake its abolition. . . .

The new publicity in regard to the social evil in itself should force the church into radical action; understanding of the sinner has ever been essential to his forgiveness; knowledge of convictions has ever preceded social reform. If it is discovered that the brothels are filled with overfatigued and underpaid girls procured by young men "too poor to marry," then it is obviously the business of the church to secure legal enactment which shall limit the hours of labor, fix a minimum wage and prescribe the conditions under which young people may be permitted to work. If it is found that the army of girls and men required in this vile business is constantly recruited from the young heedlessly looking for pleasure in vicious dance halls, on crowded excursion boats, in careless amusement parks, then it is the obligation of the church to guard and cleanse these pleasures and to provide others free from dangers.

If the new publicity continues to disclose on the one hand an enormous number of little children who are pushed into an evil life through the very congestion of the city's population, and discloses on the other hand a large number of young people in dreary country communities who are drawn into vicious practices through sheer reaction from the monotony and grayness of their lives, then a Nation-wide church in the crowded city must advocate measures to lessen the sensational evils of overcrowding, and at the same time it must offer social organization to all the solitary young people of the countryside. If it is made clear that youth is ensnared because of its ignorance of the most fundamental facts of life, then it is the duty of the church to promote public instruction for girls and boys which shall dignify sex knowledge and free it from all indecency. If it is found that degenerate children born of diseased and vicious parents become an easy prey to evil-minded men, it is clearly the obligation of the church to challenge all applicants for marriage, and to work out through modern eugenics the admonition of the

Hebrew teachers as to the responsibility unto the third and fourth generation. . . .

All over the world are traces of a changed attitude toward the social evil. Not only are American cities, such as Chicago, recommending restrictive measures looking toward final abolition, but European cities, such as Vienna, are also doubting the value of their long-established regimentation, and are therefore logically facing the same conclusion.

The medical profession is abandoning its century-old position of secrecy and connivance; leading educators are at last urging adequate instruction for all youth. Shall not the church accept the challenge and bear a valiant part in this modern crusade, whose call has come, not from a solitary hermit, as did the call for the Crusade long ago, but from a multitude of warm-hearted youth who from our streets "paved with peril, teeming with mischance," still eagerly clamor for a world made fit and fair for their budding lives?

As women all over the world are each year securing a larger measure of political power may we not expect them gradually to remedy the legislative and administrative wrongs which have grown up around the social evil and which serve to shield it from direct remedial action? Society, like the individual, always finds the contemporary test of it, spirituality, the most difficult. While it easily boasts of those already past and is unduly confident of the future it too often fails to meet the test which faces it at a given moment and which best reveals its genuine courage and sincerity.

25

⌦

"INTRODUCTION" (FROM *The Second Twenty Years at Hull-House*)

The following statement was made concerning a young Frenchman, who, in the spring of 1914, recorded his last reflection upon life:

> When we are young we do not immediately know where we shall hear those voices of our own time to which our virginal hearts will deeply and instinctively respond. They must come from figures of our own time, older than we are or they would not have found expression, but not old enough to have "arrived," so that we do not at once learn of their existence. Our teachers, as well as popular fame, thrust upon us the figures of the last generation, by whom they had themselves been inspired in youth, and these are, in general, precisely the figures to whom our instincts are most rebellious.

IT IS ALWAYS DIFFICULT for a given individual to know just when he has become "a figure of the past generation" against whom youth's instincts rebel, and I confess now to a sense of risk in writing of another twenty years—especially with autobiographical notes—the end of which brings me so very close to threescore years and ten.

But, after all, the young compose a smaller proportion of the world, year after year, as the prolongation of life increases and we are authori-

---

Note: "Introduction," in *The Second Twenty Years at Hull-House, September 1909 to September 1929 with a Record of Growing World Consciousness* (New York: Macmillan, 1930).

tatively told that never before, in the history of mankind, were there so many people—both actually and proportionately—living upon the face of the earth who are more than sixty-five years old, as are living here at present. Not that we have done very much with that increased span of life to feed our pride! In fact, the young people themselves in moments of exasperation have been known to say that many of the follies of which they are accused in cabarets and other frivolous places are really affected by older people who, equipped with the foolish clothing and the brilliant complexions of the young, are dancing and drinking to an extent that fills the actual young with dismay, and that most unfairly discredits the coming generation. Although these excessive imitators of youth may be few in number, they are symptomatic of a widespread tendency to prolong unduly the springtime of life.

Is it not possible for this newly enlarged elderly group, or at least for some of the individuals who compose it, to refrain from imitating another group simply because the latter possesses the natural glamour of youth; isn't it possible for each group to make its own contribution, if only because we know that the present moment—which after all must concern us more than the disappointing past or the iridescent future—is in the hands of the mixed lot of us; that we are of all ages and of all degrees of social usefulness; that happily the generations are never clean-cut, but are always inextricably mixed from the new-born babe to the admitted octogenarian. If these intermingling groups must push the world along as best they may, it is hardly fair for one of them, the older at that, to lazily pull out by pretending that it isn't there.

I am confident, therefore, that it is dangerous to insist upon simulating the ardors of youth, as if to be young were a virtue in itself, and that we may thus easily upset the balance; that if we carefully suppress all differences with youth even those inescapable differences of old age, we run the risk of destroying a form of variety which has a tried social value.

Our hope of achievement apparently lies in a complete mobilization of the human spirit, using all our unrealized and unevoked capacity. The situation requires limitless patience and comprehension, which ought to be supplied more readily by those who have been subjected to life's training.

One happy result has issued from the current situation. The freshly accumulated group of the elderly at least avoid giving advice, and sedulously refrain from making critical comments upon the passing show. Perhaps this multitude of "sixty-fivers and past sixty-fivers" merely shirk formulating their empirical knowledge, or have never learned to reflect, or their vision has never become sufficiently keen and purged to attract the favorable notice of the young. More likely, they have failed to demand the truth from life and are therefore disconcerted when they find that youth will brook no insincerity and is also most impatient of secondhand opinions and platitudes.

Even as I write these words I reflect that there is always a chance that the garnered wisdom of the old may turn out to be no wisdom at all, and there is an awful possibility that the aged in their strategic position of domestic tyranny and general dogmatism will retard all attempts at progress simply because such attempts necessarily imply a change in the customs with which they have been long familiar. I uneasily recall what happens in certain Oriental countries, where old age claims all its prerogatives. During a journey I once made around the world, I became much discouraged, suffragist as I was, concerning the influence of old women; those in China insisting that little girls' feet must be firmly bound, although the practice had been forbidden by law and hotly repudiated by all of Young China; the old women in India insisting upon purdah at home and veils in the street, although some of the Indian women were voting and sitting as members of the City Council of Bombay; the old women in Turkey and eastern Europe—but why continue this doleful recital, when it is quite obvious that if, or rather when, old women actually do exert themselves they become a social menace? Probably there is nothing more dangerous in the world than the leadership of prestige based solely upon the authority of age.

In contrast to this eastern attitude, I recall an eightieth birthday party, given in Chicago long ago, at a table garlanded with eighty roses and seating eighty guests. Some one asked the birthday child how she had always kept so young and she promptly replied, that it was because she had always adopted an unpopular cause; first, the abolition of slavery, when, as a young woman, she had lived in the pre-war South, and then votes for women which she thought would last her to the end. She explained that no one put you on a pedestal and treated you with respect just because you were old, if you were the advocate of an unpopular cause—you had to defend it and discuss it and take your chances with the wits of the young.

One thing is clear out of all the contradictions; that the task of youth is not only its own salvation but the salvation of those against whom it rebels, but in that case there must be something vital to rebel against and if the elderly stiffly refuse to put up a vigorous front of their own, it leaves the entire situation in a mist. Even if we, the elderly, have nothing to report but sordid compromises, nothing to offer but a disconcerting acknowledgment that life has marked us with its slow stain, it is still better to define our position. With all our errors thick upon us, we may at least be entitled to the comfort of Plato's intimation that truth itself may be discovered by honest reminiscence.

I shall attempt therefore in this record of the Second Twenty Years at Hull-House, to avoid the pretensions both of old age and of youth, in the only way possible, by setting down as carefully as I may what I deem significant in the way of experience or reflection from September 1909, to September, 1929.

The period easily divides into two decades, the first of which subdivides into five years of peace and five years of war. The second decade is continuously filled with the effect of the gregarious panic, which inevitably follows war and the rumors of its attendant revolutions.

So closely is the life of the individual or that of a public-spirited group in the modern world identified with the events enacted upon a larger arena, that such a division of the two decades, I am quite sure, seems natural to all of us.

I am honestly sorry to write so much in this book of the effects of the world war. It is idle to speculate on what an infinitesimal unit like Hull-House or any other of the millions of units composing the social order, would have been like if the world war had never taken place. But whether we care for it or not, our own experiences are more and more influenced by the experiences of widely scattered people; the modern world is developing an almost mystic consciousness of the continuity and interdependence of mankind. There is a lively sense of the unexpected and yet inevitable action and reaction between ourselves and all the others who happen to be living upon the planet at the same moment.

Perhaps no presentation is so difficult as that which treats of the growth of a new consciousness, and while I have no doubt as to the existence of this nascent world consciousness, I may so easily fail to make it clear in the following pages that I venture to quote a statement here in regard to it from one of those minds which feels the stimulus of wide surroundings and whose generous sympathies include all kinds of people. George Russell,[1] A E, as he is more generally known, after a journey in the United States in 1928 wrote in *The Irish Statesman* as follows:

What is arising or to arise in the States? I think of it as some mood of planetary consciousness. I cannot get a more precise word. . . . The biological ancestors of the people in the States are European, Asiatic, African, with some survival of the aboriginal American. Nature will find in this multitude the materials to blend to make a more complex mentality than any known before, with wide-reaching affinities in the subconscious. I notice, too, that the writers who form the spiritual germ-cell of American culture—Emerson, Whitman, Thoreau, and their school—think and write of themselves almost as naturally being children of earth, as being American citizens. That group manifest in their writings something like a cosmic consciousness. American statesmen, too, are beginning to formulate world policies, leagues of nations, world peace, a sense of duty to the world struggling up through the intense self-interest and preoccupation with their own affairs. The American benevolence is world-wide. The Rockefeller Foundation thinks of the health of humanity, not merely of the American people. . . . A planetary consciousness I surmise will grow up through centuries in this astonishing people, warring with its contrary idea which also has its own meaning and just basis. Our human faculties are burnished by their struggle with opposites in ourselves. And it is no less true of the ideas which become dominant in great civilizations. I imagine centuries in which in the higher minds in the States a noble sense of world duty, a world consciousness, will struggle with mass mentality and gradually pervade it.

It lies with us who are here now to make this consciousness—as yet so fleeting and uncertain—the unique contribution of our time to that small handful of incentives which really motivate human conduct. Such a motive has certainly been a definite factor in the last twenty years at Hull-House, and an effort to define it as well as to illustrate it, must be my apology for much of the succeeding pages which may seem unduly autobiographical and also far afield from the corner of Halsted and Polk streets, Chicago.

Notes

1. George Russell (1865–1935), Irish writer.

26

⌘

"ASPECTS OF THE WOMAN'S MOVEMENT"

THERE ARE CERTAIN DAYS which remain in our memories because we then seem to have broken through into that reality which ever lies beneath the outward appearance. I spent such a day in the summer of 1913 with delegates to a convention of the International Suffrage Alliance, traveling from Vienna by way of the Danube to the beautiful old city of Budapest. These women from many nations sitting upon the deck of a river steamer felt that curious stimulus which comes from the discovery of like-mindedness between people of varied nationalities. If culture is a combination of traits of purely local origin with those supplied by race diffusion, building up that totality which we call the unique contribution of a given race or nation, then there must be the same interest in discovering the underlying likenesses as there is in the patriotic cherishing of distinctive national traits. Whatever the reason, that day was one of those moments described by Virginia Woolf, who tells us that reality "seems to be something very erratic and very undependable, sometimes it seems to dwell in shapes too far away from us to discern what their nature is, nevertheless whatever it touches, it fixes and makes permanent." Not a breath, not a tremor of the future, ruffled the polished surface of the Danube on that summer's day. There was no haunting apprehension that these bordering states within a year's time would be firing the opening shots of the most terrible war recorded in history.

Note: "Aspects of the Woman's Movement," in *The Second Twenty Years at Hull-House, September 1909 to September 1929 with a Record of Growing World Consciousness* (New York: Macmillan, 1930), chapter 4.

Did the day acquire its curious significance later, did the glamour come in retrospect after we had realized that the end of this peaceful scene had been so near? Was it etched upon our memories as the aspect of a friend whom we have seen for the last time becomes unforgettable, not less but more impressive if we do not know that death is coming so soon?

The stories of the river told by our hostesses increased in romantic content as we approached the old cities of Buda and Pest; the tales extolled the Hungarian prowess which through the years of the Turkish wars had saved Europe from Asiatic control. Such wars seemed to us as remote as the conquests of Alexander or as the Crusades—fit subjects for poetic recital. It was the portrayal of a past grown tranquil because it was apart from life. The heroes belonged to other centuries far from our own. We could not anticipate the rough measure and poignant reproach with which our contemporary young poets would deal with war nor could we then understand that it is "only the living poets who express a feeling that is actually being made and torn out of us at the moment. We do not recognize it as poetry in the first place and too often for some reason we fear it."

Curiously enough however, a long discussion on the use of force, of military tactics versus constitutionalism, was carried on during that voyage on the Danube. Only the day before, news had been received of Emily Davison's death, incurred in her efforts to take a message to the King concerning Votes for Women.[1] It was part of the campaign carried on by a section of the English suffragists, which was at its height in that summer of 1913. Other women seeking to exercise the ancient right of petition had been intercepted by the police. Emily Davison believed that utilizing the great day of the Derby, when all England of social and political importance was gathered together, if a woman should interrupt the race and, as was probable, should be trampled to death by the panic-stricken horses that the King himself would have to know the reason; that her petition would thus reach him at last and that it would not fail because death itself would lift the minds of all the spectators to that "High Tribunal where justice is never withheld." To the friends of Emily Davison her death was a supreme illustration of their endeavor to bring the question of votes for women before the public in dramatic form. They believed that the news would travel around the world that a human life, for the sake of a great cause, had been given freely with such heroism.

Several of the women on board the Danube boat had not only known Emily Davison, but had also seen her in the hospital after the accident. From their background of personal friendship and understanding, she seemed to them to have been a martyr in the truest sense of the word, and they urged that a memorial meeting be held in Budapest preceding the convention. The English women on the boat who represented the Constitutional Society felt that any such meeting would be a great mistake, and a discussion was naturally precipitated in regard to the whole question of militant tactics. It is interesting to find that the division, *pro* and *con*, did not run along the line of reckless youth and conservative age. Among the Constitutionalists as among the Militants were many young and charming women, ardent in their advocacy of parliamentary methods. Maude Royden, whom I then met for the first time, took the position that men and women could not use force to settle a difference between them unless women were ready to lose, for certainly in the use of force men were admittedly superior![2] That the vote itself had been an historic effort to substitute reason for the sword. There were also those who advocated a passive resistance, among them Mrs. Cobden Sanderson, representing the Tax Resistance League—a body of women refusing to pay taxes to a government in which they were not directly represented. Of the able talk of these women on the Danube boat who came from many countries I recall that of a distinguished scholar quoting doctrines of Tolstoy, reminding us that the early Christians had abjured the use of force for three hundred years and that the later church had failed to work out a technique for applying this basic Christian teaching to political affairs. She somewhat wistfully expressed the hope that when Christian women received the vote they might at least experiment in this direction.

That convention in the summer of 1913 in the fine old capital of Hungary, gave an impressive view of the woman's movement. For several years I had served as vice president of the National American Woman's Suffrage Association, when Doctor Anna Howard Shaw was its brilliant president. I recall her vivid personality in many striking situations, but one in Buda-Pest remains most clearly in my mind. The old city on the Danube had long been a stronghold of Calvinism, with the result that one of the most beautiful old churches belonged to the Presbyterians. It had been decided that Doctor Shaw was to give the "congress sermon" there, but when the day arrived there was great difficulty as to a woman occupying the pulpit. The matter was finally arranged by placing a platform, with a reading desk upon it, in what was the junction of the transept and the nave of the stately old church, while the audience was seated around the platform in four different directions. In scholastic cap and gown, she stood on her raised dais and with the eloquence of which she had been past master since her early days as a pioneer Methodist preacher, she filled the vast arches with a valiant plea for the rights of women based on the old historic pleas for the rights of the individual, so dear to Calvin's heart.[3]

The status of equal suffrage reported at the Congress by the delegates from twenty-six parliamentary nations not only gave a world-wide view of the movement, but strikingly presented various evolutionary stages. The very earliest stage was doubtless represented by the women of Asia, who were making the first struggle against traditional barriers and customs rooted in primitive times. The resolution, therefore, admitting the Chinese Woman's Suffrage Society to the International Alliance was carried with prolonged applause. It seems incredible that the convention should have been told that certain Chinese women had been decapitated for the truths they had told while fighting their battle for freedom, and that at any day the men might find a reason to silence the leaders of the movement when, in their enthusiasm, they made too many converts. In spite of the somber implications of the report, the entire Convention agreed with the thrilling words of Mrs. Catt, the International President, that even as we review "the slow tragic struggle upward of the women of the West, we know there is no escape for these Eastern women, that they must follow the vision in their souls as we have done and as other women have done before us."[4]

Another stage of the women's movement was represented by the reports from such states as Bohemia, Silesia and Hungary, where women with certain property qualifications were permitted to send men as members of Parliament who would directly represent their interests. This right of women to a proxy vote had survived from the days when the ownership of property was the only basis upon which either men or women were given the franchise. But as was pointed out in the convention, these surviving votes representing a stage long past were a reproach to the existing governments which made now a greater disparity between the political status of men and women, than that which had existed three hundred years ago. It was upon such a basis that women a few centuries ago sat in the English Parliament and at that moment a small number of women were voting upon the same terms as men in the municipal government of Rangoon, in Bombay and other Indian cities.

There were also at Buda-Pest illustrations of the vote accorded to women in pioneer countries, where they had courageously endured hardships with the men who long ago gave them the franchise, in Wyoming, in Australia, and New Zealand. The fact that the latter country was able to report the lowest infant mortality rate to be found in any part of the world was accounted as a fulfillment of our hopes, and doubtless also as a confirmation of our theories. It was the northern women, however, who more than others represented the final stage of the movement. Three members of Parliament sat in the fine delegation from Finland and public servants were also found in the imposing delegation from Sweden and Norway. A most encouraging report came from Turkey, where in spite of Eastern customs, the new constitution had given women a political status, due to that tendency of each revolution to incorporate into its program the most advanced features of existing governments.

The final impression of the convention at Buda-Pest was that the movement for equal suffrage was growing, pushing and developing in all the countries upon the face of the earth, that the coming together of its representatives was no perfunctory matter, but the free exchange of genuine experiences and untrammeled hopes. The movement was everywhere surprisingly spontaneous, manifesting itself in widely separated groups within the same nation; sometimes it was sectarian and dogmatic, at others philosophic and grandiloquent; it was both amorphous and sporadic, or carefully organized and consciously directed, but it was always vital and constantly becoming more widespread. We liked to say that the entrance of women into government differed from former efforts to extend the franchise in one important aspect; that while the final entrance of the middle class was characterized by two dramatic revolutions, one in America and one in France, both of them with bloodshed, this world-wide entrance into government on the part of women was happily a bloodless one, and had been without a semblance of violence save in England, where its manifestations were not unlike those of the earlier movement among workingmen in the Chartist uprisings.

II

In those placid days before the war when we talked of suffrage we used the old abstract arguments, insisting that the adherents of representative government with its foundations laid in diversified human experiences must concede that the value of such government bears a definite relation to the area of its base, and that the history of its development is a record of new human interests, which have become subjects of governmental action and of the incorporation into the government itself of those classes who represented the new interests.

We had certainly convinced ourselves that there was a political connection between our desire for the vote and our work for social amelioration, and we constantly declared that much of the new demand for political enfranchisement arose from a desire to remedy the unsatisfactory social conditions which are responsible for so much wrong-doing and wretchedness. We argued that because of the tendency to make the state responsible for the care of the helpless and the reform of the delinquent, to safeguard by law the food we eat, and the health of children, contemporary women who were without the franchise were as much outside the real life of the world as any set of disenfranchised free men could possibly have been in all history; never before had so large an area of life found civic expression, never had Hegel's definition of the State been so nearly accurate, that "It is the realization of the moral idea."[5]

We believed that self-government must ever be built up anew in relation to changing experiences and that unless this adjustment constantly takes place, self-government itself is placed in jeopardy. We had also had practical demonstrations that if women had no votes with which to select the men upon whom her social reform had become dependent some cherished project might be so modified by uninformed legislatures during the process of legal enactment, that the law, as finally passed, injured the very people it was meant to protect. Women had discovered that the unrepresented are always liable to be given what they do not want by legislators who merely wish to placate them; a child-labor law exempts street trades, the most dangerous of all trades to a child's morals, a law releasing mothers from petty industry that they may worthily rear their children provides so inadequate a pension that overburdened women continue to face the necessity of neglecting their young in order to feed them.

The need for the franchise however, was not confined to the legislative department of the government, for the administration of social reform is often quite as important as its enactment. We found that it depended upon the personnel whether the women police should be allowed to act as veritable municipal chaperons, really guarding from danger the tired young girls who seek recreation in public dance halls, or whether the women police should be reduced to such formal duty that their very presence would give a specious sense of security. The promising movement for municipal recreation so largely fostered by women might easily be irreparably injured in the very moment of its apparent success. We sometimes considered it of doubtful advantage that more and more women were appointed to positions in administrative government, so long as the power of general direction, of determining the trend and temper of new social experiments, was lodged altogether in the hands of men responsible only to other voting men and politically free from the public opinion of the women originally concerned for the measures.

In the midst of these arguments, however, and always in the stirring conventions whether held in Europe or in the United States there remained in my mind the experiences of those simple women who could not do otherwise but make an effort for the franchise because they needed it so bitterly for their children's sake. This provided a sanction quite outside of the organized movement. One autumn during which I had spoken in five of the state campaigns for suffrage in the West, I had come away with a tremendous admiration for pioneer women; I recall an outdoor meeting on the steps of a country building in a Kansas town where a man in the crowd ventured one of the cheap jibes to which women suffragists had been so long subjected. An old lady who had come from Wisconsin to help in the campaign suddenly mounted the seat of the automobile in which she was sitting and begged leave to reply to him. To our surprise she evidently knew his name and the very county in Kansas from which he came. She told of her experiences in Kansas fifty years earlier when she had campaigned there to secure the school vote for women, and had then known the speaker's mother who was living in a remote part of the new state. This pioneer mother had borne six children without medical attendance or the ministrations of any woman and had buried two without the benefit of clergy. She had been eager for the school vote because she wanted a better school for her growing family, and in the midst of her cares had worked hard in the campaign. The simple tale of courageous living and high thinking was unfolded before her son and ended with the question directed to him: "Who can better vote on the needs of this state or on the needs of this great country than a woman like that?" He had, of course, no reply, and sheepishly disappeared in the crowd.

The vivid interest of pioneer women founded upon her own experience was not so unlike what I had seen among the Italian women of our neighborhood, such as their insistence that more attendants be provided for the lake bathing beaches to which their adventurous young sons repaired every hot night. There was instinctive wisdom behind their high handed demand that political action should concern itself with genuine human needs. It makes possible the age-long effort of women to bring the world nearer to their heart's desire—a better world for their children to live in. I was acting as judge of election in the Hull-House precinct one year when there was submitted to the voters a bond issue for a contagious disease hospital. The judge was permitted to go into the voting booth to assist illiterates to mark the ballot. When we were safely behind the little white curtain of the polling booth one woman after another would say: "Of course I am going to vote the way my man told me to, but I won't go out of this place until I vote for that hospital for catching diseases. The visiting nurses are forever taking a child to the hospital because the disease isn't catching but the very time it is, that is the time the nurse tells you that you must keep all the other children out of school to drive you plum crazy because there is no hospital for a disease as your child has got."

The American National Woman's Suffrage Association, as it was somewhat cumbersomely called, tried for years to secure suffrage state by state. After a vigorous campaign in 1910 in five states only two secured it, although the whole movement received an enormous impulse when New York State was won under the remarkable leadership of Mrs. Carrie Chapman Catt. A smaller group in Washington were pushing for a Constitutional amendment which should enfranchise us all at once, but they could obtain no monopoly on besieging Congress. For many years I had been one of a group of discouraged women to appear before the Judiciary committees both of the House and Senate as well as before the Platform committees of the National Party conventions. On one of these latter occasions the room had been prepared for the entry of the suffragists by carefully placing one of the committee members under the table. All would have gone well had he not been moved to groan aloud either in discomfort or in remorse for his drunken estate. On that occasion at least the time honored argument that women were not capable of using the franchise was not advanced.

III

Much of this activity along civic lines was the result of the Woman's Clubs throughout the country. They were organized into a National Federation which met in Chicago in June, 1914, twenty-four years after it had been organized there. In its first decade it had represented a gigantic quest for culture, at the very moment society had so prided itself upon its liberality and breadth of view that an ironic Englishman had made the statement that "it would be better to be convicted of petty larceny than to be found wanting in historic mindedness." The earlier clubs continually emphasized our common spiritual inheritance as enshrined in poetry, in history, in science, in art, in drama, in music, and believed that their study might be made a great apparatus for the evocation of cultural life. It is easy to treat lightly this period of club development, but certainly the constant coördination of these fructifying specialized studies reacted intimately on the life and character of each community. When that wave of civic emotion surged into the focus of attention which had for its watchword the city beautiful it was most important that there had long been municipal art committees, that public schools had been supplied with good pictures, that trees had been planted in barren towns, that club women had been instrumental in establishing a national park. It all gave reality and background to the movement. When the new social imperative, entitled know your city, gathered momentum far and wide, so that under its impulse and sanction there was inquiry into the facts and tendencies of city life, it was again important that women everywhere had been taught the value of inspecting milk and food, the needlessness of tuberculosis, the necessity for decent factory conditions.

For many of these efforts it was found necessary to command a public opinion not only in the city or state in which the reform was needed, but throughout the country, so that any organization less widespread than the National Federation of Women's Clubs, with interest less universal, would have availed but little. In the second decade, their quest for culture yielded to their interest in child labor, home economics and public health, housing and social hygiene. The biennial meeting in Chicago in 1914 was characteristic of this attitude of club women throughout the country including the women's clubs connected with social settlements. They could all be counted upon to aid in the many efforts at social amelioration which moved forward so rapidly during the years immediately preceding the outbreak of the World War. These efforts were municipal, state, national and international in scope, illustrated often by huge exhibits; one on Child Welfare in Chicago filled the Coliseum with throngs of visitors for a fortnight.

The social settlements from the very beginning had organized groups of women in so-called clubs; first the mothers whose children attended the kindergarten, the cooking school or some similar enterprise in which the mother's coöperation was essential. One of these at Hull-House, which was true also of other settlements, had developed into a flourishing woman's club which in time came to have its affiliations with the County, State and National Federation of Woman's Clubs and to carry its full share of the joint activities. Because its members were nearer to untoward city conditions than were the women who lived in more prosperous parts of the city, it was natural perhaps that they not only gave money but their personal services to the Visiting Nurses, to the early probation officers, to the field work of the Juvenile Protective Association, to the organization extending help to newly arrived immigrants and to many another. Yet they followed on the whole the woman's club path from culture to civic activity. The Hull-House Club not only listened to papers on many improving topics and to occasional concerts but the members themselves gave plays and musical recitals and only later added visits to the Juvenile Court to their formal visit to art galleries and museums.

Concurrently with this largest woman's club at Hull-House, whose members growing prosperous gradually moved to all parts of the city, were clubs of immigrant women divided on the language basis into Mexican, Greek and Italian, although the latter also emerged into the typical woman's club. A club of colored women obliged to meet in the evening because they were all wage earners by day were so absorbed in the housing situation and so determined to find out why their own housing conditions were so wretched that it was impossible for the first year to interest them in anything else. In point of fact all the woman's clubs connected with settlements were much given to finding out about better housing and better house furnishings. An inter-settlement federation of them in Chicago, as in several other cities, gave annual exhibits with talks by experts suggesting betterment along both lines. The Federation of Settlement Woman's Clubs in New York City claimed a distinct share in securing the state law for lessening the cost of tenement house construction. I remember addressing one of their exhibit meetings on the roof of an imposing hotel at which I received the impression that these women were taking care of their own household affairs with great intelligence and with a fine coöperative spirit which the situation required if it were to be met adequately.

During these pre-war years the settlement groups met constantly for civic discussion. I recall an incident connected with the City Club which when it was first built in Chicago was used as a meeting place for all sorts of organizations. We talked over all our causes as we ate luncheon under its hospitable roof. One day as I entered the elevator, the boy who knew me well said casually: "What are you eating with to-day—with garbage or with the social evil?" I replied: "Garbage," with as much dignity as I could command under the circumstances and he deposited me on the fourth floor where I found Mary McDowell, head of the University of Chicago Settlement, pinning on the wall blue prints of a certain garbage reduction plant. I had been a little disturbed by my conversation in the elevator, and remarked: "Isn't it amazing the way we eat and at the same time talk about these disagreeable subjects?" She went on pinning up her blue prints as she replied: "If you lived near Bubbly Creek, into which the five largest slaughterhouses in the world discharge their refuse, you would be so interested in garbage that you would talk about it at luncheon or any other time." I assured her that I was interested in garbage, and instanced the fact that I had once been a garbage inspector myself. "Yes," she said, "you are interested, but if you lived back of the Yards you could not think that any mere talk about it was disagreeable."

And so the woman's clubs were ready at least to investigate any civic situation which seemed to call for vigorous action; and because coöperation among women was new and the companionship exhilarating they were continually "borne onward with that flood of freedom which to the open sea doth flow with pomp of waters unwithstood"—a spirit characteristic of those days which later came to seem so remote—but which is still manifesting itself in new ways, such as the third conference on the Cause and Cure of War held in Washington last January, attended by six hundred delegates from nine national women's organizations. A club woman there ventured the statement that while "the culture club is still with us, discussions of international relations are more popular than papers on the poets of the seventeenth century." She added to this the opinion that "the most interesting and unexpected turn in the tide of feminine affairs is woman's intelligent and almost impassioned interest in world affairs."

IV

The French have a proverb which has always seemed to me very charming; "Men make the roads but it is women who teach children how to walk."

It was during a meeting of women from those countries which border upon the Pacific Ocean held in Honolulu in the summer of 1928 that this saying became verified in my mind. I had been asked by the Pan Pacific Union to preside over its deliberations and from the very first moment I felt a certain vitality and a special reason why women—Oriental women at least—should throw over the mechanical method of communication in favor of personal intercourse. The entire Pacific area is nearer to a basic culture founded upon human needs than are the Occidental countries where the culture taken over from Europe has become so highly mechanized in the lives of women as well as men. One felt that these women from China, Korea, Japan, Samoa, Fiji, and the Philippines, had been less mechanized than those of us who stood nearer to Western culture. We had come to regard the advance of Western civilization as a sort of game, an effort to make one type of culture predominate, which, if too hardly pushed, may break down other cultures older and more basic. We have been accustomed to say with pride that telephone poles may be set up in a jungle, that a wireless operates as easily on sea as on land, forgetting that in our absorption in communicating culture we may easily lose the patterns and customs which give it any real value.

As the Congress at Honolulu proceeded we felt that Oriental women had unique opportunities to stand free from the tyranny of mechanization and to act upon the assumption that civilization is a method of living, an attitude of equal respect for all men. The cultural outlook on life must become as aggressive as the commercial if it hopes to be effective. There is obvious need for bolder arrangements and interactions in the distribution of education, changes which can only come about if they are carried on with that same spirit of free thinking and outspoken publication that has won in the field of natural science.

The most striking figure at the Pan-Pacific Conference was a Chinese woman who is the medical director of a large hospital for women and children; I had never heard a social worker from any country give a more sympathetic interpretation of the inner lives of her clientele than a Japanese charity visitor gave at the Honolulu conference concerning the high suicide rate of the very poor in the Japanese cities whose deep oblivion is being penetrated for the first time. Finely educated Japanese women are devoting themselves to this undertaking, bringing to it the best training the West can give them in colleges and professional schools, with an understanding of the situation all their own. One could at least claim that women who dealt with living creatures, as over against industrial machines or commercial abstractions, had the best opportunity to acquire and to retain a direct approach to life itself. As woman has always had to deal with living and growing things and as the most important food plants flourish in climates which permit a relative long growing season, woman's special contribution to agriculture has been given most lavishly in the tropics where the bulk of the world's population is found.

Was it because Oriental women still retained so much of their basic occupation that they so easily took on others in spite of their ironclad customs? Women's progress, since the beginning of the nineteenth century when it became "a movement," seems to indicate that it was based upon their increasing education followed inevitably by widening opportunities to choose a course of life for themselves. Those choices not only afforded a new scope for their faculties, but so modified public opinion concerning the activities of women that the next steps became easier for all women. This occupational development is rapidly being repeated in the East; not only do young women fill the silk mills in Japan but also the new silk factory in Bokhara, although whole villages in Turkestan have risen up in angry protest against the discarding of the veil and numerous women have lost their lives in defense of the new customs. In the good old days of suffrage speeches, we always quoted the women of Burma as perhaps the freest in the world. They have lived up to expectations and it is not strange that England allowed them to vote at the age of eighteen although the women of India could not vote until they were twenty-one and the women in England itself at that moment, were not allowed to vote until they were thirty. The Burmese women carry on much of the business of the country, holding responsible positions in banking as well as commerce, and they quite frankly use the vote to further their ends. Perhaps the women in France are the only women comparable to them, and although more than two million women are engaged in business in the United States—many of them as the heads of large concerns and most of them carrying on successfully—it is only in variety of occupation that the women of these Western nations surpass Burmese women.

V

Votes for women came at last not only in the United States but in other nations as well, so soon after the war that it must be accounted as the direct result of war psychology. The suffragists had predicted during the war that it might well change woman's position, not only in industry and agriculture which it was obviously doing but that it might also make a distinct change in woman's political status. Many leaders of the suffrage movement in England and Germany as well as in the United States are convinced that votes for women came in recognition of the fine services women had rendered in war time when they had accepted the orthodox conception of loyalty to the state. It has, however, always been true that a change in woman's status has been a by-product of war and that every nation after a war has used woman's strength to recover economic losses as quickly as possible and to help rebuild what war has torn down. The wars of Napoleon permanently placed the operation of small industries and petty commercial enterprises in the hands of French women although in spite of economic emancipation, the Code Napoleon put their legal status far below the place they had held under the previous code of laws transmitted from the Romans.

It is rather curious that at the present moment it is in the Oriental countries that women are making the most surprising political advance as they are also advancing in industry. Although they received the vote in India less than ten years ago, eighty women are now members of city councils, fifty are magistrates, and a Hindu woman is deputy president of the Legislative Council of Madras, a political body representing forty-five million people. A woman is vice chancellor of the Mohammedan University at Bhopal, and hundreds of them are lawyers, doctors, and teachers. And perhaps more striking is the fact that a woman living in Samarkand is vice president of the Uzbek Republic. This may be due to the fact that in the Orient woman's interest broadened into business and professional life more concurrently with the granting of the franchise, than was true in the West. The two movements flowed together more smoothly because they synchronized or it may be because men and women having received the franchise at the same time it was naturally assumed that woman would take her place in the state. In some countries as in India this may be due to the conception of the state itself.

At the Swarajist Congress held in India, June, 1924, Gandhi made the program of the Congress so preëminently social-economic that men, primarily politicians, were virtually barred from membership. The qualifications required the spinning of two thousand yards of yarn a month by each member, a staunch support of Hindu-Mohammedan unity, equal rights for Pariahs, and development of home industry— qualifications which were certainly suggestive of woman's traditional activities.

The All India Congress of 1925 was presided over by a woman— Sarojini Naidu, a poet as well as a patriot, which was in itself a remarkable achievement for an Eastern country and could only have occurred after teachings similar to Gandhi's had penetrated the minds of many people.[6] Mrs. Naidu had been elected a member of the City Council of Bombay in the spring of 1923. I was in Bombay at the moment and had gone from one polling place to another in an effort to see a veiled woman cast a vote. I was finally rewarded by seeing one who had come out of Purdah for this modern purpose, put it through in the most matter-of-fact manner. The next day we all rejoiced at Mrs. Naidu's election, but even then no one could have predicted that she would later be made president of the city council and thus acting mayor of the city.

At that same moment in Bombay, a group of women were protesting against certain features in the houses being built for the employees of one of the large textile mills. The traditional openings in the fretted windows were so made that the women in the house could look only downward and not straight out into the street or even up to the sky above. They could see only the feet of the passer-by who, in his turn, could see nothing but a series of small openings in the stone, at one of which it might be possible to detect a human eye. The little group of women reformers were demanding a change, if only that the Purdah women might have the normal use of their eyes. I never knew until last year when Mrs. Naidu came to Hull-House that they had failed in regard to the houses which were being erected at that moment but succeeded later when the matter had finally become one of municipal regulation. . . .

The change in the status of Oriental women while affording a more striking contrast to their traditions, was scarcely more sudden in point of fact than that which occurred in southeastern Europe. Even in cosmopolitan Vienna where in 1913 I met the venerable Madam Hainisch representing the suffrage movement in Austria. When I attended one of her meetings, because women in Austria were forbidden by law to belong to any political organization, the suffrage group always pretended that it was a literary society and began each meeting with a paper on some well-worn literary theme. I returned to Vienna eight years later to find more than twenty women sitting in the Municipal Council, twelve in the lower house of the National Parliament and five in the upper house. Madam Hainisch, the mother of the president of the new republic, because she had always stood for an extension of the franchise, was eagerly honored as the leading citizen by these newly enfranchised men and women.

The Victory Convention of the National American Women's Suffrage Association and the First National Congress of the League of Women Voters were held simultaneously in Chicago, in 1920. The latter organization, with its analogous societies in all the countries in which women are voting, represents an effort to make an intelligent and effective use of the franchise which has been at last secured. The League with its combination of research, education and discipline in group thinking, with its clearly expressed objectives for its political activity demonstrates that no newly enfranchised class, from King John's barons to the workingmen, has ever prepared itself more conscientiously for the exercise of its new powers.

How long it will be necessary to keep these separate organizations for women before they unite their efforts with those of men is a question each group must decide for itself. There is no doubt that some groups remain separated too long, but that is not always the fault of the women! It is rather singular that this separation is said to be more complete in the United States than in any of the other countries.

During this first decade of suffrage women have learned that ideas change less rapidly than events, with the result that much political thought is always out of date and inappropriate to changed conditions. Perhaps their most important duty is to meet this need for constant adjustment and because they envisage the political situation afresh, they may enable the average citizen to escape from the deadening effects of worn-out conventional phrases, which so largely dominate political life. When Jeannette Rankin interrupted the roll call in the House of Representatives on April 5th, 1917, to say: "I want to stand by my country— but I cannot vote for war," the feminist movement was supposed to have received a knockout blow.[7] The patriots cried aloud that women would infect politics with pacifism, an alarm, however, which the situation in Congress twelve years later unfortunately proved unfounded. There were then eight women who were members of the lower house. They were said to "disagree on the tariff, prohibition and farm relief, but were united on the issue of national defense," which they with other members interpret into more cruisers and higher appropriations for military purposes. Some of us feel that women in politics thus far have been too conventional, too afraid to differ with the men, too ill at ease to trust their own judgments, too skeptical of the wisdom of the humble to incorporate the needs of simple women into the ordering of political life.

All these early efforts to give effective expression to new demands, demonstrating as they do the dependence of the political machine for its driving force upon many varieties of social fuel, not only made clear woman's need for a larger political participation, but demonstrated that it is much easier to dovetail into the political schemes of men than to release the innate concerns of women, which might be equivalent to a revolutionary force. I am at times inclined to agree with Chesterton when he wrote: "Many people have imagined that feminine politics would be merely pacifist or humanitarian or sentimental. The real danger of feminine politics is too much of a masculine policy."

VI

It is possible, however, that the present situation does not arise from an imitative policy but that a rather remote beginning may after all be the natural approach to political affairs, quite as our English ancestors in the beginning of their self-government were absorbed in stating general principles. Perhaps it is only fair to women to remember how long it took men in the Mother of Parliaments itself to include actual contemporaneous affairs in their formal discussions. We can all dimly recall the story of the young member of the House of Commons who was cheered to the echo when he paused and carefully corrected a false meter he had given in a quotation from Horace. The members as a whole knew their classics and considered it of the utmost importance that the new member should be so meticulous, although John Bright and Richard Cobden at that very moment were fuming in their seats because of the postponement of the discussion on the Corn Laws which in their minds might determine the starvation or survival of thousands of their fellow countrymen.[8] Women at least are starting far from such a point of abstraction and doubtless the nearer they can keep in their political life to their historic rôle in human affairs, the more valuable they may be.

That so many of the voting women have exhibited an intelligent and sustained interest in world affairs may be due to the fact that women received the vote in so many countries immediately after the war, when the relations between nations were of necessity widely discussed. Not only American and European women received the franchise at a moment when their countries were freshly involved in international interests but Oriental women as well; China had struggled for months with the problem of extraterritoriality and all it implied in relation to other nations; Burma and India in their demands for national independence were obliged to review not only their dominion status but various constitutional governments throughout the world in the light of their adaptation to Oriental concepts. Seven countries have included women in their delegations to the assembly of the League of Nations and two women sit as honored members of the Commission on Intellectual Coöperation. For the first term of eight years a woman was head of the Commission of the Secretariat dealing with many vexed social problems which could only be regulated by international action.

Perhaps it is because of the world situation that, as has been said many times, the clearest and most unmistakable evidence of the influence of women on modern affairs is to be found in the deliberations of international bodies.

Notes

1. Emily Davison (1872–1913), determined to become a martyr to the suffrage cause, succeeded by throwing herself in front of a horse at the great spectacle of the Derby when all of England high society is gathered. Addams was not drawn to these sorts of dramatic gestures.

2. Maude Royden (1876–1956), a leader of the women's suffrage effort in England.

3. Anna Howard Shaw (1847–1919), a leading American suffrage leader and president of the National American Woman Suffrage Association.

4. Catt (1859–1947), suffrage leader and president of the National American Woman Suffrage Association. Catt was considered a hardheaded pragmatist in contrast to being either a militant ideologue or a theorist.

5. Although there was a very softened version of Hegelianism in American social thought, Addams certainly did not, and could not, take Hegel neatly, for the great German philosopher saw in war the highest ethical moment of the state as the young man prepares to go forth and to die for the state as an ethical idea and am embodiment of ethical life.

6. Sarojini Naidu, a great Indian lyric poet (1879–1949) and colleague of Gandhi's in the fight for Indian home rule. Naidu visited Hull-House when she toured Chicago, and there is a famous photograph of her holding up an example of Indian pottery in the Hull-House pottery workshop.

7. Jeanette Rankin (1880–1973), U.S. representative from Montana. She voted against the United States going to war in Europe in 1917 and again in 1941.

8. John Bright and Richard Cobden were classical British liberals who joined forces in the Anti-Corn Law campaign of 1838–1846 to fight import tariffs. They were free-traders.

27

"CONTRASTS IN POST-WAR GENERATION"

IF WE OFTEN FELT THAT THE SPIRIT of intolerance had spread over our own time, choking free sensibilities and stunting the growth of the spirit, it was because we were able to compare it with pre-war times, and naturally we looked with anxiety upon the young who had grown up in this atmosphere and knew no other.

I am quite confident, however, that while the inhibitions of this post-war decade seem obvious to us, this interpretation will strike young people as most surprising, because their impression of this period would doubtless be its courage in the rejection of inhibitions. They would instance their sense of release and their new confidence in self-expression. Of course we realize that each generation clings with an almost romantic fervor to the aims of its own age and because we must always make a distinct effort in order to keep open the channels of communication with youth, it is very easy to misunderstand them. They not only think differently, so that their opinions are unlike our own, but they exhibit a tendency to surround these differences with secrecy, lest the old become horrified and try to destroy what they cannot understand. I will confess that what disturbed me during this period and what seemed most unlike my own youth, was the spirit of conformity in matters of opinion among young people especially among college students. In a city like Chicago this may be due somewhat to the

---

Note: "Contrasts in Post-War Generation," in *The Second Twenty Years at Hull-House, September 1909 to September 1929 with a Record of Growing World Consciousness* (New York: Macmillan, 1930), chapter 7.

fact that many young people who go to college and to the universities are the children of immigrants. They are anxious to appear as if their families had lived in America much longer than they really have and to conform so carefully that no one will suspect their recent coming. Conformity thus becomes a sort of protective coloring.

This situation may have been intensified beyond its normal manifestations by the fact that after the war, there was a great access of students in all the higher institutions of learning due partly to increased prosperity and partly to the new impressions which many young men had received in the army, among them being one that "the college fellows were always the officers." This increased zeal for education was all to the good of course and we are told in the young people's defense that we misinterpret their desire for conformity to their own standards, that it is really a defiance of the authority which is so often associated with obsolete standards. But this would mean that in the very assertion of independence each one feels that he must be bolstered by others, and must constantly reassure himself that he is, after all, very much like the people with whom he is identified.

It is doubtless true that in the heart of every young person lies a certain fear that he may not make good, for he is conscious of a weakness in himself that he is not sure of in anyone else. It may be that our contemporary young people in addition to this inevitable burden of youth, are carrying their share of that fear-control so apparent throughout the nation and everywhere expressing itself in a dread of change, in a desire to play safe and to let well enough alone. We may easily believe that the combination has overwhelmed their nascent strength and forced them into an undue conformity. Or are we all equally afraid of what will happen to us if we do not carefully conform, and do the young simply conform more obviously in their anxiety to do it properly quite as they are more meticulous as to their hats and shoes?

Every thoughtful traveler who came to America during the early post-war period remarked upon our excessive conformity, and explained it in various ways. One well-known philosopher said:

> Although machinery makes man collectively more lordly in his attitude toward nature, it tends to make the individual more subservient to his group. Perhaps this is one cause of the fact that the herd instinct is so much more insistent in America than in England,

and that individual liberty is less respected, both socially and politically. I think, however, that the more important cause is the mixture of races and nationalities in the United States which makes herd instinct a necessary, unifying force.

Whether or not we accept these explanations we must agree that the opening of the windows to vigorous thought, to pungent criticism which "the man from the soil" was long supposed to bring into academic halls, at present has lost ground in American colleges. There is no doubt that this conformity and lack of independence current among American students are often incomprehensible to their fellow students in other countries.

In Calcutta, where I was once addressing an audience composed largely of young men, I found myself briskly heckled: it began when a young man with a very Oxfordian accent asked me if the people in the United States still believe that all men were created free and equal. I discovered that I was being grilled because the day before the United States Supreme Court had sustained a decision that a Hindu could not become an American citizen. These Hindu students all thought this decision a great unfairness for it not only hurt their race pride but they considered it a blow to their nationalistic movement. But what bewildered them most of all was that no protest came from the student body in the United States who they felt should be defending the basic doctrines upon which the new nations, including the United States, had been founded. They believed that the young throughout the world were united in upholding these doctrines and they could not understand indifference when this breach of principle had been made.

II

Because the effect of war on our social institutions was responsible for a period of political and social sag, did the young people attempting to recapture life just when democratic advance had been discredited, when political and social changes were inhibited, inevitably push forward their own experimentation into the more intimate areas of life? The new psychology had stressed the importance of those subconscious deep-lying strata of personality, which profounder than reason are a direct product of racial experience. In addition, the Freudian theories as to dangers of repression were seized upon by agencies of publicity, by half-baked lecturers and by writers on the new psychology and finally interpreted by reckless youth as a warning against self-control. All of this profoundly influenced the attitude of children to parents and the attitude of the sexes toward each other.

It was impossible, of course, that the experiences of war should not have made changes in the conception of the family unit which responds to social pressure as do other social institutions, and the pressure brought upon the family during the war was tremendous. According to English writers, under the post-war conditions young people demanded personal happiness as theirs by right, decried sentimentalism and exalted sex; they were opposed to all hampering social conventions and even to established reticences. Sir Philip Gibbs has written of this period:

> Sex was a mother of hysteria in a civilization which had created innumerable disharmonies between the body and the mind, among people who were oversensitive and overstrained—and yet without this passion there would be no beauty, no joy, no life.—How could one get the balance between its good and evil, its spiritual fulfillment and its thwarted impulses, its loyalties and its treacheries? The balance of life had been upset somehow. The old controls had weakened. There was no faith in self-sacrifice or future compensations for earthly suffering. There was a fierce demand for happiness here and now lest all should be lost.[1]

In their revolt against Victorian prudery, against innuendoes and distrust of natural impulses, they made a cult of frankness. They derided especially the doctrine that "there is no conduit to the mastery of the world other than the mastery of self." Many of them were amused at the appeal to what they called "The priceless mid-Victorian notion of duty." Nevertheless, it seemed at moments to their elders as if the prophecy in Wordsworth's *Ode to Duty,* although couched in the jingling rhythm the young so heartily despise had been fulfilled. "Serene would be our days and bright, And happy would our natures be, If joy were an unerring light, And love its own security." The last line states the question, is the joy of self-expression an unerring light and is love its own security. Upon the assumption of an affirmative reply these unresisting believers in the power of the subconscious easily arrive at a de-

nial of the value of self-criticism and of self-discipline. In their refusal
to be tied to conceptions of duty they threaten to become abject followers of blind forces admittedly beyond their control. In a moment of exasperation Epicurus is reported to have exclaimed that he would rather
be a slave to the old gods of the vulgar than to the forces of Destiny
evoked by the philosophers of his day. The fear of missing some emotional stimulus may well become a tyranny worse than the austere
guidance of reason.

On the other hand, if all that makes for self-expression and self-
development and the determination to secure a new freedom in sex relations seems at moments to absorb the entire reforming energy of the
young, it is also obvious to them that the previous generation was too
exclusively concerned for the masses, too intent upon the removal of
what seemed unfair restrictions for the man at the bottom of society.
Have these contemporary young people inevitably gone back to liberty
for the individual? Does the pendulum have to swing back and forth
from individual to collective effort and does it always seem inconsistent
as the two advocates pass one another? Of this I recall a striking instance; we had tried to interest a group of people who, through their
own journal, had long stressed individual liberty, in the political liberty
of the inhabitants of Haiti, which at the moment was occupied by
United States Marines. A committee in which the Women's International League had been represented had visited the island and came
back to urge public opinion in favor of self-government of Haiti. Political liberty, however, seemed of no consequence to this journal, so committed to the liberty of the individual, and as we talked to them about
it, we seemed to be speaking two different languages. Apparently, to
this set of people as to many another, freedom meant unlimited opportunities for self-development with the recognition on the part of society
that such freedom was important and the next step in social reform.
This desired freedom and self-development was always associated in
some way with the breaking down of sex taboos and with the establishment of new standards of marriage.

III

Perhaps this astounding emphasis upon sex was the less comprehensible because of the unique element in the social situation during the last

half century regarding the rôle played by the educated, unmarried woman.

For a considerable period after the door of opportunity began to be slowly opened to woman, she was practically faced with an alternative of marriage or a career. She could not have both apparently for two reasons. Men did not at first want to marry women of the new type, and women could not fulfill the two functions of profession and home-making until modern inventions had made a new type of housekeeping practicable, and perhaps one should add, until public opinion tolerated the double rôle. Little had been offered to the unmarried women of the earlier generations but a dependence upon relatives which was either grudged or exploited, with the result that the old maid herself was generally regarded as narrow and unhappy and, above all, hopelessly embittered. Changing conditions, however, gradually produced a large number of women, selected by pioneer qualities of character and sometimes at least by the divine urge of intellectual hunger, who were self-supporting and devoted to their chosen fields of activity. I asked one of the finest of them, my friend Emily Greene Balch, who for twenty years had been head of the Department of Economics in Wellesley College, and who through years of study in Europe and as the first secretary of the Woman's International League knew the women in many countries, to give me her impression of the situation. I quote the following from her illuminating reply:

> Men had normally given hostages to fortune in the shape of families. Professional women were far freer in general to risk their jobs for the sake of unpopular principles and tabooed forms of activity. They had, too, a quite special spur in the desire to prove incorrect the general belief that they were congenitally incapable. They found a tingling zest in discovering that it is not true, as woman had been brought up to believe, that she was necessarily weaker and more cowardly, incapable of disinterested curiosity, unable to meet life on her own merits. Much good feminine energy went astray in proving that women could do this and that which had been marked taboo, when perhaps this or that was not the most desirable thing to do. There was also another incentive in the sense of opening the way to others and the sharing of an interesting experiment. Is it compatible with the modern theories about sex that

two generations of professionally trained women lived, without vows or outward safeguards, completely celibate lives with no sense of its being difficult or of being misunderstood? Some of them later married; most of them did not. Now they are old or oldish women, how do they feel about it? They are rather a reserved lot but quite willing to admit that it has been a serious loss, certainly, to have missed what is universally regarded as the highest forms of woman's experience but there is no evidence that they themselves or those who know them best find in them the abnormality that the Freudian psychoanalysts of life would have one look for. They are strong, resistant and active, they grow old in kindly and mellow fashion; their attitude to life is based upon active interests; they are neither excessively repelled nor excessively attracted to that second-hand intimacy with sexuality which modern science and modern literature so abundantly display. It is, however, strange to them to read interpretations of life, in novels, plays, and psychological treatises that represent sex as practically the whole content of life; family feeling, religion and art, as mere camouflaged libido, and everything that is not concerned with the play of desire between men and women as without adventure, almost without interest. If the educated unmarried women of the period between the Civil War and the World War represent an unique phase, it is one that has important implications which have not yet been adequately recognized by those who insist upon the imperious claims of sex.

If this period in which the unmarried woman played her part was marked by an undue interest in social and economic reform it was perhaps natural that the next generation should choose other objects for its endeavor.

Possibly the whole difference between the generations rests upon a basis quite outside of personal experience. Certain authorities contend that the attitude of an age toward the great problems of life tends to become symbolized in catchwords which are often associated with its own scientific discoveries. One of the younger generation himself has written of this: "Evolution was the watchword of rebels against social injustice; relativity is becoming the watchword of rebels against the tyrannies of absolute moral judgments and too inflexible rules of life."

He further explains: "Relativity soon ceases to be simply a doctrine of higher physics and becomes a way of looking at things which is valuable in the age-long fight of the younger generation of the moment, against the tyranny of tradition." As our generation endeavored to ameliorate untoward conditions and to abolish unfair restrictions because we believed that each human being had a right to develop to his utmost capacity, so the next generation in turn is bent upon the same quest. The motivation is undoubtedly similar although the field of activity is changed. It is not all a struggle of opposing interests. There is also "the battle of the angels."

IV

The current endeavor of the new generation is characterized by a widespread and sustained effort in the fields of education and public health but above all by a marked increase of interest in world affairs. There is a new awareness of other people, a lively interest in foreign matters and at least the stirrings of a will to organize this politically chaotic world. In the midst of the new militarism there is a conscious demand for political action looking toward a peaceful world; an insistence that although governments were originally evolved for competitive fighting and are hard to move in any other direction, nevertheless the time has now come when governments must move on to effective action for world organization.

If the formula is trustworthy that a behaving organism reacts to the stimulus of its entire environment, certainly the young people of the post-war generation who have so enormously enlarged their environmental interest, are facing the possibility of discovering and utilizing new motivations. They are out for an honest, frank and efficiently hard world. In approaching life by a new synthesis they evince a fine sense of social adventure and of course utilize the tireless energy of discovery, which belongs so preëminently to youth.

Typical of the directness and efficiency put into international relations by the younger generation is the No More War Movement in England with its scathing descriptions of the shattered world which has been handed over to the contemporary generation. Such fresh statements on the part of post-war youth broke into the self-righteousness which so persistently dogs the feet of the sober middle aged and the elderly and which has always wrought its share of havoc. Our self-righteousness was pretty well disabled when we were reminded by the Youth Movement that of all the generations of men who have lived upon the face of the earth, our generation has the least claim to advise the next. The responsible adults living in the world in 1914 had been unable to avert the great war which resulted in the annihilation of ten million young men. The occurrence of such a catastrophe must have been due to the lack of adequate political arrangements between the nations so that when difficult international situations arose the statesmen were unable to compose them. It must inevitably appear that the commercial and industrial development of the world outran the political arrangements, and above all, that there was no morality vigorous enough and sufficiently international in outlook to forestall such a disaster, nor to keep it within bounds when it did occur. The next generation will never know what its own world would have been, had the millions of young men killed in the war survived, and had they been able to bring to its tangled affairs their experience and understanding. One of the young soldiers, a survivor, has written:

> And that is just why they let us down so badly. For us lads of eighteen they ought to have been mediators and guides to the world of maturity, the world of work, of duty, of culture, of progress—to the future. We often made fun of them and played jokes on them, but in our hearts we trusted them. The idea of authority, which they represented, was associated in our minds with a greater insight and manlier wisdom. But the great war shattered this belief. We had to recognize that our generation was more to be trusted than theirs. They surpassed us only in phrases and in cleverness. The first bombardment showed us our mistake, and under it the world as they had taught it to us, broke in pieces.

At least the insufferable assumption that the older generation is *per se* wiser has been cleared out of the way. All of us, of whatever age should therefore find it easier to work together and have the resulting enormous advantage. Because of the sense of struggle between them, the two generations inevitably face a period of conflict unless they are open to that conception of the social forces which comes from integration in the sphere of activities rather than in that of ideas. What we want is not mere argument, certainly not suppression of any sort, but the release of energy and the evocation of new powers in common action. . . .

VI

Possibly the younger people are more naturally sensitive to a nascent world consciousness than the older ones. Perhaps the outgoing generation is only too aware that war as an institution blasts the hopes of mankind, and is apprehensive that if cherished social movements should be again well under way, they might again be destroyed and scattered to the winds by another war. There may be a poetic justice in the fact that our generation will be crippled forevermore by the effects of the war which we failed to avert, so that we must humbly depend upon the untrammelled hopes of the young.

Certainly the most successful efforts to secure more adequate international arrangements are carried on in the United States by citizens of all ages and degrees of education. In this new urge to know the world the two generations are heartily united, as a brief review of their common undertakings will indicate.

The enormous increase of interest in foreign affairs, in what was happening in other parts of the world, was registered in the United States the very day before the Armistice was declared when the Foreign Policy Association was founded in New York City. It was designed to aid in the solution of after-the-war problems, through submitting them to the test of thorough discussion: "To carry on research and educational activities to aid in the understanding and constructive development of American foreign policy."

During the war we had been very proud of the fact that while the League for Democratic Control in England was endeavoring to have all treaties in the future submitted to the House of Commons before they were validated, we had always had that provision for treaties in the United States Senate. But the whole nation suddenly became alive to the fact that a democracy which undertakes to control its own foreign relations must know something about them, and similar associations were gradually organized in one American city after another. . . .

It was the fashion in the United States just then to call the Assembly [of the League of Nations] a mere debating society, to say that the actual responsibility was vested in the Council with the big powers in control. It seemed to some of us that even if this were a correct estimate such a departure in international affairs was in itself most significant. We might all be grateful that there should be a small area on the earth's surface to which governments might send their representatives to debate upon questions of world-wide importance and where the big powers should be challenged by the smaller ones. In line with this, I recall an incident in which a humble man made a moral appeal to the 1923 Assembly to which the delegates enthusiastically responded. He himself was a delegate from Haiti—a small republic of colored men in which the United States at the moment was maintaining marines—who got up to protest concerning an incident which had happened in Africa in one of the mandated territories, when the South African Free State had bombed villages from an aeroplane in order to secure a prompt payment of taxes from their inhabitants. The Haitian submitted that this was no way to collect taxes, and on that ground made an appeal to the moral sentiment of the Assembly. Almost immediately three very distinguished Englishmen explained, no nation ever apologizes, that the incident had been reported to Parliament and the man responsible had been recalled; that the British Empire was far-flung and occasionally unfortunate things occurred which no one regretted so much as the government itself, and they assured the Assembly that everything was being done to prevent a recurrence of such an unfortunate action.

The significance of the incident was that a man from a small nation, speaking on behalf of his race, found a place provided for him in the Assembly of the League where such an appeal could be made, where world opinion could actually estimate the moral value of a nation quite irrespective of its diplomatic skill or the size of its navy. . . .

All over the world there were many non-governmental efforts to secure better international relations. Immediately after the Peace Conference in Paris—perhaps because it was seen that the position of official representatives was almost impossibly difficult—Englishmen and Americans attached to their respective delegations, feeling the need of freer and more thorough study, organized the Royal Institute of International Affairs in London and the Council on Foreign Relations in New York City. Later there was organized through the efforts of the Pan-Pacific Union an Institute of Pan-Pacific Relations which has come to be considered almost official in questions affecting the countries of the Pacific area. While the United States has through Congress attempted to preserve its traditional isolation, we have been unable to ignore the interlocking character of world politics and the rapid extension of financial and political interests has forced the country to take part in this new conference method. Several universities have developed institutes for promoting discussion of international relations; among them the University of Chicago, the University of Virginia and a dozen others. Perhaps the most significant approach to international affairs from the scientific standpoint is the Walter Hines Page School for International Relations established at Johns Hopkins University in 1926. The founders acknowledged that:

> The very nationalist feeling which strengthens democratic government at home is, in itself, a barrier to the discovery of facts in the international field, particularly when these facts turn out to be unpleasant or unpopular to the electorate.
>
> As a result of this, the primary purpose of diplomatic intelligence is to promote national interest. We have what might be called an industry of foreign relations, but we have no science; we have a trade, but no art. And so far no definite effort has been made to train scientists in this important field. . . .

VII

The proposition to outlaw war by international agreement was first made by a well-known attorney in Chicago and after a campaign exhibiting great devotion on the part of the originator and of its first adherents. Outlawry of War became a popular cause throughout the United States and finally resulted in the Pact of Paris more popularly known as the Kellogg Pact.[2] This Pact eclipsed all former treaties by outlawing war itself as an institution, by making war as such, illegal; the signatories to the treaty pledged themselves never to use war as an instrument in international affairs. This comprehensive treaty illustrates, as nothing in all history has done, the genuine movement for peace taking place all over the world. It has been endorsed and ratified by government officials and voted upon favorably by hard-headed, even by hard-boiled politicians. The difficulties ahead lie in the enforcement of this high resolve and unless it is to prove an example, like the Prohibition Amendment, of government action outrunning public opinion every effort for popular backing must be made along both educational and empirical lines. Ramsay MacDonald has said in connection with these treaties that the mentality of the people must be transformed from a dependence upon military security to a dependence upon political security, the latter "rooted in public opinion and enforced by a sense of justice in a civilized world."

This is the task awaiting this post-war generation. It will require all their efficiency to accomplish that in which their immediate predecessors so completely failed. After all it is not so much that different generations are hostile to each other as that they find each other irrelevant. This reaction is in part instinctive and in part self-conscious. The son shrugs his shoulders at the watchwords that thrilled his father, but out of his more fragmentary experience searches desperately for new ones to meet his own need. The wisdom in the ancient phrase "the great god liveth and never groweth old" may save the situation. If our generations pool the increasing knowledge conscious that all we know of this strange old world is that which has passed through the human mind, we will find that our intellectual interests have become part of its texture. If we continue to unite our unremitting efforts to organize for a more reasonable life upon the earth's surface, we will gradually make possible the utilization of a new dynamic. We will almost inevitably begin to grope our way toward what our generation calls human brotherhood but which the post-war generation would, I am sure, rather designate as a wider participation in life.

Notes

1. Sir Philip Gibbs, British writer (1877–1962).
2. The Kellogg-Briand Pact is widely derided as an act of naivete and folly that helped to lull much of Western Europe as Germany rearmed.

28

"A REVIEW OF BREAD RATIONS
AND WOMAN'S TRADITIONS"

As THE EUROPEAN WAR CONTINUED and new relief organizations developed for the care of the wounded and orphaned, the
members of our group felt increasingly the need for the anodyne of
work, although it was difficult to find our places. For instance, the
American Red Cross, following the practice of the British society, had
become part of the military organization as it had never done before
and its humanitarian appeal for funds had fully utilized the war enthusiasms. Such a combination made it not only more difficult for pacifists
to become identified with the Red Cross, but all war activities which
were dependent upon public funds became very timid in regard to pacifist co-operation. This was, of course, quite natural as the newspapers
constantly coupled the words traitor and pro-German with the word
pacifist, as if they described one and the same person. There were in
fact many examples arising from the fear of imperiling a good cause by
having a pacifist identified with it, that resulted in individual pacifists
withdrawing from organizations which they had themselves founded or
fostered. But although our feelings were sometimes hurt at the moment
when it was made obvious that one or another was *persona non grata,*
I think, on the whole, we frankly recognized the instinct for practical
politics as responsible for certain incidents; at any rate, we learned to
take our rebuffs without a sense of grievance. Personally, I found these
incidents easier to bear than the occasional persecutions which came

---

Note: "A Review of Bread Rations and Woman's Traditions," in *Peace and
Bread in Time of War* (New York: Macmillan, 1922), chapter 4.

the other way around; when enthusiastic and fanatical pacifists openly challenged the honesty and integrity of their former associates who had become convinced of the necessity for the war.

With many other Americans I, therefore, experienced a great sense of relief when Congress finally established a Department of Food Administration for the United States and when Mr. Hoover, who had spent two and a half years in Europe in intimate contact with the backwash of war, made his first appeal to his fellow countrymen in the name of the food shortage of the entire world, insisting that "the situation is more than war, it is a problem of humanity."

Certainly here was a line of activity into which we might throw ourselves with enthusiasm, and if we were not too conspicuous we might be permitted to work without challenge. The latter was perhaps too much to hope for. But although the challenge came from time to time, in my case at least it did not prove a deterrent and I was soon receiving many more invitations than I could possibly accept to speak on food conservation in relation to European needs; some of these invitations were under the auspices of the Federal Department of Food Administration, and in California, Texas, Colorado and other states under the auspices of the State. But what I cared most for was an opportunity to speak to women's organizations, because I not only believed, as I somewhat elaborately stated, that "in this great undertaking women may bear a valiant part if they but stretch their minds to comprehend what it means in this world crisis to produce food more abundantly and to conserve it with wisdom," but I also believed that we might thus break through into more primitive and compelling motives than those inducing so many women to increase the war spirit. There was something as primitive and real about feeding the helpless as there was about the fighting and in the race history the tribal feeding of children antedated mass fighting by perhaps a million years. Anthropologists insist that war has not been in the world for more than 20,000 years. It is in fact so recent that existing remnants of primitive people do not understand it. They may be given to individual murder but not to the collective fighting of numbers of men against other masses of men. Could not the earlier instinct and training in connection with food be roused and would it be strong enough to overwhelm and quench the later tendency to war? Each individual within himself represented something of both strains: I used to remind myself that although I had had ancestors who fought in all the American wars since 1684, I was also the daughter, granddaughter and the great grand-daughter of millers. My earliest recollection was of being held up in a pair of dusty hands to see the heavy stone mill wheels go round. The happiest occupation of my childhood was to watch the old foaming water wheel turning in the back of the mill. I could tell by the sounds of the mill when the old wheel was used, which occurred occasionally long after the turbines were established. Watching the foaming water my childish mind followed the masses of hard yellow wheat through the processes of grinding and bolting into the piled drifts of white flour and sometimes further into myriad bowls of bread and milk.

Again, those two strains of War and Bread mingled in my memory of months of travel. Certainly drilling soldiers and the constant reviewing of troops were seen in all the capital cities of Europe but there were also the peasant women who, all the world over, are still doing such a large part of the work connected with the growing and preparation of foods. I recalled them everywhere in the fields of vast Russia as in the tiny pastures of Switzerland; by every roadside in Palestine they were grinding at the hand mills; in Egypt they were forever carrying the water of the Nile that the growing corn might not perish.

The newspapers daily reported the changing fortunes of war on both fronts and our souls turned sick with anxiety and foreboding because all that the modern world held dear hung upon the hazards of battle. But certainly the labor for bread, which to me was more basic and legitimate than war, was still going on everywhere. In my desire to uncover it, to make clear woman's traditional activity with something of its poetry and significance, I read endlessly in Fraser's "Golden Bough," two large volumes of which are given over to the history and interpretation of the innumerable myths dealing with the Spirits of the Corn. These spirits are always feminine and are usually represented by a Corn Mother and her daughter, vaguely corresponding to the Greek Demeter—the always fostering Earth, and her child Persephone.

At the risk of breaking into the narrative of this book, so far as there is one, I am venturing to repeat some of the material which brought a touch of comfort to me and which, so far as I was able at that moment, I handed on to other women. Fraser discovers that relics of the Corn Mother and the Corn Maiden are found in nearly all the harvest fields of Europe; among many tribes of North American Indians; the Eastern world has its Rice Mother, for whom there are solemn ceremonies when the seed rice, believed to contain "soul stuff," is gathered. These deities are always feminine, as is perhaps natural from the association with fecundity and growth, and about them has gathered much of the poetry and song in the sowing of the grain and the gathering of the harvest, and those saddest plaints of all expressing the sorrows of famine.

Myths centering about the Corn Mother but dimly foreshadowed what careful scientific researches have later verified and developed. Students of primitive society believe that women were the first agriculturists and were for a long time the only inventors and developers of its processes. The men of the tribe did little for cultivating the soil beyond clearing the space and sometimes surrounding it by a rough protection. The woman as consistently supplied all cereals and roots eaten by the tribe as the man brought in the game and fish, and in early picture writing the short hoe became as universally emblematic of woman as the spear of the hunter, or the shield and battle axe of the warrior. In some tribes it became a fixed belief that seeds would not grow if planted by a man, and apparently all primitive peoples were convinced that seeds would grow much better if planted by women. In Central Africa to this day a woman may obtain a divorce from her husband and return to her father's tribe, if the former fails to provide her with a garden and a hoe.

It is said that every widespread myth has its counterpart in the world of morals. This is certainly true of the "fostering Mother." Students in the origin of social customs contend that the gradual change from the wasteful manner of nomadic life to a settled and much more economic mode of existence may be fairly attributed to these primitive agricultural women. Mothers in order to keep their children alive had transplanted roots from the forest or wild grains from the plains, into patches of rudely cultivated ground. We can easily imagine when the hunting was poor or when the flocks needed a new pasture, that the men of the tribe would be for moving on, but that the women might insist that they could not possibly go until their tiny crops were garnered; and that if the tribe were induced to remain in the same caves or huts until after harvest the women might even timidly hope that they could use the same fields next year, and thus avert the loss of their children, sure to result from the alternation of gorging when the hunt was good and of starving when it was poor. The desire to grow food for her children led to a fixed abode and to the beginning of a home, from which our domestic morality and customs are supposed to have originated.

With such a historic background, it seemed to me that women might, in response to the food saving and food production appeals issued in one country after another, so enlarge their conception of duty that the consciousness of the world's needs for food should become the actual impulse of their daily activities.

It also presented another interesting aspect; from the time we were little children we have all of us, at moments at least, cherished overwhelming desires to be of use in the great world to play a conscious part in its progress. The difficulty has always been in attaching our vague purposes to the routine of our daily living, in making a synthesis between our ambitions to cure the ills of the world on the one hand, and the need to conform to household requirements on the other.

It was a very significant part of the situation, therefore, that at this world's crisis the two had become absolutely essential to each other. A great world purpose could not be achieved without woman's participation founded upon an intelligent understanding and upon the widest sympathy, at the same time the demand could be met only if it were attached to her domestic routine, its very success depending upon a conscious change and modification of her daily habits.

It was no slight undertaking to make this synthesis, it afforded probably the most compelling challenge which has been made upon woman's constructive powers for centuries. It required all her human affection and all her clarity of mind to make the kind of adjustment which the huge scale of the situation demanded.

It is quite understandable that there was no place for woman and her possible contribution in international affairs under the old diplomacy. Such things were indeed not "woman's sphere." But it was possible that as women entered into politics when clean milk and the premature labor of children became factors in political life, so they might be concerned with international affairs when these at last were dealing with such human and poignant matters as food for starving peoples who could be fed only through international activities.

I recall a great audience in Hot Springs, Arkansas, made up of the members of the General Federation of Women's Clubs. It seemed to me that every woman there might influence her community "back home," not only to produce and to save more food, but to pour into the war torn world such compassion as would melt down its animosities and bring back into it a gregarious instinct older and more human than the motives responsible for war. I believed that a generous response to this world situation might afford an opportunity to lay over again the foundations for a wider, international morality, as woman's concern for feeding her children had made the beginnings of an orderly domestic life. We are told that when the crops of grain and roots so painstakingly produced by primitive women began to have a commercial value their production and exchange were taken over by the men, as men later turned the manufacturing of pottery and other of woman's early industries into profit making activities. Such a history suggested that this situation might be woman's opportunity if only because foods were, during the war, no longer considered primarily in regard to their money-making value but from the point of view of their human use. Because the production of food was for the moment, dependent upon earlier motives it had fallen back into woman's hands. There had developed a wide concern for the feeding of hungry people, an activity with which women were normally connected.

As I had felt the young immigrant conscripts caught up into a great world movement, which sent them out to fight, so it seemed to me the millions of American women might be caught up into a great world purpose, that of conservation of life; there might be found an antidote to war in woman's affection and all-embracing pity for helpless children.

Certainly compassion is not without its social utility. Up to the present moment the nations, in their foreign policies, have conspicuously lacked that humane quality which has come in their domestic policies through the increasing care for the poor, and the protection of children. These have been responsible for all sorts of ameliorative legislation during the later years, in one nation after another. In their relations to each other, however, nations have been without such motives of humanitarian action until the Allied nations, during the war, evolved a strikingly new foreign policy in their efforts to relieve the starvation and distress throughout widespread areas.

There are such unexpected turnings in the paths of moral evolution that it would not be without precedent that a new and powerful force might be unloosed in the world when the motive for producing and shipping food on the part of great nations was no longer a commercial one but had for the moment shifted to a desire to feed hungry people with whose governments they had entered into obligations. Such a force might in the future have to be reckoned with as a factor in international affairs.

In those dark years, so destructive of the old codes, the nations were forced back to their tribal function of producing and conserving food in contrast to the methods of modern commerce. All food supplies had long been collected and distributed through the utilization of the commercial motive. When it was commercially valuable to a man, to a firm or nation, food was shipped; when it was not commercially valuable, food was withheld or even destroyed. At that moment, however, the Allied Nations were collecting and conserving a common food supply and each nation was facing the necessity of making certain concessions to the common good that the threat of famine for all might be averted. A new internationalism was being established day by day; the making of a more reasonable world order, so cogently urged by the President of the United States, was to some extent already under way, the war itself forming its matrix.

There was a substitution of the social utility motive for that of commercial gain, energized pity for that of business enterprise. Mr. Hoover had said: "The wheat loaf has ascended in the imagination of enormous populations as the positive symbol of national survival." It seemed as if the age-long lack of organization between the nations, the dearth of human relationships in world politics, was about to be corrected, because an unspeakable disaster had forced the nations to consider together the primitive questions of famine and pestilence. It was possible that a new international ethic was arising from these humble beginnings, as the defense and feeding of the dependent members of the tribe had laid the foundations of tribal loyalty and of national existence itself. In spite of the great mass of social data accumulated in the last century, in spite of widespread intellectual training, there has been no successful attempt to reduce the chaos of human affairs into a rational world order. Society failed to make a community of nations and was at last tragically driven to the beginnings of one along the old primitive folkways, as if in six thousand years no other method could have been devised.

It seemed, therefore, a great historic achievement that there should have been devised a workable method for the collective purchase of food, to prohibit profiteering in "the precious stuff that men live by," even for the duration of the war. . . .

To transfer this concern for food into the international field was to enlarge its functions enormously as well as to increase its proportions. The

Allied Nations had seriously undertaken to solve the problem of producing with the utmost economy of human labor the largest amount of food and of distributing that food to the points of greatest need; they had been forced to make international arrangements for its distribution, exactly as intelligently as they were producing war supplies.

It was easier to do this because each of the Allied Nations, in addition to feeding the soldiers and the munition makers who were directly concerned in the tragic business of "winning the war," had also become responsible for feeding its entire civilian population. The appointment of food controllers, the issuing of bread cards and the system of rationing, was undertaken quite as much in the interest of just dealing in food supplies as for food conservation itself. The British government, in the winter of 1916, when we were constantly speaking on food conservation as such, had undertaken the responsibility of providing the British Isles with all its imported food, and other belligerent and neutral nations had been obliged to pursue the same course in order to avert starvation. Commercial competition had been suppressed, not in response to any theory, but because it could not be trusted to feed the feeble and helpless. The European governments had been compelled to undertake, as the consequence of the shortage in materials, the single-handed purchase of their supplies both for civil and military purposes. There had grown up an enormous consolidation of buying for a hundred and twenty million European people—a phenomenon never before witnessed in the economic history of the world.

With this accomplishment, it seemed reasonable to hope for world order in other directions as well. Certainly some of the obstructions were giving way. An English economist had said in 1917, "The war has, so far, in Europe generally, thrown the customs tariff flat." Were they, perhaps, disappearing under this onslaught of energized pity for world-wide needs, and was a motive power new in the relations between nations being evolved in response to hunger and dependence as the earliest domestic ethics had been? It was becoming clear that nations cannot oppose their political frontiers as an obstacle to free labor and exchange without suffering themselves and causing suffering; that the world was faced with a choice between freedom in international commerce or international conflicts of increasing severity. Under this new standard of measurement, preferential tariffs would inevitably disappear because the nation denied the open door must suffer in its food supplies; the control of strategic waterways or interstate railroad lines by any one nation which might be tempted to consider only the interest of its own commerce, would become unthinkable. . . .

Certainly during the winter of 1916–17, I, personally, came to believe it possible that the more sophisticated questions of national grouping and territorial control would gradually adjust themselves if the paramount human question of food for the hungry were fearlessly and drastically treated upon an international basis. I ventured further, that the League of Nations, upon which the whole world, led by President Wilson, was fastening its hopes, might be founded not upon broken bits of international law, but upon ministrations to primitive human needs.

Much had been said during the war about primitive emotion and instinctive action, but certainly their use need not be reserved to purposes of destruction. After all, the first friendly communication between tribe and tribe came through the need of food when one or the other was starving and too weak to fight; primitive human compassion made the folkway which afterward developed into political relationships. I dared to believe that this early human instinct to come together in order to avert widespread starvation could not be forever thwarted by appeals to such later separatist instincts as nationalism and therefore urge that the gates be opened and that these primitive emotions be allowed to flood our devastated world. By all means let the beneficent tide be directed and canalized by the proposed League of Nations which was, after all, the outgrowth of century old dreams.

29

"Personal Reactions in Time of War"

AFTER THE UNITED STATES had entered the war there began to appear great divergence among the many types of pacifists, from the extreme left, composed of non-resistants, through the middle-of-the-road groups, to the extreme right, who could barely be distinguished from mild militarists. There were those people, also, who although they felt keenly both the horror and the futility of war, yet hoped for certain beneficent results from the opportunities afforded by the administration of war; they were much pleased when the government took over the management of the railroads insisting that governmental ownership had thus been pushed forward by decades; they were also sure that the War Labor Policies Board, the Coal Commission and similar war institutions would make an enormous difference in the development of the country, in short, that militarism might be used as an instrument for advanced social ends. Such justifications had their lure and one found old pacifist friends on all the war boards and even in the war department itself. Certainly we were all eager to accept whatever progressive social changes came from the quick reorganization demanded by war, and doubtless prohibition was one of these, as the granting of woman suffrage in the majority of the belligerent nations was another. But some of us had suspected that social advance depends as much upon the process through which it is secured as upon the result itself; if railroads are nationalized solely in order to secure rapid transit

Note: "Personal Reactions in Time of War," in *Peace and Bread in Time of War* (New York: Macmillan, 1922), chapter 7.

of ammunition and men to points of departure for Europe, when that governmental need no longer exists what more natural than that the railroads should no longer be managed by the government?

My temperament and habit had always kept me rather in the middle of the road; in politics as well as in social reform I had been for "the best possible." But now I was pushed far toward the left on the subject of the war and I became gradually convinced that in order to make the position of the pacifist clear it was perhaps necessary that at least a small number of us should be forced into an unequivocal position. If I sometimes regretted having gone to the Woman's Congress at The Hague in 1915, or having written a book on Newer Ideals of Peace in 1911 which had made my position so conspicuously clear, certainly far oftener I was devoutly grateful that I had used such unmistakable means of expression before the time came when any spoken or written word in the interests of Peace was forbidden.

It was on my return from The Hague Congress in July, 1915, that I had my first experience of the determination on the part of the press to make pacifist activity or propaganda so absurd that it would be absolutely without influence and its authors so discredited that nothing they might say or do would be regarded as worthy of attention. I had been accustomed to newspaper men for many years and had come to regard them as a good natured fraternity, sometimes ignorant of the subject on which they asked an interview, but usually quite ready to report faithfully albeit somewhat sensationally. Hull-House had several times been the subject of sustained and inspired newspaper attacks, one, the indirect result of an exposure of the inefficient sanitary service in the Chicago Health Department had lasted for many months; I had of course known what it was to serve unpopular causes and throughout a period of campaigning for the Progressive Party I had naturally encountered the "opposition press" in various parts of the country, but this concerted and deliberate attempt at misrepresentation on the part of newspapers of all shades of opinion was quite new in my experience. After the United States entered the war, the press throughout the country systematically undertook to misrepresent and malign pacifists as a recognized part of propaganda and as a patriotic duty. We came to regard this misrepresentation as part of the war technique and in fact an inevitable consequence of war itself, but we were slow in the very beginning to recognize the situation, and I found my first experience which came long before the United States entered the war rather overwhelming.

Upon our return from the Woman's International Congress at The Hague in 1915, our local organization in New York City with others, notably a group of enthusiastic college men, had arranged a large public meeting in Carnegie Hall. Dr. Anna Howard Shaw presided and the United States delegates made a public report of our impressions in "war stricken Europe" and of the moral resources in the various countries we visited that might possibly be brought to bear against a continuation of the war. We had been much impressed with the fact that it was an old man's war, that the various forms of doubt and opposition to war had no method of public expression and that many of the soldiers themselves were far from enthusiastic in regard to actual fighting as a method of settling international difficulties. War was to many of them much more anachronistic than to the elderly statesmen who were primarily responsible for the soldiers presence in the trenches.

It was the latter statement which was my undoing, for in illustration of it I said that in praticality every country we had visited, we had heard a certain type of young soldier say that it had been difficult for him to make the bayonet charge (enter into actual hand to hand fighting) unless he had been stimulated; that the English soldiers had been given rum before such a charge, the Germans ether and that the French were said to use absinthe. To those who heard the address it was quite clear that it was not because the young men flinched at the risk of death but because they had to be inflamed to do the brutal work of the bayonet, such as disembowelling, and were obliged to overcome all the inhibitions of civilization.

Dr. Hamilton and I had notes for each of these statements with the dates and names of the men who had made them, and it did not occur to me that the information was new or startling. I was however, reported to have said that no soldier could go into a bayonet charge until he was made half drunk, and this in turn was immediately commented upon, notably in a scathing letter written to the New York Times by Richard Harding Davis, as a most choice specimen of a woman's sentimental nonsense.[1] Mr. Davis himself had recently returned from Europe and at once became the defender of the heroic soldiers who were being traduced and belittled. He lent the weight of his name and his very able pen to the cause but it really needed neither, for the misstatement was repeated, usually with scathing comment, from one end of the country to the other.

I was conscious, of course, that the story had struck athwart the popular and long-cherished conception of the nobility and heroism of the soldier as such, and it seemed to me at the time that there was no possibility of making any explanation, at least until the sensation should have somewhat subsided. I might have repeated my more sober statements with the explanation that whomsoever the pacifist held responsible for war, it was certainly not the young soldiers themselves who were, in a sense, its most touching victims, "the heroic youth of the world whom a common ideal tragically pitted against each other." Youth's response to the appeal made to their self-sacrifice, to their patriotism, to their sense of duty, to their high-hearted hopes for the future, could only stir one's admiration, and we should have been dull indeed had we failed to be moved by this most moving spectacle in the world. That they had so responded to the higher appeals only confirms Ruskin's statement that "we admire the soldier not because he goes forth to slay but to be slain."[2] The fact that many of them were obliged to make a great effort to bear themselves gallantly in the final tests of "war's brutalities" had nothing whatever to do with their courage and sense of devotion. All this, of course, we had realized during our months in Europe.

After the meeting in Carnegie Hall and after an interview with President Wilson in Washington, I returned to Chicago to a public meeting arranged in the Auditorium; I was met at the train by a committee of aldermen appointed as a result of a resolution in the City Council. There was an indefinite feeling that the meeting at The Hague might turn out to be of significance, and that in such an event its chairman should have been honored by her fellow citizens. But the bayonet story had preceded me and every one was filled with great uneasiness. To be sure, a few war correspondents had come to my rescue—writing of the overpowering smell of ether preceding certain German attacks; the fact that English soldiers knew when a bayonet charge was about to be ordered because rations of rum were distributed along the trenches. Some people began to suspect that the story, exaggerated and grotesque as it had become, indicated not cowardice but merely an added sensitiveness which the modern soldier was obliged to overcome. Among the many letters on the subject which filled my mail for weeks, the bitter and abusive were from civilians or from the old men to whom war experiences had become a reminiscence, the large number and the most understanding ones came from soldiers in active service.

Only once did I try a public explanation. After an address in Chautauqua, New York, in which I had not mentioned bayonets, I tried to remake my original statement to a young man of the associated press only to find it once more so garbled that I gave up in despair, quite unmoved by the young man's letter of apology which followed hard upon the published report of his interview.

I will confess that the mass psychology of the situation interested me even then and continued to do so until I fell ill with a serious attack of pleuro-pneumonia, which was the beginning of three years of semi-invalidism. During weeks of feverish discomfort I experienced a bald sense of social opprobrium and wide-spread misunderstanding which brought me very near to self pity, perhaps the lowest pit into which human nature can sink. Indeed the pacifist in war time, with his precious cause in the keeping of those who control the sources of publicity and consider it a patriotic duty to make all types of peace propaganda obnoxious, constantly faces two dangers. Strangely enough he finds it possible to travel from the mire of self pity straight to the barren hills of self-righteousness and to hate himself equally in both places.

From the very beginning of the great war, as the members of our group gradually became defined from the rest of the community, each one felt increasingly the sense of isolation which rapidly developed after the United States entered the war into that destroying effect of "aloneness," if I may so describe the opposite of mass consciousness. We never ceased to miss the unquestioning comradeship experienced by our fellow citizens during the war, nor to feel curiously outside the enchantment given to any human emotion when it is shared by millions of others. The force of the majority was so overwhelming that it seemed not only impossible to hold one's own against it, but at moments absolutely unnatural, and one secretly yearned to participate in "the folly of all mankind." Our modern democratic teaching has brought us to regard popular impulses as possessing in their general tendency a valuable capacity for evolutionary development. In the hours of doubt and self-distrust the question again and again arises, has the individual or a very small group the right to stand out against millions of his fellow countrymen? Is there not a great value in mass judgment and in instinctive mass enthusiasm, and even if one were right a thousand times over in conviction, was he not absolutely wrong in abstaining from this communion with fellows? The misunderstanding on the part of old friends and associates and the charge of lack of patriotism was far easier to bear than those dark periods of faint-heartedness. We gradually ceased to state our position as we became convinced that it served no practical purpose and, worse than that, often found that the immediate result was provocative.

We could not, however, lose the conviction that as all other forms of growth begin with a variation from the mass, so the moral changes in human affairs may also begin with a differing group or individual, sometimes with the one who at best is designated as a crank and a freak and in sterner moments is imprisoned as an atheist or a traitor. Just when the differing individual becomes the centro-egotist, the insane man, who must be thrown out by society for its own protection, it is impossible to state. The pacifist was constantly brought sharply up against a genuine human trait with its biological basis, a trait founded upon the instinct to dislike, to distrust and finally to destroy the individual who differs from the mass in time of danger. Regarding this trait as the basis of self-preservation it becomes perfectly natural for the mass to call such an individual a traitor and to insist that if he is not for the nation he is against it. To this an estimated nine million people can bear witness who have been burned as witches and heretics, not by mobs, for of the people who have been "lynched" no record has been kept, but by order of ecclesiastical and civil courts.

There were moments when the pacifist yielded to the suggestion that keeping himself out of war, refusing to take part in its enthusiasms, was but pure quietism, an acute failure to adjust himself to the moral world. Certainly nothing was clearer than that the individual will was helpless and irrelevant. We were constantly told by our friends that to stand aside from the war mood of the country was to surrender all possibility of future influence, that we were committing intellectual suicide, and would never again be trusted as responsible people or judicious advisers. Who were we to differ with able statesmen, with men of sensitive conscience who also absolutely abhorred war, but were convinced that this war for the preservation of democracy would make all future wars impossible, that the priceless values of civilization which were at stake could at this moment be saved only by war? But these very dogmatic statements spurred one to alarm. Was not war in the interest of democracy for the salvation of civilization a contradiction of terms, whoever said it or however often it was repeated?

Then, too, we were always afraid of fanaticism, of preferring a consistency of theory to the conscientious recognition of the social situation, of a failure to meet life in the temper of a practical person. Every student of our time had become more or less a disciple of pragmatism and its great teachers in the United States had come out for the war and defended their positions with skill and philosophic acumen. There were moments when one longed desperately for reconciliation with one's friends and fellow citizens; in the words of Amiel, "Not to remain at variance with existence but to reach that understanding of life which enables us at least to obtain forgiveness." Solitude has always had its demons, harder to withstand than the snares of the world, and the unnatural desert into which the pacifist was summarily cast out seemed to be peopled with them. We sorely missed the contagion of mental activity, for we are all much more dependent upon our social environment and daily newspaper than perhaps any of us realize. We also doubtless encountered, although subconsciously, the temptations described by John Stuart Mill: "In respect to the persons and affairs of their own day, men insensibly adopt the modes of feeling and judgment in which they can hope for sympathy from the company they keep."[3]

The consciousness of spiritual alienation was lost only in moments of comradeship with the like minded, which may explain the tendency of the pacifist in war time to seek his intellectual kin, his spiritual friends, wherever they might be found in his own country or abroad.

It was inevitable that in many respects the peace cause should suffer in public opinion from the efforts of groups of people who, early in the war, were convinced that the country as a whole was for peace and who tried again and again to discover a method for arousing and formulating the sentiments against war. I was ill and out of Chicago when the People's Council held a national convention there, which was protected by the city police but threatened with dispersion by the state troops, who, however, arrived from the capital several hours after the meeting was adjourned. The incident was most sensational and no one was more surprised than many of the members of the People's Council who thus early in the war had supposed that they were conducting a perfectly legitimate convention. The incident gave tremendous 'copy' in a city needing rationalizing rather than sensationalizing at that moment. There is no doubt that the shock and terror of the "anarchist riots" occurring in Chicago years ago have left their traces upon the nervous system of the city somewhat as a nervous shock experienced in youth will long afterwards determine the action of a mature man under widely different circumstances.

On the whole, the New York groups were much more active and throughout the war were allowed much more freedom both of assembly and press, although later a severe reaction followed expressed through the Lusk Committee and other agencies. Certainly neither city approximated the freedom of London and nothing surprised me more in 1915 and again in 1919 than the freedom of speech permitted there.

We also read with a curious eagerness the steadily increasing number of books published from time to time during the war, which brought a renewal of one's faith or at least a touch of comfort. These books broke through that twisting and suppressing of awkward truths, which was encouraged and at times even ordered by censorship. Such manipulation of news and motives was doubtless necessary in the interest of war propaganda if the people were to be kept in a fighting mood. Perhaps the most vivid books came from France, early from Romain Rolland, later from Barbusse, although it was interesting to see how many people took the latter's burning indictment of war merely as a further incitement against the enemy. On the scientific side were the frequent writings of David Starr Jordan and the remarkable book of Nicolai on "The Biology of War." The latter enabled one, at least in one's own mind, to refute the pseudo-scientific statement that war was valuable in securing the survival of the fittest. Nicolai insisted that primitive man must necessarily have been a peaceful and social animal and that he developed his intelligence through the use of the tool, not through the use of the weapon; it was the primeval community which made the evolution of man possible, and cooperation among men is older and more primitive than mass combat which is an outgrowth of the much later property instinct. No other species save ants, who also possess property, fights in masses against other masses of its own kind.[4] War is in fact not a natural process and not a struggle for existence in the evolutionary sense. He illustrated the evolutionary survival of the fittest by two tigers inhabiting the same jungle or feeding ground, the one who has the greater skill and strength as a hunter survives and the other starves, but the strong one does not go out to kill the weak one, as the war propagandist implied; or by two varieties of mice living in the same field or barn in the biological struggle, the variety which grows a thicker coat survives the winter while the other variety freezes to extinction, but if one variety of mice should go forth to kill the other, it would be absolutely abnormal and quite outside the evolutionary survival which is based on the adjustment of the organism to its environment. George Nasmyth's book on Darwinism and the Social Order was another clear statement of the mental confusion responsible for the insistence that even a biological progress is secured through war.[5] Mr. Brailsford wrote constantly on the economic results of the war and we got much comfort from John Hobson's "Toward International Government," which gave an authoritative account of the enormous amount of human activity actually carried on through international organizations of all sorts, many of them under governmental control. Lowes Dickenson's books, especially the spirited challenge in "The Choice Before Us," left his readers with the distinct impression that "war is not inevitable but proceeds from definite and removable causes."[6] From every such book the pacifist was forced to the conclusion that none save those interested in the realization of an idea are in a position to bring it about and that if one found himself the unhappy possessor of an unpopular conviction, there was nothing for it but to think as clearly as he was able and be in a position to serve his country as soon as it was possible for him to do so.

But with or without the help of good books a hideous sensitiveness remained, for the pacifist, like the rest of the world, has developed a high degree of suggestibility, sharing that consciousness of the feelings, the opinions and the customs of his own social group which is said to be an inheritance from an almost pre-human past. An instinct which once enabled the man-pack to survive when it was a question of keeping together or of perishing off the face of the earth is perhaps not underdeveloped in any of us. There is a distinct physical as well as moral strain when this instinct is steadily suppressed or at least ignored.

The large number of deaths among the older pacifists in all the warring nations can probably be traced in some measure to the peculiar strain which such maladjustment implies. More than the normal amount of nervous energy must be consumed in holding one's own in a hostile world. These older men, Kier Hardie and Lord Countney in England, Jenkin Lloyd Jones, Rauchenbusch, Washington Gladden in the United States, Lammasch and Fried in Austria, had been honored by their fellow citizens because of marked ability to interpret and understand them. Suddenly to find every public utterance wilfully misconstrued, every attempt at normal relationship repudiated, must react in a baffled suppression which is health-destroying even if we do not accept the mechanistic explanation of the human system. Certainly by the end of the war we were able to understand, although our group certainly did not endorse the statement of Cobden, one of the most convinced of all internationalists: "I made up my mind during the Crimean War that if ever I lived in the time of another great war of a similar kind between England and another power, I would not as a public man open my mouth on the subject, so convinced am I that appeals to reason, conscience or interest have no force whatever on parties engaged in war, and that exhaustion on one or both sides can alone bring a contest of physical force to an end."

On the other hand there were many times when we stubbornly asked ourselves, what after all, has maintained the human race on this old globe despite all the calamities of nature and all the tragic failings of mankind, if not faith in new possibilities, and courage to advocate them. Doubtless many times these new possibilities were declared by a man who, quite unconscious of courage, bore the "sense of being an exile, a condemned criminal, a fugitive from mankind." Did every one so feel who, in order to travel on his own proper path had been obliged to leave the traditional highway? The pacifist, during the period of the war could answer none of these questions but he was sick at heart from causes which to him were hidden and impossible to analyze. He was at times devoured by a veritable dissatisfaction with life. . . . No one knew better than we how feeble and futile we were against the impregnable weight of public opinion, the appalling imperviousness, the coagulation of motives, the universal confusion of a world at war. . . . We were well aware that the modern liberal having come to conceive truth of a kind which must vindicate itself in practice, finds it hard to hold even a sincere and mature opinion which from the very nature of things can have no justification in works. The pacifist in war time is literally starved of any gratification of that natural desire to have his own decisions justified by his fellows.

That, perhaps, was the crux of the situation. We slowly became aware that our affirmation was regarded as pure dogma. We were thrust into the position of the doctrinnaire, and although, had we been permitted, we might have cited both historic and scientific tests of our so-called doctrine of Peace, for the moment any sanction even by way of illustration was impossible.

It therefore came about that ability to hold out against mass suggestion, to honestly differ from the convictions and enthusiasms of one's best friends did in moments of crisis come to depend upon the categorical belief that a man's primary allegiance is to his vision of the truth and that he is under obligation to affirm it.

Notes

1. Richard Harding Davis (1864–1916) was an author of romantic novels and is widely regarded as one of the greatest journalists of his generation. He was especially successful as a daring war reporter. Davis fanned the flames of the campaign against Addams for her alleged slur against the courage of men in uniform on the Western front.

2. Anyone familiar with the literature of war is struck by the pervasive theme of self-sacrifice. See Jean Bethke Elshtain, *Women and War* (New York: Basic Books, 1987; 2nd ed., University of Chicago Press, 1994).

3. John Stuart Mill (1806–1873) is the greatest liberal political theorist of the nineteenth century whose tract *On Liberty* is a classic of liberal political thought. He was also an ardent supporter of women's suffrage.

4. We now know, of course, that there is a good bit more organized violence in the animal kingdom, including among the higher primates, than Jane Addams here allows for, based on the evidence circulating in her own era.

5. George Nasmyth (1882–1920) was the author of a major work, *Social Progress and the Darwinian Theory*, published in 1916.

6. Lowes Dickinson (1862–1932) is no relation to Emily Dickinson, the great poet.

30

"Address of Miss Addams at Carnegie Hall" (The Revolt Against War)

I AM SURE WE WOULD CALL all of this a tribute to the cause of peace. It is very fine that peace can be as rousing almost as war. It is very difficult to try to formulate one's experiences when one has been brought face to face with so much genuine emotion and high patriotism as Europe exhibits at the present moment, and one becomes very much afraid of generalizing. In the first place, the situation is so confused, so many wild and weird things are said about it, that one is afraid to add one word that is not founded upon absolutely first-hand impressions and careful experience, because for the world one would not add a bit to this already overwhelming confusion. And one does not come back—at least I do not—from these various warring countries with any desire to let loose any more emotion upon the world. I feel that what is needed above all else is some careful understanding, some human touch, if you please, in this over-involved and over-talked-up situation in which so much of the world finds itself in dire confusion and bloodshed. One gets afraid of tall talk; and one does not know where words may lead the people to whom one is speaking. They seem to have acquired such fearful significance and to have power over the very issues of life and death itself. And so I should like, if I might, for a few moments, to tell as simply as I can the experiences which we had at The Hague.

Note: "Address of Miss Addams at Carnegie Hall" (The Revolt Against War), *Survey*, vol. 34 (July 17, 1915).

People are much too kind who call me the leader of that movement, for I was not that in any sense of the word. The meeting was convened and called together by a group of European women, and only after all the arrangements had been made did we know about it in America, and consent to go. They were anxious to have a woman from a neutral country to serve as president, and it was safer to have the neutral country as far away as possible, and America was the furthest away. Therefore, I think, America was chosen. But I beg of you to look at it, if we may, for a few moments together, in its simplest terms. After all, the women who called the Congress were sure that, although during this last year none of the great international congresses, in science or arts or the most abstract subjects have dared to meet, yet the women who had been meeting during many years in such conventions as Dr. Shaw has described, at least a few of them, could come together and in all sobriety and in all friendliness discuss their common aims and the terrible stake which they all had together in this war. And, of course, that faith, as you know, was well grounded, and for three days and a half, with much less friction than is usual in the ordinary meetings of men or women, so far as I know them, the women met there at The Hague and formulated their series of resolutions. I will confess that the first day we were a little cautious. We skated, as it were, more or less on thin ice, because we did not know how far we dared venture in freedom of expression. One of the Dutch Committee came to me and whispered almost in a stage whisper, "I think you ought to know that the hall is full of police, not only those supplied by The Hague, but some of them supplied by the Government itself, because they feared disorder." I said, "Very well, we will be very happy indeed to have the police hear our declarations, and if we need their services, we will be very glad to call upon them." It seemed as if every one were nervous, and I will admit that there was an element of risk, if you please, in asking these women to come, but they did come from twelve different countries, in the midst of the strain under which Europe is now laboring.

On the last day of that conference it was suggested that the resolutions be carried by committees to the various governments of Europe, and to the President of the United States. Some of us felt that the congress was ending very happily, that we had proceeded day by day in good will and understanding, and that it was perhaps unfortunate to venture further. But the resolution was passed, and two committees set forth. One committee, consisting of a woman from the side of the Allies, a woman from the side of the Germans, and two women from the neutral nations, went to the north, to visit the Scandinavian countries and Russia. . . . The other committee, I hope, will make a report, and I am sure they will have a most interesting one to make. This second committee, consisting of the vice-president and the president of the congress, women from the two neutral nations, Holland and America, set forth to visit the other countries.

I should like, if I may, to reproduce in the minds of this audience. . . some of the impressions made by this pilgrimage of ours, if you choose to call it so, going from one government to another, to nine governments in all, as we did in the space of five weeks.

The first thing which is striking is this, that everywhere one heard the same phrases, the identical phrases, given as the causes and as the reasons for the war. Each of the warring nations, I solemnly assure you, is fighting under the impulse of self-defense. Each of the warring nations, I assure you, is fighting to preserve its own traditions and its own ideals from those who would come in to disturb and destroy those high traditions and those ideals. And from one tongue or another it was translated. . . . I almost knew what to expect, what phrases were coming next, after a foreign minister had begun. We were received in each of the capitals, in London, in Berlin, in Vienna, in Budapest, in Rome, in Havre, where the Belgium government is now established, and we also took in Switzerland, although it was neutral, and Holland, although that was neutral, we were received in each of those countries in each case by the minister of foreign affairs, and by the chancellor or prime minister, and in all of the countries we saw members of Parliament and other men who are responsible for governmental policies.

It is, of course, difficult in any wise to sum up these experiences, but I will try to tell you another thing which we found very striking. In practically all of the foreign offices and especially in two of the foreign offices which I supposed to be leading, one on one side, and one on the other side of this conflict, the men said, again in very similar phrases, that a nation at war cannot make negotiations, that a nation at war cannot even express a willingness to receive negotiations, for if it does either, the enemy will at once construe it as a symptom of weakness, and under the terms which are made the side which first suggested negotiations will suffer as being considered the side that was weaker and was suing for peace. But they said in all of these different foreign offices that if some other power will present propositions, if neutral peoples, however they may be gotten together, peoples who will command the respect of the foreign offices to whom their propositions are represented, if a small group is willing to get together to study the situation seriously and to make propositions... until some basis is found upon which negotiations might commence, there is none of the warring nations that would not be glad to receive such service. That came to us unequivocally. We presented to each of the chancelleries our resolutions, but we talked for the most part about the possibility of substituting negotiations for military processes. It is very easy for a minister to say, "This country will never receive negotiations. We are going to drive the enemy out inch by inch." But it is pretty hard for him to say that to one or two or three or four women who are sitting there, and who ask, "If a proposition were presented to you, which seemed to you feasible, if something were presented to you which might mean the beginning of further negotiations between yourselves and your enemies, would you decline such a proposition, would you feel justified to go on sacrificing the young men of your country in order to obtain through bloodshed what might be obtained through negotiations, the very thing for which your foreign office was established?" No minister, of course, is willing to say that he would, and no minister would be willing, of course, to commit himself for a moment to such a policy. That we found true everywhere.

Then there was another thing that was impressed upon us all the time, and this was that in all of the great countries which we visited, although the people are tremendously united within the countries at the present moment, although there is no break that can be seen or heard anywhere on the part of the people fighting together, still they wish the war to cease, or they are going to divide into parties, one party to oppose the other. While they are united in this tremendous national consciousness, there are in every single country two general lines of approach. One is through the military party, which believes that the matter can be settled only upon a military basis, and the other is through a civil party, which very much deprecates this exaltation of militarism, which says that the longer the war goes on, the more the military authorities will be established, as censors of the press are established in all sorts of places which they ordinarily did not occupy; the longer the war goes on, the more the military power is breaking down all the safeguards of civil life and of civil government, and that consequently it will be harder for civil life and for the rights of civil life to resuscitate themselves and regain their place over the rights and power of the military. And that goes on through the mere continuation of the war, and the military becomes more strongly intrenched in these countries every month, and the longer the war goes on, and the more desperately the people cling to their armies for their salvation, the more absolute are the power and the glory of that army. And the people, who represent the civil view of life, in the midst of their patriotic fervor, in the midst of their devotion to the army see that, and long for some other form of settlement, for some other form of approach to this terribly confused situation, long for it in each succeeding month more than they did in the month before.

And one can only say as one goes from one country to another, one can only say for oneself and say it to the citizens as one has opportunity, that if this war is ever to be settled through negotiations ... Why not begin now before the military becomes even further entrenched? Why not begin now when you still have enough power to hold them to their own statements, to hold them to their own purposes, and not allow them to rule and control the absolute destinies of the nation.

I am quite aware that in every country we met, broadly speaking, the civil people and not the military people. I am quite aware that it was natural for us to see the pacificists, if you please—although they are hardly known under that name—it was more natural for us to meet and know the people who were on that side of life, instead of those on the military side of life. But because we did meet dozens of them, I am willing to believe that there must be many more of the same type of mind in every country, quite as loyal as the military people, quite as eager for the growth and development of their own ideals and their own standard of living, but believing with all their hearts that the military message is a wrong message and cannot in the end establish those things which are so dear to their hearts.

That is something to work upon, and when peace comes it must come through the people within those countries having some sort of claim upon the same type of mind and the same type of people in other countries. At present they have no communication. They say under the censorship of the press one man cannot tell how many other men are feeling as he does or believing as he does. Although he is a comrade in mind, and may be living in the next town, may be living in the next street, he does not know how many there are; he cannot get them together because, as you know, in our large cities with their huge agglomerations of human beings, we can communicate largely only through the daily press. We cannot find out the public opinion in any other way. Poor method as it seems, it is all that we have worked out as yet—and in the warring countries nothing goes into the press excepting those things which the military censor deems fit and proper.

So, as we went about, people would say to us, in regard to the press, "If you see so and so, say a word about lessening the censorship of the press." And we said, "No, we can talk about but this one thing. We cannot carry messages from the citizens to their governments." But over and over again this request was made. And as we got back to one country they would say. "Are people talking like that there? That is just the way we are talking here." But they do not know each other from one country to another, and the individuals cannot find each other within the country itself.

Another thing which seems to me very striking is this: in each of the warring nations there is this point of similarity; generally speaking, we heard it everywhere—this was not universal, but we heard it everywhere—that this was an old man's war; that the young men who were dying, the young men who were doing the fighting, were not the men who wanted the war, and were not the men who believed in the war; that somewhere, in Church and State, somewhere in the high places of society, elderly people, the middle aged people, had established themselves and had convinced themselves that this was a righteous war, that this war must be fought out, and, as a young man put it, in a certain country, "and we young fellows have to do the fighting."

This is a terrible indictment, and I admit that I cannot substantiate it, I can only give it to you as an impression, but I should like to bring one or two details before you to back it up, so to speak. I thought when I got up I should not mention the word "German" or the word "Allies," but perhaps if I give an example from Germany and then an example from the Allies, I will not get into trouble.

We met a young German in Switzerland. He had been in the trenches for three months and a half. He had been wounded in the lungs and had been sent to Switzerland to be cured. A physician, I think, would hardly say that he was going to be cured. I think a careful physician would say he had tuberculosis and would die. But he thought he was being cured, and he was speaking his mind before he went back to the trenches. He was, I suppose, what one would call a fine young man, but not an exceptional young man. He had had a gymnasium education. He had been in business with his father, had traveled in South Africa, had traveled in France, England and Holland, in the line of business, and had come to know men, as he said, as "menschen." Good "menschen" night be found in every land. And now here he was, at twenty-eight, facing death, because he was quite sure when he went back to the trenches death awaited him. But this is what he said: never during that three months and a half had he once shot his gun in a way that could possibly hit another man; nothing in the world could make him kill another man. He could be ordered into the trenches; he could be ordered to go through the motions, but the final act was in his own hands and with his own conscience. And he said, "My brother is an officer"—he gave the name of his brother; he gave the name of his rank; he wasn't concealing anything; he was quite too near death's door to have any shifting and concealing—"he never shoots anything; he never shoots in a way that will kill. And I know dozens and dozens of young men who do not."

We had a list given to us by the woman at the head of a hospital in one German city of live young Germans who had been cured and were ready to be sent back to the trenches who had committed suicide, not because they were afraid of being killed, but because they were afraid they might be put into a position where they would have to kill some one else.

We heard stories of that sort from France, while we talked with nurses in hospitals, with convalescent soldiers, with the mothers of soldiers who had come back on furlough and had gone again into the trenches; and in all of those countries there are surprising numbers of young men and older men who will not do any fatal shooting, because they think that no one has the right to command them to do that thing.

Now I would like to give my testimony from England, in order to be quite fair and square. This was published in the Cambridge Magazine at Cambridge University. It was written by a young man who had gone from Cambridge. . . "The greatest trial that this war has brought is that it has released the old men from all restraining influences, and has let them loose upon the world. The city editors, the retired majors, the amazons"—women are included, you see—"and last but not least, the venerable archdeacons have never been so free from restraint. Just when the younger generation was beginning to take its share in the affairs of the world this war has come to silence us, permanently or temporarily as the case may be. Meanwhile the old men are having field days of their own. In our name and for our sakes, as they imagine, they are doing their very utmost, it would seem, to perpetuate by their appeals to hate, to intolerance and revenge, those very follies which have produced the present conflict."

I am not going to tell of many things that were said, because I think there have been for the present too many things said, but the mothers said to us repeatedly, "It was hard to see that boy go, because he did not believe in war. He did not belong to the generation that believes in war."

One of the leading men of Europe, whose name you would instantly recognize if I felt at liberty to give it, said, "If this war could have been postponed for ten years, perhaps," he said, "I will be safe and say, twenty years, war would have been impossible in Europe, because of the tremendous revolt against it in the schools and the universities."

I am quite sure when I say that, that it is a partial view. I am quite sure that there are thousands of young men in the trenches feeling that they are performing the highest possible duties. I am quite sure that the spirit of righteousness is in the hearts of most of them, at least of many of them. But I am also sure that throughout there are to be found these other men who are doing violence to the highest teachings they know. It seemed to me at times as if the difference between the older generation and the new was something which was apprehended dimly in each country; that the older men believed more in abstractions, shall I say, that when they talked of patriotism, when they used certain words, certain theological or nationalistic words, these meant more to them than they did to the young men; that the young men took life much more from the point of view of experience. . . they took life much more empirically, and when they went to the trenches and tested it out they concluded that it did not pay, that it was not what they wanted to do with their lives.

I saw an old Quaker in England who said, "My sons are not fighting, they are sweeping mines." They allow themselves to sweep mines, but they do not allow themselves to fire mines. "My sons are doing this, that and the other thing. It is strange to me, because they never went to Quaker meetings, but they are awfully keen now on being consistent." Now, there you are. I think it was the older generation, the difference again between the older and the new. This again may be a superficial impression, but such as it is, we had it in every single country, one after the other.

I would like to say just a word about the women in the various countries. The belief that a woman is against war simply and only because she is a woman and not a man, of course, does not hold. In every country there are many, many women who believe that the war is inevitable and righteous, and that the highest possible service is being performed by their sons who go into the army, just as there are thousands of men believing that in every country. The majority of women and men doubtless believe that. But the women do have a sort of pang about it. Let us take the case of an artist, an artist who was in an artillery corps, let us say, and was commanded to fire upon a wonderful thing, say St. Mark's at Venice, or the Dome at Florence, or any other great architectural and beautiful thing. I am sure he would have just a little more compunction than the man who had never given himself to creating beauty and did not know the cost of it. And there is certainly that deterrent on the part of the women who have nurtured these soldiers from the time they were little things, who brought them into the world, and brought them up to the age of fighting, and then see them destroyed. That curious revolt comes out again and again, even in the women who are most patriotic, and who say, "I have five sons, and a son-in-law, in the trenches. I wish I had more sons to give." Even those women when they are taken off their guard, give a certain protest, a certain plaint against the whole situation which very few men, I think, are able to formulate.

Now, what is it that these women do in the hospitals? They nurse the men back to health and send them to the trenches, and the soldiers say to them, "You are so good to us when we are wounded; you do everything in the world to make life possible and to restore us; why do you not have a little pity for us when we are in the trenches; why do you not put forth a little of this same effort and this same tenderness to see what might be done to pull us out of those miserable places?" That testimony came to us, not from the nurses of one country, and not from the nurses who were taking care of the soldiers on one side, but from those who were taking care of them upon every side. And it seems to make it quite clear that whether we are able to recognize it or not, there has grown up a generation in Europe, as there has doubtless grown up a generation in America, who have revolted against war. It is a God they know not of, and they are not willing to serve him, because all of their inmost sensibilities and the training upon which their highest ideals depend, revolt against the whole situation. Now, it seems to me this is true—and I have no plan and the papers were much too kind when they said that I was going to advise the President. I never dreamed of going to advise the President, and I never dreamed of coming home with any plan, for if any plans are to be formulated, it will have to be when the others have returned. I should never venture alone to do anything of the sort. But this, it seems to me, broadly speaking, might be true, that if some set of people could be gotten together who were international out of their own experience—you know, of course, that the law is the least international thing we have. We have an international body of science. A man takes the knowledge of the science to which he is devoted, and deals with that knowledge, and he doesn't ask whether it was gathered together by Englishmen or Germans. We have an international postal system, a tremendous international commerce, and a tremendous international finance—internationalism in all sorts of fields. But the law lags behind, and perhaps will lag behind for a long time, just as many of our most settled customs have never been embodied in law at all. If men could be brought together who had international experience, who had had it so long and so unconsciously that they had come to think not in nationalistic terms, but in the terms of the generation in which they were living, whether concerning business or labor or any other thing which has become so tremendously international, if they could be brought together and could be asked to try to put the very best mind they had, not as they represented one country or another, but as they represented human life and human experience as it has been lived during the last ten years in Europe, upon the question of what has really brought about this situation—Does Servia need a seaport? Is that what is the matter with Servia? I won't mention any of the other warring countries because I might get into difficulties, but is this thing or that thing needed? What is it from the human standpoint, from the social standpoint? Is it necessary to feed the people of Europe who are, as you know, so underfed in all of the southern portions of Europe.

Is it necessary in order to feed them to get the wheat out of Russia? In Heaven's name then, let us have more harbors in order to get that wheat out of Russia. Let us not consider it from the point of view of the claims of Russia, or the counterclaims of some one else, but let us consider it from the point of view of the needs of Europe—I believe if men with that temper, and that experience, and that sort of understanding of life were to begin to make propositions to the various governments which would not placate the claims of one government and set it over against the claims of another government, but would look at the situation from a humane standpoint. I am quite sure, I say from the knowledge of dozens of men in all of the countries who talk about the situation, that that sort of negotiation would be received. That does not seem an impossible thing, does it?

Perhaps the most shocking impression left upon one's mind is this, that in the various countries the temper necessary for continuing the war is worked up and fed largely by the things which have occurred in the war itself. Germany has done this, the Allies have done that, somebody else tried to do this, and we foiled them by doing that, and what awful people they are, and they must therefore be crushed. Now I submit that any, shall I say plain mother, any peasant woman who found two children fighting, not for any cause which they stated, but because he did that and I did this, and therefore he did that to me, that such a woman would say: That can't go on; that leads to nothing but continued hatred and quarreling. Let us say that there are two gangs of boys in a boys' club who are fighting. Yes, we did this because the other fellows did that. You would simply have to say: "I won't go into the rights and wrongs of this; this thing must stop, because it leads nowhere and gets you nowhere." And let us go on with larger groups. We all know the strikes that have gone on for weeks with the original cause quite lost sight of. I submit that something of the same sort is happening in Europe now. They are going on because of the things which have been done in the war, and that certainly is a very curious reason for continuing the war. And what it needs, it seems to many of us, is a certain touch of human nature. The human nature in the trenches would be healed over, the kindly people in the various countries would not support the war longer, and foreign officers themselves would resume their own business, that of negotiation versus that of military affairs, if the thing could be released instead of being fed and kept at the boiling pitch as it is all the time by outrages here and there and somewhere else.

I do not know how that could be brought about, but I will submit it is a very simple analysis of a very complex situation. But when you go about you see the same sort of sorrow, the tremendous loss of life in these countries, and you can't talk to a woman on any subject, not on the subject of peace and war, not on the subject of the last time she traveled here or there, if you please, without finding at once that she is in the deepest perplexity, that she is carrying herself bravely, and going on with her accustomed activities because she thinks thereby she is serving her country. But her heart is being torn all the time. At last human nature must revolt. This fanatic feeling which is so high in every country, and which is so fine in every country, cannot last. The wave will come down of course. The crest cannot be held indefinitely, and then they will soberly see the horrible things which have happened, and they will have to soberly count up the loss of life and the debt they have settled upon themselves for years to come.

I could go on and tell you many things which we saw. We spoke with Cardinals. The Pope himself gave us an audience of half an hour. Those are men of religious responsibility, men who feel keenly what has happened in Europe. And yet there they all are apparently powerless to do the one thing which might end it. We did not talk peace as we went about; it would merely confuse the issue, but isn't it hideous that whole nations find the word peace intolerable. We said, why not see what can be done to arrive at some way of coming together to discover what might he done in place of the settlement which is now being fought out by military processes. And that was as far as we were able to go with clearness and safety, and upon that platform we were met with the greatest—some one said courtesy—it was to my mind more than courtesy, it was indeed as though we brought a breath of fresh air, some one coming in at last to talk of something that was not of war. We went into the room of one of the prime ministers of Europe—and I never have a great deal of self-confidence, I am never so dead sure I am doing the right thing, and I said to him. "This probably seems to you very foolish, to have women going about in this way," and he said: "Foolish? Not at all. These are the first sensible words that have been uttered in this room for ten months." He said "That door opens from time to time, and people come in and say, 'Mr. Minister, we must have more men, we must have more ammunition, we must have more money. We cannot go on with this war without more of something else,'" and he continued: "At last that door opens and two people walk in and say. 'Mr. Minister, could not negotiations be begun.'" After all I may not represent his country very worthily, but he is an officer of the government in a high place, and that is what he said. I give it to you for what it is worth. And there are other testimonials of the same sort from all kinds of people in office and they are part of the peoples who are at war and unable to speak for themselves.

There is one more thing I should like to say and I will close: that is, that one feels that the talk against militarism, and the belief that it can he crushed by a counter-militarism is, as has been uttered so many times, one of the greatest illusions which can possibly seize the human mind. England likes to talk and does talk sharply against what it calls militarism, but if they have conscription in England, the militarism which they think they are lighting will, at least for the moment, have conquered England itself, which had always been so proud that it had a free army, not a conscriptive army. All of the young men of France between certain ages come to their deaths in their effort to move people out of trenches from which they cannot be moved, because they are absolutely built in of concrete on both sides—and even military men say that you cannot budge these without tremendous loss of life—if these young men are convinced that France must arm as never before, that she must turn herself into a military nation, then, of course, the militaristic idea has conquered in France; and the old belief that you can drive a belief into a man at the point of a bayonet is in force once more. And yet it seems almost as foolish to think that, if militarism is an idea and an ideal, it can be changed and crushed by counter-militarism or by a bayonet charge. And the young men in these various countries say of the bayonet charges: "That is what we cannot think of." We heard in all countries similar statements in regard to the necessity for the use of stimulants before men would engage in certain bayonet charges, that they have a regular formula in Germany, that they give them rum in England, and absinthe in France. They all have to give them the "dope" before the bayonet charge is possible. Think of that. No one knows who is responsible. All the nations are responsible, and they indict themselves. But in the end human nature must reassert itself. The old elements of human understanding and human kindliness must come to the fore, and then it may well be that they will reproach the neutral nations and will say: "What was the matter with the rest of the world that they kept quiet while this horrible thing was happening, that men for a moment had lost their senses in this fanaticism of national feeling all over Europe." They may well say, "You were far enough away from it not to share in it, and yet you wavered until we had lost the flower of the youth of all Europe." That is what they said in various tongues and according to their various temperaments, and that is what enables them to fight for their countries when they are at war, believing as they did in the causes for which they were fighting. The women who came to the congress were women who were impelled by a genuine feeling of life itself, which compelled them to come and see if it could hold for three days and a half composed of women. Now they say: "Oh, yes, we see it can be done; we thought it could not be done." Three or four scientific societies who saw it said, "Perhaps we can do it. We were not at all sure that, if we tried to do it, we could do it." But we women got there, and there it is standing for what it is worth. Now, please do not think we are overestimating a very slight achievement, or taking too seriously the kindness with which we were received abroad, but we do wish to record ourselves as being quite sure that the peoples in these various countries were grateful for the effort, trifling as it was. The people say, "We do not want this war." They say that the governments are making this war, and the governments say, "We do not want this war. We will be grateful to anybody who will help us stop it." We did not reach the military offices, but we did talk to a few military men, and we talked to some of them who said that they were sick to death of this war, and I have no doubt there were many others who, if they spoke freely, would say the same thing. And without abandoning their causes, and without lowering, if you please, the real quality of their patriotism, whatever it is which these various nations want, the women's resolutions said to them, and we said it to them as long as they permitted us to talk, "Whatever it is you want, and whatever it is you feel you ought to have with honor, why in the world can't you submit your case to a tribunal of fair minded men. If your cause is as good as you say it is, or you are sure it is, certainly those men will find the righteousness which adheres within it." And they all say that if the right medium can be found the case will be submitted.

31

"WOMEN'S MEMORIES —
CHALLENGING WAR"

I WAS SHARPLY REMINDED OF an obvious division between high
tradition and current conscience in several conversations I held during the great European war with women who had sent their sons to the
front in unquestioning obedience to the demands of the State, but who,
owing to their own experiences, had found themselves in the midst of
that ever-recurring struggle, often tragic and bitter, between two conceptions of duty, one of which is antagonistic to the other.

One such woman,[1] who had long been identified with the care of
delinquent children and had worked for many years towards the establishment of a Children's Court, had asked me many questions concerning the psychopathic clinic in the Juvenile Court in Chicago,
comparing it to the brilliant work accomplished in her own city
through the coöperation of the university faculty. The Imperial government itself had recently recognized the value of this work and at
the outbreak of the war was rapidly developing a system through
which the defective child might be discovered early in his school career, and might not only be saved from delinquency but such restricted abilities as he possessed be trained for the most effective use.
"Through all these years," she said, "I had grown accustomed to the
fact that the government was deeply concerned in the welfare of the
least promising child. I had felt my own efforts so identified with it
that I had unconsciously come to regard the government as an agency

Note: "Women's Memories—Challenging War," in *The Long Road of
Woman's Memory* (New York: Macmillan, 1916), chapter 5.

for nurturing human life and had apparently forgotten its more primitive functions.

"I was proud of the fact that my son held a state position as professor of Industrial Chemistry in the University, because I knew that the research in his department would ultimately tend to alleviate the harshness of factory conditions, and to make for the well-being of the working classes in whose children I had become so interested.

"When my son's regiment was mobilized and sent to the front I think that it never occurred to me, any more than it did to him, to question his duty. His professional training made him a valuable member of the Aviation Corps, and when, in those first weeks of high patriotism his letters reported successful scouting or even devastating raids, I felt only a solemn satisfaction. But gradually through the months, when always more of the people's food supply and constantly more men were taken by the government for its military purposes, when I saw the state institutions for defectives closed, the schools abridged or dismissed, women and children put to work in factories under hours and conditions which had been legally prohibited years before, when the very governmental officials who had been so concerned for the welfare of the helpless were bent only upon the destruction of the enemy at whatever cost to their fellow-citizens, the State itself gradually became for me an alien and hostile thing.

"In response to the appeal made by the government to the instinct of self-preservation, the men of the nation were ardent and eager to take any possible risks, to suffer every hardship, and were proud to give their lives in their country's service. But was it inevitable, I constantly asked myself, that the great nations of Europe should be reduced to such a primitive appeal? Why should they ignore all the other motives which enter into modern patriotism and are such an integral part of devotion to the state that they must in the end be reckoned with?

"I am sure that I had reached these conclusions before my own tragedy came, before my son was fatally wounded in a scouting aëroplane and his body later thrown overboard into a lonely swamp. It was six weeks before I knew what had happened and it was during that period that I felt most strongly the folly and waste of putting men, trained as my son had been, to the barbaric business of killing. This tendency in my thinking may have been due to a hint he had given me in the very last letter I ever received from him, of a change that was taking place within himself. He wrote that whenever he heard the firing of a huge field-piece he knew that the explosion consumed years of the taxes which had been slowly accumulated by some hard-working farmer or shopkeeper, and that he unconsciously calculated how fast industrial research would have gone forward, had his department been given once a decade the costs of a single day of warfare, with the government's command to turn back into alleviation of industrial conditions the taxes which the people had paid. He regretted that he was so accustomed to analysis that his mind would not let the general situation alone but wearily went over it again and again; and then he added that this war was tearing down the conception of government which had been so carefully developed during this generation in the minds of the very men who had worked hardest to fulfill that conception.

"Although the letter sounded like a treatise on government, I knew there was a personal pang somewhere behind this sombre writing, even though he added his old joking promise that when their fathers were no longer killed in industry, he would see what he could do for my little idiots.

"At the very end of the letter he wrote, and they were doubtless the last words he ever penned, that he felt as if science herself in this mad world had also become cruel and malignant.

"I learned later that it was at this time that he had been consulted in the manufacture of asphyxiating gases, because the same gases are used in industry and he had made experiments to determine their poisonousness in different degrees of dilution. The original investigation with which he had been identified had been carried on that the fumes released in a certain industrial process might be prevented from injuring the men who worked in the factory. I know how hard it must have been for him to put knowledge acquired in his long efforts to protect normal living to the brutal use of killing men. It was literally a forced act of prostitution."

As if to free her son's memory from any charge of lack of patriotism, after a few moments she continued: "These modern men of science are red-blooded, devoted patriots, facing dangers of every sort in mines and factories and leading strenuous lives in spite of the popular conception of the pale anæmic scholar, but because they are equally interested in scientific experiments wherever they may be carried on, they inevitably cease to think of national boundaries in connection with their work. The international mind, which really does exist in spite of the fact, that it is not yet equipped with adequate organs for international government, has become firmly established, at least among scientists. They have known the daily stimulus of a wide and free range of contacts. They have become interpenetrated with the human consciousness of fellow scientists all over the world.

"I hope that I am no whining coward—my son gave his life to his country as many another brave man has done, but I do envy the mothers whose grief is at least free from this fearful struggle of opposing ideals and traditions. My old father, who is filled with a solemn pride over his grandson's gallant record and death, is most impatient with me. I heard him telling a friend the other day that my present state of mind was a pure demonstration of the folly of higher education for women; that it was preposterous and more than human flesh could bear to combine an intellectual question on the function of government with a mother's sharp agony over the death of her child. He said he had always contended that women, at least those who bear children, had no business to consider questions of this sort, and that the good sense of his position was demonstrated now that such women were losing their children in war. It was enough for women to know that government waged war to protect their firesides and to preserve the nation from annihilation; at any rate, they should keep their minds free from silly attempts to reason it out. It's all Bertha von Suttner's book and other nonsense that the women are writing, he exploded at the end."[2]

Then as if she were following another line of reminiscence she began again. "My son left behind him a war bride, for he obeyed the admonition of the statesmen, as well as the commands of the military officers in those hurried heroic days. But the hasty wooing betrayed all his ideals of marriage quite as fighting men of other nations did violence to his notions of patriotism, and the recklessness of a destructive air raid outraged his long devotion to science. Of course his child will be a comfort to us and his poor little bride is filled with a solemn patriotism which never questions any aspect of the situation. When she comes to see us and I listen to the interminable talk she has with my father, I am grateful for the comfort they give each other, but when I hear them repeating those hideous stories of the conduct of the enemy which accumulate every month and upon which the war spirit continually feeds itself, I with difficulty refrain from crying out upon them that he whose courage and devotion they praise so loudly would never have permitted such talk of hatred and revenge in his presence; that he who lived in the regions of science and whose intrepid mind was bent upon the conquest of truth, must feel that he had died in vain did he know to what exaggerations and errors the so-called patriotism of his beloved country had stooped.

"I listen to them thinking that if I were either older or younger it would not be so hard for me, and I have an unreal impression that it would have been easier for my son if the war had occurred in the first flush of his adventurous youth. Eager as he had been to serve his country, he would not then have asked whether it could best be accomplished by losing his life in a scouting aëroplane or by dedicating a trained mind to industrial amelioration. He might then easily have preferred the first and he certainly would never have been tormented by doubts. But when he was thirty-one years old and had long known that he was steadily serving his country through careful researches, the results of which would both increase the nation's productivity and protect its humblest citizens, he could not do otherwise than to judge and balance social values. I am, of course, proud of his gallant spirit, that did not for a moment regret his decision to die for his country, but I can make the sacrifice seem in character only when I place him back in his early youth.

"At times I feel immeasurably old, and in spite of my father's contention that I am too intellectual, I am consciously dominated by one of those overwhelming impulses belonging to women as such, irrespective of their mental training, in their revolt against war. After all, why should one disregard such imperative instincts? We know perfectly well that the trend of a given period in history has been influenced by 'habits of preference' and by instinctive actions founded upon repeated and unrecorded experiences of an analogous kind; that desires to seek and desires to avoid are in themselves the very incalculable material by which the tendencies of an age are modified. The women in all the belligerent countries who feel so alike in regard to the honor and human waste of this war and yet refrain from speaking out, may be putting into jeopardy that power inherent in human affairs to right themselves through mankind's instinctive shifting towards what the satisfactions recommend and the antagonisms repulse. The expression of such basic impulses in regard to human relationships may be most important in this moment of warfare which is itself a reversion to primitive methods of determining relations between man and man or nation and nation.

"Certainly the women in every country who are under a profound imperative to preserve human life, have a right to regard this maternal impulse as important now as was the compelling instinct evinced by primitive women long ago, when they made the first crude beginnings of society by refusing to share the vagrant life of man because they insisted upon a fixed abode in which they might cherish their children. Undoubtedly women were then told that the interests of the tribe, the diminishing food supply, the honor of the chieftain, demanded that they leave their particular caves and go out in the wind and weather without regard to the survival of their children. But at the present moment the very names of the tribes and of the honors and glories which they sought are forgotten, while the basic fact that the mothers held the lives of their children above all else, insisted upon staying where the children had a chance to live, and cultivated the earth for their food, laid the foundations of an ordered society.

"My son used to say that my scientific knowledge was most irregular, but profound experiences such as we are having in this war throw to the surface of one's mind all sorts of opinions and half-formed conclusions. The care for conventions, for agreement with one's friends, is burned away. One is concerned to express only ultimate conviction even though it may differ from all the rest of the world. This is true in spite of the knowledge that every word will be caught up in an atmosphere of excitement and of that nervous irritability which is always close to grief and to moments of high emotion.

"In the face of many distressing misunderstandings I am certain that if a minority of women in every country would clearly express their convictions they would find that they spoke not for themselves alone but for those men for whom the war has been a laceration,—'an abdication of the spirit.' Such women would doubtless formulate the scruples of certain soldiers whose 'mouths are stopped by courage,' men who months ago with closed eyes rushed to the defence of their countries.

"It may also be true that as the early days of this war fused us all into an overwhelming sense of solidarity until each felt absolutely at one with all his fellow-countrymen, so the sensitiveness to differences is greatly intensified and the dissenting individual has an exaggerated sense of isolation. I try to convince myself that this is the explanation of my abominable and constant loneliness, which is almost unendurable.

"I have never been a Feminist and have always remained quite un-moved by the talk of the peculiar contribution women might make to the State, but during the last dreadful months, in spite of women's widespread enthusiasm for the war and their patriotic eagerness to make the supreme sacrifice, I have become conscious of an unalterable cleavage between Militarism and Feminism. The Militarists believe that government finally rests upon a basis of physical force, and in a crisis such as this, Militarism, in spite of the spiritual passion in war, finds its expression in the crudest forms of violence.

"It would be absurd for women even to suggest equal rights in a world governed solely by physical force, and Feminism must necessar-ily assert the ultimate supremacy of moral agencies. Inevitably the two are in eternal opposition.

"I have always agreed with the Feminists that, so far as force plays a great part in the maintenance of an actual social order, it is due to the presence of those elements which are in a steady process of elimination; and of course as society progresses the difficulty arising from woman's inferiority in physical strength must become proportionately less. One of the most wretched consequences of war is that it arrests these benef-icent social processes and throws everything back into a coarser mould. The fury of war, enduring but for a few months or years, may destroy slow-growing social products which it will take a century to recreate— the 'consent of the governed,' for instance. . . .

"But why do I talk like this! My father would call it one of my un-trained and absurd theories about social progress and the functions of government concerning which I know nothing, and would say that I had no right to discuss the matter in this time of desperate struggle. Nevertheless it is better for me in these hideous long days and nights to drive my mind forward even to absurd conclusions than to let it fall into one of those vicious circles in which it goes round and round to no purpose."

In absolute contrast to this sophisticated, possibly oversophisticated, mother was a simple woman who piteously showed me a piece of shrapnel taken from her son's body by his comrades, which they had brought home to her in a literal-minded attempt at comfort. They had told her that the shrapnel was made in America and she showed it to me, believing that I could at sight recognize the manufactured products of my fellow-countrymen. She apparently wished to have the statement either confirmed or denied, because she was utterly bewildered in her feeling about the United States and all her previous associations with it. In her fresh grief, stricken as she was, she was bewildered by a sudden reversal of her former ideals. Many of her relatives had long ago emigrated to America, including two brothers living in the Western states, whom she had hoped to visit in her old age. For many reasons, throughout her youth and early womanhood, she had thought of that far-away country as a kindly place where every man was given his chance and where the people were all friendly to each other irrespective of the land in which they had been born. To have these same American people send back the ammunition which had killed her son was apparently incomprehensible to her.

She presented, it seemed to me, a clear case of that humble internationalism which is founded not upon theories, but upon the widespread immigration of the last fifty years, interlacing nation to nation with a thousand kindly deeds. Her older brother had a fruit ranch which bordered upon one of those co-operative Italian colonies so successful in California, and he had frequently sent home presents from his Italian neighbors with his own little cargoes. The whole had evidently been prized by his family as a symbol of American good-will and of unbounded opportunity. Her younger brother had attained some measure of success as a contractor in an inland town, and when he had written home of the polyglot composition of the gangs of men upon whose labors his little fortune had been founded, she had taken it as an example of all nationalities and religions working happily together. He had also served one term as mayor, obviously having been elected through his popularity with the same foreign colonies from which his employes had been drawn.

For many reasons therefore she had visualized America as a land in which all nationalities understood each other with a resulting friendliness which was not possible in Europe, not because the people still living in Europe were different from those who had gone to America, but because the latter, having emigrated, had a chance to express their natural good-will for everybody. The nations at war in Europe suggested to her simple mind the long past days of her grandmother's youth when a Protestant threw stones at a Catholic just because he was "different."

The religious liberty in America was evidently confused in her mind with this other liberalism in regard to national differences.

Holding this conception of actual internationalism as it had been evolved among simple people, crude and abortive though it was, she had been much more shocked by the fact that friendly Americans should make ammunition to be used for killing any human being than by the actual war itself, because the war was taking place in Europe, where it was still quite natural for a German to fight against a Frenchman or an Italian against an Austrian.

Her son had been a Socialist and from the discussions he sometimes held with his comrades in her house, she had grown familiar with certain phrases which she had taken literally and in some curious fashion had solemnly come to believe were put into practice in her El Dorado of America.

The arguments I had used so many times with her fellow-countrymen to justify America's sale of ammunition, ponderously beginning with The Hague conventions of 1907, I found useless in the face of this idealistic version of America's good-will.

She was evidently one of those people whose affections go out to groups and impersonal causes quite as much as to individuals, thus often supplementing and enlarging harsh and narrow conditions of living. She certainly obtained a curiously personal comfort out of her idealization of America. Her conversation revealed what I had often vaguely felt before when men as well as women talked freely of the war, that her feelings had been hurt, that her very conception of human nature had received a sharp shock and set-back. To her the whole world and America in particular would henceforth seem less kind and her spirit would be less at home. She was tormented by that ever recurring question which perhaps can never be answered for any of us too confidently in the affirmative, "Is the Universe friendly?" The troubled anguish in her old eyes confirmed her statement that the thought of the multitude of men who were being killed all over the world oppressed her day and night. This old woman had remained faithful to the cause of moral unity and bore her humble testimony to one of the noblest and profoundest needs of the human spirit.

These efforts at spiritual adjustment necessitated by the war are attempted by many people, from the simple souls whose hard-won conceptions of a friendly universe have been brought tumbling about their ears, to the thinking men who are openly disappointed to find civilized nations so irrational. Such efforts are encountered in all the belligerent nations as well as in the neutral ones, although in the former they are often inhibited and overlaid by an overwhelming patriotism. Nevertheless, as I met those women who were bearing their hardships and sorrows so courageously, I often caught a glimpse of an inner struggle, as if two of the most fundamental instincts, the two responsible for our very development as human beings, were at strife with each other. The first is tribal loyalty, such unquestioning acceptance of the tribe's morals and standards that the individual automatically fights when the word comes; the second is woman's deepest instinct, that the child of her body must be made to live.

We are told that the peasants in Flanders, whose fields border upon the very trenches, disconsolately came back to them last Spring and continued to plough the familiar soil, regardless of the rain of shrapnel falling into the fresh furrows; that the wine growers of Champagne last Autumn insistently gathered their ripened grapes, though the bombs of rival armies were exploding in their vineyards; why should it then be surprising that certain women in every country have remained steadfast to their old occupation of nurturing life, that they have tenaciously held to their anxious concern that men should live, through all the contagion and madness of the war fever which is infecting the nations of the earth.

In its various manifestations the struggle in women's souls suggests one of those movements through which, at long historic intervals, the human spirit has apparently led a revolt against itself, as it were, exhibiting a moral abhorrence for certain cherished customs which, up to that time, had been its finest expression. A moral rebellion of this sort was inaugurated three thousand years ago both in Greece and Judea against the old custom of human sacrifice. That a man should slay his own child and stand unmoved as the burning flesh arose to his gods was an act of piety, of courage, and of devotion to ideals, so long as he performed the rite wholeheartedly. But after there had gradually grown up in the minds of men first the suspicion, and then the conviction, that it was unnecessary and impious to offer human flesh as a living sacrifice, courage and piety shifted to the men who refused to conform to this long-established custom. At last both the Greeks and the Jews guarded themselves against the practice of human sacrifice with every possible device. It gradually became utterly abhorrent to all civilized peoples, an outrage against the elemental decencies, a profound disturber of basic human relations. Poets and prophets were moved to call it an abomination; statesmen and teachers denounced it as a hideous barbarism, until now it is so nearly abolished by the entire race that it is no longer found within the borders of civilization and exists to-day only in jungles and hidden savage places.

There are indications that the human consciousness is reaching the same stage of sensitiveness in regard to war as that which has been attained in regard to human sacrifice. In this moment of almost universal warfare there is evinced a widespread moral abhorrence against war, as if its very existence were more than human nature could endure. Citizens of every nation are expressing this moral compunction, which they find in sharp conflict with current conceptions of patriotic duty. It is perhaps inevitable that women should be challenged in regard to it, should be called upon to give it expression in such stirring words as those addressed to them by Romain Rolland, "Cease to be the shadow of man and of his passion of pride and destruction. Have a clear vision of the duty of pity! Be a living peace in the midst of war—the eternal Antigone refusing to give herself up to hatred and knowing no distinction between her suffering brothers who make war on each other."

This may be a call to women to defend those at the bottom of society who, irrespective of the victory or defeat of any army, are ever oppressed and overburdened. The suffering mothers of the disinherited feel the stirring of the old impulse to protect and cherish their unfortunate children, and women's haunting memories instinctively challenge war as the implacable enemy of their age-long undertaking.

Notes

1. The following conversation is a composite made from several talks held with each of two women representing both sides of the conflict. Their opinions and observations are merged into one because in so many particulars they were either identical or overlapping. Both women called themselves patriots, but each had become convinced of the folly of war. [Note: This is a Jane Addams note, not one of mine. J.B.E.]

2. Bertha von Suttner (1843–1914), important German antiwar activist and writer.

32

"PATRIOTISM AND PACIFISTS IN WARTIME"

T HE POSITION OF THE PACIFIST in time of war is most difficult, and necessarily he must abandon the perfectly legitimate propaganda he maintained before war was declared. When he, with his fellow countrymen, is caught up by a wave of tremendous enthusiasm and
is carried out into a high sea of patriotic feeling, he realizes that the
virtues which he extols are brought into unhappy contrast to those
which war, with its keen sense of a separate national existence, places
in the foreground.

Nevertheless, the modern peace movement, since it was inaugurated
three hundred years ago, has been kept alive throughout many great
wars and during the present war some sort of peace organization has
been maintained in all of the belligerent nations. Our Woman's International Committee for Permanent Peace, for instance, of which I have the
honor to be chairman, is in constant communication with our branches
organized since this war began in such fighting nations and colonies as
Australia, Austria, Belgium, Canada, Finland, Germany, Great Britain,
Ireland, Hungary, British India, Italy, France, Poland and Russia, in addition to the neutral countries of Europe and one or two of South America.

Surely the United States will be as tolerant to pacifists in time of war as
those countries have been, some of which are fighting for their very existence, and fellow-citizens, however divided in opinion, will be able to discuss those aspects of patriotism which endure through all vicissitudes.

Note: "Patriotism and Pacifists in Wartime," *City Club of Chicago Bulletin*,
vol. 10 (June 18, 1917).

Before taking up the subject of this paper, it may be well to state that there are many types of pacifists, from the extreme left, composed of non-resistants, through the middle-of-the-road groups, to the extreme right, who can barely be distinguished from mild militarists; and that in our movement, as well as in many others, we must occasionally remind ourselves of Emerson's saying, that the test of a real reformer is his ability to put up with the other reformers.

In one position, however, we are all agreed, and to this as to an abstract proposition, we must hold at all times, even after war has been declared: that war, although exhibiting some of the noblest qualities of the human spirit, yet affords no solution for vexed international problems; and that moreover after war has been resorted to, its very existence, in spite of its superb heroisms and sacrifices which we also greatly admire, tends to obscure and confuse those faculties which might otherwise find a solution.

In the stir of the heroic moment when a nation enters war, men's minds are driven back to the earliest obligations of patriotism, and almost without volition the emotions move along the worn grooves of blind admiration for the soldier and of unspeakable contempt for him who, in the hour of danger, declares that fighting is unnecessary. We pacifists are not surprised, therefore, when apparently striking across and reversing this popular conception of patriotism, that we should not only be considered incapable of facing reality, but that we should be called traitors and cowards. It makes it all the more incumbent upon us, however, to demonstrate, if we can that in our former advocacy we urged a reasonable and vital alternative to war, and that our position now does not necessarily imply lack of patriotism or cowardice.

To take up the three charges in order:

PACIFISTS AND "PASSIVISM"

First: The similarity of sound between the words "passive" and "pacifism" is often misleading, for most pacifists agree with such statements as that made by Mr. Brailsford in *The New Republic* of March 17th — that wonderful journal, *The New Republic*, from which so many preachers are now taking their texts in preference to the New Testament. Mr. Brailsford, an Englishman, said: "This war was an act of insurgence against the death in life which acquiesces in hampered conditions and unsolved problems. There was in this concerted rush to ruin and death the force of a rebellious and unconquerable life. It was bent on a change, for it knew that the real denial and surrender of life is not a physical death but the refusal to move and progress." Agreeing substantially with this analysis of the causes of the present war, we pacifists, so far from passively wishing nothing to be done, contend on the contrary that this world crisis should be utilized for the creation of an international government able to make the necessary political and economic changes when they are due; we feel that it is unspeakably stupid that the nations should have failed to create an international organization through which each one, without danger to itself, might recognize and even encourage the impulse toward growth in other nations.

Pacifists believe that in the Europe of 1914, certain tendencies were steadily pushing towards large changes which in the end made war, because the system of peace had no way of effecting those changes without war, no adequate international organization which could cope with the situation. The conception of peace founded upon the balance of power or the undisturbed *status quo* was so negative that frustrated national impulses and suppressed vital forces led to war, because no method of orderly expression had been devised.

We are not advocating the mid-Victorian idea that good men from every country meet together at The Hague or elsewhere, where they shall pass a resolution, that "wars hereby cease" and that "the world hereby be federated." What we insist upon is that the world can be organized politically by its statesmen as it has been already organized into an international fiscal system by its bankers or into an international scientific association by its scientists. We ask why the problem of building a railroad to Bagdad, of securing corridors to the sea for a land-locked nation, or warm water harbors for Russia, should result in war. Surely the minds of this generation are capable of solving such problems as the minds of other generations have solved their difficult problems. Is it not obviously because such situations transcend national boundaries and must be approached in a spirit of world adjustment, while men's minds still held apart by national suspicions and rivalries are unable to approach them in a spirit of peaceful adjustment?

The very breakdown exhibited by the present war reinforces the pacifists' contention that there is need of an international charter — a Magna Charta indeed — of international rights, to be issued by the nations great and small, with large provisions for economic freedom.

THE PATRIOTISM OF PACIFISTS

In reply to the old charge of lack of patriotism, we claim that we are patriotic from the historic viewpoint as well as by other standards. American pacifists believe — if I may go back to those days before the war, which already seem so far away — that the United States was especially qualified by her own particular experience to take the leadership in a peaceful organization of the world. We then ventured to remind our fellow citizens that when the founders of this republic adopted the federal constitution and established the Supreme Court, they were entering upon a great political experiment of whose outcome they were by no means certain. The thirteen colonies somewhat slowly came into the federation, and some of them consented very reluctantly to the use of the supreme court. Nevertheless, the great political experiment of the United States was so well established by the middle of the 19th century, that America had come to stand to the world for the principle of federal government and for a supreme tribunal whose decisions were binding upon sovereign states.

We pacifists hoped that the United States might perform a similar service in the international field, by demonstrating that the same principles of federation and of an interstate tribunal might be extended among widely separated nations as they had already been established between contiguous states. Stirred by enthusiasm over the great historical experiment of the United States, it seemed to us that American patriotism might rise to a supreme effort. We hoped that the United States might refuse to follow the beaten paths of upholding the rights of a separate nationalism by war, because her own experience for more than a century had so thoroughly committed her to federation and to peaceful adjudication as to every-day methods of government. The President's speech before the Senate embodied such a masterly restatement of these early American principles that thousands of his fellow citizens dedicated themselves anew to finding a method for applying them in the wider and more difficult field of international relationships.

THE TASK OF ORGANIZATION

We also counted upon the fact that this great war had challenged the validity of the existing status between nations as it had never been questioned before, and that radical changes were being proposed by the most conservative of men and of nations. As conceived by the pacifist, the constructive task laid upon the United States in the recent crisis called for something more than diplomacy and the old type of statesmanship.

It demanded a penetration which might discover a more adequate moral basis for the relationship between nations and the sustained energy to translate the discovery into political action. The exercise of the highest political intelligence, we hoped, might not only establish a new scale of moral values, but might hasten to a speedy completion for immediate use, that international organization which has been so long discussed and so ardently anticipated. For there is another similarity between the end of the 18th century and the present time; quite as the Declaration of Independence and the adoption of the Constitution had been preceded by much philosophic writing on the essential equality of all men and on the possibility of establishing self government among them, so the new internationalism has long had its thinkers who have laid a foundation of abstract principle. Then, as now, however, the great need was not for more writing, nor even for able propaganda, but for a sober attempt to put them into practice, to translate them into concrete acts.

AMERICAN PRECEDENTS

We were more hopeful of this from the fact that the test of experience had already been applied by the United States to such a course of actions at least so far as to substitute adjudication for war. Four times before now has our country become involved in the fringe of European wars, and in three instances the difficulties were peacefully adjudicated.

In 1798, when the French Revolution had pulled most of Europe into war, George Washington, who was then President — perhaps because he was so enthusiastic over our Supreme Court — refused to yield to the clamor of his countrymen to go to war on the side of France, our recent friend, against Great Britain, out recent enemy, and sent Chief Justice John Jay over to London to adjust the difficulties which had arisen in connection with our shipping. Because John Jay was successful in his mission, George Washington became for the time so unpopular that he publicly expressed the wish that he had never been born — although he does not seem to have permanently lost his place in the hearts of his countrymen.

Four years later, when France violated our neutral rights on the seas, John Adams, as President, sent commissioners to Paris who adjudicated the matter. Although keeping the peace made Adams so unpopular that be failed of his second term, many years later, as an old man, he said that his tombstone might well be inscribed with the words: "He kept the peace with France."

Adams' successor, Thomas Jefferson, encountered the same difficulty, and in spite of grave mistakes. succeeded in keeping the country out of war. He was finally rewarded by the peaceful acquisition of the vast Louisiana territory.

The War of 1812 was the result of a disregard of neutral rights incident to the Napoleonic upheaval and made the first break in the chain of international adjudications instituted by Chief Justice Jay, which had become known as the American plan.

Although both England and France had violated our rights at sea, the United States was drawn into war with England at the moment when she was in a death grapple with Napoleon, and so irrational is war, that in the final terms of peace, the treaty did not mention the very matter upon which war had been declared. Perhaps, however, three adjudications out of five instances in which the shipping of the United States has become involved in European war is as much as can be hoped for.

PACIFISTS AGAINST ISOLATION

With such a national history back of us, as pacifists we are thrown into despair over our inability to make our position clear when we are accused of wishing to isolate the United States and to keep our country out of world politics. We are, of course, urging a policy exactly the reverse, that this country should lead the nations of the world into a wider life of coordinated political activity; that the United States should boldly recognize the fact that the vital political problems of our time have become as intrinsically international in character as have the commercial and social problems so closely connected with them; that modern wars are not so much the result of quarrels between nations as of the rebellion against international situations inevitably developed through the changing years, which admit of adequate treatment only through an international agency not yet created. The fact that such an agency has been long desired, the necessity for it clearly set forth by statesmen in all the civilized nations, and that a splendid beginning had already been made at The Hague, makes the situation only more acute.

AMERICA'S RESOURCES FOR LEADERSHIP

We had also hoped much from the varied population of the United States, for whether we will or not, our very composition would make it easier for us than for any other nation to establish an international organization founded upon understanding and good will did we but possess the requisite courage and intelligence to utilize it.

There are in this country thousands of emigrants from the Central Powers, to whom a war between the United States and the fatherland means exquisite torture. They and their inheritances are a part of the situation which faces us. They are a source of great strength in an international venture, as they are undoubtedly a source of weakness in a purely nationalistic position of the old-fashioned sort. These ties of blood, binding us to all the nations of the earth, afford a unique equipment for a great international task if the United States could but push forward into the shifting area of internationalism.

Modern warfare is an intimately social and domestic affair. The civilian suffering and, in certain regions, the civilian mortality, is as great as that endured by the soldiers. There are thousands of our fellow citizens who cannot tear their minds away from Poland, Galicia, Syria, Armenia, Serbia, Roumania, Greece, where their own relatives are dying from diseases superinduced by hardship and hunger. To such sore and troubled minds war had come to be a hideousness which belongs to Europe alone and was part of that privation and depression which they had left behind them when they came to America. Newly immigrated Austrian subjects of a dozen nationalities came to their American friends during the weeks of suspense, utterly bewildered by the prospect of war. They had heard not three months before that the President of the United States did not believe in war — for so the Senate speech has been interpreted by many simple minds — and they had concluded that whatever happened, some more American way would be found.

The multitude of German subjects who have settled and developed certain parts of the United States had, it seems to me, every right to be considered as important factors in the situation, before war was declared. President Wilson himself said, in February, after the U-boat campaign had been announced, that he was giving due weight to the legitimate rights of the American citizens of German descent. The men of '48 are as truly responsible for our national ideals as the Puritans of New England, the Quakers of Pennsylvania, or the Russian revolutionists of the '90s. How valuable that gallant spirit of '48, spreading as it did from one European country to another, could be made in an international venture it is difficult to estimate.

It has been said that this great war will prove the bloody angle at which mankind turns from centuries of warfare to the age of peace. But certainly this will not happen automatically nor without leadership founded upon clear thinking and international sympathies.

It is very easy to go to war for a well defined aim which changes imperceptibly as the war progresses, and to continue the war or even end it on quite other grounds. Shifting aims is one of the inherent characteristics of war as an institution.

Pacifists hoped that this revolution in international relationships, which has been steadily approaching for three hundred years and is long over-due might have been obtained without our participation in the war; but we also believe that it may be obtained after the war, if the United States succeeds in protecting and preserving the higher standards of internationalism.

NATIONAL UNSELFISHNESS

Pacifists recognize and rejoice in the large element of national unselfishness and in the recognition of international obligation set forth by President Wilson as reasons for our participation in the great war. We feel that the exalted sense of patriotism in which each loses himself in the consciousness of a national existence has been enlarged by an alliance with nations across the Atlantic and across the Pacific with whom we are united in a common purpose. Let the United States, by all means, send a governmental commission to Russia; plans for a better fiscal system to bewildered China; food to all nations wherever little children are starving; but let us never forget that the inspiring and overwhelming sense of a common purpose, which an alliance with fifteen or sixteen nations gives us, is but a forecast of what might be experienced if the genuine international alliance were achieved, including all the nations of the earth.

In so far as we and our allies are held together by the consciousness of a common enemy and the fear of a common danger, there is a chance for the growth of the animosity and hatred which may yet overwhelm the attempt at international organization to be undertaken after the war, as it has defeated so many high-hearted attempts in the past.

May we not say in all sincerity that for thirty-three months Europe has been earnestly striving to obtain through patriotic wars, that which can finally be secured only through international organization? Millions of men, loyal to one international alliance, are gallantly fighting millions of men loyal to another international alliance, because of Europe's inability to make an alliance including them all. Can the United States discharge her duty in this situation save as she finally makes possible the establishment of a genuine international government?

AMERICA'S SENSE OF FAILURE

Ever since the European war began, the United States has been conscious of a failure to respond to a moral demand; she has vaguely felt that she was shirking her share in a world effort toward the higher good; she has had black moments of compunction and shame for her own immunity and safety. Can she hope through war to assuage the feverish thirst for action she has felt during all those three years? There is no doubt that she has made the correct diagnosis of her case, of her weariness with a selfish, materialistic life, and of her need for concerted, self-forgetting action. But is blood-letting a sufficiently modern remedy in such a diagnosis? Will she lose her sense of futility and her consciousness of moral failure, when thousands of her young men are facing the dangers of war? Will she not at the end of this war still feel her inadequacy and sense of failure unless she is able to embody in a permanent organization the cosmopolitanism which is the essence of her spirit? Will she be content, even in war time, to organize food supplies of one group of nations and to leave the women and children of any nation still starving?

Is not the government of the United States somewhat in the position of those of us who have lived for many years among immigrants? It is quite impossible for us to ask just now whether the parents of a child who needs food are Italians, and therefore now our allies, or Dalmatians. and therefore now our "alien enemies." Such a question is as remote as if during the Balkan war we had anxiously inquired whether the parents were Macedonians or Montenegrins, although that was then a distinction of paramount importance to thousands of our neighbors.

It has been officially declared that we are entering this war "to make the world safe for democracy." While we are still free to make terms with our allies, are we not under obligation to assert that the United States owes too much to all the nations of the earth whose sons have developed our raw prairies into fertile fields, to allow the women and children of any of them to starve?

It is told of the recent Irish uprising that after Sheehy Skeffington had been arrested, an English soldier was placed on guard in the house lest Mrs. Skeffington and her little boy might destroy possibly incriminating papers; that the soldier, after standing for a long time in the presence of the woman and child, finally shifted his position and, looking uneasily at Mrs. Skeffington, said, "You see, I didn't enlist exactly for this."

Would it not be possible for the United States to tell her allies that she had not enlisted in this great war for the purpose of starving women and children? When the United States entered the war the final outcome was apparently to be decided by food supply rather than by force of arms. Could Germany hold out during the spring and early summer until the new crop was garnered? Could England feed herself were the U-boat campaign in any degree successful, were the terrible questions in men's minds.

For decades civilized nations had confidently depended upon other nations for their supply of cattle and of grain until long continued war brought the primitive fear of starvation back into the world with so many other obsolete terrors.

NATIONAL BOUNDARIES AND FOOD SUPPLY

Such an international organization as the United States is now creating in connection with her allies for the control of their common food supply is clearly transcending old national bounds. It may be a new phase of political unification in advance of all former achievements, or it may be one of those shifting alliances for war purposes of which European history affords so many examples. Simply because food is so strategic, as it were, we lay ourselves open to the latter temptations. Could we not free ourselves from this and at the same time perform a great service if we urge that an international commission sit at Athens during the rest of this war, as an international commission sat in London during the Balkan wars? Such a commission might at once insist upon a more humane prosecution of the war, at least so far as civilian populations are concerned, a more merciful administration of the lands occupied, and distribution of foodstuffs to all conquered peoples.

MILITARY COERCION OR SOCIAL CONTROL?

The United States has to her credit a long account of the spread of democratic institutions during the years when she was at peace with the rest of the world. Her own experiment as a republic was quickly followed by France, and later by Switzerland, and to the south of her a vast continent contains no nation which fails — through many vicissitudes though it be — to maintain a republican form of government.

It has long been the aim of this government of ours and of similar types of government the world over to replace coercion by the full consent of the governed, to educate and strengthen the free will of the people through the use of democratic institutions, and to safeguard even the rights of minorities. This age-long process of obtaining the inner consent of the citizen to the outward acts of his government is of necessity violently interrupted and thrown back in war time; but we all realize that some day it must be resumed and carried forward again, perhaps on an international basis. Let us strive to keep our minds clear regarding it.

Some of us once dreamed that the cosmopolitan inhabitants of this great nation might at last become united in a vast common endeavor for social ends. We hoped that this fusing might be accomplished without the sense of opposition to a common enemy which is an old method of welding people together, better fitted for military than for social use. If this for the moment is impossible, let us at least place the spirit of cooperation above that of bitterness and remember the wide distinction between social control and military coercion.

It is easy for all of us to grow confused in a moment like this for the pacifist, like the rest of the world, has developed a high degree of suggestibility; we too share that sensitiveness to the feelings, the opinion, and the customs of our own social group which is said to be an inheritance from an almost prehuman past. An instinct which once enabled the man-pack to survive when it was a question of keeping a herd together, or of perishing off the face of the earth is perhaps not under-developed in any of us.

ARE PACIFISTS COWARDS?

When as pacifists we urge a courageous venture into international ethics, which will require a fine valor as well as a high intelligence, we experience a sense of anti-climax when we are told that because we do not want war, we are so cowardly as to care for "safety first," that we place human life, physical life, above the great ideals of national righteousness.

But surely that man is not without courage who, seeing that which is invisible to the majority of his fellow countrymen, still asserts his conviction and is ready to vindicate its spiritual value over against the world. Each advance in the zigzag line of human progress has traditionally been embodied in small groups of individuals, who have ceased to be in harmony with the *status quo* and have demanded modifications. Such modifications did not always prove to be in the line of progress, but whether they were or not, they always excited opposition, which from the nature of the case was never so determined as when the proposed changes touched moral achievements which were greatly prized and had been secured with much difficulty.

Bearing in mind the long struggle to secure and maintain national unity, the pacifist easily understands why his theories seem particularly obnoxious just now, although in point of fact our national unity is not threatened, and would be finely consummated in an international organization.

PEACE AND JUSTICE

With visions of international justice filling our minds, pacifists are always a little startled when those who insist that justice can only be established by war, accuse us of caring for peace irrespective of justice. Many of the pacifists in their individual and corporate capacity have long striven for social and political justice with a fervor perhaps equal to that employed by the advocates of force, and we realize that a sense of justice has become the keynote to the best political and social activity in this generation. Although this ruling passion for juster relations between man and man, group and group, or between nation and nation, is not without its sterner aspects, among those who dream of a wider social justice throughout the world there has developed a conviction that justice between men or between nations can be achieved only through understanding and fellowship, and that a finely tempered sense of justice, which alone is of any service in modern civilization, cannot be secured in the storm and stress of war. This is not only because war inevitably arouses the more primitive antagonisms, but because the spirit of fighting burns away all of those impulses, certainly towards the enemy, which foster the will to justice.

We believe that the ardor and self sacrifice so characteristic of youth could be enlisted for the vitally energetic role which we hope our beloved country will inaugurate in the international life of the world. We realize that it is only the ardent spirits, the lovers of mankind, who will be able to break down the suspicion and lack of understanding which has so long stood in the way of the necessary changes upon which international good order depends; who will at last create a political organization enabling nations to secure without war, those high ends which they now gallantly seek to obtain upon the battlefield.

With such a creed, can the pacifists of today be accused of selfishness when they urge upon the United States not isolation, not indifference to moral issues and to the fate of liberty and democracy, but a strenuous endeavor to lead all nations of the earth into an organized international life worthy of civilized men?

33

"FRIENDSHIP WITH FLORENCE KELLEY—NATIONAL CONFERENCE ON SOCIAL WORK"

A S THE EDUCATIONAL ACTIVITIES at Hull-House were gradually developed, we found many young people to whom it was useless to offer educational advantages because the promise of youth had
been frustrated by premature labor or by malnutrition in childhood. It
was not only the greed of employers but of consumers and even of parents which had to be curbed before leisure for education could be secured for such children, and it was perhaps inevitable that efforts to secure a child labor law should have been our first venture into the field
of state legislation.

Florence Kelley who came into residence at Hull-House in the winter
of 1891, galvanized us all into more intelligent interest in the industrial
conditions all about us. She was especially concerned for the abolition
of child labor and the sweating system and she urged such remedial
measures as shorter hours, and the elimination of night work. Writing
of her Edith Abbott says:

> The method of social progress in which Florence Kelley believed al-
> most devoutly was that of direct assault. She brought magnificent
> weapons to bear on the enemy. Sleepless, tireless, indefatigable, she

---

Note: "Friendship with Florence Kelley—National Conference on Social
Work," in *My Friend, Julia Lathrop* (New York: Macmillan, 1935), chapter 8.

was always on the alert. Life was never dull and the world was never indifferent where she lived and moved.

We all felt the stimulus of her magnetic personality and during that first winter the foundation of a lifelong friendship was laid between her and Julia Lathrop.

It was as a result of Mrs. Kelley's energy that a Commission was sent up from the Illinois legislature to investigate sweat shops in Chicago, and through the co-operation of the labor unions and other public bodies the first factory act of Illinois went into operation July 1, 1893, with Florence Kelley as chief factory inspector. . . .

It was during the same winter after the World's Fair of 1893 that William Stead often visited us at Hull-House, and his brilliant monologues on a Sunday evening or at a prolonged dinner table were very exhilarating although his indictments often seemed unduly severe.[1] He had recently published "The Bitter Cry of Outcast London" and had been most unfairly sent to prison because of his methods of securing information. But he made us all very uncomfortable by his assertion that an international white slave traffic actually existed and had ramifications in Chicago. Some years later the fact was established with the finding in the Immigration Commission's report in 1911.

Mr. Stead was much struck by the way Hull-House seemed to have become the center of a fight against the smallpox epidemic which the World's Fair had bequeathed to Chicago. I quote from a description of this experience written years afterwards by Judge Bruce:

> I knew Florence Kelley at the time of the smallpox epidemic when both she and Julia Lathrop were risking their lives in the sweatshop districts of Chicago and were fearlessly entering the rooms and tenements of the west side and not merely alleviating the sufferings of the sick but preventing the sending abroad of the disease-infected garments to further contaminate the community. I saw these two women do that which the health department of the great city of Chicago could not do. The authorities were afraid not only of personal contagion but of damage suits if they destroyed the infected garments. They therefore said that there was no smallpox in Chicago. Later as the result of a joint attack by Miss Julia Lathrop and Mrs. Florence Kelley they were induced to act and they de-

stroyed thousands of dollars worth of clothing. That attack illustrates the difference between these two tremendously useful women. Julia Lathrop, the diplomat, reasoned and cajoled. Mrs. Kelley, the fighter, asked me to file a mandamus suit to compel action. Each acted in her own way, but each fought for the same cause and each risked her life in the same conflict. Working together, they saved hundreds perhaps thousands of human lives.

One day I heard a young doctor remonstrate with Julia Lathrop that while she might consider it her duty to put the smallpox patients into the contagious disease hospital, it was really not necessary to follow them there and to be "a messenger of cheer between them and their families." She replied that there must be some human method of communication and that she certainly knew better how to keep free from contagion than their families did and that she had many more opportunities for cleanliness.

One of the Hull-House residents says: "Hull-House I verily believe was the most interesting place in the world when Julia Lathrop and Mrs. Kelley were both there. There were always Mrs. Kelley's quick characterizations for the benefit of the group of residents gathered about her after she came back from her night school. All were packed into the Octagon, where Miss Lathrop would start one of her meandering sentences which, after amusing people all the way, suddenly wound up with some unexpected twist."

The persons who knew both of these brilliant women at Hull-House tend to associate them together and vividly recall the long and scintillating discussions between them not only when both were residents but long afterwards when they often met there. Their most doughty debates centered around court decisions. Florence Kelley constantly saw what she considered beneficent legislation thrown out by the decision of the supreme courts in the states and in the nation. For instance the eight-hour law for women, which as state factory inspector she had administered for a year, was declared unconstitutional by the Supreme Court of Illinois and she later saw the minimum wage measures which had been enacted into laws by state legislatures made inoperative because they were declared unconstitutional by the Supreme Court of the United States. This was true of an attempt to limit the hours of work for the bakers of New York State, of the minimum wage law for women in Oregon, and of similar legislation. Mrs. Kelley contended that this judicial nullification of beneficent legislation on the ground of unconstitutionality set a distinct limitation to the experiments through which the nation might increase its fund of social knowledge and that it curtailed the opportunity for utilizing experimentation as a method for progressive government. She pointed out that over and over again intelligent attempts to deal with a social evil, if made the basis of legal enactment, were less likely to receive judicial approval than an outworn method of dealing with the same evil which had the doubtful value of an early precedent under conditions long obsolete. She devoutly believed and was afterward upheld by Justice Holmes in minority opinions of Supreme Court decisions, that the process of adjustment to current conditions is a necessity if constitutional government is to endure.

In these discussions Julia Lathrop usually was found defending the actions of the courts, insisting that we must proceed by precedent broadening into precedent and she held to this during the very disappointing decision of the Supreme Court in regard to the constitutionality of the federal Child Labor law which she was then administering as chief of the Children's Bureau. It is fair to her changing position however to quote from a speech that she once made to the League of Women Voters:

> As citizens of the United States, whatever our differences of opinion, we have turned of late to our Declaration of Independence and to our Constitution with a new sense of their vitality. Some of us think the Constitution ought not to be touched but that like the ark it is a complete and finished vehicle of a sacred utterance. Others of us believe that the Constitution is a living testament of adaptations to the changes which are taking place in our country. All of us respect the patriotism, the courage and the statesmanship of the men who wrote it. Even those of us who have no legal training feel that human struggle to reach just agreements of which our Constitution is the result. Men of differing lives and characters and social traditions came together eleven years after the Declaration of Independence to try to find a way by which they could agree upon a joint expression of the essential principles on which they believed the union of the states must rest.

*   *   *

They never thought they had written a perfect thing. They knew they had set up after many compromises the minimum framework of a common government. And it stands with repeated modifications after one hundred and fifty years of extraordinary national growth.

Julia Lathrop had long attended the sessions of the National Conference of Social Work, many of them when it was called the National Conference of Charities and Correction. Although in later years its delegates were not so largely representative of governmental institutions, a certain number of public officials registered in its membership every year with the thousands of citizens from every state in the Union who were engaged in all sorts of philanthropy. . . . She was profoundly interested that the state and county officials who attended the conference should be kept in close touch with the experiences and attitudes of the volunteer social workers and be pushed towards better administration of existing laws. She realized how easy it was to consider a given measure as secure when the government has taken it over but perhaps no one in the conference knew better than she how necessary it is that social workers should still feel interested in the measures they have advocated and should identify themselves with the officials charged with difficult and sometimes experimental administration. This attitude of hers occasionally appeared to the younger and ardent would-be sociologists in the conference like a throw-back to the old days of the Conference of Charities and Correction although it was greatly to the special interests of these young people that the measures they were thrusting into governmental agencies should be properly administered. Another reason why she was so deeply concerned for the development of public social service of a high professional standard was that only the public agency can be absolutely comprehensive and really continuous. The comprehensiveness was always a goal, for this meant that all who needed it were to be included in the service provided. On one occasion Florence Kelley spoke vigorously before a large general session of the National Conference of Social Work discussing methods of caring for widows and their children. "The thing to do for widows and orphans," she said quickly, "is to abolish them!"—and she went on speedily to laws concerning industrial accidents and workmen's compensation. Julia Lathrop of course agreed with her—she could always be trusted to take a large view of any situation,—but she warned the social workers at the conference that even such measures would not help the hard lot of the poor unless the officials in charge of administration knew actual conditions. . . .

Throughout Julia Lathrop's years in attendance at the conferences she was almost universally recognized as able to apply to perplexing social situations as they arose, the ability which can best be described as that of statesmanship. A host of her colleagues in social work would heartily agree with Graham Taylor's tribute: "Miss Lathrop was attracted to social work as a statesman, seeing in statesmanship a gigantic lever for wide social reform."

That Julia Lathrop was elected President of the National Council of Social Work in 1917 with the enthusiastic backing of all the young and radical members demonstrated once again how thoroughly she and the young people understood each other.

The following extracts from her letters written to Florence Kelley reveal something of the range and continuity of their mutual interests. The first have to do with efforts to secure legislation:

April 28, 1923

> *This week we had our first bout with the Illinois legislature. You would be surprised a little I think to find the amount of mis-statement [sic] which is lavishly circulated among our best citizens especially among the ladies of high standing and which is in some cases lapped up as if it were wholesome. I do not know how we shall come out. I think the deep basic difficulty which paralyzes our effort lies in the bad political situation in our state as a whole, which has put into the hands of physicians responsibility not to their profession but to politicians who control the medical service of the state. It is a strange situation— perhaps it must last until the end of this administration. Perhaps we shall be beaten but I try to remember that lobbying is an alluring indoor sport if properly played. . . .*

Oct. 4, 1926

If you all decide on the meeting in Washington I will come if it seems clear that I can help. Myself I doubt if I could be useful. While I have a few friendly connections I am ashamed to think of some legislators who detest me. It will not be easy for me to come but you know—or rather you cannot possibly know that my instinct is to do anything you ask, and I am not ready to refuse this although for various good personal reasons I earnestly hope it may prove undesirable for our purpose.

The next letters refer to international matters:

January 27, 1927

I think that I must go to the Child Welfare Committee[2] meeting in Geneva. There has been great dissatisfaction because it appeared that none of the Western Assessors or committee members are coming. Hence with my usual luck I seem to go. And then I believe in the Committee if it can be equipped for research and study. On the whole I am not sure that much ground was lost at the last session. In view of the whole situation the triumph of our cause was remarkable and leaves us a breathing space and a spark of life.

GENEVA, SWITZERLAND, *May 2, 1927*

Our news is so complete and prompt and competently set forth that if it were only factual we would be the best informed newspaper readers in the world. I do not think the European press is any more factual—.

I do not blame other countries for disliking us nor for failing to dissemble but one is too conscious of the feeling to make attendance at even such meetings as this, a pure joy. One finds valued friends of course and politeness, but the air is not too warm otherwise. . . .

From a letter written to Florence Kelley at the death of her daughter just after she had entered Smith College I venture to quote the following paragraphs:

September 30, 1905

I am sure from the brief words of your telegram that you must already find a solace in the fact of the swift unconsciousness and painlessness of Margaret's death. When I think of her as I saw her last, so beautiful, so charmingly maternal and whimsical with the little Greek baby at Hull-House, so proud of you and with such a gay independence at the same time, I can hardly imagine a daughter more perfectly filling your own ideal. That she has been yours all these growing years and had reached that wonderful youth which leads on the imagination of every older observer into an earthly paradise and that she remains to all of us forever young, forever fair—all this seems to me in itself a wonderful possession and joy.

November 11, 1931

Dearest F. K.—How could you have the heart to stay weeks and weeks in a hospital and never let me know! Only when I ask a silly favor of you do you order your precious eldest born to write me as to a thing of no consequence about which I should not have troubled you when you were in the best of health. . . . I have an uneasy feeling about any of our precious H.-H. society daring to be ill or anything, and not telling me.

Because I am afraid that in presenting these two brilliant women I have stressed their zeal too much and their grace too little, I am adding an article Julia Lathrop wrote for *The Survey* only a few weeks before her own death, revealing as to both of these good friends.

Florence Kelley—1859–1932

To those who read this inadequate page the name of Florence Kelley is well known. Many of you know her as a personal friend and feel for her an intimate affection and a deep respect. None of us can quite bear yet to speak of her as if she had gone away from this world which she so tenderly loved, and the more we consider what she has given to it the more we realize that she had exemplified a spirit and method of social study and social work in the full sense of the words which will survive as long as those who come after her desire to continue her efforts, not looking down meticulously for her footprints, but in her spirit, heads up, looking forward, as she would wish.

Some of you knew Florence Kelley in her childhood or perhaps you went to school with her. I had no such privilege but we know that she was born to a conventional and luxurious life in Philadelphia, her father, William D. Kelley, one of the ablest lawyers and most distinguished political leaders of his time; her mother of a fine Quaker family, a woman of an exceptionally gentle and retiring nature. Both must have seen with rare wisdom that this brilliant intellectual child was not of the stuff to be driven or led in the old way of education but rather that she must be helped to find her own path. Thus she received a formal education indeed, but one of exceptional interest and breadth which she pursued from school in Philadelphia to Cornell University whose door just then was opened to women—there she was graduated with a brilliant record and thence she went to the University of Zurich. And it should be added here that years later when she felt that for her work as chief state factory inspector in Illinois she needed more knowledge of law, she quietly entered the classroom of the Northwestern University Law School, took the required courses in her spare time and received her degree in 1894.

Mrs. Kelley was an accomplished linguist and fine translations stand to her credit. Of course she was a Phi Beta Kappa. She was always by taste and attainments genuinely a scholar, with a scholar's choice contempt for pretentious writing and thinking. She became absorbed in economic and social study, in the practical as well as the student's view of the labor problem, in public education as the only substitute for child labor and in all the aspects of the struggling advance toward a just social order.

I first met Mrs. Kelley when she came to Chicago in 1891. She at once became a resident of Hull-House where she lived during the eight crowded years she spent in Illinois. Her coming was timely and she helped from the first. Miss Addams and she understood each other's powers and worked together in the wonderfully effective way many of us well remember.

Soon a new opportunity opened. John P. Altgeld, who became governor of Illinois in 1893, was a man of great independence of thought and action and entirely on his own initiative, so far as I have been able to learn, he determined to appoint qualified women to various administrative and advisory positions in the state service. These appointments, carefully made and non-political, surprised everyone and gratified at least the women of the state. The most important and difficult place was that of chief factory inspector and for this position the governor selected Mrs. Kelley and as first assistant appointed Mrs. Alzina P. Stevens of Chicago, a well known leader in women's labor organizations. A legend exists to the effect that when the announcement of these two appointments was made someone remonstrated in a friendly way, saying that two such "big women" would never be able to work together, to which the governor replied, according to the legend: "If they are big enough for the job, they will get along together well enough." The event proved that the governor was right.

Mrs. Kelley, her assistant and staff, worked courageously and ably in enforcing the Illinois statute restricting the work of women and girls in manufacture to eight hours in one day and forty-eight hours in one week, but the statute was short-lived. In 1895 the Supreme Court of Illinois pronounced the provision unconstitutional.

Mrs. Kelley remained in Chicago at Hull-House, always doing whatever came to her hand, studying, writing, teaching, speaking, always stimulating, until she seemed an essential element of Chicago. But in 1899 she became general secretary of the National Consumers' League whose office was in New York and from that office she reached out across our country and beyond for the rest of her life.

In New York she lived for some years at the Nurses' Settlement with Miss Wald and there as in Hull-House she gave invaluable help.

It was from this settlement background in two cities that she drew much of her intimate knowledge of human-kind, her interest in working women, in children, in Negroes and in immigrants.

In Mrs. Kelley's book, "Some Ethical Gains Through Legislation," published in 1905, we find a plan for a United States commission for children whose scope and purpose was carried out in concise form in the Children's Bureau Act of 1912. Its passage was aided by such support from the settlements as perhaps few of us realize.

We all know how lavishly and modestly Mrs. Kelley gave herself, how faithfully she attended conventions and conferences and committees, speaking in that flute-like voice as if she was delighted to have the privilege, praising and stimulating others, asking nothing for herself. She gave herself so unsparingly that sometimes it seemed as if her life was too hard, but as I think now of her life I think she had much happiness. She was surrounded by friends known and unknown—she must have felt that. Always her mind to her a kingdom was. She must have had happiness in ruling it for the common good. More precious than all else she had her beloved family, her sons, her grandchildren. Yes, hers was a nobly rich and generous life. We know its influence must reach far beyond her day and ours.

Notes

1. William Stead, a celebrated British muckraking journalist, wrote a book exposing social conditions in Chicago (*If Christ Came to Chicago*), which exerted a profound influence on Jane Addams and her generation of reformers. Stead went to his death bravely, helping other passengers during the sinking of the *Titanic*.

2. A subcommittee of the Commission on the Welfare of Children and Young Persons of the League of Nations, of which Miss Lathrop was appointed an assessor by the Council of the League in 1925.

Part Four

Introduction:
Culture, Character, and
the Power of Memory

J ANE ADDAMS HAD LEARNED from the great George Eliot, one
of her favorite writers, the importance of memory in human life.
Pity and faithfulness are intertwined with our memories. Memory
can unlock preserves of ancient legend absorbed with our mother's
milk. One of her most famous essays, "The Devil Baby at Hull-House,"
was so much in demand that she incorporated a version of it into two
of her books. Here I include the version that appeared in *The Long
Road of Woman's Memory* (1916). The essay is an exercise in cultural
and interpretive anthropology and gives us entrée into Jane Addams's
method of "sympathetic understanding." When three Italian women
turned up at the door of Hull-House demanding to be shown a "devil
baby" born at Hull-House to an unwed mother or, perhaps, to a pious
girl married to an atheist—there were "a hundred variations" on the
tale, Addams tells us—she used the occasion, and the saga it precipitated, as a lesson in dredging contemporary meaning from ancient
myths. She found that different national traditions had their own variations of the devil-baby tale. What united them all was the sense that the
misdeeds or even impiety of the father may well be visited upon the
child as a visible sign, punishment, and torment to the evildoer. The old
women in the neighborhood and beyond, enchanted by the story and
the prospect of seeing a devil baby up close, "loosed their tongues," she
tells us, and the possibility helped them to "condense that mystic wisdom which becomes deposited" in human hearts. Many women had
faced tragic experiences in their own lives, sadly too often at the hands

of a miscreant husband-father who had brutalized, deserted, and taxed them to the very limit of human endurance.

The devil-baby story, taking the form of a deep, folklorish tradition that had been papered over but never died out entirely, speaks not only to a universal moral sense and conviction that misdeeds will not go unmarked any more than good deeds but also to an aesthetic sensibility Addams credited as part of the natural human makeup; hence, the inclusion here of "The Play Instinct and the Arts," drawn from the second volume of her autobiography, *The Second Twenty Years at Hull-House* (1930). This play instinct points to the undeniable fact that human beings need more than an opportunity to maximize their own self-interests; they also need to play. Hull-House afforded young people an opportunity to express and to develop this play instinct through its art, music, and drama clubs and through its Boys and Girls Clubs. Given our extraordinary human propensity to play and to create something aesthetically satisfying, it is essential to incorporate this dimension into education at every level and, as well, to be vigilant about those popular media that may exert an almost hypnotic power on susceptible youth—the movies, in Addams's day. She would certainly, were she still alive today, have pointed comments to make on the way our play instinct and aesthetic yearnings get twisted in consumerist ideologies and obsessions and in those representations in television, films, and the Internet. Addams's concern would be that these show human beings in degraded and degrading ways without offering any ethical interpretation or reflections on such degradation. Education is not just about learning basic subject matter, she insisted, but about instilling what the great observer of the American scene, Alexis de Tocqueville, called "habits of the heart" that call us into community life with our fellow citizens.[1] This need for moral exemplars is expressed in her essay "Tolstoy and Gandhi" (1931), for without such exemplary persons, ethical life would soon falter and fall to the lowest common denominator.

In a culturally prescient reflection, Addams anticipated the fact that women had many years stretching before them when they reached the age of fifty. Given that women's lives were no longer absorbed entirely by domestic tasks and imperatives, there was no need for the women over fifty to feel old; indeed, given her relative freedom from the intense and absorbing tasks of childrearing, she could turn to the needs of her immediate wider community, her nation, and even the wider world.

Here, "ever-widening channels are gradually being provided through which woman's increasing moral energy may flow," and women are obliged to pay attention and to draw themselves into these wider channels of human life, thereby making their own contribution. She addressed this theme in her column in *Ladies Home Journal*, in Addams's day a magazine devoted in part to serious political and cultural topics. Post–childrearing lives spent in pure leisure and self-indulgence cannot satisfy, she insisted, because they do not speak to our human complexity, our desire to be of service and to add our own individual story to the larger story of our society. This urgency begins when we are young and turns on the proper education of the moral sentiments.

No society can simply rely on human instinct to assert itself. Instead, society must train young people in what Addams called character, hence, we include her essay "Pen and Book as Tests of Character" (1913). For her, all education should be geared toward the building of character, toward what is called in German *Bildung*, the shaping and forming of a self over time. She would not support separate courses in "character education" so much as she would, and did, insist that *all* education, formal and informal, should be a training in character. When we are young our characters need to be formed. As we grow older our characters need to be sustained and strengthened. When we reach the ends of our lives, our characters help to give us a sturdy sense of where we have been, who we are, and what story we are going to leave behind.

The story of Jane Addams is a great one. She lived a remarkable, rich, varied life, and she left behind a singular tale for the telling. As long as stories like hers are told, it is not too much to hope that the "better angels of our natures" will rise to the fore and enrich us as persons, families, and communities in a nation honored for the quality of the lives its citizens live rather than exclusively for its wealth and its power.

Notes

1. Alexis de Tocqueville, *Democracy in America*, trans. George Lawrence (New York: Harper and Row, 1969). Tocqueville's great work has played a major role in the recent revival of interest in democratic civil society. Addams's vision fits squarely within the civil-society approach.

34

⟡

"PEN AND BOOK AS TESTS OF CHARACTER"

THE HOUSE OF REPRESENTATIVES by its recent affirmative vote upon the Burnett Bill reported from the Committee on Immigration and Naturalization registered itself in favor of the literacy test for immigrants arriving in the United States. Much of the discussion in the House and in the press was particularly objectionable because of the emphasis placed upon racial differences. The old and new immigration were frequently contrasted with the traditional odiousness resulting from comparisons. The epithet of "inferior races" was constantly applied to certain peasant groups who, as the result of isolation and lack of opportunity are doubtless backward, but who do not therefore belong to an inferior stock, and who exhibit no greater differences to other groups of their own race than those which often obtain between branches of the same family. Striking differences are certainly found between certain family groups in America, one of which has remained for five generations stranded in the mountains of Virginia or Tennessee, in contrast to their cousins whose forefathers crossed over the mountains into fertile valleys. Many mountain whites of America are illiterate and totally unacquainted with the advances of civilization, but they do not thereby change their race nor their capacity for development.

After all, literacy is neither a test of character nor of ability; it is merely an index of the educational system of the community in which a man has been reared. The literacy test will always work in favor of the

Note: "Pen and Book as Tests of Character," *Survey*, vol. 29 (January 4, 1913).

man from the city and discriminate against the man from the country. On the face of it, it would seem safer to admit a sturdy peasant from the mountains of Calabria than a sophisticated Neapolitan, familiar with the refined methods of police graft which have made the Camorra famous. In addition to that, the peasant finds work waiting for him, the educated man "above manual labor" often has a pitiful struggle to keep himself from starvation. Our experience at Hull House is similar to that of the friends of the immigrant everywhere. We recall an Italian editor, a Greek professor, a Russian medical student, an Armenian Master of Arts, for whom it was impossible to obtain anything but manual work which they finally undertook in bitterness of spirit and with insufficiency of muscle. A settlement constantly sees the deterioration of highly educated foreigners under the strain of maladjustment, in marked contrast to the often rapid rise of the families of illiterate immigrants.

One of the most gifted boys ever connected with Hull House, who is now a rising man in his profession and in the civic life of Chicago, is the son of immigrant parents who can neither read nor write, while one of our most baffling cases is the refined and educated son of a Greek clergyman who can find no work which he does not consider beneath his educational qualifications.

The only service America is universally eager to render to the immigrant and his children, and moreover the only one it is thoroughly equipped to offer, is free education. By the same token, so eager are the immigrants to avail themselves of America's educational opportunities for their children, that the census figures show greater illiteracy among native whites of native parentage than among native white of foreign parentage. The average illiteracy of native white of native parentage is 5.7 per cent and of native white of foreign parents 1.6 per cent. In the light of these figures it would seem clear that illiteracy is the one defect most easily remedied and that American experience does not justify the use of literacy as a fair test for entrance.

Throughout the discussion concerning the literacy test the "oversupply of unskilled labor" was constantly referred to although no comprehensive inquiry has ever been undertaken which could demonstrate this. We have no national system of labor exchanges which might show how much of the apparent unemployment is maladjustment of the supply to the demand and how much is oversupply. Certainly underemployment, casual work, long hours, poor wages, unsanitary shops, are found in industries in which the "unskilled immigrant man" is not employed. Limiting the supply by restricting immigration will cure none of these, and it merely confuses the issue to claim that it will. Until industrial conditions in America are faced, the immigrant will continue to be blamed for conditions for which the community is responsible. There is no doubt that America has failed to make legislative provisions against those evils as other countries have done, partly because the average citizen holds a contemptuous attitude toward the "foreigner" and is not stirred to action on his behalf.

In line with this lack of clear thinking and even of definite information on the subject is the constant assertion commonly made that one million immigrants a year are coming into this country; yet Secretary Nagel's annual report for the fiscal year ending June 30, 1912, shows that in the year 838,172 immigrants and 178,983 non-immigrant aliens entered. The total of these is 1,017,155. But during the year departed from the country 615,292 aliens, of whom 333,262 were of the emigrant and 282,030 of the non-emigrant class. The net or actual increase in the alien population for the fiscal year 1912, therefore, was 401,863; the corresponding increase in 1911 was 512,085, averaging less than half a million a year. Before Congress legislates further upon this subject of immigration should it not provide that copies of the valuable report issued by the Immigration Commission be given to the country that we may at least be supplied with accurate information?

35

"WOMEN'S MEMORIES — TRANSMUTING THE PAST, AS ILLUSTRATED BY THE STORY OF THE DEVIL BABY"

QUITE AS IT WOULD BE HARD for any one of us to select the summer in which he ceased to live that life, so ardent in childhood and early youth, when all the real happenings are in the future, so it must be difficult for old people to tell at what period they began to regard the present chiefly as a prolongation of the past. There is no doubt, however, that such instinctive shiftings and reversals have taken place for many old people who, under the control of Memory [sic], are actually living much more in the past than in the ephemeral present.

It is most fortunate, therefore, that in some subtle fashion these old people, reviewing the long road they have travelled, are able to transmute their own untoward experiences into that which seems to make even the most wretched life acceptable. This may possibly be due to an instinct of self-preservation, which checks the devastating bitterness that would result did they recall over and over again the sordid detail of events long past; it is even possible that those people who were not able thus to inhibit their bitterness have died earlier, for as one old man recently reminded me, "It is a true word that worry can kill a cat."

Note: "Women's Memories—Transmuting the Past, as Illustrated by the Story of the Devil Baby," in *The Long Road of Woman's Memory* (New York: Macmillan, 1916), chapter 1.

This permanent and elemental function of Memory was graphically demonstrated at Hull-House during a period of several weeks when we were reported to be harboring within its walls a so-called "Devil Baby."

The knowledge of his existence burst upon the residents of Hull-House one day when three Italian women, with an excited rush through the door, demanded that he be shown to them. No amount of denial convinced them that he was not there, for they knew exactly what he was like with his cloven hoofs, his pointed ears and diminutive tail; the Devil Baby had, moreover, been able to speak as soon as he was born and was most shockingly profane.

The three women were but the forerunners of a veritable multitude; for six weeks from every part of the city and suburbs the streams of visitors to this mythical baby poured in all day long and so far into the night that the regular activities of the settlement were almost swamped.

The Italian version, with a hundred variations, dealt with a pious Italian girl married to an atheist. Her husband in a rage had torn a holy picture from the bedroom wall saying that he would quite as soon have a devil in the house as such a thing, whereupon the devil incarnated himself in her coming child. As soon as the Devil Baby was born, he ran about the table shaking his finger in deep reproach at his father, who finally caught him and, in fear and trembling, brought him to Hull-House. When the residents there, in spite of the baby's shocking appearance, wishing to save his soul, took him to church for baptism, they found that the shawl was empty and the Devil Baby, fleeing from the holy water, was running lightly over the backs of the pews.

The Jewish version, again with variations, was to the effect that the father of six daughters had said before the birth of a seventh child that he would rather have a devil in the family than another girl, whereupon the Devil Baby promptly appeared.

Save for a red automobile which occasionally figured in the story and a stray cigar which, in some versions, the new-born child had snatched from his father's lips, the tale might have been fashioned a thousand years ago.

Although the visitors to the Devil Baby included persons of every degree of prosperity and education, even physicians and trained nurses, who assured us of their scientific interest, the story constantly demonstrated the power of an old wives' tale among thousands of men and women in modern society who are living in a corner of their own, their vision fixed, their intelligence held by some iron chain of silent habit. To such primitive people the metaphor apparently is still the very "stuff of life," or rather no other form of statement reaches them; the tremendous tonnage of current writing for them has no existence. It was in keeping with their simple habits that the reputed presence of the Devil Baby should not reach the newspapers until the fifth week of his sojourn at Hull-House—after thousands of people had already been informed of his whereabouts by the old method of passing news from mouth to mouth.

For six weeks as I went about the house, I would hear a voice at the telephone repeating for the hundredth time that day, "No, there is no such baby"; "No, we never had it here"; "No, he couldn't have seen it for fifty cents"; "We didn't send it anywhere, because we never had it"; "I don't mean to say that your sister-in-law lied, but there must be some mistake"; "There is no use getting up an excursion from Milwaukee, for there isn't any Devil Baby at Hull-House"; "We can't give reduced rates, because we are not exhibiting anything"; and so on and on. As I came near the front door, I would catch snatches of arguments that were often acrimonious: "Why do you let so many people believe it, if it isn't here?" "We have taken three lines of cars to come and we have as much right to see it as anybody else"; "This is a pretty big place, of course you could hide it easy enough"; "What are you saying that for, are you going to raise the price of admission?"

We had doubtless struck a case of what the psychologists call the "contagion of emotion" added to that "æsthetic sociability" which impels any one of us to drag the entire household to the window when a procession comes into the street or a rainbow appears in the sky. The Devil Baby of course was worth many processions and rainbows, and I will confess that, as the empty show went on day after day, I quite revolted against such a vapid manifestation of even an admirable human trait. There was always one exception, however; whenever I heard the high eager voices of old women, I was irresistibly interested and left anything I might be doing in order to listen to them. As I came down the stairs, long before I could hear what they were saying, implicit in their solemn and portentous old voices came the admonition:—

"Wilt thou reject the past
Big with deep warnings?"

It was a very serious and genuine matter with the old women, this story so ancient and yet so contemporaneous, and they flocked to Hull-House from every direction; those I had known for many years, others I had never known and some whom I had supposed to be long dead. But they were all alive and eager; something in the story or in its mysterious sequences had aroused one of those active forces in human nature which does not take orders, but insists only upon giving them. We had abruptly come in contact with a living and self-assertive human quality!

During the weeks of excitement it was the old women who really seemed to have come into their own, and perhaps the most significant result of the incident was the reaction of the story upon them. It stirred their minds and memories as with a magic touch, it loosened their tongues and revealed the inner life and thoughts of those who are so often inarticulate. They are accustomed to sit at home and to hear the younger members of the family speak of affairs quite outside their own experiences, sometimes in a language they do not understand, and at best in quick glancing phrases which they cannot follow; "More than half the time I can't tell what they are talking about," is an oft-repeated complaint. The story of the Devil Baby evidently put into their hands the sort of material with which they were accustomed to deal. They had long used such tales in their unremitting efforts at family discipline, ever since they had frightened their first children into awed silence by tales of bugaboo men who prowled in the darkness.

These old women enjoyed a moment of triumph—as if they had made good at last and had come into a region of sanctions and punishments which they understood. Years of living had taught them that recrimination with grown-up children and grandchildren is worse than useless, that punishments are impossible, that domestic instruction is best given through tales and metaphors.

As the old women talked with the new volubility which the story of the Devil Baby had released in them, going back into their long memories and urging its credibility upon me, the story seemed to condense that mystical wisdom which becomes deposited in the heart of man by unnoticed innumerable experiences.

Perhaps my many conversations with these aged visitors crystallized thoughts and impressions I had been receiving through years, or the tale itself may have ignited a fire, as it were, whose light illumined some of my darkest memories of neglected and uncomfortable old age, of old peasant women who had ruthlessly probed into the ugly depths of human nature in themselves and others. Many of them who came to see the Devil Baby had been forced to face tragic experiences, the powers of brutality and horror had had full scope in their lives and for years they had had acquaintance with disaster and death. Such old women do not shirk life's misery by feeble idealism, for they are long past the stage of make-believe. They relate without flinching the most hideous experiences: "My face has had this queer twist for now nearly sixty years; I was ten when it got that way, the night after I saw my father do my mother to death with his knife." "Yes, I had fourteen children; only two grew to be men and both of them were killed in the same explosion. I was never sure they brought home the right bodies." But even the most hideous sorrows which the old women related had apparently subsided into the paler emotion of ineffectual regret, after Memory had long done her work upon them; the old people seemed, in some unaccountable way, to lose all bitterness and resentment against life, or rather to be so completely without it that they must have lost it long since.

None of them had a word of blame for undutiful children or heedless grandchildren, because apparently the petty and transitory had fallen away from their austere old age, the fires were burnt out, resentments, hatreds, and even cherished sorrows had become actually unintelligible.

Perhaps those women, because they had come to expect nothing more from life and had perforce ceased from grasping and striving, had obtained, if not renunciation, at least that quiet endurance which allows the wounds of the spirit to heal. Through their stored-up habit of acquiescence, they offered a fleeting glimpse of the translucent wisdom, so often embodied in the old, but so difficult to portray. It is doubtless what Michael Angelo [sic] had in mind when he made the Sybils old, what Dante meant by the phrase "those who had learned of life," and the age-worn minstrel who turned into song a Memory which was more that of history and tradition than his own.

In contrast to the visitors to the Devil Baby who spoke only such words of groping wisdom as they were able, were other old women who, although they had already reconciled themselves to much misery, were still enduring more: "You might say it's a disgrace to have your son beat you up for the sake of a bit of money you've earned by scrubbing—your own man is different—but I haven't the heart to blame the boy for doing what he's seen all his life, his father forever went wild when the drink was in him and struck me to the very day of his death. The ugliness was born in the boy as the marks of the Devil was born in the poor child up-stairs."

Some of these old women had struggled for weary years with poverty and much childbearing, had known what it was to be bullied and beaten by their husbands, neglected and ignored by their prosperous children, and burdened by the support of the imbecile and the shiftless ones. They had literally gone "Deep written all their days with care."

One old woman actually came from the poorhouse, having heard of the Devil Baby "through a lady from Polk Street visiting an old friend who has a bed in our ward." It was no slight achievement for the penniless and crippled old inmate to make her escape. She had asked "a young bar-keep in a saloon across the road" to lend her ten cents, offering as security the fact that she was an old acquaintance at Hull-House who could not be refused so slight a loan. She marvelled at some length over the goodness of the young man, for she had not had a dime to spend for a drink for the last six months, and he and the conductor had been obliged to lift her into the street car by main strength. She was naturally much elated over the achievement of her escape. To be sure, from the men's side, they were always walking off in the summer and taking to the road, living like tramps they did, in a way no one from the woman's side would demean herself to do; but to have left in a street car like a lady, with money to pay her own fare, was quite a different matter, although she was indeed "clean wore out" by the effort. However, it was clear that she would consider herself well repaid by a sight of the Devil Baby and that not only the inmates of her own ward, but those in every other ward in the house would be made to "sit up" when she got back; it would liven them all up a bit, and she hazarded the guess that she would have to tell them about that baby at least a dozen times a day.

As she cheerfully rambled on, we weakly postponed telling her there was no Devil Baby, first that she might have a cup of tea and rest, and then through a sheer desire to withhold a blow from a poor old body who had received so many throughout a long, hard life.

As I recall those unreal weeks, it was in her presence that I found myself for the first time vaguely wishing that I could administer comfort by the simple device of not asserting too dogmatically that the Devil Baby had never been at Hull-House.

Our guest recalled with great pride that her grandmother had possessed second sight; that her mother had heard the Banshee three times and that she, herself, had heard it once. All this gave her a certain proprietary interest in the Devil Baby and I suspected she cherished a secret hope that when she should lay her eyes upon him, her inherited gifts might be able to reveal the meaning of the strange portent. At the least, he would afford a proof that her family-long faith in such matters was justified. Her misshapen hands lying on her lap fairly trembled with eagerness.

It may have been because I was still smarting under the recollection of the disappointment we had so wantonly inflicted upon our visitor from the poorhouse that the very next day I found myself almost agreeing with her whole-hearted acceptance of the past as of much more importance than the mere present; at least for half an hour the past seemed endowed also for me with a profounder and more ardent life.

This impression was received in connection with an old woman, sturdy in her convictions, although long since bedridden, who had doggedly refused to believe that there was no Devil Baby at Hull-House, unless "herself" told her so. Because of her mounting irritation with the envoys who one and all came back to her to report "they say it ain't there," it seemed well that I should go promptly before "she fashed herself into the grave." As I walked along the street and even as I went up the ramshackle outside stairway of the rear cottage and through the dark corridor to the "second floor back" where she lay in her untidy bed, I was assailed by a veritable temptation to give her a full description of the Devil Baby, which by this time I knew so accurately (for with a hundred variations to select from I could have made a monstrous infant almost worthy of his name), and also to refrain from putting too much stress on the fact that he had never been really and truly at Hull-House.

I found my mind hastily marshalling arguments for not disturbing her belief in the story which had so evidently brought her a vivid interest long denied her. She lived alone with her young grandson, who went to work every morning at seven o'clock and save for the short visits made by the visiting nurse and by kind neighbors, her long day was monotonous and undisturbed. But the story of a Devil Baby, with his existence officially corroborated as it were, would give her a lodestone which would attract the neighbors far and wide and exalt her once more into the social importance she had had twenty-four years before when I had first known her. She was then the proprietor of the most prosperous second-hand store on a street full of them, her shiftless, drinking husband and her jolly, good-natured sons doing exactly what she told them to do. This, however, was long past, for "owing to the drink," in her own graphic phrase, "the old man, the boys, and the business, too, were clean gone" and there was "nobody left but little Tom and me and nothing for us to live on."

I remember how well she used to tell a story when I once tried to collect some folk-lore for Mr. Yeats to prove that an Irish peasant does not lose his faith in the little people nor his knowledge of Gaelic phrases simply because he is living in a city.[1] She had at that time told me a wonderful tale concerning a red cloak worn by an old woman to a freshly dug grave. The story of the Devil Baby would give her material worthy of her powers, but of course she must be able to believe it with all her heart. She could live only a few months at the very best, I argued to myself; why not give her this vivid interest and through it awake those earliest recollections of that long-accumulated folklore with its magic power to transfigure and eclipse the sordid and unsatisfactory surroundings in which life is actually spent? I solemnly assured myself that the imagination of old age needs to be fed and probably has quite as imperious a claim as that of youth, which levies upon us so remorselessly with its "I want a fairy story, but I don't like you to begin by saying that it isn't true." Impatiently I found myself challenging the educators who had given us no pedagogical instructions for the treatment of old age, although they had fairly overinformed us as to the use of the fairy tale with children.

The little room was stuffed with a magpie collection, the usual odds and ends which compose an old woman's treasures, augmented in this case by various articles which a second-hand store, even of the most flourishing sort, could not sell. In the picturesque confusion, if anywhere in Chicago, an urbanized group of the little people might dwell; they would certainly find the traditional atmosphere which they strictly require, marvelling, faith and unalloyed reverence. At any rate, an eager old woman aroused to her utmost capacity of wonder and credulity was the very soil, prepared to a nicety, for planting the seed-thought of the Devil Baby. If the object of my errand had been an hour's reading to a sick woman, it would have been accounted to me for philanthropic righteousness, and if the chosen reading had lifted her mind from her bodily discomforts and harassing thoughts so that she forgot them all for one fleeting moment, how pleased I should have been with the success of my effort. But here I was with a story at my tongue's end, stupidly hesitating to give it validity, although the very words were on my lips. I was still arguing the case with myself when I stood on the threshold of her room and caught the indomitable gleam of her eye, fairly daring me to deny the existence of the Devil Baby, her slack dropsical body so responding to her overpowering excitement that for the moment she looked alert in her defiance and positively menacing.

But, as in the case of many another weak soul, the decision was taken out of my hands, my very hesitation was enough, for nothing is more certain than that the bearer of a magic tale never stands dawdling on the door-step. Slowly the gleam died out of the expectant old eyes, the erect shoulders sagged and pulled forward, and I saw only too plainly that the poor old woman had accepted one more disappointment in a life already overflowing with them. She was violently thrown back into all the limitations of her personal experience and surroundings, and that larger life she had anticipated so eagerly was as suddenly shut away from her as if a door had been slammed in her face.

I never encountered that particular temptation again, though she was no more pitiful than many of the aged visitors whom the Devil Baby brought to Hull-House. But, perhaps as a result of this experience, I gradually lost the impression that the old people were longing for a second chance at life, to live it all over again and to live more fully and wisely, and I became more reconciled to the fact that many of them had little opportunity for meditation or for bodily rest, but must keep on working with their toil-worn hands, in spite of weariness or faintness of heart.

The vivid interest of so many old women in the story of the Devil Baby may have been an unconscious, although powerful, testimony that tragic experiences gradually become dressed in such trappings in order that their spent agony may prove of some use to a world which learns at the hardest; and that the strivings and sufferings of men and women long since dead, their emotions no longer connected with flesh and blood, are thus transmuted into legendary wisdom. The young are forced to heed the warning in such a tale, although for the most part it is so easy for them to disregard the words of the aged. That the old women who came to visit the Devil Baby believed that the story would secure them a hearing at home was evident, and as they prepared themselves with every detail of it, their old faces shone with a timid satisfaction. Their features, worn and scarred by harsh living, as effigies built into the floor of an old church become dim and defaced by rough-shod feet, grew poignant and solemn. In the midst of their double bewilderment, both that the younger generation was walking in such strange paths and that no one would listen to them, for one moment there flickered up the last hope of a disappointed life, that it may at least serve as a warning, while affording material for an exciting narrative.

Sometimes in talking to a woman who was "but a hair's breadth this side of the darkness," I realized that old age has its own expression for the mystic renunciation of the world. Their impatience with all nonessentials, the craving to be free from hampering bonds and soft conditions, recalled Tolstoy's last impetuous journey, and I was once more grateful to his genius for making clear another unintelligible impulse of bewildered humanity.

Often, in the midst of a conversation, one of these touching old women would quietly express a longing for death, as if it were a natural fulfilment of an inmost desire, with a sincerity and anticipation so genuine that I would feel abashed in her presence, ashamed to "cling to this strange thing that shines in the sunlight and to be sick with love for it." Such impressions were, in their essence, transitory, but one result from the hypothetical visit of the Devil Baby to Hull-House will, I think, remain: a realization of the sifting and reconciling power inherent in Memory itself. The old women, with much to aggravate and little to soften the habitual bodily discomforts of old age, exhibited an emotional serenity so vast and so reassuring, that I found myself perpetually speculating upon how soon the fleeting and petty emotions which now seem unduly important to us might be thus transmuted; at what moment we might expect the inconsistencies and perplexities of life to be brought under this appeasing Memory with its ultimate power to increase the elements of beauty and significance and to reduce, if not to eliminate, all sense of resentment.

Notes

1. William Butler Yeats (1865–1939) was a great Irish writer, one of many writers and artists she met on her travels. Because of the Hull-House art and literature emphasis, visiting artists included Hull-House on their Chicago itineraries as well.

36

⌒◯⌒

"WOMEN'S MEMORIES — REACTION ON LIFE, AS ILLUSTRATED BY THE STORY OF THE DEVIL BABY"

D URING THE WEEKS WHEN the Devil Baby seemed to occupy every room in Hull-House, I was conscious that all human vicissitudes are, in the end, melted down into reminiscence, and that a metaphorical statement of the basic experiences which are implicit in human nature itself, however crude in form the story may be, has a singular power of influencing daily living.

At moments we also seemed to glimpse the process through which such tales had been evolved. As our visitors to the Devil Baby came day by day, it gradually became evident that the simpler women were moved not wholly by curiosity, but that many of them prized the story as a valuable instrument in the business of living. From them and from the surprising number of others who had been sent by the aged and the bed-ridden to secure an exact history and description of the child, the suggestion finally became quite irresistible that such a story, outlining a great abstraction, may once have performed the high service of tradition and discipline in the beginnings of a civilized family life.

The legend exhibited all the persistence of one of those tales which has doubtless been preserved through the centuries because of its taming effects upon recalcitrant husbands and fathers. Shamefaced men

Note: "Women's Memories—Reaction on Life, as Illustrated by the Story of the Devil Baby," in *The Long Road of Woman's Memory* (New York: Macmillan, 1916), chapter 2.

brought to Hull-House by their women folk to see the baby, but ill concealed their triumph when there proved to be no such visible sign of retribution for domestic derelictions. On the other hand, numbers of men came by themselves, one group from a neighboring factory on their "own time" offered to pay twenty-five cents, a half dollar, two dollars apiece to see the child, insisting that it must be at Hull-House because "the women had seen it." To my query as to whether they supposed we would, for money, exhibit a poor little deformed baby, if one had been born in the neighborhood, they replied: "Sure, why not?" and "it teaches a good lesson, too," they added as an afterthought, or perhaps as a concession to the strange moral standards of a place like Hull-House. All the members in this group of hard-working men, in spite of a certain swagger towards one another and a tendency to bully the derelict showman, wore a hang-dog look betraying that sense of unfair treatment which a man is so apt to feel when his womankind makes an appeal to the supernatural. In their determination to see the child, the men recklessly divulged much more concerning their motives than they had meant to do. Their talk confirmed my impression that such a story may still act as a restraining influence in the sphere of marital conduct which, next to primitive religion, has always afforded the most fertile field for irrational taboos and savage punishments.

What story could be better than this to secure sympathy for the mother of too many daughters and contumely for the irritated father; the touch of mysticism, the supernatural sphere in which it was placed, would render a man quite helpless.

The story of the Devil Baby, evolved in response to the imperative needs of anxious wives and mothers, recalls the theory that woman first fashioned the fairy story, that combination of wisdom and romance, in an effort to tame her mate and to make him a better father to her children, until such stories finally became a crude creed for domestic conduct, softening the treatment men accorded to women. Because such stories, expressing the very essence of human emotion, did not pretend to imitate the outside of life, they were careless of verisimilitude and absolutely indifferent to the real world. They did, however, meet an essential requirement of the good story, in that they dealt with fundamental experiences.

These first pitiful efforts of women were so widespread and powerful that we have not yet escaped their influence. As subconscious memories, they still cast vague shadows upon the vast spaces of life, shadows that are dim and distorted because of their distant origin. They remind us that for thousands of years women had nothing to oppose against unthinkable brutality save "the charm of words," no other implement with which to subdue the fiercenesses of the world about them. Only through words could they hope to arouse the generosity of strength, to secure a measure of pity for themselves and their children, to so protect the life they had produced that "the precious vintage stored from their own agony" might not wantonly be spilled upon the ground. Possibly the multitude of life's failures, the obscure victims of unspeakable wrong and brutality, have embodied their memories in a literature of their own, of which the story of the Devil Baby is a specimen, crude and ugly in form, as would be inevitable, but still bringing relief to the surcharged heart.

During the weeks that the Devil Baby drew multitudes of visitors to Hull-House, my mind was opened to the fact that new knowledge derived from concrete experience is continually being made available for the guidance of human life; that humble women are still establishing rules of conduct as best they may, to counteract the base temptations of a man's world. I saw a new significance in the fact that thousands of women, for instance, make it a standard of domestic virtue that a man must not touch his pay envelope, but bring it home unopened to his wife. High praise is contained in the phrase, "We have been married twenty years and he never once opened his own envelope," or covert blame in the statement, "Of course he got to gambling; what can you expect from a man who always opens his own pay?"

These humble domestic virtues, of which women see the need so much more vividly than men do, have furthermore developed their penalties. The latter, too, are put into aphorisms which, in time, when Memory has done her work upon them, may become legendary wisdom.

Such a penalty was recently illustrated in our neighborhood by the fate of an old man who was found in his room almost starved to death. He was pointed out by many of our neighbors as an example of the inevitable fate of one who deserts his family and therefore, "without a woman to keep him straight," falls into drink and shiftlessness and the endless paths of wrongdoing, so that loneliness and destitution inevitably overtake his old age.

The women were so fatalistically certain of this relation of punishment to domestic sin, of reward to domestic virtue, that when they talked about them, as they so constantly did in connection with the Devil Baby, it often sounded as if they were using the words of a widely known ritual. Among the visitors to the Devil Baby were many foreign-born peasant women who, when they had come to America, had been suddenly subjected to the complicated and constantly changing environment of city life, and, finding no outlet for many inherited tendencies, might easily have been thrown into that state described by psychologists as one of "baulked disposition."[1] To them this simple tale, with its direct connection between cause and effect, between wrong-doing and punishment, brought soothing and relief, and restored a shaken confidence as to the righteousness of the universe. They used the story not only to tame restless husbands, but mothers threatened their daughters that if they went to dance halls or out to walk with strange young men, they would be eternally disgraced by devil babies. As the story grew, the girls themselves seized upon it as a palpable punishment to be held over the heads of reckless friends. That the tale was useful was evidenced by many letters similar to the anonymous epistle here given.

> me and my friends we work in talor shop and when we are going home on the roby street car where we get off that car at blue island ave. we will meet some fellows sitting at that street where they drink some beer from pail. they keep look in cars all time and they will wait and see if we will come sometimes we will have to work, but they will wait so long they are tired and they dont care they get rest so long but a girl what works in twine mill saw them talk with us we know her good and she say what youse talk with old drunk man for we shall come to thier dance when it will be they will tell us and we should know all about where to see them that girl she say oh if you will go with them you will get devils baby like some other girls did who we knows. she say Jane Addams she will show one like that in Hull House if you will go down there we shall come sometime and we will see if that is trouth we do not believe her for she is friendly with them old men herself when she go out from her work they will wink to her and say something else to. We will go down and see you and make a lie from what she say.

Because the Devil Baby embodied an undeserved wrong to a poor mother whose tender child had been claimed by the forces of evil, his merely reputed presence had power to attract to Hull-House hundreds of women who had been humbled and disgraced by their children; mothers of the feeble-minded, of the vicious, of the criminal, of the prostitute. In their talk it was as if their long rôle of maternal apology and protective reticence had at last broken down, as if they could speak out freely because for once a man responsible for an ill-begotten child had been "met up with" and had received his deserts. Their sinister version of the story was that the father of the Devil Baby had married without confessing a hideous crime committed years before, thus basely deceiving both his innocent young bride and the good priest who performed the solemn ceremony; that the sin had become incarnate in his child which, to the horror of the young and trusting mother, had been born with all the outward aspects of the devil himself.

As if drawn by a magnet, these forlorn women issued forth from the many homes in which dwelt "the two unprofitable goddesses, Poverty and Impossibility." Occasionally it seemed to me that the women were impelled by a longing to see one good case of retribution before they died, as a bullied child hopes to deal at least one crushing blow at his tormentor when he "grows up," but I think, on the whole, such an explanation was a mistake; it is more probable that the avidity of the women demonstrated that the story itself, like all interpretative art, was "one of those free, unconscious attempts to satisfy, outside of life, those cravings which life itself leaves unsatisfied." At moments, however, baffled desires, sharp cries of pain, echoes of justices unfulfilled, the original material from which such tales are fashioned, would defy Memory's appeasing power and break through the rigid restraints imposed by all Art, even that unconscious of itself.

With an understanding quickened, perhaps, through my own acquaintance with the mysterious child, I listened to many tragic reminiscences from the visiting women; of premature births, "because he kicked me in the side"; of children maimed and burnt because "I had no one to leave them with when I went to work"; women had seen the tender flesh of growing little bodies given over to death because "he wouldn't let me send for the doctor," or because "there was no money to pay for the medicine." But even these mothers, rendered childless through insensate brutality, were less pitiful than some of the others, who might well have cried aloud of their children as did a distracted mother of her child centuries ago:

"That God should send this one thing more
Of hunger and of dread, a door
Set wide to every wind of pain!"

Such was the mother of a feeble-minded boy who said: "I didn't have a devil baby myself, but I bore a poor 'innocent' who made me fight devils for twenty-three years." She told of her son's experiences from the time the other little boys had put him up to stealing that they might hide in safety and leave him to be found with "the goods on him," until grown into a huge man he fell into the hands of professional burglars; he was evidently the dupe and stool-pigeon of the vicious and criminal until the very day he was locked into the State Penitentiary. "If people played with him a little, he went right off and did anything they told him to, and now he's been sent up for life. We call such innocents 'God's Fools' in the old country, but over here the Devil himself gets them. I've fought off bad men and boys from the poor lamb with my very fists; nobody ever came near the house except such-like and the police officers, who were always arresting him."

There were a goodly number of visitors to the Devil Baby of the type of those to be found in every large city, who are on the verge of nervous collapse, or who exhibit many symptoms of mental aberration, and yet are sufficiently normal to be at large most of the time, and to support themselves by drudgery which requires little mental effort, although the exhaustion resulting from the work they are able to do is the one thing from which they should be most carefully protected. One such woman, evidently obtaining inscrutable comfort from the story of the Devil Baby even after she had become convinced that we harbored no such creature, came many times to tell of her longing for her son, who had joined the army eighteen months before and was now stationed in Alaska. She always began with the same words.

"When Spring comes and the snow melts so that I know he could get out, I can hardly stand it. You know I was once in the Insane Asylum for three years at a stretch, and since then I haven't had much use of my mind except to worry with. Of course I know that it is dangerous for me, but what can I do? I think something like this: 'The snow is melting, now he could get out, but his officers won't let him off and if he runs away he'll be shot for a deserter—either way I'll never see him again; I'll die without seeing him'—and then I begin all over again with the snow."

After a pause, she said: "The recruiting officer ought not to have taken him, he's my only son and I'm a widow. It's against the rules, but he was so crazy to go that I guess he lied a little—at any rate, the government has him now and I can't get him back. Without this worry about him my mind would be all right; if he were here he would be earning money and keeping me and we would be happy all day long."

Recalling the vagabondish lad, who had never earned much money and had certainly never "kept" his hard-working mother, I ventured to suggest that, even if he were at home, he might not have work these hard times, that he might get into trouble and be arrested—I did not need to remind her that he had already been arrested twice—that he was now fed and sheltered and under discipline, and I added hopefully something about his seeing the world. She looked at me out of her withdrawn, harried eyes, as if I were speaking a foreign tongue. "That wouldn't make any real difference to me—the work, the money, his behaving well and all that, if I could cook and wash for him. I don't need all the money I earn scrubbing that factory. I only take bread and tea for supper and I choke over that, thinking of him."

She ceased to speak, overcome by a thousand obscure emotions which could find no outlet in words. She dimly realized that the facts in the case, to one who had known her boy from childhood, were far from creditable, and that no one could understand the eternally unappeased idealism which, for her, surrounded her son's return. She was even afraid to say much about it, lest she should be overmastered by her subject and be considered so irrational as to suggest a return to the Hospital for the Insane.

Those mothers who have never resisted fate nor buffeted against the black waters, but have allowed the waves to close over them, worn and bent as they are by hard labor, subdued and misshapen by the brutality of men are at least unaffrighted by the melodramatic coarseness of life, which Stevenson more gently describes as "the uncouth and outlandish strain in the web of the world." The story of the Devil Baby may have made its appeal through its frank presentation of this very demoniac quality to those who live under the iron tyranny of that poverty which threatens starvation, and under the dread of a brutality which may any dark night bring them or their children to extinction; to those who have seen both virtue and vice go unrewarded and who have long since ceased to explain.

This more primitive type embodies the eternal patience of those humble, toiling women who through the generations have been held of little value, save as their drudgery ministered to their men. One of them related her habit of going through the pockets of her drunken son every pay day, and complained that she had never found so little as the night before, only twenty-five cents out of fifteen dollars he had promised for the rent, long overdue. "I had to get that as he lay in the alley before the door; I couldn't pull him in, and the copper who helped him home, left as soon as he heard me coming and pretended he didn't see me. I have no food in the house, nor coffee to sober him up with. I know perfectly well that you will ask me to eat something here, but, if I can't carry it home, I won't take a bite nor a sup. I have never told you so much before. Since one of the nurses said he could be arrested for my non-support, I have been awful close-mouthed. It's the foolish way all the women in our street are talking about the Devil Baby that's loosened my tongue, more shame to me."

A sorrowful woman clad in heavy black, who came one day, exhibited such a capacity for prolonged weeping that it was evidence in itself of the truth of at least half her statement, that she had cried herself to sleep every night of her life for fourteen years in fulfilment of a "curse" laid upon her by an angry man, that "her pillow would be wet with tears as long as she lived." Her respectable husband had a shop in the Red Light district because he found it profitable to sell to the men and women who lived there. She had kept house in the room over the "store" from the time she was a bride newly come from Russia, and her five daughters had been born there, but never a son to gladden her husband's heart.

She took such a feverish interest in the Devil Baby that, when I was obliged to disillusion her, I found it hard to take away her comfort in the belief that the Powers that Be are on the side of the woman when her husband resents too many daughters. But, after all, the birth of daughters was but an incident in her tale of unmitigated woe, for the scoldings of a disappointed husband were as nothing to the curse of a strange enemy, although she doubtless had a confused impression that if there were retribution for one in the general scheme of things, there might be for the other. When the weeping woman finally put the events of her disordered life in some sort of sequence, it became clear that about fifteen years ago she had reported to the police a vicious house whose back door opened into her own yard. Her husband had forbidden her to do anything about it and had said that it would only get them into trouble, but she had been made desperate one day when she saw her little girl, then twelve years old, come out of the door, gleefully showing her younger sister a present of money. Because the poor woman had tried for ten years without success to induce her husband to move from the vicinity of such houses, she was certain that she could save her child only by forcing out "the bad people" from her own door yard. She therefore made her one frantic effort, found her way to the city hall and there reported the house to the chief himself. Of course, "the bad people stood in with the police" and nothing happened to them save, perhaps, a fresh levy of blackmail, but the keeper of the house, beside himself with rage, made the dire threat and laid the curse upon her. In less than a year from that time he had enticed her daughter into a disreputable house in another part of the district. The poor woman, ringing one door-bell after another, had never been able to find her, but her sisters, who in time came to know where she was, had been dazzled by her mode of life. The weeping mother was quite sure that two of her daughters, while still outwardly respectable and "working downtown," earned money in the devious ways which they had learned all about when they were little children, although for the past five years the now prosperous husband had allowed the family to live in a suburb, where the two younger daughters were "growing up respectable."

Certain of the visitors, although confronted by those mysterious and impersonal wrongs which are apparently inherent in the very nature of things, gave us glimpses of another sort of wisdom than that expressed in the assumptions that the decrees of Fate are immutable.

Such a glimpse came to me through a conversation with a woman whose fine mind and indomitable spirit I had long admired: I had known her for years, and yet the recital of her sufferings, added to those the Devil Baby had already induced other women to tell me, pierced me afresh. The story of the Devil Baby may have incited these women to put their experiences more vividly than they had hitherto been able to do. It may have been because they were unconsciously spurred by the hope that a supernatural retribution might intervene even for them, or because they were merely comforted by the knowledge that it had once done so for some one else that they spoke with more confidence than they had ever done before.

"I had eleven children, some born in Hungary and some born here, nine of them boys; all of the children died when they were little but my

dear Liboucha. You know all about her. She died last winter in the Insane
Asylum. She was only twelve years old when her father, in a fit of delir-
ium tremens, killed himself after he had chased us around the room, trying to kill us first. She saw it all, the blood splashed on the wall stayed in
her mind the worst; she shivered and shook all that night through, and
the next morning she had lost her voice, couldn't speak out loud for terror. After a while she went to school again and her voice came back, although it was never very natural. She seemed to do as well as ever and
was awful pleased when she got into High School. All the money we had
I earned scrubbing in a public dispensary, although sometimes I got a little more by interpreting for the patients, for I know three languages, one
as well as the other. But I was determined that whatever happened to me,
Liboucha was to be educated. My husband's father was a doctor in the
old country, and Liboucha was always a clever child. I wouldn't have her
live the kind of life I had, with no use for my mind except to make me
restless and bitter. I was pretty old and worn out for such hard work, but
when I used to see Liboucha on a Sunday morning ready for church in
her white dress, with her long yellow hair braided round her beautiful
pale face, lying there in bed as I was, being brought up a free-thinker, and
needing to rest my aching bones for the next week's work, I'd feel almost
happy, in spite of everything. But of course no such peace could last in
my life; the second year at High School Liboucha began to seem different
and to do strange things. You know the time she wandered away for
three days and we were all wild with fright, although a kind woman had
taken her in and no harm came to her. I could never be easy after that;
she was always gentle, but she was awful sly about running away and at
last I had to send her to the asylum. She stayed there off and on for five
years, but I saw her every week of my life and she was always company
for me, what with sewing for her, washing and ironing her clothes, cooking little things to take out to her, and saving a bit of money to buy fruit
for her. At any rate, I had stopped feeling so bitter, and got some comfort
out of seeing the one thing that belonged to me on this side of the water,
when all of a sudden she died of heart failure and they never took the
trouble to send for me until the next day."

She stopped as if wondering afresh that the Fates could have been so
casual, but with a sudden illumination, as if she had been awakened
out of the burden and intensity of her restricted personal interests into
a consciousness of those larger relations that are, for the most part, so

strangely invisible. It was as if the young mother of the grotesque Devil Baby, that victim of wrong doing on the part of others, had revealed to this tragic woman much more clearly than soft words had ever done, that the return of a deed of violence upon the head of the innocent is inevitable; as if she had realized that, although she was destined to walk all the days of her life with the piteous multitude who bear the undeserved wrongs of the world, she would walk henceforth with a sense of companionship.

At moments it seemed possible that these simple women, representing an earlier development, eagerly seized upon the story because it was primitive in form and substance. Certainly, one evening, a long-forgotten ballad made an unceasing effort to come to the surface of my mind as I talked to a feeble woman who, in the last stages of an incurable disease from which she soon afterwards died, had been helped off the street car in front of Hull-House. The ballad tells how the lover of a proud and jealous mistress, who demanded as a final test of devotion that he bring her the heart of his mother, had quickly cut the heart from his mother's breast and impetuously returned to his lady, bearing it upon a salver; and how, when stumbling in his gallant haste, he stooped to replace upon the silver plate his mother's heart, which had rolled to the ground, the heart, still beating with tender solicitude, whispered the hope that her child was not hurt. The ballad itself was scarcely more exaggerated than the story of our visitor that evening, who had made the desperate effort of a journey from home in order to see the Devil Baby. I was familiar with her vicissitudes; the shiftless, drinking husband and the large family of children, all of whom had brought her sorrow and disgrace, and I knew that her heart's desire was to see again, before she died, her youngest son, who was a life prisoner in the penitentiary. She was confident that the last piteous stage of her disease would secure him a week's parole, founding this forlorn hope upon the fact that "they sometimes let them out to attend a mother's funeral, and perhaps they'd let Joe come a few days ahead; he could pay his fare afterwards from the insurance money. It wouldn't take much to bury me." Again we went over the hideous story: Joe had violently quarrelled with a woman, the proprietor of the house in which his disreputable wife was living, because she had withheld from him a part of his wife's "earnings," and in the altercation had killed her—a situation, one would say, which it would be difficult for even a mother to condone. But not at all, her thin gray face worked with emotion, her trembling hands restlessly pulled at her shabby skirt as the hands of the dying pluck at their sheets, but she put all the vitality she could muster into his defence. She told us he had legally married the girl, who supported him, "although Lily had been so long in that life that few men would have done it. Of course, such a girl must have a protector or everybody would fleece her. Poor Lily said to the day of her death that he was the kindest man she ever knew, and treated her the whitest; that she herself was to blame for the murder because she told on the old miser, and Joe was so hotheaded she might have known that he would draw a gun for her." The gasping mother concluded: "He was always that handsome and had such a way. One winter, when I was scrubbing in an office building, I'd never get home much before twelve o'clock, but Joe would open the door for me just as pleasant as if he hadn't been waked out of a sound sleep." She was so triumphantly unconscious of the incongruity of a sturdy son in bed while his mother earned his food, that her auditors said never a word, and in silence we saw a hero evolved before our eyes, a defender of the oppressed, the best beloved of his mother, who was losing his high spirits and eating his heart out behind prison bars. He could well defy the world even there, surrounded as he was by that invincible affection which assures both the fortunate and unfortunate alike that we are loved, not according to our deserts, but in response to some profounder law.

This imposing revelation of maternal solicitude was an instance of what continually happened in connection with the Devil Baby. In the midst of the most tragic reminiscences, there remained that something in the memories of these mothers which has been called the great revelation of tragedy, or sometimes the great illusion of tragedy; that which has power in its own right to make life palatable and at rare moments even beautiful.

Notes

1. Although Jane Addams had some harsh things to say about pseudo-Freudian lecturers traveling the country and preaching what was, for her, a spurious doctrine of personal liberation, she worked with a psychological theory that is very similar to the psychodynamics of psychoanalysis. Her discussion of "baulked disposition" is very like the Freudian category of repression.

37

"A PERSONAL EXPERIENCE IN INTERPRETING MEMORY"

SEVERAL YEARS AGO, during a winter spent in Egypt, I found within myself an unexpected tendency to interpret racial and historic experiences through personal reminiscences. I am therefore venturing to record in this closing chapter my inevitable conclusion that a sincere portrayal of a widespread and basic emotional experience, however remote in point of time it may be, has the power overwhelmingly to evoke memories of like moods in the individual.

The unexpected revival in my memory of long-forgotten experiences may have been due partly to the fact that we have so long been taught that the temples and tombs of ancient Egypt are the very earliest of the surviving records of ideas and men, that we approach them with a certain sense of familiarity, quite ready to claim a share in these "family papers and title deeds of the race."

We also consider it probable that these primitive human records will stir within us certain early states of consciousness, having learned, with the readiness which so quickly attaches itself to the pseudo-scientific phrase, that every child repeats in himself the history of the race. Nevertheless, what I, at least, was totally unprepared to encounter, was the constant revival of primitive and overpowering emotions which I had experienced so long ago that they had become absolutely detached from myself and seemed to belong to some one else—to a small person with whom I was no longer intimate, and who was certainly not in the

---

Note: "A Personal Experience in Interpreting Memory," in *Peace and Bread in Time of War* (New York: Macmillan, 1922), chapter 6.

least responsible for my present convictions and reflections. It gradually became obvious that the ancient Egyptians had known this small person quite intimately and had most seriously and naïvely set down upon the walls of their temples and tombs her earliest reactions in the presence of death.

At moments my adult intelligence would be unexpectedly submerged by the emotional message which was written there. Rising to the surface like a flood, this primitive emotion would sweep away both the historic record and the adult consciousness interested in it, leaving only a child's mind struggling through an experience which it found overwhelming.

It may have been because these records of the early Egyptians are so endlessly preoccupied with death, portraying man's earliest efforts to defeat it, his eager desire to survive, to enter by force or by guile into the heavens of the western sky, that the mind is pushed back into that earliest childhood when the existence of the soul, its exact place of residence in the body, its experiences immediately after death, its journeyings upward, its relation to its guardian angel, so often afforded material for the crudest speculation. In the obscure renewal of these childish fancies, there is nothing that is definite enough to be called memory; it is rather that Egypt reproduces a state of consciousness which has so absolutely passed into oblivion that only the most powerful stimuli could revive it.

This revival doubtless occurs more easily because these early records in relief and color not only suggest in their subject-matter that a child has been endowed with sufficient self-consciousness to wish to write down his own state of mind upon a wall, but also because the very primitive style of drawing to which the Egyptians adhered long after they had acquired a high degree of artistic freedom, is the most natural technique through which to convey so simple and archaic a message. The square shoulders of the men, the stairways done in profile, and a hundred other details, constantly remind one of a child's drawings. It is as if the Egyptians had painstakingly portrayed everything that a child has felt in regard to death, and having, during the process, gradually discovered the style of drawing naturally employed by a child, had deliberately stiffened it into an unchanging convention. The result is that the traveller, reading in these drawings which stretch the length of three thousand years, the long endeavor to overcome death, finds that the experience of the two—the child and the primitive people—often become confused, or rather that they are curiously interrelated.

This begins from the moment the traveller discovers that the earliest tombs surviving in Egypt, the mastabas,—which resemble the natural results of a child's first effort to place one stone upon another,—are concerned only with size, as if that early crude belief in the power of physical bulk to protect the terrified human being against all shadowy evils were absolutely instinctive and universal. The mastabas gradually develop into the pyramids, of which Breasted says that "they are not only the earliest emergence of organized men and the triumph of con-certed effort, they are likewise a silent, but eloquent, expression of the supreme endeavor to achieve immortality by sheer physical force." Both the mastabas at Sahkara and the pyramids at Gizeh, in the sense of Tolstoy's definition of art as that which reproduces in the spectator the state of consciousness of the artist, at once appeal to the child sur-viving in every adult, who insists irrationally, after the manner of chil-dren, upon sympathizing with the attempt to shut out death by strong walls.

Certainly we can all vaguely remember, when death itself, or stories of ghosts, had come to our intimate child's circle, that we went about saying to ourselves that we were "not afraid," that it "could not come here," that "the door was locked, the windows tight shut," that "this was a big house," and a great deal more talk of a similar sort.

In the presence of these primitive attempts to defeat death, and with-out the conscious aid of memory, I found myself living over the emo-tions of a child six years old, saying some such words as I sat on the middle of the stairway in my own home, which yet seemed alien be-cause all the members of the family had gone to the funeral of a relative and would not be back until evening, "long after you are in bed," they had said. In this moment of loneliness and horror, I depended ab-solutely upon the brick walls of the house to keep out the prowling ter-ror, and neither the talk of kindly Polly, who awkwardly and unsuccess-fully reduced an unwieldy theology to child-language, nor the strings of paper dolls cut by a visitor, gave me the slightest comfort. Only the blank wall of the stairway seemed to afford protection in this bleak moment against the formless peril.

Doubtless these huge tombs were built to preserve from destruction the royal bodies which were hidden within them at the end of tortuous and carefully concealed passages; but both the gigantic structures in the vicinity of Memphis, and the everlasting hills, which were later utilized at Thebes, inevitably give the impression that death is defied and shut out by massive defences.

Even when the traveller sees that the Egyptians defeated their object by the very success of the Gizeh pyramids—for when their overwhelming bulk could not be enlarged and their bewildering labyrinths could not be multiplied, effort along that line perforce ceased—there is something in the next attempt of the Egyptians to overcome death which the child within us again recognizes as an old experience. One who takes pains to inquire concerning the meaning of the texts which were inscribed on the inner walls of the pyramids and the early tombs, finds that the familiar terror of death is still there although expressed somewhat more subtly; that the Egyptians are trying to outwit death by magic tricks.

These texts are designed to teach the rites that redeem a man from death and insure his continuance of life, not only beyond the grave but in the grave itself. "He who sayeth this chapter and who has been justified in the waters of Natron, he shall come forth the day after his burial." Because to recite them was to fight successfully against the enemies of the dead, these texts came to be inscribed on tombs, on coffins, and on the papyrus hung around the neck of a mummy. But woe to the man who was buried without the texts: "He who knoweth not this chapter cannot come forth by day." Access to Paradise and all its joys was granted to any one, good or bad, who knew the formulæ, for in the first stages of Egyptian development, as in all other civilizations, the gods did not concern themselves with the conduct of a man toward other men, but solely with his duty to the gods themselves.

The magic formulæ alone afforded protection against the shadowy dangers awaiting the dead man when first he entered the next world and enabled him to overcome the difficulties of his journey. The texts taught him how to impersonate particular gods and by this subterfuge to overcome the various foes he must encounter, because these foes, having at one time been overcome by the gods, were easily terrified by such pretence.

When I found myself curiously sympathetic with this desire "to pretend," and with the eager emphasis attached by the Egyptians to their magic formulæ, I was inclined to put it down to that secret sympathy with magic by means of which all children, in moments of rebellion against a humdrum world, hope to wrest something startling and thrilling out of the environing realm of the supernatural; but beyond a kinship with this desire to placate the evil one, to overcome him by mysterious words, I found it baffling to trace my sympathy to a definite experience. Gradually, however, it emerged, blurred in certain details, surprisingly alive in others, but all of it suffused with the selfsame emotions which impelled the Egyptian to write his Book of the Dead.

To describe it as a spiritual struggle is to use much too dignified and definite a term; it was the prolonged emotional stress throughout one cold winter when revival services—protracted meetings, they were then called—were held in the village church night after night. I was, of course, not permitted to attend them, but I heard them talked about a great deal by simple adults and children, who told of those who shouted aloud for joy, or lay on the floor "stiff with power" because they were saved; and of others—it was for those others that my heart was wrung—who, although they wrestled with the spirit until midnight and cried out that they felt the hot breath of hell upon their cheeks, could not find salvation. Would it do to pretend? I anxiously asked myself, why didn't they say the right words so that they could get up from the mourners' bench and sit with the other people, who must feel so sorry for them that they would let them pretend? What were these words that made such a difference that to say them was an assurance of heavenly bliss, but if you failed to say them you burned in hell forever and ever? Was the preacher the only one who knew them for sure? Was it possible to find them without first kneeling at the mourners' bench and groaning? These words must certainly be in the Bible somewhere, and if one read it out loud all through, every word, one must surely say the right words in time; but if one died before one was grown up enough to read the Bible through—to-night, for instance—what would happen then? Surely nothing else could be so important as these words of salvation. While I did not exactly scheme to secure them, I was certainly restrained only by my impotence, and I anxiously inquired from everyone what these magic words might be; and only gradually did this childish search for magic protection from the terrors after death imperceptibly merge into a concern for the fate of the soul.

Perhaps, because it is so impossible to classify one's own childish experiences or to put them into chronological order, the traveller at no time feels a lack of consistency in the complicated attitude toward death which is portrayed on the walls of the Egyptian temples and tombs. Much of it seems curiously familiar; from the earliest times, the Egyptians held the belief that there is in man a permanent element which survives—it is the double, the Ka, the natural soul in contradistinction to the spiritual soul, which fits exactly into the shape of the body but is not blended with it. In order to save this double from destruction, the body must be preserved in a recognizable form.

This insistence upon the preservation of the body among the Egyptians, antedating their faith in magic formulæ, clearly had its origin, as in the case of the child, in a desperate revolt against the destruction of the visible man.

Owing to this continued insistence upon corporeal survival, the Egyptians at length carried the art of embalming to such a state of perfection that mummies of royal personages are easily recognized from their likenesses to portrait statues. Such confidence did they have in their own increasing ability to withhold the human frame from destruction that many of the texts inscribed on the walls of the tombs assure the dead man himself that he is not dead, and endeavor to convince his survivors against the testimony of their own senses; or rather, they attempt to deceive the senses. The texts endlessly repeat the same assertion, "Thou comest not dead to thy sepulchre, thou comest living"; and yet the very reiteration, as well as the decorations upon the walls of every tomb, portray a primitive terror lest after all the body be destroyed and the element of life be lost forever. One's throat goes dry over this old fear of death expressed by men who have been so long dead that there is no record of them but this, no surviving document of their once keen reactions to life.

Doubtless the Egyptians in time overcame this primitive fear concerning the disappearance of the body, as we all do, although each individual is destined to the same devastating experience. The memory of mine came back to me vividly as I stood in an Egyptian tomb: I was a tiny child making pothooks in the village school, when one day—it must have been in the full flush of Spring, for I remember the crab-apple blossoms—during the afternoon session, the A B C class was told that its members would march all together to the burial of the mother of one of the littlest girls. Of course, I had been properly taught that people went to heaven when they died and that their bodies were buried in the cemetery, but I was not at all clear about it, and I was certainly totally unprepared to see what appeared to be the person herself put deep down into the ground. The knowledge came to me so suddenly and brutally that for weeks afterward the days were heavy with a nameless oppression and the nights were filled with horror.

The cemetery was hard by the school-house, placed there, it had always been whispered among us, to make the bad boys afraid. Thither the A B C class, in awestruck procession, each child carefully holding the hand of another, was led by the teacher to the edge of the open grave and bidden to look on the still face of the little girl's mother.

Our poor knees quaked and quavered as we stood shelterless and unattended by family protection or even by friendly grownups; for the one tall teacher, while clearly visible, seemed inexpressively far away as we kept an uncertain footing on the freshly spaded earth, hearing the preacher's voice, the sobs of the motherless children, and, crowning horror of all, the hollow sound of three clods of earth dropped impressively upon the coffin lid.

After endless ages the service was over and we were allowed to go down the long hill into the familiar life of the village. But a new terror awaited me even there, as the street and the last of the way home was therefore solitary. I remember a breathless run from the blacksmith shop, past the length of our lonely orchard until the carriage-house came insight, through whose wide-open doors I could see a man moving about. One last panting effort brought me there, and after my spirit had been slightly reassured by conversation, I took a circuitous route to the house that I might secure as much companionship as possible on the way. I stopped at the stable to pat an old horse who stood munching in his stall, and again to throw a handful of corn into the poultry yard. The big turkey gobbler who came greedily forward gave me great comfort because he was so absurd and awkward that no one could possibly associate him with anything so solemn as death. I went into the kitchen where the presiding genius allowed me to come without protest although the family dog was at my heels. I felt constrained to keep my arms about his shaggy neck while trying to talk of familiar things— would the cake she was making be baked in the little round tins or in the big square one? But although these idle words were on my lips, I wanted to cry out, "Their mother is dead; whatever, whatever will the children do?" These words, which I had overheard as we came away from the graveyard, referred doubtless to the immediate future of the little family, but in my mind were translated into a demand for definite action on the part of the children against this horrible thing which had befallen their mother.

It was with no sense of surprise that I found this long forgotten experience spread before my eyes on the walls of a tomb built four thousand years ago into a sandy hill above the Nile, at Assuan. The man so long dead, who had prepared the tomb for himself, had carefully ignored the grimness of death. He is portrayed as going about his affairs surrounded by his family, his friends, and his servants: grain is being measured before him into his warehouse, while a scribe by his side registers the amount; the herdsmen lead forth cattle for his inspection; two of them, enraged bulls, paying no attention to the somber implication of tomb decoration, lower their huge heads, threatening each other as if there were no such thing as death in the world. Indeed, the builder of the tomb seems to have liked the company of animals, perhaps because they were so incurious concerning death. His dogs are around him, he stands erect in a boat from which he spears fish, and so on from one marvelous relief to another, but all the time your heart contracts for him, and you know that in the midst of this elaborately prepared nonchalance he is miserably terrified by the fate which may be in store for him, and is trying to make himself believe that he need not leave all this wonted and homely activity; that if his body is but properly preserved he will be able to enjoy it forever.

Although the Egyptians, in their natural desire to cling to the familiar during the strange experience of death, portrayed upon the walls of their tombs many domestic and social habits whose likeness to our own household life gives us the quick satisfaction with which the traveler encounters the familiar and wonted in a strange land, such a momentary thrill is quite unlike the abiding sense of kinship which is founded upon the unexpected similarity of ideas, and it is the latter which are encountered in the tombs of the eighteenth century dynasty. The paintings portray a great hall, at the end of which sits Osiris, the god who had suffered death on earth, awaiting those who come before him for judgment. In the center of the hall stands a huge balance in which the hearts of men are weighed, once more reminiscent of a childish conception, making clear that as the Egyptians became more anxious and scrupulous they gradually made the destiny of man dependent upon morality, and finally directed the souls of men to heaven or hell according to their merits.

There is a theory that the tremendous results of good and evil, in the earliest awakening to them, were first placed in the next world by a primitive people sore perplexed as to the partialities and injustices of mortal life. This simple view is doubtless the one the child naturally takes. In Egypt I was so vividly recalled to my first apprehension of it, that the contention that the very belief in immortality is but the postulate of the idea of reward and retribution seemed to me at the moment a perfectly reasonable one.

The incident of my childhood around which it had formulated itself was very simple. I had been sent with a message—an important commission it seemed to me—to the leader of the church choir that the hymn selected for the doctor's funeral was "How blest the righteous when he dies." The village street was so strangely quiet under the summer sun that even the little particles of dust beating in the hot air were more noiseless than ever before. Frightened by the noonday stillness and instinctively seeking companionship, I hurried toward two women who were standing at a gate talking in low tones. In their absorption they paid no attention to my somewhat wistful greeting, but I heard one of them say with a dubious shake of the head that "he had never openly professed nor joined the church," and in a moment I understood that she thought the doctor would not go to heaven. What else did it mean, that half-threatening tone? Of course the doctor was good, as good as any one could be. Only a few weeks before he had given me a new penny when he had pulled my tooth, and once I heard him drive by in the middle of the night when he took a beautiful baby to the miller's house; he went to the farms miles and miles away when people were sick, and everybody sent for him the minute they were in trouble. How could any one be better than that?

In defiant contrast to the whispering women, there arose in my mind, composed doubtless of various Bible illustrations, the picture of an imposing white-robed judge seated upon a golden throne, who listened gravely to all those good deeds as they were read by the recording angel from his great book, and then sent the doctor straight to heaven.

I dimly felt the challenge of the fine old hymn in its claim of blessings for the righteous, and was defiantly ready at the moment to combat the theology of the entire community. Of my own claim to heaven I was most dubious, and I simply could not bring myself to contemplate the day when my black sins should be read aloud from the big book; but when the claim of reward in the next world for well-doing in this came to me in regard to one whose righteousness was undoubted, I was eager to champion him before all mankind and even before the judges in the shadowy world to come.

This state of mind, this mood of truculent discussion, was recalled by the wall paintings in the tomb of a nobleman in the Theban hills. In an agonized posture he awaits the outcome of his trial before Osiris. Thoth, the true scribe, records on the wall the just balance between the heart of the nobleman, which is in one pan of the scale, and the feather of truth which is in the other. The noble appeals to his heart, which has thus been separated from him, to stand by him during the weighing and not to bear testimony against him. "Oh, heart of my existence, rise not up against me; be not an enemy against me before the divine powers; thou art my Ka that is in my body, the heart that came to me from my mother." The noble even tries a bribe by reminding the Ka that his own chance of survival is dependent on his testimony at this moment. The entire effort on the part of the man being tried is to still the voice of his own conscience, to maintain stoutly his innocence even to himself.

The attitude of the self-justifying noble might easily have suggested those later childish struggles in which a sense of hidden guilt, of repeated failure in "being good," plays so large a part, and humbles a child to the very dust. That the definite reminiscence evoked by the tomb belonged to an earlier period of rebellion may indicate that the Egyptian had not yet learned to commune with his gods for spiritual refreshment.

Whether it is that the long days and magical nights on the Nile lend themselves to a revival of former states of consciousness, or that I had come to expect landmarks of individual development in Egypt, or, more likely still, that I had fallen into a profoundly reminiscent mood, I am unable to state; but certainly, as the Nile boat approached nearer to him "who sleeps in Philæ," something of the Egyptian feeling for Osiris, the god to whom was attributed the romance of a hero and the character of a benefactor and redeemer, came to me through long-forgotten sensations. Typifying the annual "great affliction," Osiris, who had submitted himself to death, mutilation, and burial in the earth, returned each Spring when the wheat and barley sprouted, bringing not only a promise of bread for the body but healing and comfort for the torn mind; an intimation that death itself is beneficent and may be calmly accepted as a necessary part of an ordered universe.

Day after day, seeing the rebirth of the newly planted fields on the banks of the Nile, and touched by a fresh sense of the enduring miracle of Spring with its inevitable analogy to the vicissitudes of human experience, one dimly comprehends how the pathetic legends of Osiris, by providing the Egyptian with an example for his own destiny, not only opened the way for a new meaning in life, but also gradually vanquished the terrors of death.

Again there came a faint memory of a child's first apprehension that there may be poetry out-of-doors, of the discovery that myths have a foundation in natural phenomena, and at last a more definite reminiscence.

I saw myself a child of twelve standing stock-still on the bank of a broad-flowing river, with a little red house surrounded by low-growing willows on its opposite bank, striving to account to myself for a curious sense of familiarity, for a conviction that I had long ago known it all most intimately, although I had certainly never seen the Mississippi River before. I remember that, much puzzled and mystified, at last I gravely concluded that it was one of those intimations of immortality that Wordsworth had written about and I went back to my cousin's camp in so exalted a frame of mind that the memory of the evening light shining through the blades of young corn growing in a field passed on the way has remained with me for more than forty years.

Was that fugitive sense of having lived before nearer to the fresher imaginations of the Egyptians, as it is nearer to the mind of a child? and did the myth of Osiris make them more willing to die because the myth came to embody a confidence in this transitory sensation of continuous life?

Such ghosts of reminiscence, coming to the individual as he visits one after another of the marvellous human documents on the banks of the Nile may be merely manifestations of that new humanism which is perhaps the most precious possession of this generation, the belief that no altar at which living men have once devoutly worshipped, no oracle to whom a nation long ago appealed in its moments of dire confusion, no gentle myth in which former generations have found solace, can lose all significance for us, the survivors.

Is it due to this same humanism that, in spite of the overweight of the tomb, Egypt never appears to the traveller as world-weary, or as a land of the dead? Although the slender fellaheen, whom he sees all day pouring the water of the Nile on their parched fields, use the primitive shaduf of their remote ancestors, and the stately women bear upon their heads water-jars of a shape unchanged for three thousand years, modern Egypt refuses to belong to the past and continually makes the passionate living appeal of those hard-pressed in the struggle for bread.

Under the smoking roofs of the primitive clay houses lifted high above the level of the fields, because resting on the ruins of villages which have crumbled there from time immemorial, mothers feed their children, clutched by the old fear that there is not enough for each to have his portion; and the traveller comes to realize with a pang that the villages are built upon the bleak, barren places quite as the dead are always buried in the desert because no black earth can be spared, and that each new harvest, cut with sickles of a curve already ancient when Moses was born, in spite of its quick ripening, is garnered barely in time to save the laborer from actual starvation.

Certain it is that through these our living brothers, or through the unexpected reactions of memory to racial records, the individual detects the growth within of an almost mystical sense of the life common to all the centuries, and of the unceasing human endeavor to penetrate into the unseen world. These records also afford glimpses into a past so vast that the present generation seems to float upon its surface as thin as a sheet of light which momentarily covers the ocean and moves in response to the black waters beneath it.

38

⌑

"THE PLAY INSTINCT AND THE ARTS"

BECAUSE THE MODERN INDUSTRIAL city is so new, we are as yet ignorant of its ultimate reactions upon human life, and we know little of the impressions and even of the scars which this new type of living makes upon that most highly sensitized material, the body and mind of the young at the moment they are most acutely alive to their surroundings. We only know that young people, with their new-born instincts, whether walking in crowded streets or in the open fields, continually test the achievements and shortcomings of the life about them by standards of romance new to them but as old as the world.

Because the youth of Chicago have been brought together from all parts of the world into one cosmopolitan community, in sentimental moments certain lines of Swinburne seem so appropriate that we can almost imagine them chanting together:

> WE MIX FROM MANY LANDS
> WE MARCH FROM VERY FAR
> THE LIGHT WE WALK IN
> DARKENS SUN AND MOON AND STAR.

We realize afresh that it is the business of youth to reaffirm the beauty and joy in the world that such spontaneity may become a source of new vitality, a wellspring of refreshment to a jaded city. It is easy to

---

Note: "The Play Instinct and the Arts," in *The Second Twenty Years at Hull-House* (New York: Macmillan, 1930), chapter 11.

fail to utilize it, the artists are preoccupied trying to recapture it after the first bloom has escaped them and only occasionally do the educators demonstrate that each child lives not only in an actual environment visible to all, but in enchanted surroundings which may be reproduced by the child himself.

The early School of Education at the University of Chicago, founded by Dr. John Dewey, demonstrated that a child after an historic period had made itself at home in his imagination would wholeheartedly live in it for weeks at a time.[1] He energetically dug, built, wove and cooked, sometimes according to his need in a primitive hut, at other times in a medieval castle surrounded by a moat. But because this fresh imaginative life with its instinct for play is in a sense the mission of art itself we have found at Hull-House that our educational efforts tend constantly toward a training for artistic expression; in a music school, a school of dramatics, classes in rhythm and dancing and the school of the plastic and graphic arts. In the last which we call the Hull-House Art School the children are given great freedom in the use of color and clay and other media through which they may express those images which are perpetually welling up from some inner fountain, and which suggest not only their secret aspirations, but, curiously enough, something of their historic background.

Because Hull-House is in an immigrant district, we have the great advantage that children in the art school are of many races and nationalities and to a surprising degree they are familiar with the backgrounds of culture which their parents represent. The other day in one of our pottery classes where the children were trying historic subjects, the Scandinavian boy made a Viking bowl, the Mexican an Indian hut, the Greek the capital of a Corinthian column, the Italian the dome of St. Peter's. The variety was interesting, but not nearly so significant as the fact that each boy recognized what the other boy had made and called it by name. They were disconcerted only by an Egyptian pylon which a sophisticated elder was modeling, and they excused themselves by saying that they didn't have any Egyptians in the school, but they hoped after a while that one would come. This school gives the children space, time and tools, and is sure that they will find their own way, although of course the teachers help them over difficulties of material and push them toward a clearer expression. There is apparently in each material new suggestions and a new joy in manipulating it, as each child finds a chance to make his own contribution. One of the younger teachers considers it her chief business to discover and remove inhibitions, because she finds that joy is the most important factor in freeing the child's expression, she has apparently discovered with Count Keyserling, that an inhibited artist is of no use in the practical world.[2] Norah Hamilton, the head of our little art school, says that if such artistic children have no early outlet for their gifts they may never find a real place in the world about them and their possible contribution will be lost.[3] She further adds:

> The children seem to find in their inner lives a world of color and beauty in which they are perfectly at home. They work with freedom and endless facility, with faith in their own way of seeing, and with faith in hands and material to carry out their vision. They give their best, and take it for granted that what they give is good. They are free from our inhibitions, use their full selves and make use also, perhaps, of an instinctive self. They give the reality as it comes to them but the reality is living and filled with the spirit of play, that "other seeing" that finds the play world as real as the material world "peopled with psychic beings kin to them," as were the hills and streams to the Greeks, the kings of all artists. To sum up the charm of the children's work, they give us a new world seen with new eyes. Perhaps, with the great primitives, they follow nature's very ways, are close to her rhythm; perhaps obey some law inherent in things as they are.

Included in the art school program are talks given with photographic reproductions of the early Italian painters shown to the pupils by Miss Starr when they spend an evening in her bookbindery.[4] She is often impressed by their quick recognition of the message which the picture would convey and by the admiration bestowed by her young visitors upon the ability of the artist "to get it over." Excursions are often arranged to other parts of the city. It is both travel and adventure for the children to visit a museum and they refer to these trips years afterwards as to great events, also the sense of contrast apparently makes them see their own part of the city with a new sense of romance. Sketching classes are held every summer at the Bowen Country Club and almost every member of the school spends at least one week-end there every year. They vie with each other as to which season was found to be the most beautiful and defend certain aspects of light and color with genuine enthusiasm. Most of them also have two weeks vacation there in the summer and recount not only the excursions and sports of country life but tell a great deal about its beauty as well. It may possibly be easier for Italian children to talk openly about such matters because the life of an artist is familiar to them and they know that it is a national asset that thousands of people come to Italy every year to admire the beauty so lavishly found there. . . .

III

Social life and art have always seemed to go best together at Hull-House. This is shown in what has been called the Big Studio, the large room where young people come year after year, partly making their own atmosphere and partly led by Enella Benedict, a teacher at the Art Institute, an early Hull-House resident, who brings books, pictures, reproductions, for them to share. Between them all, there seems to be created an atmosphere in which each can find his own way in art. Even here the medium is varied, for they make batiks in the studio and also use the adjoining room which contains a complete etching outfit.

From the beginnings in this studio a group of professional artists has been developed, four of whom are residents at Hull-House, occupying studios built upon the roofs of our two taller buildings. Two of these artists, who married each other, are now spending two years abroad with the keenest pleasure and profit; another who received a European scholarship at the Art Institute in Chicago was able, because of his habits of frugal living, to take another man from the studio with him and they even stretched the scholarship into a second year of study which they spent in Spain. This fact caused a much more stirring interest in the studio than the news that one of the older men had received ten thousand dollars for a portrait in New York, and was fast growing famous. An illustration showing that the students felt more at home in the studio than anywhere else was afforded when one of their number returned from the war suffering from shell shock and insisted upon living there day and night for many weeks until he slowly recovered. He slept on a cot which his studio friends installed for him. They brought him food from the coffee house below and heated it upon the gas ring used for batiks. He painted hard and furiously by day and at last slept peacefully at night, gradually readjusting himself to the world outside. It is rather interesting that out of ten of these artists who may be said to have "arrived," at least half of them are Jewish. This may be partly because the Jewish youth seems more persistent in the pursuit of his object and partly because the family are willing to free the time of a gifted young man, as Jewish families, however meager their resources, have for ages supported the Talmud scholar.

The people who seize upon the plastic arts with the most enthusiasm are the Mexicans. A few weeks spent in Mexico one gorgeous spring convinced me that the Mexicans took their art seriously. We saw the enthusiasm on the part of Saens, assistant secretary of Education, of Vasconcelos who was previously secretary, of the school of gifted artists who decorated the vast halls of the educational buildings with scenes from the history of Mexico. The artists always bear in mind the progressive educational theory as they conceive it. They showed us a wall in a boys' school upon which the paintings had been deliberately defaced because the French artists who did them "had violated the canons of the new education" and had "imitated the frivolities of a dead art."

One of the resident artists at Hull-House spends several months of every year in Mexico, and comes back with fresh material and fresh enthusiasm for the possibilities of all their abundant talent. A few of the Mexicans in the neighborhood of Hull-House come from the Indian tribes in which the making of pottery has been traditional. Several of these men are able to support themselves by what they produce in our shops and in a little factory set up in the basement of one of our buildings called the Hull-House Kilns which we hope may fill a definite need in the scheme of the art school. It is not only that the children are under the economic stress and pressure of life more and more as they grow older and that their families ask for promise of some practical returns upon their work, but that the faculty of the art school itself is constantly driven to make plans out of respect for the talent which the school uncovers. They want to give young talent a chance to try itself out, young powers an opportunity to make good while they are young.

Critics of the Cizek School in Vienna and of other attempts to connect the play instinct with forms of art, are always certain to point out that at the period of adolescence when the child becomes self-conscious and actually looks at the world about him his work suffers a collapse, sometimes he refuses to go on with it and often continues only half-heartedly. The reply to such an indictment must be that the educational methods are at fault, that a gradual adaptation should be made to the inner changes which come so gradually to the child. The environment which the child encounters in real life may also have to be modified, but what better clue could be followed in making needed changes in our industries. Certainly the Hull-House Kilns which were started three years ago under the able direction of Mrs. French, the head of the department of Ceramics in the Art Institute, who is also a resident at Hull-House, have been very satisfactory. One of our most gifted young men finds permanent occupation there as foreman. He had earned much more money as a prize fighter with a reputation growing beyond the Italian colony into national fame. He yielded at last to the lure of creative activity, perhaps the most intriguing occupation vouchsafed to mankind.

IV

It is to be hoped that such experiments as are carried on in the art school at Hull-House and in many other places in America, including the advanced public schools, will at last influence the entire system of public education. To give every child in our schools the ability to use his hands with ease and pleasure, not upon the narrow basis of fitting him for factory life as educated clerks have been formerly prepared for the merchants, but in order to retain that power of unfolding human life which is implicit in the play instinct. If it had a natural expression it would normally develop into the art impulse with that power of variation which industry so sadly needs to redeem it from its extreme mechanization. In the minority report on the English Poor Law, all the English speaking world was told that it was a mistake to put young people under eighteen at work which did not have educational content; that England was preparing for herself a new crop of dependents and unemployables. We might add that the immature human creature should not be put into a certain type of monotonous work because society is losing something too valuable by thus prematurely extinguishing that variety and promise and bloom of life which are the unique possession of youth and the basis of the arts.

The United States perhaps more than any other country in the world can demonstrate what applied science has accomplished for industry through invention of machinery and the utilization of all sorts of un-promising raw material. It would be unfortunate if we should become content with this achievement and oblivious to the fact that the next in-dustrial advance lies in the discovery and education of the workman himself to the end that his mind, his power of variation and his instinct for art may ultimately be reflected in the industrial product. The pur-chasing public including both consumers and producers—although it is impossible to regard them as two classes if we accept the dictum that the nation is most prosperous in which its producers are at the same time its best consumers—may in time refuse to be surrounded by man-ufactured objects which do not represent some gleam of intelligence on the part of the men who made them. Hundreds of people have already taken that very short step so far as all decoration and ornament are concerned. Such a change in industry will be but a recognition of the play instinct, of the charm and spontaneity of life which might be re-flected in the most prosaic of products. But first industry must be seized upon by the educators who now either avoid it altogether or beg the question by teaching a tool industry, advocated by Ruskin and Morris in their first revolt against the iniquities of the present system.[5]

The result of monotonous factory work is quickly registered by the most premature of the workers in whom the play instinct is extremely difficult to repress. A study reported in the *Survey* in 1927 demonstrated that a surprising number of young people between the ages of sixteen and eighteen meet with accidents in industry because they are bungling and do not give attention to their work. In one sense these accidents are an attempt on the part of nature itself to protect them, strange as it may seem, from the deadening effects of mechanical work by the irresistible urge to play. Many of them revolt and throw up the job altogether, searching only half-heartedly for another one. Prematurely monotonous work seems to produce two types of unemployables, one type becomes vagrant and one type develops into those men who become criminals in the effort to "live without working." This repression of the natural in-stincts of youth sometimes results in actual retrogression. A careful study made in England of working boys between the ages of fourteen and twenty years, came to the conclusion that when these boys left school at the age of fourteen they had a better vocabulary, a larger range of ideas, more things they could talk about and did talk about, than was true of the same boys when they were twenty years of age. During the six years after they went to work their minds were contracted and they lost the power of using certain words and phrases, and were not only less valuable at twenty in the industrial world than many of them had been at fourteen, but were actually less educated and in every way less fitted to face life. I do not believe that this state of affairs is more true of England than of the United States. I have known Italian children who leave school able to read quite readily in the third and fourth readers, and who five or six years afterwards could not read a sentence from a newspaper. After leaving school they had worked in a factory with other Italians and at home had used the same tongue, until their hard-earned education had simply fallen away from them. It was found that the only things they really remembered were those which the daily task required them to use—the subjects which were put into use were not only remembered but were quite often extended. We have also discovered that as boys become familiar with electricity and machinery, understanding something of the application of modern science to industry, they are more receptive and eager to develop their general knowledge, rising occasionally to intellectual interests.

There are many indications that public education is moving in this direction. Public schools equipped for electrical engineering, aviation, automobile construction and other of the mechanical arts are filled day after day by young workers who are in the continuation schools, with attendance arranged out of their employers' time. The present development is the result of much effort on the part of many people to secure freedom from too early labor and also the prolongation of education for self-supporting youth. . . .

VI

Perhaps one of the most notable expressions of the play instinct in these later times has been connected with the amateur drama. Many years ago a little theater was built for Hull-House which has sheltered many interesting plays in many tongues. Perhaps nothing better illustrates the connection between the play instinct and the arts than the history of six dramatic clubs which were all started with very young children and have preserved their continuity through the years, their membership at the present moment numbering almost three hundred persons. Some of the individual members of these clubs have become successful actors and have long had their headquarters in New York. One of them is the leading male dancer at La Scala Theater in Milan. He gave a recital in Chicago one Sunday afternoon recently to an audience which held many of his proud countrymen but no one there had a greater sense of participation than the Marionette Club, of which he had been a member for many years. One young woman who began her training at Hull-House as a little child is now a member of the faculty in the Department of Dramatics at Yale University. These achievements as professionals have been in a sense secondary to the fact that the young people as a whole have been able to refine the play instinct into dramatic expression, to realize the pleasure which a devotion to an art entails. I should like to describe these clubs by quoting from an address given by their gifted director, Edith de Nancrede,[6] at the Yale Drama Conference, held in 1927, to those representing at least a few of the three thousand little theaters scattered all over the United States:

> One of the interesting facts that Hull-House has brought out in its dramatic work is the almost unique power a dramatic club has of holding a group of people together from childhood, through adolescence and into maturity. The need of some means of making life more interesting and beautiful, the need of something to stimulate the mind and imagination, is peculiarly felt in neighborhoods such as that of Hull-House.
>
> Through such plays as "Mid-Summer Night's Dream," the "Sunken Bell," "Prunella," with their opportunity for beautiful and imaginative settings and lovely incidental music, a real love and appreciation of beauty has been developed. Fortunately there are several artists and musicians among the Hull-House residents and, in the groups themselves, there are young artists and musicians developed by our Music School and our Art School. The dramatic clubs care so much for the beauty of their performances that they spend a tremendous amount of time and energy, and all the money that they take in at their productions, upon costumes, scenery and lighting. As all of the members, including the director, are engaged all day in earning a living, the painting of scenery and experimenting in lighting, as well as all rehearsals, are done at night. And often, just before a play, the work on the stage goes on all night. The result of such devotion is that the Hull-House productions are often quite

beautiful to look at, and the music, performed by a quartette trained in the Music School, is lovely to listen to. . . .

After observing for some twenty-five years its remarkable results in the form of charming and interesting young people, I am fully convinced that there is no force so powerful as that of the drama in awakening and stimulating an interest in intellectual and beautiful things. And to me it has an even greater quality—the power of freeing people from inhibitions and repressions. It seems to me the drama is like Josephine Preston Peabody's "Piper"—always letting things out of cages—and sometimes, as I watch some young, self-conscious creature expanding and growing under the influence of the inspiring or poetic thought he is expressing, the drama seems to me like one of those Eastern magicians, who puts a seed into the earth and immediately before one's eyes, it sends forth roots, branches, leaves, buds, and opens wide a flower. I have seen such miracles, such incredible growth on the Hull-House stage.

The National Federation of Settlements which has been so great a factor in unifying settlement activities throughout the country, has sustained committees on dramatics, on music—the latter has been able to report an astonishing growth in music schools in Philadelphia, New York and in other cities—and one on poetry. The last both encourages children to care for poetry and to write it if they choose. One of the best methods of obtaining the first object is to have the children recite in chorus somewhat in the spirit of the speaking choruses, which John Masefield has so skillfully encouraged in England that hundreds of people, the timbre of whose voices has been carefully selected, can recite together with great beauty. We find the children at Hull-House will fit their rhythm to music or easily chant to a distinct meter. We have had one or two rather heartbreaking experiences with regard to composition. The following verse was written by a little girl whose uncle had been executed for murder. There was no possible way of knowing that the child would select such a theme of which these are the last lines:

> HE WAS DOOMED TO DIE THAT NIGHT
> OH, IT WAS A DREADFUL SIGHT
> THEY BROUGHT HIM COFFEE TO MAKE IT RIGHT
> BUT A SHOCK CAME AND HE WAS DEAD.

VII

Perhaps I can best illustrate the aims of our music school by quoting from the journal published quarterly by the National Federation of Settlements. The review was written by the editor, Albert Kennedy.

> *The Merman's Bride* is a cantata by Eleanor Smith, one of the most finely creative minds in the Hull-House group, a composer of note, and founder and director of the Hull-House Music School. It is naturally a matter of considerable significance to all who are interested in Settlements when a work of art of notable quality comes to birth in a Neighborhood House. An agency such as the Settlement, whose basic purpose is to raise the quality of civilization cannot but thrill when its angel grants it the supreme joy of participating in a creative process. . . . The score of *The Merman's Bride* calls for two pianos, a string quartette, four solo voices, a chorus, actors and dancers to mime the characters of the story. The junior division of the Hull-House Dramatic Department takes the responsibility of the visual presentation upon the stage. . . .
>
> The pupils of the Music School are peculiarly fortunate in being permitted to participate in bringing so distinguished a composition to performance. There is an enlargement that comes with being involved in a creative process. Possibly the cantata was conceived through some vital interplay between the children of the school and their director. One feels both in the story and in the choruses something of the actual life of these girls who sing and play. Quite obviously its melodies had already become part of their mental and emotional heritage, and as the years go by they will recall the birth of the work as one of the choicest experiences of their lives. Of all the gifts that the creator, the artist and the teacher can give to youth, surely none is so precious as this, that the pupil is included within the vital creative process of his master. Some among these children already appreciate this and all will be affected by it, however slightly.

Again the factor of continuity has been important. The young matron who sang the leading rôle of the bride had been a member of the Music School since she was a child in the Hull-House kindergarten.

The music she had sung and composed and taught there had been in a very real sense an abiding and continuing interest, not only as a craft but in very truth as an art. To take a quotation from another article on the Hull-House Music School:

> It is the system of all great artists to leave egotism aside by loving something very superior—here is the very basis and essence of a true system such as Plato recommended.

The arts have, I think, always been embodied in the ultimate aims of Hull-House. From time to time in moments of depression or of exhilaration over some public undertaking to which the residents were committed, we have urged Miss Smith to phrase in music the social compunction which at the moment it seemed impossible to express in any other way. This might be considered a demonstration that the function of art was germane to the group and that the teaching of music was not akin to the motive of the Vermont farmer who "only raised wheat for seed." When we came to the twenty-fifth anniversary of the opening of Hull-House in September, 1914, only a few weeks after the beginning of the World War, it seemed impossible to arrange for an occasion of rejoicing at such a moment. We decided, however, to record the ending of our first quarter of a century by publishing five Hull-House songs composed by the head of the Music School. The four songs written in response to public efforts were on the protection of sweatshop workers, the abolition of child labor, the relief of the anthracite coal miners during a great strike, and the movement for granting votes to women. The fifth song set to a poem of Matthew Arnold's was really a prayer to be saved from the eternal question as to whether in any real sense the world is governed in the interest of righteousness. It voices the doubt which so inevitably dogs the footsteps of all those who venture into the jungle of social wretchedness. Because old-fashioned songs, with the exception of those of religion and patriotism, chiefly expressed the essentially individualistic emotions of love, hope or melancholy, it is perhaps all the more imperative that socialized emotions should also find musical expression, if the manifold movements of our contemporaries are to have the inspiration and solace they so obviously need. We believed that all the songs in this collection fulfilled the highest mission in music, first in giving expression to the type of emotional experience which quickly tends to get beyond words, and second in affording an escape from the unnecessary disorder of actual life, into the wider region of the spirit which, under the laws of a great art, may be filled with an austere beauty and peace.

VIII

The release function of art, the offering of an escape from the monotony of daily living, is doubtless provided most widely by the movie and its new child the talkie. Whether the audience in a movie house is composed of adults or children, there is no doubt that they all come with a simple desire to be amused or a willingness to be instructed if done entertainingly. The fact that a tired man has to be jerked away from his preoccupation rather violently may account for the popularity of the detective and murder plays. They seem as innocent as any other form of puzzle although they doubtless tend to a view of crime which is at once romantic and sordid, losing sight of the human and social reactions and abstracting all moral judgments. Interest centers on the cleverness of the two parties to the game, the criminal and the detective and he wins who "gets away with it." The exception to the desire for pure entertainment is afforded by the girls who frankly announce that some films are valuable in showing them how to secure a husband and that other films are no good for that purpose. It is also said that a certain sort of young man tests a girl's resistance by what she will stand for in a movie, and that he boasts that it is possible, by a continuous selection of movies, to undermine a girl's standards, a new type of seduction as it were, as if the moving picture films still exhibited traces of their furtive origin in the peep shows.

But allowing for these disabilities and many others which could readily be found there is no doubt that the function of release in neighborhoods such as ours, is marvelously performed by the movies. It is no small achievement that millions of men, women and children with no hope for an opportunity for travel, are still easily familiar with ships on wide seas, with a moon shining on snow-capped mountains, with the rice fields of China, and the temples in India and Egypt. To have made thousands of immigrants familiar with the life of the wild west is to give them the background for at least one aspect in our national development. One may safely assume that certain standard pictures will arise in the minds of the simplest audience when given subjects are discussed.

From my own experience I should say that one of the most beneficent features of the movie is the recreation and release it offers to old people. I recall an old Scotchwoman whose declining years were quite made over by the movies. She lived in an apartment house on Halsted Street, whose lower floor of two stores had been turned into a moving picture house. By using the back stairs she did not need to go out of doors and the kind proprietor saved her a seat night after night so near to her point of entrance that she could reach it unobserved and, therefore, she "never had to dress for the show." As she sat there in the dark her poverty, her deafness and all her other disabilities slipped from her and she was transported to one absorbing scene after another. At first she saved out Wednesday evenings for prayer meeting, but as she had the genuine excuse of the difficulty of walking three blocks with a lame knee, she gradually gave that up, and for a modest lump sum was entitled to the first performance during six nights a week, for her Presbyterianism held out against Sunday night until the very end. Her old eyes would shine with the light of youth as she told us of yet another wonderful experience in this world of ours which she had never had a chance to explore until she was about to leave it.

It is impossible to attend international meetings of any sort without encountering discussion upon motion pictures, their influence upon international opinion, and upon the estimate accorded by one nation to another. In a congress of Pan-Pacific women, I heard an Australian delegate tell of a governmental investigation into the cinema situation, especially as to how far the film portrayal of Western civilization affected the attitude of the village population toward the mother country; in India, a similar investigation had been made of the films exhibited there, seventy per cent of which were manufactured in America. The Pan-Pacific women passed a resolution which was sent to various producers, begging them to send representations of the better type of Western life and not so often of the baser. Certainly we all recall seeing cinemas in foreign countries which had little to do with the higher values of life. "Chicago, oh, yes; that is where they pursue the thief over the tops of the roofs," was said to me in Tokio. At the moment, the Japanese newspapers were full of what they termed a new stage in the "westernization" of Japan. The criminal element in Japan was, according to their news reports, copying the West in its methodology and the police were greatly worried over the change in tactics of the lawless element with which they had to deal. They credited these marked changes in violence to the criminal procedure of Chicago and other Western metropolitan centers, as presented by the "cultural medium" of the movies.

A sponsoring committee is being organized, with headquarters in New York, for "A Proposed Study of the Influence of Motion Pictures on International Relations, especially as regards the Attitudes set up in Foreign Lands towards Americans and America." It is impossible to anticipate the report, but that a committee of responsible people should be committed to such an arduous undertaking is in itself a testimony of the gravity of the situation.

This sordid condition may have come about because so-called recreation has been allowed to get too far away from art expression which while universal in its interests still imposes long-established restraints upon a portrayal of the individual experience, connecting it in some subtle fashion with those permanent experiences forming the basis of our human heritage.

I recall that H. G. Wells once contended that mankind is developing a genuine pleasure in cooperation and is evincing a new craving for that sort of associative effort which transcends personal motives.[7] He believes that we can in time count upon this new factor in human affairs as we have already learned to depend upon intellectual curiosity which also only gradually became disinterested. Doubtless our scientific advance depends more upon disinterested intellectual curiosity than upon any other human trait but we may be faced at this moment with an opportunity to so revitalize our own experiences that we may score as never before in the very Art of Living itself. We may drink from a fountain into which are flowing fresh waters from remote mountain ranges which only the artists could have discovered and made part of our familiar world.

Notes

1. Dewey is, of course, associated with that movement in education called "progressive education," although the phrase by now has so many possible meanings it isn't very useful.

2. Count Keyserling (1880–1946) was famous for something called the School of Wisdom, a pedagogical philosophy and method.

3. Norah Hamilton (1873–1945) is best known today as the illustrator of *Twenty Years at Hull-House*; her sketches are reproduced in contemporary edi-

tions. She was part of a trio of astonishingly accomplished sisters, including the redoubtable Dr. Alice Hamilton, Hull-House resident, and Edith Hamilton, the distinguished scholar of the Greek world.

4. Miss Starr is, of course, Ellen Gates Starr, cofounder of Hull-House and a lifelong friend of Addams.

5. William Morris (1834–1896) was, like John Ruskin, an artist and activist with an antimechanical, antiindustrial bent.

6. Edith de Nancrede (1877–1936) was director of Hull-House Theater. She was a Hull-House resident from 1898 until her death. Hull-House theater is acknowledged as the beginning of Chicago's vibrant theater tradition.

7. H. G. Wells (1866–1946), a British writer much admired by Addams.

39

⚜

"NEED A WOMAN OVER
FIFTY FEEL OLD?"

ONE OF THE REMARKABLE CHANGES in the lives of women in
this country has been the postponement of old age. Chiefly because they had nothing else to do, our grandmothers, after their children had been reared and safely launched into homes of their own, expected to give their remaining years to a general oversight of the
households of their sons and daughters and to the upbringing of their
grandchildren, conforming both as nearly as possible to their own excellent although somewhat inflexible standards.

It is useless to deny that this admirable and highly domestic occupation occasionally led to difficulties. A vigorous woman, accustomed to
the cares of a large household in which her word was law, when deprived of an absorbing occupation could not at all once reduce herself
to a negligible quantity, and the traditional "mother-in-law" was quite
as much the victim of circumstances as were cherished family upon
whom her unused energies were expended.

The easy assumption of old age under the circumstances is readily
understood, for when the individual valued herself largely as a repository of wisdom and tradition it was quite in character to don a cap, and
to sit, knitting innumerable pairs of stockings, where she might easily
be consulted. Almost any family album will reveal these sweet-faced
women, a fold of linen over their placid breasts, a cap upon their
smooth hair, whom we are happy to claim as our grandmothers, and

Note: "Need a Woman over Fifty Feel Old?" *Ladies Home Journal*, vol. 31
(October 1914).

yet if we knew their exact ages, in almost every instance we would be surprised to discover how young they were, many of them scarcely fifty years old. They assumed that life was over for them at the very time their husbands were still in the midst of business and professional activities, often receiving their honest honors and rendering their most distinguished public services after they were fifty years old.

We regret the passing of these charming women and we certainly deplore those women of seventy years occasionally seen rushing from one social function to another, attired in modish gowns, with picture hats surmounting their elaborately coifed [sic] heads. Although so dissimilar it is nevertheless true that both types of women are without adequate activity. The former dissembled a placidity which certainly they could not have felt in every instance; the latter continue a round of vapid occupations which they fear to drop lest they be faced by an insupportable leisure. Both are obviously without absorbing interests.

Happily there is another type of woman between the ages of fifty and seventy years of whom every section of America has its shining examples; first discovered perhaps through church sewing circles and missionary societies, although the widely spread Woman's Christian Temperance Union organizations had much to do with enabling her to find herself. The Woman's Club movement has also been a great factor in developing the powers of women who are over fifty years old. Many of them learned to write papers, to address audiences, to preside over meetings, to organize committees for the first time after they had passed that age. The women's clubs also gave to thousands of women their first sense of responsibility in regard to public education and civic reform. It was largely through the efforts of these older club women that kindergartens, manual training and domestic science were introduced into the public-school system of America. In many cities these women were also the pioneers in agitating for public playgrounds and vacation schools.

These same elderly women who, in their youth, had been sheltered from any knowledge of crime and the ways of criminals, and who would have considered it most unladylike even to refer to a disreputable woman, were often responsible for securing matrons in the police stations, teachers in the jails, the establishment of juvenile courts and the abolition of vice districts. These women are now in no small measure responsible for municipal concerts, for crafts and trades schools and for exhibitions for the encouragement of local artists. In their childhood they knew no exercise more violent than playing croquet, no dietary more rigid than preserves and sponge cake for supper, no notion but that all diseases were Heaven-sent, and that a certain number of children must inevitably die in infancy, but they are now agitating for public gymnasiums and municipal baths, for pure food laws and a clean milk supply; they are quite tigerlike in insisting that all children shall be protected from contagious diseases through school nursing and medical inspection, and they have come to consider a high death rate among infants as a disgrace and a reproach to the community. . . .

One woman of sixty whom I know is most widely useful in many church activities, not only in the local circles of her denomination but also as president of a State organization. Her husband died several years ago, her children are both married and living in two distant cities. It would be hard to imagine a more desolate life than hers might be did she not have an outlet, not only for her splendid energy, but also for her social gifts and her affection. Her small but charming house does not give an impression of emptiness, but is as if it were the center of beneficent activity, a place where a woman dwelt not alone but surrounded by the affection of countless friends. It would be absurd to say that if she had remained "quietly at home," exchanging social amenities with her neighbors, her life would have been so filled with satisfactory interests.

Another woman over fifty years old is the executive head of a National organization which has for years urged and secured better conditions for working women and children, both through legislation and voluntary effort. She has moved from one difficult piece of social organization to another until probably no one else in America is more conversant with the conditions surrounding working women and children in every part of the country, with the laws which have been enacted in their behalf and with the efficiency of their enforcement.

Another woman over fifty years of age has brought into her public services the resources of large wealth, as well as the matured powers of an energetic nature and unusual capacity. For seven years she was president of the Juvenile Court Committee of Chicago, and it was she who suggested and formed, out of this committee, the Juvenile Protective Association. She has been influential in securing the specialization and socialization of the Chicago Municipal Courts, the Court of Domestic Relations, the Morales [sic] Court, and, last of all, the Boys' Court. She has become an extremely able speaker, and continually presents, through addresses and publications, the needs of the boys in the jails, the lack of industrial opportunity for colored young people, the temptations of young women employed in department stores, hotels and restaurants, the dangers to young girls on excursion boats and in amusement parks, the disastrous effect of street trading on boys and girls, and many other similar subjects.

That weariness and dullness, which inhere in both domestic and social affairs when they are carried on by men alone, will no longer be a necessary attribute of public life when such gracious and gray-haired women became a part of it, and when new social movements, in which men as well as women are concerned, naturally utilize woman's experience and ability.

Ever-widening channels are gradually being provided through which woman's increasing moral energy may flow, and it is not too much to predict that in the end public affairs will be amazingly revivified from those new fountainheads fed in the upper reaches of woman's natural capacity.

40

"TOLSTOY AND GANDHI"

THOUSANDS OF PEOPLE IN EVERY nation are eagerly watching Gandhi's great experiment in India. It may be his seizure of the moral initiative, his courageous endurance of suffering, the news interest in his tactical surprises and untried maneuvers, which create such a high degree of suggestibility in the spectators; but it is as if Gandhi at the present moment, as Tolstoy before him, had given a "suggestion needed to free the pent-up energies of good will among men. I have been much interested in this reaction, and find myself continually comparing it to certain experiences during the decade of 1890 when we first read Tolstoy's masterly exposition of the doctrine of non-resistance. Both men demonstrate that when this doctrine is clearly set forth it easily speaks over the head of whatever else may be happening in the world, and both men exemplify the value of conduct as a medium of propaganda.

Tolstoy came to the doctrine of non-resistance as a political method fifty years ago when, during the 1870's he was often urged to join the movement of revolt against the oppressive government of the tsar by the eager young people who keenly felt the opposition of the government to all their efforts to ameliorate the conditions of the peasants. They were disappointed that ten years of the reign of Alexander II had not justified the high hopes which the emancipation of the serfs had engendered. Tolstoy never joined them; although he sympathized with their sense of wrong, he disapproved of their methods. In 1878 the movement resulted in terrorism, and the assassination of the tsar in 1881 demonstrated Tolstoy's position that the inciting of revolution against wrong is sure to end in a resort to violence.

Note: "Tolstoy and Gandhi," *Christian Century*, vol. 48 (November 25, 1931).

What Tolstoy wished to do was to substitute moral forces for all those forces which are at present aroused in warfare. He pointed out that as war develops, it means more expensive equipment, which only the stronger party to the conflict is able to supply, and thus daily the fight becomes more unequal, until there is nothing left but the exertion of moral power, in which alone men are equal. So Tolstoy considered it a matter of wisdom to overthrow oppressive government by the use of this principle from the start, rather than later when much force has been wasted and worse than wasted, for it has raised anger and a spirit of opposition making it more difficult for men to use reason and good will. This position was carefully stated by Tolstoy in his book entitled "My Religion," with the contention that to oppose one wrong with another is to get away ever further from the teachings of the New Testament in regard to overcoming evil with good.

It was not until the later years of his life that Tolstoy himself saw his theory put into practice in an actual political situation; an attempt was at length made to overcome governmental domination without hatred or violence. Tolstoy, who collected examples of non-resistance as an enthusiastic numismatist amasses rare coins, wrote before his death that he regarded Gandhi's activities in the Transvaal as the most important of all the work being done in the world.

Curiously enough, Gandhi's first public activity after he had left London in 1891, where he had studied law for three years, had taken place in South Africa.[1] For twenty years in the Transvaal he had devoted his splendid capacities to the tireless task of protecting his countrymen from a long series of discriminatory enactments designed to prevent serious competition from the free Indian workers who had been brought into the country as indentured laborers. Their former masters did not wish to hire them because they preferred to import new indentured labor, and the citizens of the Transvaal feared the competition of the free Indians as farmers and merchants. Gandhi, as their attorney, finally learned the use of non-cooperation as a successful means of obtaining legal redress. For seven years, without hatred or violence, the indomitable Indian community refused to obey oppressive laws and cheerfully accepted the consequences, although approximately 10,000 of them were sent to jail.

The strategy finally succeeded in 1914 so that Gandhi, in the interest of his clients, found himself in England in the opening days of the world war. In spite of his experience in South Africa, Gandhi at that time often expressed his great admiration for the British colonial system as perhaps the best in the world. He devoted his energies throughout the war to recruiting soldiers and securing money to be sent from India in the support of Great Britain in the world war, although he himself served only as a stretcher bearer.

It was during the armistice that his attitude towards the British rule in India underwent a drastic change, and in a year he had become a tireless opponent of the British rule in India and had joined his fellow countrymen whose resentment against foreign domination had long been accumulating in the nationalist movement. But instead of an armed uprising, which has been the historic method of throwing off the domination of a foreigner, when in 1920 India had reached the breaking point, Gandhi eloquently advocated the use of non-violent non-cooperation as the strategy to be adopted. His experience in its successful use and his fervent convictions resulted in a response to his appeal which was unparalleled. For a moment it appeared that the bewildering strategy of non-cooperation would sweep all before it.

Gandhi often acknowledges his indebtedness to the teachings of Tolstoy, whose books he had eagerly read, although the doctrine of non-resistance and the gospel of returning good for evil had also been reinforced by his reading of the Hindu scriptures and his study of the sermon on the mount. He has never believed in acquiescence to injustice. On the contrary, he has advocated the utmost opposition to wrongdoing, even to the extent, if necessary, of laying down one's life in the effort. But only by the use of non-violent means. Hatred must be resisted by love, violence by meekness, cruelty by suffering, inhumanity by forgiveness. Not hopeless resignation nor violent antagonism, but an unceasing effort to overcome evil by doing good. Gandhi's attitude toward the established government in India was not unlike Tolstoy's attitude toward the tsar's government, which was represented to the peasant only by the tax-gatherer and the conscription officer. Tolstoy uses this primitive form of government as the embodiment of sheer force. He says that because we have the policeman, the army and the courts, all of which embody governmental force, we rely upon them to such an extent that we do not exert our own moral energy.

Although throughout the campaign in India Gandhi had pleaded for good will toward Englishmen while urging ceaseless opposition to the British policy, and although his followers were exhorted to accept any humiliation and to endure any suffering rather than to retaliate with violence, popular riots occurred in several places, one of them accompanied by hideous barbarities. These riots were undoubtedly due to the panic of undisciplined troops on their first battlefield. Apparently the leaders of non-violence must control the emotion of anger and the instinct of pugnacity in the same way and to the same extent that military discipline controls the emotion of fear and the instinct of flight.

Gandhi's followers were not sufficiently drilled in the new technique and had simply dropped back into the old patterns of conduct. In deep agony of spirit, he decided on the drastic policy of calling off the campaign of mass non-cooperation, and declared that he could not think of starting mass "civil disobedience" until he was sure of peace being retained in spite of government provocation. It was only a month later that Gandhi was arrested and sentenced to prison after one of the most notable trials recorded in legal history.

The message of Gandhi is similar to Tolstoy's in its indictment of western civilization and equally insistent in its call to labor and simple living. Gandhi faces an agricultural situation which it is hard for the people of the west to envisage, for we can scarcely imagine the depths of misery in which hundreds of millions of Indians live, nine-tenths of them in agricultural villages where they cultivate incredibly small plots of ground with resulting unemployment for half of the year. To ask these hard-driven peasants to plant a few rows of cotton and to spin and weave their own clothing, is the most sensible advice in the world. Spinning is a simple process and if by this means a person saves or earns only five cents per day for 180 days, the amount thus received is equivalent to half a year's income for the average peasant in India. He could eat more of his produce if he were not obliged to take out enough to buy even his simple clothing; this margin might easily save him from starvation and prove the truth of Gandhi's statement that "the whole nation is starving for want of a large productive occupation ancillary to agriculture."

This is at the base of the home industry movement, and quite naturally the spinning-wheel has become the emblem of the nationalists. Gandhi himself uses it daily and when I visited his ashram near Ahmedabad, his followers showed me the long-fibered cotton which they are raising in the hope that they may eventually improve the quality of cotton for the peasants.

In addition to that aspect, Gandhi contends that India should avoid the difficulties which have occurred in Japan and England and to a certain extent in the United States, by allowing agriculture to become dependent upon industry. Indications of this dependency can already be seen in India; in the neighborhood of Bombay, the villages from which the young people have gone to the textile mills and to which they have brought back their wages, show improvement in housing and tillage, as is true of certain Japanese villages near the large new silk mills. In both countries such villages are in sharp contrast to those in which the inhabitants have depended solely upon agriculture. The farmers, to a large extent, in England and also in certain parts of the United States have become dependent in the same way upon what "the boys who have left the farm" are able to send back. But these western countries are predominantly industrial and in a very different situation from India with her overwhelmingly agricultural population.

Through identification with the lives of the peasants who obtain so inadequate a living from their tiny strips of earth, both Tolstoy and Gandhi, with convictions attained in middle age, committed themselves to a daily portion of manual labor. Gandhi has embraced poverty as Tolstoy had done; neither of them, however, as St. Francis did, in response to the counsel of perfection, but through the desire to use no force, governmental or other, for the protection of their persons or property.

Gandhi, like Tolstoy, constantly resents the heavy taxation to which the humblest are subjected, and he continually demands that the whole revenue system be so revised as to make the good of the peasant its primary concern. It was therefore in a spirit of challenge to the entire revenue system that Gandhi, in August, 1930, inaugurated the civil disobedience campaign by marching to the sea with a group of his followers and conspicuously making salt from its waters, in defiance of the salt tax which he considers "the tax most iniquitous of all, from the standpoint of the poor man."

Both these men have expounded the religious foundation of nonresistance and have insisted that it is as old as the teaching of the sermon on the mount. This modern manifestation has as yet no term which exactly defines it. Tolstoy's non-resistance is a very inadequate name for overcoming evil with good, and Gandhi's soul-force is slow to come into English usage. It is sometimes said that Gandhi may be a great religious teacher but that he has no political acumen nor statesmanship. Such critics ignore the fact that religion is the great preoccupation of India; that no man could be a leader there nor even evoke widespread public interest unless he made the religious appeal and validated it with his daily living; that the saint is still the popular political hero in the east. It is as if Gandhi's vigorous activity had evoked a response in the policy of the British government itself, which is also changing as the result of a situation he has in part created. The response is not to a fixed environment but to newly discovered relationships.

The political world is just now beginning to count up the deadening effects and waste of opposing force to force, exhausting both in the process and often producing a mutual canceling out. Because almost every modern state is founded upon a rebellion against the domination of a master group and owes its existence to success in arms, there grew up, in the western races at least, the classic pattern of domination and conflict, succeeding one another in almost rhythmic order. In addition to this, it was evident that physical clash between men strikes sparks of high tension of will, of emotion, of heroism, as the clash of minds in debate and argument sharpens wits and heightens intellectual voltage. Conflict was at last prized for itself and gradually became conventionalized into opposing armies on the field of battle, into opposing parties in parliaments, and into lawyers for the prosecution and defense in the courts.

Yet, all over the world at the present moment there is an amazing tendency to experiment with this new technique and to see what it can do. The masterful foreman in a factory has been replaced by the personnel director; the domineering pedagogue has fled the field in favor of a new type of educator who evokes the ability of his students, as in medicine the doctor thinks it important as never before to win the cooperation of his patient; the judge of the juvenile court neither acquits nor condemns, but uses every available means, including the moral energy of the offender himself, to rectify a given situation. Everywhere men are eager to find a technique fitted to cope with the extraordinary complications of the modern world.

Notes

1. Mohandes K. Gandhi (1869–1948), called the "Mahatma," or Great Soul, is one of the singular figures of the twentieth century. His method of militant nonviolence (*satygraha*) exerted a profound influence on Martin Luther King Jr. and the social activism of the Southern Christian Leadership Conference in combating segregation. Gandhi was assassinated in 1948, following the simultaneous celebration of independence for India but the tragedy, to his mind, of partition between predominantly Hindu India and predominantly Muslim Pakistan.

41

"OUR NATIONAL SELF-RIGHTEOUSNESS"

OUR NATIONAL SELF-RIGHTEOUSNESS, often honestly disguised as patriotism, in one aspect is part of that adolescent self-assertion which the United States has never quite outgrown, and which is sometimes crudely expressed, both by individuals and nations, in sheer boasting. In another aspect it is that complacency which we associate with the elderly who, feeling justified by their own successes, have completely lost the faculty of self-criticism. Innocent as such a combination may be, it is unfortunate that it should have been intensified at this particular moment when humility of spirit and a willingness to reconsider existing institutions are so necessary to world salvation.

To illustrate—Senator Borah suggested that the cancellation of war debts owed by the allied European nations to the United States be considered with the provision that the nations which take advantage of the offer shall consent to reduce their armaments. And yet the United States makes no proposition to disarm itself! This is doubtless due to the fact that we are fully convinced of our own righteousness, of our own beneficent intentions; but this very attitude toward ourselves may make the offer unacceptable to other nations.

It is not difficult to trace the historic beginning of such a national self-righteousness. The persecuted religious sects which first settled so much of the Atlantic Coast were naturally convinced that they bore witness to the highest truth and were therefore the chosen people.

Note: Our National Self-Righteousness," *University of Chicago Magazine,* vol. 26 (November 1933).

William Penn, who bought from the Indians every acre of land in his own royal grant, said that he visited the various communities "who were of a separating and seeking turn of mind," and in spite of his insistence upon religious freedom, he was ever surrounded by a good many "come-outers."[1] These very separatists, from Plymouth to Philadelphia, who ultimately federated into the Thirteen Colonies, probably achieved it as much through a similarity of temperament as through a common devotion to political doctrines. They undoubtedly bequeathed both to their successors, and certainly the former made a very good foundation for this national trait.

Another historic manifestation of the spirit of superiority so easily turned into self-righteousness, is discovered as early as 1830 in a national attitude toward the European immigrants who came over in ever increasing numbers until by 1913 the annual arrivals were over a million. A consciousness of superiority constantly tended to exalt the earlier Americans and to put the immigrants into a class by themselves, until it became an obvious deterrent and was responsible for several social maladjustments.

First, for our tardiness in passing protective legislation. Since every approach to labor problems in the United States had to do with immigrants, because they form the bulk of the wage-earning population, it eventually came to be considered patriotic to oppose governmental measures for workmen's compensation, for unemployment insurance, and for old-age security. Over-crowded tenements, sweating systems, a high infant death-rate, and many another familiar aspect of unregulated industry also became associated in the public mind with the immigrant. Unlike the impassioned study of poverty made in England during the '80's, resulting in the belief that a representative government was performing its legitimate function when it considered such matters, we in the United States in the very same decade, found an alibi for all of our disturbing industrial problems and put them off on the immigrant.

William Penn affords an antithesis of all this and presents a direct method of avoiding the difficulties of self-righteousness in his relations with the aliens who confronted him—the North American Indians, for more than a century regarded by the New England colonies as untamed savages. His 1682 treaty with them, impressively consummated [sic] by two self-respecting political entities, was made as between equals and was mutually binding. Moreover, he assured the non-English settlers in his colony—the Dutch, the Swedes, and the Germans, that "you shall be governed by laws of your own making, and live a free and if you will, sober and industrious people," and each group at once received the franchise. The laborers, who represented many European nationalities, were to be provided for at the expiration of their terms of service. The despised negro was to be free after fourteen years, and furnished land, tools, and stock. William Penn manumitted his own slaves in 1701. Such was his confidence in his fellowman that he gave to his conglomerate colony the first constitution in the world which provided for its own amendment. . . .

Our national self-righteousness might be indicted for another policy towards labor—the widespread belief that differing opinions may be controlled by force. European immigrants have been held responsible for strikes and other industrial disorders, since it was assumed that they held all sorts of beliefs contrary to basic American doctrines. Therefore to scatter strikers by the police and even by the militia and the regulars came to be considered a patriotic duty. Yet William Penn reached the conclusion when he was imprisoned in the Tower as a young man that real protection lay in mutual understanding and confidence; "that love and persuasion have more force than weapons of war." He stood for this conviction when in the vast wilderness stretching around him groups of white settlers were being attacked and sometimes massacred by the Indians.

A third result of our national attitude toward the immigrant is that we have become indifferent to the protection of human life. Unfortunately the earliest outbreaks of gang violence in Chicago—more or less typical of those throughout the country—were associated with colonies of immigrants. Although we all knew that the bootleggers and other racketeers could not have continued without political protection, the community was slow to act, because so long as the Sicilians, who composed the first powerful boot-legging gang, killed only one another, it was considered of little consequence. From January 1928 to January 1932 we had in Chicago 232 gang killings, in which the law-enforcing agencies failed to bring even one to trial. Such preferential treatment of crime—an obvious symptom of a breakdown in Democratic government—may be an indirect result of an unjustifiable habit of considering one human being of less consequence than another. Never was William Penn's ideal of religion, founded upon fraternity and righteousness, so sorely needed.

This leads quite naturally to the fourth indictment arising out of our attitude toward the immigrant—our dilemma in regard to prohibition. Because the Simon-pure American did make an exception of himself, he often voted for laws which he would like to see enforced upon others without any intention of keeping them himself. Many Southern men voted for the Eighteenth Amendment because they wanted to keep drink away from the negro; other Northern men, because they needed sober immigrant labor. William Penn set an example even here. He did not sell liquor to the Indians because of the terms of an agreement which they had *voluntarily* entered into with him. In one more instance he had achieved his purpose by the moral coöperation of those he was trying to serve, and of course there is no other way. . . .

Another aspect of our national self-righteousness, much more sinister in its influence, is the demand for conformity on pain of being denounced as a "red" or a "traitor." Perhaps never before in our history has there been within the framework of orderly government such impatience with differing opinion. Such a stultifying situation is more than ever dangerous just now when the nation needs all the free and vigorous thinking which is available. To illustrate the danger of holding fast to a social concept which is no longer useful, but which has not yet been superseded by the new, because the new one is considered dangerous, Dr. Nicholas Murray Butler said within recent weeks to the students of Columbia University, "We are living in the backwash of ultra nationalism following the Great War, ignoring the fundamental and controlling fact that the world today is an international world."[2] He also quoted the concluding words of a report signed by leading members of the Finance Committee of the League of Nations: "It may be truly said that international trade is gradually being strangled to death. If the process continues, millions of people in this economically interlocked world must inevitably die of starvation." Would it not be humiliating for a world to starve in the midst of a plethora of food because the constructive and collective intelligence of mankind was unable to make a distinction between political nationalism and economic internationalism, and serenely sacrificed the latter to the first?. . .

The corrective supplied by William Penn on this point is very clear. Nothing could have been more difficult in his day and generation than his long advocacy of religious freedom—that each man must worship God in his own way. Religion, it is only fair to remember, was the absorbing interest of the 17th century. Dynasties rose and fell upon theological issues, and great families disappeared when they found themselves on the side of the oppressed instead of the oppressor. William Penn took his stand for the freedom of worship of all sects, for the Roman Catholics, no less than for the Quakers. With invincible courage he put the truth as God gave him to see the truth to the test of action, in the new world among alien Indians, as well as in the old.

One could make a long list of William Penn's advances beyond his contemporaries. In education, he was expelled from Oxford, because the Universities saw that the inspirational preacher might interfere with the stiff scholasticism which produced their dull and learned clergy. Regarding the education of children he expressed ideas which might easily be ascribed to John Dewey or Bertrand Russell. In international affairs we have hardly caught up to him yet. A hundred years before the thirteen colonies were federated, for example, he had worked out a plan for a "Dyet or Parliament of Europe to settle trouble between nations without war." William Penn appealed from tradition to experience; from intrenched [sic] authority to life, and in his absorbed devotion to his colony, calmly followed his own rule, "Though there is a regard due to education and the tradition of our fathers, Truth will ever deserve, as well as claim, the preference." In this spirit he suppressed the hunting of witches, declared the spiritual equality of men and women, reduced from two hundred to two the number of offenses punishable by death, declared that all prisons should be workshops, and literally taxed slavery out of existence. Such right thinking and courageous acting is doubtless what we need at this moment more than anything else. Sir Arthur Salter, in a recent number of *Foreign Affairs* believes that the choice before the world today is between trying to build up world trade, based on world order, or moving further toward a system of closed units, each aiming to be self-sufficient. The choice of the United States in this world decision has come to have an undue influence, and yet we all know that there exists an overwhelming danger that America may leave unaided and thus unwantonly cripple the supreme political effort of these later centuries— the effort to make international relations more rational and human. Several years ago at Williamstown, Arnold Toynbee boldly warned us against what he described as a rather low type of religion—the worship of some sixty or seventy gods called Sovereign National States, declaring that such idolatry of nationalism was not patriotism but suicide. . . .

I find it a great temptation to conclude with an exhortation to those who represent a seat of learning; certainly the scholar, who is always impatient of intellectual apathy and incapacity, may find a formula which shall preserve "that spirit of nationality in which for many years the aspirations of man for liberty and free development have found their expression, and yet prevent the abuse of that nationality which now threatens with destruction all that it has given or promised." Is it not true that the contemporary world, based upon the search for private profit and for national advantage, has come in conflict with the newer principle of social welfare and the zeal for practical justice in our human affairs? Must we wait for another William Penn to show us the unique opportunity it affords once more to make politics further the purposes of religion and to purge religion itself from all taint of personal and national self-righteousness?

Notes

1. William Penn (1644–1718), leader of the Quaker-dominated colony of Pennsylvania.

2. Dr. Butler, president of Columbia University, shared the Nobel Prize for Peace with Jane Addams in 1931.

BIBLIOGRAPHY OF THE PRINTED
WORKS OF JANE ADDAMS

Note: This bibliography of the printed works of Jane Addams is included as copied from John C. Farrell's *Beloved Lady: A History of Jane Addams' Ideas on Reform and Peace* (Baltimore: Johns Hopkins University Press, 1967). It is reproduced with their permission.

1. "Plated Ware," *Rockford Seminary Magazine,* VI (April, 1878), 60–2.
2. "The Element of Hopefulness in Human Nature," *ibid.,* VII (May, 1879), 120–2.
3. "Summary of 'Marks,'" a Play, *ibid.,* p. 130.
4. "One Office of Nature," *ibid.,* VII (June, 1879) , 154–6.
5. "Home Items," *ibid.,* VII (July, 1879), 199–202.
6. Speech to the Vesperian Society, October 3, 1879, ibid., VII (November, 1879), 242.
7. "The Girl Who Had Too Much To Do," *ibid.,* pp. 235–7. The article was co-authored by Sarah F. Anderson.
8. "The Macbeth of Shakespeare," *ibid.,* VIII (January, 1880), 13–6.
9. "Bread Givers," Rockford *Daily Register,* April 21, 1880.
10. "Self Tradition," Rockford Seminary Magazine, IX (April, 1881), 97–101.
11. "Valedictory," ibid., IX (July, 1881), 219–22.
12. "Three Days on the Mediterranean Subjectively Related," *ibid.,* XIV (January, 1886), 11–7.
13. "Rockford Seminary Endowment," in *Memorials of Anna Peck Sill, First Principal of Rockford Female Seminary,* 1849–1889 (Rockford, Ill., 1889), pp. 70–5.
14. "How Would You Uplift the Masses?" *Sunset Club [of Chicago] Yearbook* (1891/1892), pp. 118–21.
15. "With the Masses," *Advance* (Chicago), XXV (February 18, 1892), 133. This is a revision of number 14.
16. "Hull House, Chicago: an Effort toward Social Democracy," *Forum,* XIV (October, 1892), 226–41.
17. "A New Impulse to an Old Gospel," *ibid.,* XIV (November, 1892),345–58.

18. "The Subjective Necessity for Social Settlements," in Henry C. Adams (ed.), *Philanthropy and Social Progress, Seven Essays by Miss Jane Addams, Robert A. Woods, Father J. O. S. Huntington, Professor Franklin H. Giddings and Bernard Bosanquet Delivered before the School of Applied Ethics at Plymouth, Mass., during the Session of 1892* (New York, 1893), pp. 1–26. This is the same as number 17.

19. "Objective Value of a Social Settlement," in *ibid.*, pp. 27–56. This is the same as number 16.

20. "What Shall We Do for Our Unemployed?" *Sunset Club [of Chicago] Yearbook* (1893/1894), pp. 81–2.

21. "Domestic Service and the Family Claim," in May Wright Sewall (ed.), *A Historical Resume for Popular Circulation of the World Congress of Representative Women, Convened in Chicago on May 15, and Adjourned on May 22, 1893, under the Auspices of the Woman's Branch of the World's Congress Auxiliary* (Chicago & New York, 1894), II, 626–31.

22. Address at Western Reserve College for Women, *College Folio,* II (June, 1894), 129–31.

23. "Art-Work Done by Hull-House," *Forum,* XIX (July, 1895), 614–7.

24. "Prefatory Note," *Hull-House Maps and Papers, by Residents of Hull-House, A Social Settlement, a Presentation of Nationalities and Wages in a Congested District of Chicago, Together with Comments and Essays on Problems Growing out of the Social Conditions* (New York, 1895), pp. vii-viii.

25. "The Settlement as a Factor in the Labor Movement," ibid., pp. 183–204.

26. "The Settlement" in Illinois State Conference of Charities and Correction, Proceedings, I (1896), 54–8.

27. "A Belated Industry," *American Journal of Sociology,* I (March, 1896), 536–50. This is a revision with additions of number 21.

28. "The Objects of Social Settlements," *Union Signal,* XXII (March 5, 1896), 148–9.

29. "The Problem of Domestic Servants Viewed Scientifically," *Review of Reviews,* XII (May, 1896), pp. 604–5. This is excerpted from number 27.

30. "Foreign-Born Children in the Primary Grades," in National Education Association, *Journal of Proceedings and Addresses* (1897), pp. 104–12.

31. "Social Settlements," in National Conference of Charities and Correction, *Proceedings* (1897), pp. 338–46.

32. Discussion of after-care of convalescent and recovered insane patients, in *ibid.,* pp. 464–6.

33. Discussion of social settlements, in *ibid.,* pp, 472–6.

34. "Growth of Corporate Consciousness" in Illinois State Conference of Charities and Correction, *Proceedings,* II (1897), 40–2.

35. *Study of the Milk Supply of Chicago.* ("Illinois Agricultural Experiment Station Circular," No.13.) Urbana, 1898. Pp. 1–8. The circular was co-authored by H. S. Grindley.

36. "Ethical Survivals in Municipal Corruption," *International Journal of Ethics*, VIII (April, 1898), 273–91.

37. "Why the Ward Boss Rules," *Outlook*, LVIII (April 2, 1898), 879–82. This is excerpted from number 36.

38. "A Study in Municipal Politics," *Review of Reviews*, XVII (May, 1898), 605–6. This is excerpted from number 36.

39. "The College Woman and the Family Claim," *The Commons*, III (September, 1898), 3–7.

40. "The Significance of Organized Labor," *Machinist's Monthly Journal*, X (September, 1898), 551–2.

41. "Woman's Work for Chicago," *Municipal Affairs*, II (September, 1898), 502–8.

42. "Christmas Fellowship," *Unity*, XLII (December 22, 1898), 308–9.

43. "Democracy or Militarism," in Central Anti-Imperialist League of Chicago, *Liberty Tract*, I (1899), 35–9.

44. "Trade Unions and Public Duty," *American Journal of Sociology*, IV (January, 1899), 448–62.

45. "The Subtle Problems of Charity," *Atlantic Monthly*, LXXXIII (February, 1899), 163–78.

46. "The Charity Visitor's Perplexities," *Outlook*, LXI (March 11, 1899), 598–600. This is excerpted from number 45.

47. "A Function of the Social Settlement," *Annals*, XIII (May, 1899), 323–45.

48. "What Peace Means," *Unity*, XLIII (May 4, 1899), 178. This is a reprinting of number 43.

49. "Social Settlement and University Extension," *Review of Reviews*, XX (July, 1899), 93. This is excerpted from number 47.

50. "Trade Unions and Public Duty," *Railroad Trainman's Journal*, XVI (December, 1899), 1070–86. This is a reprinting of number 44.

51. "Social Education of the Industrial Democracy," *The Commons*, V (June 30, 1900), 17–20.

52. "The Hull-House Labor Museum," *Current Literature*, XXIX (October, 1900). This is excerpted from number 51.

53. "What Is the Greatest Menace to Twentieth Century Progress?" Sunset Club [of Chicago] Yearbook (1899/1901), pp. 338–41.

54. *The Greatest Menace to Progress.* Chicago, 1901. This is a separate publication of number 53.

55. "Respect for Law," *Independent*, LIII (January 3, 1901), 18–20.

56. "One Menace to the Century's Progress," *Unity*, XLVII (April 4, 1901), 71–2. This is a reprinting of number 53.

57. "College Women and Christianity," *Independent*, LIII (August 8, 1901), 1852–5.

58. *First Report of the Labor Museum at Hull-House, Chicago*, 1901/1902. Chicago, 1902. This pamphlet is unsigned, but it was reprinted under Miss Addams's signature. See number 61.

59. Speech, in University Settlement Association of New York, *Annual Report,* XVI (1902), 51–6.

60. *Democracy and Social Ethics.* New York, 1902. Chapter II is a revision, with additions, of number 45. Chapter III includes excerpts from number 39. Chapter IV is a revision, with additions, of number 27. Chapter V contains some sections originally published in number 44. Chapter VI is a revision of number 30. Chapter VII is a revision, with additions, of number 36.

61. "First Report of the Labor Museum at Hull House, Chicago, 1901–1902," *Unity,* XLIX (March 13, 1902), 20–23.

62. "What the Theatre at Hull-House Has Done for the Neighborhood People," *Charities,* VIII (March 29, 1902), 284–6.

63. "The Housing Problem in Chicago," and discussion, *Annals,* XX (July, 1902), 99–107.

64. "Newer Ideals of Peace," *Chautauqua Assembly Herald,* XXVII (July 8, 1902), 5.

65. "Arts and Crafts and the Settlement," *ibid.,* XXVII (July 9, 1902), 2.

66. "The Newer Ideals of Peace," *ibid.,* XXVII (July 10, 1902), 6.

67. "Count Tolstoy," *ibid.,* XXVII (July 11, 1902), 5.

68. "Tolstoy's Theory of Life," *ibid.,* XXVII (July 14, 1902), 2–3.

69. "Child Labor and Pauperism," in National Conference of Charities and Correction, *Proceedings* (1903), pp. 114–21.

70. Discussion and summary on child labor, in *ibid.,* pp. 546–8.

71. "Address of Miss Jane Addams," in Chicago Union League Club, *Exercises in Commemoration of the Birthday of Washington, 23 February 1903* (Chicago, 1903), pp. 6–9.

72. "The Friendship of Settlement Work," *Charities,* X (March 28, 1903), 315–6. This is excerpted from number 59.

73. "Women's Clubs versus Child Labor," *The Commons,* VIII (July, 1903), 1–2. This letter is co-signed by Florence Kelley and Caroline D. G. Granger. It is included in Mrs. A. O. Granger, "The Work of the General Federation of Women's Clubs against Child Labor," Annals, XXV (May, 1905), 516–7.

74. "The Servant Problem," *Good Housekeeping,* XXXVII (September, 1903), 233–40.

75. "Child Labor and Pauperism," *Charities,* XI (October 3, 1903) , 300–4. This is a reprinting of number 69.

76. "Henry Demarest Lloyd, His Passion for a Better Social Order," *The Commons,* VIII (December, 1903), 1–3.

77. "The Responsibilities and Duties of Women toward the Peace Movement," in Universal Peace Congress, *Official Report,* XIII (1904), 120–2.

78. "The Interests of Labor in International Peace," in *ibid.,* pp. 145–7.

79. Address, in *ibid.,* pp. 261–2.

80. "Neighborhood Improvement," in National Conference of Charities and Correction, *Proceedings* (1904), pp. 456–8, and repeated at pp. 560–2.

81. Remarks as chairman of discussion, in *ibid.,* pp. 608–17.

82. Address, in *Dedication of the Hull-House Organ Given in Memory of Sarah Rozet Smith, Sunday, March 27, 1904* (n.p., n.d. [1904]), unpaged.

83. "Henry Demarest Lloyd, His Passion for a Better Social Order," *The Commons,* IX (January, 1904), 20–2. This is a reprinting of number 76.

84. "Henry Demarest Lloyd, His Passion for a Better Social Order," in Chicago Teachers' Federation, *Bulletin,* III (January 29, 1904), 1–3. This is a reprinting of number 76.

85. "Educational Methods as They Relate to Labor Unions," *ibid.,* III (March 25, 1904), pp. 1–2. This is excerpted from Chapter VI of number 60.

86. "Humanizing Tendency of Industrial Education," *Chautauquan,* XXXIX (May, 1904), 266–72.

87. "Hull-House and Its Neighbors," *Charities,* XII (May 7, 1904), 450–1.

88. "Larger Social Groupings," ibid., XII (June 25, 1904), 675. This is a brief summary of number 80.

89. "The Present Crisis in Trades-Union Morals," *North American Review,* CLXXIX (August, 1904), 178–93.

90. "Woman's Peace Meeting—Jane Addams's Address," *Woman's Journal,* XXXV (October 22, 1904), 337, 340–1.

91. "Child Labor Legislation: a Requisite for Industrial Efficiency," in National Child Labor Committee, New York, *Child Labor, the Proceedings of the First Annual Conference, New York City, February 14–16, 1905* (New York, 1905), pp. 128–36.

92. "Child Labor Legislation: a Requisite for Industrial Efficiency," in National Child Labor Committee, New York, *Pamphlet,* XIII (1905). This is a reprinting of number 91.

93. "Speech at the Hull House Memorial Meeting, Chicago, January 21, 1905," in *Jessie Bross Lloyd, September 27, 1844–December 29, 1904* (n.p. [Chicago), n.d. [1905]), pp. 41–3.

94. "Speech at the Winnetka Memorial Meeting, February 12, 1905," in *ibid.,* pp. 57–62.

95. "Immigrants and American Charities," in Illinois Conference of Charities and Correction, *Proceedings* (1905), 11–8.

96. "Problems of Municipal Administration," *American Journal of Sociology,* X (January, 1905), 425–44.

97. "Recent Immigration, a Field Neglected by the Scholar," *University [of Chicago) Record,* IX (January, 1905), 274–84.

98. "'Recent Immigration, a Field Neglected by the Scholar," *The Commons,* X (January, 1905), 9–19. This is a reprinting of number 97.

99. "Recent Immigration, a Field Neglected by the Scholar," *Unity,* LIV (January 19, 1905), pp. 328–33. This is a reprinting of number 97.

100. "Recent Immigration," *Education Review,* XXIX (March, 1905), 245–63. This is a reprinting of number 97.

101. "Child Labor," *Journal of Education,* LXI (March 16, 1905), 289.

102. "A House Stands on a Busy Street," *Unity,* L V (March 30, 1905), p. 85.

103. "The Subjective Necessity of Social Settlements," *Social Service,* XI (April, 1905), 38–47. This is excerpted from number 17.

104. "A House Stands on a Busy Street," *The Commons,* X (April, 1905), 225. This is a reprinting of number 101.

105. "Child Labor Legislation: a Requisite for Industrial Efficiency," *Annals,* XXV (May, 1905), 542–50. This is a reprinting of number 91.

106. Speech at the civic dedication of the Abraham Lincoln Center, *Unity,* LV (May 27, 1905), 364–5.

107. "Work and Play as Factors in Education," *Chautauquan,* XLII (November, 1905), 251–5.

108. "Day Nurseries—Do They Foster Parental Irresponsibility?" *Charities and The Commons,* XV (December 30, 1905), 411–2.

109. Ed. of, Henry Demarest Lloyd. *Man, the Social Creator,* New York, 1906. Anne Withington edited this book with Miss Addams.

110. "The Modern City and the Municipal Franchise for Women," in National American Woman Suffrage Association, *Woman Suffrage, Arguments and Results* (n.p., n.d. [1906?]), variously paged.

111. "Operation of the Illinois Child Labor Law," in National Child Labor Committee, New York, *Child Labor, a Menace to Industry, Education and Good Citizenship, the Proceedings of the Second Annual Conference, Washington, December 8–10, 1905* (New York, 1906), pp. 69–72.

112. "Operation of the Illinois Child Labor Law," in National Child Labor Committee, New York, *Pamphlet,* XXIX (1906). This is a reprinting of number 111.

113. Letter to the Speaker of the United States House of Representatives, June 11, 1906, U. S. *Congressional Record.* 59th Cong., 1st Sess., 1906, XL, Part 9, p. 8515.

114. "Social Settlements in Illinois," Transactions of the Seventh Annual Meeting of the Illinois State Historical Society, in Illinois State Historical Library, *Publication,* XI (1906), 162–71.

115. "Child Labor and Other Dangers of Childhood," in American Humane Association, *Report of the Proceedings of the Annual Convention* (1906) , pp. 28–30.

116. "On Behalf of the Community," *Unity,* LVI (January 18, 1906), 366–7.

117. "Jane Addams on Judge Tuley," *Woman's Journal,* XXXVII (January 27, 1906), 14. This is excerpted from number 116.

118. "Jane Addams' Own Story of Her Work: Fifteen Years at Hull House," *Ladies' Home Journal,* XXIII (March, 1906), 13–4.

119. "Operation of the Illinois Child Labor Law," *Annals,* XXVII (March, 1906), 327–30. This is a reprinting of number 111.

120. "Some Childhood Experiences of Jane Addams," *Unity,* LVII (March I, 1906), II. This is excerpted from number 118.

121. "Judge Tuley," *Charities and The Commons,* XV (March 3, 1906), 752–3. This is a reprinting of number 116.

122. "Probation Work under Civil Service," *ibid.*, XV (March 17, 1906), 881.

123. "Jane Addams' Own Story of Her Work: the First Five Years at Hull House," *Ladies' Home Journal*, XXIII (April, 1906), 11–2.

124. "The Modern City and the Municipal Franchise for Women," *Woman's Journal*, XXXVII (April 7, 1906), 53–5. This is a reprinting of number 110.

125. "Woman's Relations to Civic Housekeeping," *Public*, IX (April 28, 1906), 86–7. This is excerpted from number 110.

126. "Jane Addams' Own Story of Her Work: How the Work at Hull House Has Grown," *Ladies' Home Journal*, XXIII (May, 1906), 11–2.

127. Statement concerning Judge Ben B. Lindsey, *Public*, IX (October 20, 1906), 691–2.

128. *Newer Ideals of Peace.* New York, 1907. Chapters II and III are revisions, with additions, of number 96 and 97. Chapter V includes material originally published in number 89. Chapter VII is a revision, with additions, of number 110. Chapter VIII includes material originally used in numbers 43 and 97.

129. Address, in *A Living Memorial to John A. Davis, Colonel 46th Illinois Volunteer Infantry* (Chicago, 1907), pp. 15–8.

130. "New Ideals of Peace," in National Arbitration and Peace Congress, *Proceedings* [I] (1907), pp. 106–10.

131. "New Internationalism," in *ibid.*, pp. 213–6.

132. "National Protection for Children," in National Child Labor Committee, New York, *Child Labor and the Republic, the Proceedings of the Third Annual Conference, Cincinnati, Ohio, 13–15 December 1906* (New York, 1907), pp. 57–60.

133. "National Protection for Children," in National Child Labor Committee New York, *Pamphlet*, XLVII (1907). This is a reprinting of number 132.

134. "Problems of Municipal Administration," in Howard J. Rogers (ed.), *International Congress of Arts and Science, Universal Exposition, St. Louis, 1904* (Boston & New York, 1905–7), VII, 434–50. This is a revision of number 96.

135. "An Interpretation of the Chicago Industrial Exhibit," in *Handbook of the Chicago Industrial Exhibition, Brooke's Casino, March 11–17, 1907* (Chicago, 1907), pp. 20–3.

136. "Class Conflict in America," in American Sociological Society, *Papers and Proceedings*, II (1907), pp. 152–5.

137. "National Protection for Children," *Annals*, XXIX (January, 1907), 57–60. This is a reprinting of number 132.

138. Address, in National Society for the Promotion of Industrial Education, *Bulletin*, I (January, 1907), 37–44.

139. "Newer Ideals of Peace," *Charities and The Commons*, XVII (January 5, 1907), 599–606. This is a reprinting of Chapter I, number 128.

140. "National Program," *ibid.*, pp. 641–2. This is excerpted from number 132.

141. "How Shall We Approach Industrial Education?" Educational *Bi-Monthly,* I (February, 1907), 183–90. This is a reprinting of number 138.
142. Memorial address for John A. Davis, *Unity,* LIX (May 30, 1907), 201. This is a reprinting of number 129.
143. "Public Recreation and Social Morality," *Charities and The Commons,* XVIII (August 3, 1907), 492–4.
144. "Why Girls Go Wrong," *Ladies' Home Journal,* XXIV (September, 1907), pp. 13–4.
145. "Do We Want Rifle Practice in the Public Schools?" in Peace Association of Friends, *Do We Want Rifle Practice in the Public Schools* (Philadelphia, 1908), pp. 5–6.
146. "Hull House," in William D. P. Bliss (ed.), *New Encyclopedia of Social Reform* (New York, 1908), pp. 587–90.
147. "The Public School and the Immigrant Child," in National Education Association, *Journal of Proceedings and Addresses* (1908), pp. 99–102.
148. "The Home and the Special Child," in *ibid.,* pp. 1127–31.
149. "Woman's Conscience and Social Amelioration," in Charles Stelzle *et al., Social Application of Religion* ("Merrick Lectures, Ohio Wesleyan University, Delaware, Ohio," 1907–1908, Cincinnati, 1908), pp. 41–60.
150. "Child Labor and Education," in National Conference of Charities and Correction, *Proceedings* (1908), pp. 364–9.
151. "The Relation of 'Settlements' and Religion; or, the place of Religion as It May Be Experienced in the Settlement," *Unity,* LX (January 9, 16, 1908), 295–7, 311–3. Jane Addams presided at this discussion which included addresses by Mary Kingsbury Simkhovitch and Mary E. McDowell.
152. Address, *Journal of Education,* LXVII (February 13, 1908), 175–6. This is inaccurately excerpted from number 157.
153. "The Relation of Women to Industry and Social Relations," *Woman's Journal,* XXXIX (March 28, 1908), p. 42.
154. "Working Women and the Ballot," *Woman's Home Companion,* XXXV (April, 1908), 19.
155. Address, *Playground,* II (April, 1908), 25–8.
156. Address at Smith College, *Woman's Journal,* XXXIX (April 4, 1908), 56.
157. Discussion, in National Society for the Promotion of Industrial Education, *Bulletin,* VI, Part 2 (May, 1908), 92–7.
158. "The Chicago Settlements and Social Unrest," *Charities and The Commons,* XX (May 2, 1908), 155–66.
159. "Advantages and Disadvantages of a Broken Inheritance," *Atlanta University Bulletin,* CLXXXIII (June, 1908), 1–2.
160. Speech at the Abraham Lincoln Center, *Unity,* LXI (July 2, 1908), 280.
161. "The 'Piece-Work' System as a Factor in The Tuberculosis of Wage-Workers," in International Congress on Tuberculosis, Proceedings, VI, Section 5 (September, 1908), 139–40. Dr. Alice Hamilton co-authored this article.

162. "Some Reflections on the Failure of the Modern City to Provide Recreation for Young Girls," *Charities and The Commons,* XXI (December 5, 1908), 365–8. This is a reprinting of number 155.

163. *Hull House, 1889–1909.* Chicago, n.d. [1909].

164. *The Spirit of Youth and the City Streets.* New York, 1909. Chapter I used material which was originally published as number 155. Chapter III includes number 144.

165. "Modern Devices for Minimizing Dependencies," in U.S. Senate, *Proceedings of the Conference on the Care of Dependent Children, Washington, 25–26 January 1909,* Senate Document 721, 60th Cong., 2nd Sess., 1909, pp. 99–101.

166. "Report of the Committee on Immigrants," in National Conference of Charities and Correction, *Proceedings* (1909), pp. 213–5.

167. "The Federal Children's Bureau—a Symposium," in National Child Labor Committee, New York, *Child Workers of the Nation, the Proceedings of the 5th Annual Conference, Chicago, Illinois, January 21–23, 1909* (New York, 1909), pp. 28–30.

168. "Street Trading," in *ibid.,* pp. 237–8.

169. "The Federal Children's Bureau—a Symposium," in National Child Labor Committee, New York, *Pamphlet,* CI (1909), 8–10. This is a reprinting of number 167.

170. "Street Trading," in *ibid.,* CXIV (1909), 8–9. This is a reprinting of number 168.

171. "Woman's Special Training for Peacemaking," in American [National Arbitration and] Peace Congress, *Proceedings,* II (1909), 252–4.

172. "The Federal Children's Bureau—a Symposium," *Annals,* XXXIII, Supplement (March, 1909), 28–30. This is a reprinting of number 167.

173. "Street Trading," *ibid.,* pp. 232–3. This is a reprinting of number 168.

174. "The Reaction of Modern Life upon Religious Education," *Religious Education,* IV (April, 1909), 23–9.

175. "Reaction of Moral Instruction upon Social Reform," *Survey,* XXII (April 3, 1909), 17–9. This is a shorter version, partially rewritten, of number 174.

176. "Immigrants," *ibid.,* XXII (June 26, 1909), 453–4. This is a reprinting of number 166.

177. "Bad Boy of the Streets," *Ladies' Home Journal,* XXVI (October, 1909), 17. This is excerpted from Chapter III of number 164.

178. "When Youth Seeks a Mate," *ibid.,* XXVI (November, 1909), 22. This is excerpted from Chapter II of number 164.

179. "Foreword," in Immigrants' Protective League, Chicago, *Annual Report* (1909/1910), p. 4.

180. *Twenty Years at Hull-House with Autobiographical Notes.* New York, 1910.

181. "Charity and Social Justice," in National Conference of Charities and Correction, *Proceedings* (1910), pp. 1–18.

182. "Woman Suffrage and the Protection of the Home," *Ladies' Home Journal,* XXVII (January, 1910), 21.

183. "Gospel of Recreation," *Northwestern Christian Advocate,* LVIII (January 5, 1910), 9–10. This is excerpted from Chapter I of number 164.

184. "Autobiographical Notes upon Twenty Years at Hull-House. A Wartime Childhood," *American Magazine,* LXIX (April, 1910), 723–34. This is a reprinting of Chapters I and II of number 180.

185. "Autobiographical Notes upon Twenty Years at Hull-House. Early Undertakings at Hull-House," *ibid.,* LXX (June, 1910), 192–202. This is a reprinting of Chapter VII of number 180.

186. "Charity and Social Justice," *Survey,* XXIV (June 11, 1910), 441–9. This is a reprinting of number 181.

187. "Charity and Social Justice," *North American Review,* CXCII (July, 1910), 68–81. This is a reprinting of number 181.

188. "Autobiographical Notes upon Twenty Years at Hull House. Problems of Poverty," *American Magazine,* LXX (July, 1910), 338–48. This is a reprinting of Chapter VIII of number 180.

189. "Autobiographical Notes upon Twenty Years at Hull-House. Resources of Immigrants," *ibid.,* LXX (August, 1910), 494–505. This is excerpted from Chapters XI and XV of number 180.

190. "Autobiographical Notes upon Twenty Years at Hull-House. Echoes of the Russian Revolution," *ibid.,* LXX (September, 1910), 638–46. This is a reprinting of Chapter XVII of number 180.

191. "Stage Children," *Survey,* XXV (December 3, 1910), pp. 342–3.

192. "Child Labor on the Stage," in National Child Labor Committee, New York, *Uniform Child Labor Laws, the Proceedings of the 7th Annual Conference of the National Child Labor Committee, Birmingham, Alabama, 9–12 March 1911* (New York, 1911), pp. 60–5.

193. "Ten Years' Experience in Child Labor Legislation in Illinois," in *ibid.,* pp. 144–8.

194. "What Does Child Labor Reform Cost the Community?" in National Child Labor Committee, New York, *Pamphlet,* CLV (1911). This is a reprinting of number 193.

195. "Symposium—Child Labor on the Stage," in i*bid.,* CLXV (1911) .This is a reprinting of number 192.

196. "Recreation as a Public Function in Urban Communities," in American Sociological Society, *Publications,* VI (1911), 35–9.

197. "Opening of the Exhibit," in Chicago Child Welfare Exhibit, 1911, *The Child in the City, a Handbook of the Child Welfare Exhibit,* 11–25 *May* 1911, *Chicago Coliseum* (Chicago, 1911), pp. 4–5.

198. "The Child Welfare Exhibit—a Foreword in Explanation," in *ibid.,* p. 5.

199. "The Hull House Labor Museum," in *ibid.,* pp. 410–4.

200. Address, in University Settlement Society of New York, *Annual Report,* XXV (1911), 21–4.

201. "Standards of Education for Industrial Life," in National Conference of Charities and Correction, *Proceedings* (1911) , pp. 162–4.

202. "The Call of the Social Field," in *ibid.,* pp. 370–2.

203. "Social Control," *Crisis, a Record of the Darker Races,* I (January, 1911), 22–3.

204. "A Visit to Tolstoy," *McClure's Magazine,* XXXVI (January, 1911), 295–302. This is a reprinting of Chapter XII of number 180.

205. "The Ballot for Health and Beauty," *Woman's Journal,* XLII (February 11, 1911), 48.

206. "The Social Situation: Religious Education and Contemporary Social Conditions," Religious Education, VI (June, 1911), 145–52.

207. Speech, *Woman's Journal,* XLII (June 17, 1911), 185–6.

208. "Child Labor on the Stage," *Annals,* XXXVIII, Supplement (July, 1911), 60–5. This is a reprinting of number 192.

209. "Ten Years Experience in Child Labor Legislation in Illinois," *ibid.,* pp. 144–8. This is a reprinting of number 193.

210. "Why Women Should Vote," *Woman's Journal,* XLII (October 28, 1911), 337.

211. "A New Conscience and an Ancient Evil, Chapter I," *McClure's Magazine,* XXXVIII (November, 1911), 2–13.

212. "A New Conscience and an Ancient Evil, Chapter II: Economic Pressure and Its Inevitable Results," *ibid.,* XXXVIII (December, 1911), pp. 232–40.

213. "The Church and the Social Evil," in *Men and Religion Forward Movement: Messages of the Men and Religion Movement* (New York, 1912), II, 130–41.

214. "Child at the Point of Greatest Pressure," in National Conference of Charities and Correction, *Proceedings* (1912), pp. 26–30.

215. "Remarks," in U.S. House of Representatives, Committee on the Judiciary, *Hearings on Woman Suffrage, 13 March 1912,* Serial 2, 62nd Cong., 2nd Sess., 1912, pp. 7–8.

216. Speech seconding Theodore Roosevelt's nomination for President at the Progressive convention, in U.S. *Congressional Record,* XL VIII, Part 12, Appendix, 62nd Cong., 2nd Sess., 1912, pp. 564–5.

217. *A New Conscience and an Ancient Evil.* New York, 1912. Chapter I is a reprinting of number 211. Chapter III is a reprinting of number 212.

218. "A New Conscience and an Ancient Evil, Chapter III: Lack of Moral Education and Its Dangers," *McClure's Magazine.* XXXVIII (January, 1912), 338–44. This is a reprinting of Chapter IV of number 217.

219. "Mrs. J. T. Bowen," *American Magazine,* LXXIII (January, 1912), 292–6.

220. "A New Conscience and an Ancient Evil, Chapter IV: Tragedies of Lonely and Unprotected Girls," *McClure's Magazine,* XXXVIII (February, 1912), 471–8. This is a reprinting of Chapter V of number 217.

221. "Recreation as a Public Function in Urban Communities," *American Journal of Sociology*. This is a reprinting of number 196.
222. "A New Conscience and an Ancient Evil, Chapter V: Social Control," *McClure's Magazine*, XXXVIII (March, 1912), 592–8. This is a reprinting of Chapter VI of number 217.
223. "A New Conscience and an Ancient Evil," *Woman's Journal*, XLIII (March 16, 1912), 82. This is excerpted from Chapter VI of number 217.
224. "Humanitarian Value of Civil Service," *Survey*, XXVIII (April 6, 1912), 14–6.
225. "The Church and the Social Evil," *Vigilance*, XXV (May, 1912), 1–6. This is a reprinting of number 213.
226. "A Challenge to the Contemporary Church," *Survey*, XXVIII (May 4, 1912), 195–8. This is a reprinting of number 213.
227. Speech, in *City Club [of Chicago] Bulletin*, V (May 27, 1912), 212–3.
228. "The Civic Value of Higher Education for Women," *Bryn Mawr Alumnae Quarterly*, VI (June, 1912), 59–67.
229. "Votes for Women and Other Votes," *Survey*, XXVIII (June 1, 1912).
230. "Votes for Women and Other Votes," *Woman's journal*, XLIII (June 15, 1912) , 191. This is excerpted from number 229.
231. "Why I Seconded Roosevelt's Nomination," *ibid.*, XLIII (August 17, 1912), 257.
232. "The Church and the Social Evil; Christian Responsibility for a Terrible Modern Scourge," *Methodist Quarterly Review*, LXI (October, 1912), 665–72. This is a reprinting of number 213.
233. "Pragmatism in Politics," *Survey*, XXIX (October 5, 1912), 11–2.
234. "Woman in Politics," *Progress, a Progressive Monthly Review, Political Social, Economic*, I (November, 1912), 37–40. I have been unable to verify this article.
235. "The Progressive Party and the Negro," *Crisis; a Record of the Darker Races*, V (November, 1912), 30–1.
236. "My Experiences as a Progressive Delegate," *McClure's Magazine*, XL (November, 1912), 12–4.
237. "The Progressive's Dilemma—the New Party," *American Magazine*, LXXV (November, 1912), 12–4.
238. "A Modern Lear," *Survey*, XXIX (November 2, 1912), 131–7.
239. "Indirect Influence," *Woman's Journal*, XLIII (November 23, 1912), 373.
240. "Lessons of the Election," *City Club [of Chicago] Bulletin*, V (November 27, 1912), 361–4.
241. "Communion of the Ballot," *Woman's Journal*, XLIII (December 14, 1912), 397.
242. *Plea for More Play, More Pay and More Education for Our Factory Boys and Girls, from the Writings of Jane Addams*. N.p. [Chicago], n.d. [1913]. An editorial note in *Survey*, XXX (August 30, 1913), p. 671 identifies this pamphlet.

243. Introduction, in Graham Taylor, *Religion in Social Action* (New York, 1913), pp. xi–xxxv.

244. "Why Women Should Vote," in Frances Maule (ed.), *Woman Suffrage, History, Arguments and Results* (New York, 1913), pp. 139–58. This is a reprinting of number 182.

245. Foreword, in Robert A. Woods and Albert J. Kennedy (eds.), *Young Working Girls* (Boston & New York, 1913), pp. xi–xiii.

246. "Struggle for Life above the Poverty Line," National Federation of Settlements, Conference, III (1913), 16–9.

247. Jane Addams' page, *Ladies' Home Journal*, XXX (January, 1913), 25.

248. "Pen and Book as Tests of Character," *Survey*, XXIX (January 4, 1913), 419–20.

249. Jane Addams' page, *Ladies' Home Journal*, XXX (February, 1913), 23.

250. "Has the Emancipation Act Been Nullified by National Indifference?" *Survey*, XXIX (February 1, 1913), 565–6.

251. Jane Addams' page, *Ladies' Home Journal*, XXX (March, 1913), 27.

252. Jane Addams' page, *ibid.*, XXX (April, 1913), 27.

253. Jane Addams' page, *ibid.*, XXX (May, 1913), 27.

254. Jane Addams' page, *ibid.*, XXX (June, 1913), 21.

255. Jane Addams' page, *ibid.*, XXX (July, 1913), 19.

256. Jane Addams' page, *ibid.*, XXX (August, 1913), 19.

257. "Solving the Problem of the Unemployed," *ibid.*, XXX (September, 1913), 23.

258. "The 'Juvenile-Adult' Offender," *ibid.*, XXX (October, 1913), 24.

259. "The Sheltered Woman and the Magdalen," *ibid.*, XXX (November, 1913), 25. This is a revision with additions of number 213.

260. "Should the Chicago Aldermanic Elections Next Spring Be Non-Partisan?" *City Club [of Chicago] Bulletin*, VI (November 7, 1913), 302–4.

261. "Peace on Earth," *Ladies' Home Journal*, XXX (December, 1913), 27.

262. "Why Women Are Concerned with the Larger Citizenship," in Shailer Mathews (ed.), *Woman Citizen's Library* (Chicago, 1913–4), IX, 2123–42.

263. "Women's Clubs and Public Policies," in General Federation of Women's Clubs, *Biennial Convention*, XII (1914), 24–30.

264. "The Immigrant Woman as She Adjusts Herself to American Life," *ibid.*, 370–4.

265. "Humanitarian Aspects of the Merit System," in National Civil Service Reform League, *Proceedings at the Annual Meeting* (1914), pp. 108–13.

266. Testimony, in U.S. House of Representatives, [Sub-] Committee on Woman Suffrage of the Committee on Rules, *Hearing on Resolution Establishing a Committee on Woman Suffrage*, House Document 754, 63rd Cong., 2nd Sess., 1914, pp. 13–8.

267. "Democracy and Social Ethics," in Andrew C. McLaughlin and Albert Bushnell Hart (eds.), *Cyclopedia of American Government* (New York, 1914), I, 563–4.

268. Preface, in Louise DeK. Bowen, *Safeguards for City Youth at Work and at Play* (New York, 1914), pp. vii–xiii.

269. "Social Justice through National Action," in *Speeches Delivered at the Second Annual Lincoln Day Dinner of the Progressive Party, Hotel Astor, New York City, 12 February 1914* (New York, 1914), pp. 6–9.

270. "Unexpected Reactions of a Traveler in Egypt," *Atlantic Monthly*, CXIII (February, 1914), 178–86.

271. Telegram on woman suffrage, *Outlook*, CVI (March 7, 1914), 511.

272. Telegram, *Independent*, LXXVII (March 16, 1914), 366. This is excerpted from number 271.

273. "The Girl Problem—Its Community Aspects," *American Youth*, III (April, 1914), 81–5.

274. "The Need of a Constructive Appeal," *Child Labor Bulletin*, III (May, 1914), 11–3.

275. "A Modern Devil Baby," *American Journal of Sociology*, XX (July, 1914), 117–8.

276. "Passing of the War Virtues," *Craftsman*, XXVII (October, 1914), 79–80. This is excerpted from number 128.

277. "Need a Woman over Fifty Feel Old?" *Ladies' Home Journal*, XXXI (October, 1914), 7.

278. "Is the Peace Movement a Failure?" *ibid.*, XXXI (November, 1914), 5.

279. "Larger Aspects of the Woman's Movement," *Altltals*, LVI (November, 1914), 1–8. This is a reprinting with slight changes of number 229.

280. "A Memory (Caroline M. Severance)," *California Outlook*, XVII (December 12, 1914), 9.

281. Introduction, in Eleanor Smith, *Hull-House Songs* (Chicago, n.d. [1915]), p. 2.

282. "A Modern Lear, a Parenthetical Chapter," in Graham Romeyn Taylor, *Satellite Cities, a Study of Industrial Suburbs* (New York & London, 1915), pp. 68–90. This is a reprinting of number 238.

283. "Presidential Address," in International Congress of Women at The Hague, 28th April–1st May, 1915, *Report* (1915), pp. 18–22.

284. "Women and War," in Lucia Ames Mead (ed.), *The Overthrow of the War System* (Boston, 1915), pp. 1–9. This is a reprinting of number 283.

285. Address, in *Report of the International Congress of Women at The Hague ... President's Address, Resolutions Adopted; Report of Committees Visiting European Capitols* (Chicago, 1915), pp. 6–9. This is a reprinting of number 283.

286. "Filial Relations," in John Milton Berdan *et al.* (eds.), *Modern Essays* (New York, 1915), pp. 369–86. This is a reprinting of Chapter III of number 60.

287. "Why Women Should Vote," in Frances M. Bjorkman and Anne G. Porritt (eds.), *Woman Suffrage, History, Arguments and Results* (New York, 1915), pp. 131–50. This is a reprinting of number 182.

288. *Women at The Hague, the International Congress of Women and Its Results.* New York, 1915. This was co-authored by Emily G. Balch and Alice Hamilton. Miss Addams contributed Chapter III, "The Revolt against War," Chapter IV, "Factors in Continuing the War," and Chapter VII, "Women and Internationalism."

289. "Address," in Woman's Peace Party, *Addresses Given at the Organization Conference of the Woman's Peace Party, Washington, D.C., January 10, 1915* (Chicago, n.d. [1915]), pp. 10–2.

290. "The Unemployment Question," *City Club [of Chicago] Bulletin,* VIII (February 24, 1915), pp. 63–6.

291. "What War Is Destroying," *Advocate of Peace,* LXXVII (March, 1915), 64–5. This is a reprinting of number 289.

292. "Songs for the Hull House Quarter Century," *Survey,* XXXIII (March 6, 1915), 597. This is a reprinting of number 281.

293. Foreword to "War and Social Reconstruction," *ibid.,* p. 603.

294. "Towards the Peace That Shall Last," *ibid.,* Part II, unpaged. This statement is signed also by seventeen others.

295. "Towards the Peace That Shall Last," *Unity,* LXXV (March 25, 1915), 54–7. This is a reprinting with minor changes of number 294.

296. "The President's Address," *Jus Suffragii,* IX (June 1, 1915), 303–4. This is a reprinting of number 283.

297. "The Revolt against War," *Survey,* XXXIV (July 17, 1915), 355–9. This includes excerpts from Chapter III, Chapter IV, and Chapter VII of number 288.

298. "Address of Miss Jane Addams, Delivered at Carnegie Hall, Friday, July 9, 1915," *Christian Work,* XCIX (July 31, 1915), 145–8. This is a reprinting of number 297.

299. "Women, War, and Babies," *Harper's Weekly,* LXI (July 31, 1915), 101.

300. "As I See Women," *Ladies' Home Journal,* XXXII (August, 1915), 11.

301. "The Revolt against War," *Unity,* LXXV (August 5, 1915), 358–63. This is a reprinting of number 297.

302. "Europe Would Welcome Peace," *Christian Herald,* XXXVIII (August 11, 1915), 218–19. This is excerpted from number 297.

303. "Jane Addams and World Peace," *Congregationalist and Christian World,* C (August 12, 1915), 218–9. This is extracted from number 297.

304. "Peace and the Press," *Independent,* LXXXIV (October 11, 1915), 55–6. This is excerpted from Chapter IV of number 288.

305. "Woman Suffrage," *Survey,* XXXV (October 23, 1915), 85.

306. Letter to President Wilson, *Commoner,* XV (November, 1915), 6. The letter was also signed by Lucia Ames Mead, Anna Garlin Spencer, Alice Thatcher Post, and S. P. Breckinridge.

307. "Women, War and Suffrage," *Survey,* XXXV (November 6, 1915), 148–50. This is excerpted from Chapter VII of number 288.

308. "The Food of War," *Independent*, LXXXIV (December 13, 1915), 430–1. This is excerpted from Chapter IV of number 288.

309. "Towards Internationalism," in U.S., Second Pan American Scientific Congress, *Report on Women's Auxiliary Conference held in Washington in Connection with 2nd Pan American Scientific Congress, December 28, 1915–January 7, 1916*, prepared by Mrs. Glen Levin Swiggert (Washington, 1916), pp. 59–60. This also appeared in a Spanish edition.

310. *The Long Road of Women's Memory*. New York, 1916. Chapter VI is a shortened version of number 270.

311. Address, in Woman's Peace Party, *Yearbook* (1916), pp. 21–4.

312. Testimony, in U.S. House of Representatives, Committee on Military Affairs, *To Increase Efficiency of the Military Establishment of the United States (Hearings on National Defense) (13 January 1916)*, 64th Cong., 1st Sess., 1916, pp. 201–13.

313. Testimony, in U.S. House of Representatives, Committee on Foreign Affairs, *United States and the Orient, Hearing on H. R. 16661 (to Provide for a Commission on Relations between the U.S. and the Orient) 12 December 1916*, 64th Cong., 2nd Sess., 1916, pp. 10–2.

314. Testimony, in U.S. House of Representatives, Committee on Foreign Affairs, *Commission for Enduring Peace (Hearings on H. R. 6921 and H. J. Resolution 32) (11 January 1916)*, 64th Cong., 1st Sess., 1916, pp. 3–17.

315. "Towards the Peace That Shall Last," in Randolph Bourne (ed.), *Towards an Enduring Peace, a Symposium of Peace Proposals and Programs, 1914–1916* (New York, n.d. [1916]), pp. 230–9. This is co-signed by Lillian Wald and Paul U. Kellogg. This is a reprinting of number 294.

316. "Conference of Neutrals," *Survey*, XXXV (January 22, 1916), 495.

317. "Reaction of Simple Women to Trade Union Propaganda," *ibid.*, XXXVI (July 1, 1916), 364–6. This is excerpted from Chapter IV of number 310.

318. "War Times Challenging Woman's Traditions," *ibid.*, XXXVI (August 5, 1916), 475–8. This is excerpted from Chapter V of number 310.

319. "The Devil Baby at Hull House," *Atlantic*, CXVIII (October, 1916), 441–51. Material included in this article appeared as Chapters I and II of number 310.

320. "Disturbing Conventions," *Survey*, XXXVII (October 7, 1916), 1–5. This is a reprinting of Chapter III of number 310.

321. "Why Women Should Vote," in Frances M. Bjorkman and Anna G. Porritt (eds.), *Woman Suffrage, History, Arguments and Results* (New York, 1917), pp. 110–29. This is another edition of number 287, and a reprinting of number 182.

322. Testimony, in U.S. House of Representatives, Committee on the Judiciary, *Espionage and Interference with Neutrality, Hearings on H. R. 291, April 9 and 12, 1917*, Serial LIII, Part 2, 65th Cong., 1st Sess., 1917, pp. 50–52.

323. Statement, in U.S. House of Representatives, Committee on Military Affairs, *Volunteer and Conscription System*, 65th Cong., 1st Sess., 1917, pp. 20–2.

324. Statement, in U.S. House of Representatives, Committee on Military Affairs, *Selective-Service Act, Hearings on the Bill Authorizing the President to Increase Temporarily the Military Establishment of the United States*, 65th Cong., 1st Sess., 1917, pp. 238–40. This is a reprinting of number 323.

325. "What Jane Addams Learned from the Devil Baby," *Current Opinion*, LXII (January, 1917), 44–5. This is excerpted from number 319.

326. "Patriotism and Pacifists in Wartime," *City Club [of Chicago] Bulletin*, X (June 18, 1917), 184–90.

327. "Labor as a Factor in the Newer Conception of International Relationships," in Academy of Political Science, *Proceedings*, VII (July, 1917) , 282–8.

328. "Are Pacifists Cowards?" *Unity*, LXXIX (July 19, 1917), 331. This is excerpted from number 326.

329. "Tolstoy and the Russian Soldiers," *New Republic*, XII (September 29, 1917), 240–2.

330. "Devil Baby at Hull House," in *Atlantic Classics, Second Series* (Boston, 1918), pp. 52–77. This is a reprinting of number 319.

331. "World's Food and World's Politics," in National Conference of Social Work, *Proceedings* (1918), pp. 650–6.

332. Discussion of state child care, *ibid.*, pp. 395–6.

333. "World's Food and World's Politics," in National Conference of Social Work, *Pamphlet*, CCXVIII (1918). This is a reprinting of number 331.

334. "Lest We Forget Toynbee Hall and Canon Barnett," in National Federation of Settlements, *Conference Report*, VIII (1918), 4–5.

335. "World's Food Supply and Woman's Obligation," in General Federation of Women's Clubs, *Biennial Convention*, XIV (1918), 251–63.

336. "World's Food Supply and Woman's Obligation," in National Education Association, *Journal of Addresses and Proceedings* (1918), pp. 108–13. This is a reprinting of number 335.

337. "Tolstoy and the Russian Soldiers," *Friends' Intelligencer*, LXXV (19th First Month 1918), 35–6. This is a reprinting of number 329.

338. "Tolstoy and the Russian Soldiers," *Unity*, LXXX (January 31, 1918), pp. 344–6. This is a reprinting of number 329.

339. "World's Food Supply and Woman's Obligation," *General Federation Magazine*, XVII (July, 1918), 11–5. This is a reprinting of number 335.

340. "World's Food Supply and Woman's Obligation," *Journal of Home Economics*, X (September, 1918), 389–400. This is a reprinting of number 335.

341. "The Corn Mother," *World Tomorrow*, I (November, 1918), 277–80. This is excerpted from number 335.

342. Memorial address for Jenkins Lloyd Jones, *Unity*, LXXXII (November 28, 1918), 148–9.

343. "Newer Ideals of Peace," in H. Stanley Redgrove and Jeanne Heloise Rowbottom, *An Indictment of War* (London, 1919), pp. 24–6. This is excerpted from number 128.

344. "Americanization," in American Sociological Society, *Publications,* XIV (1919), 206–14.

345. "A Tribute to Mary H. Wilmarth," in *Funeral Services for Mary Hawes Wilmarth at Hubbard Woods, Illinois, August 30, 1919* (n.p. [Chicago], n.d. [1919]), unpaged.

346. "Theodore Roosevelt—a Social Worker," *Survey,* XLI (January 18, 1919), 523.

347. Message, *Towards Peace and Freedom* (August, 1919), p. 1. This is excerpted from number 180.

348. "A Belated Industry," *Journal of Home Economics,* XI (August, 1919), 355–64. This is excerpted from number 27.

349. "After the Lean Years, Impressions of Food Conditions in Germany when Peace Was Signed," *Survey,* XLII (September 6, 1919), 793–97. The article was co-authored by Dr. Alice Hamilton.

350. "A Tribute (in Memory of Mary H. Wilmarth)," in Chicago Women's Club, *Bulletin,* III (October, 1919), 5–7. This is a revision of number 345.

351. "Report of Jane Addams and Dr. Hamilton to the American Friends' Service Committee on the Situation in Germany," in American Friends' Service Committee, *Bulletin,* XXV (November, 1919). This is a revision of number 349.

352. "Where the Christmas Spirit Will Wane," *Life Boat* (Hinsdale, Ill.), XXII (December, 1919), 353–6. This is excerpted from number 351.

353. Presidential address, International Congress of Women, Zurich, May 12–17, 1919, *Report,* 1920, pp. 1–3.

354. Speech, *ibid.,* pp. 195–8.

355. Closing address, *ibid.,* pp. 235–7.

356. "Immigration: a Field Neglected by the Scholar," in Philip Davis and Bertha Swartz (comps.), *Immigration and Americanization* (Boston, 1920), pp. 3–22. This is a reprinting of number 97.

357. "The Spirit of Social Service," in National Conference of Social Work, *Proceedings* (1920), pp. 41–3.

358. "The Immigrant and Social Unrest," in *ibid.,* pp. 59–62.

359. "Nationalism—a Dogma?" *Survey,* XLIII (February 7, 1920), 524–6. This is a reprinting of number 344.

360. Speech dedicating the Jenkins Lloyd Jones Chair of English Literature, *Unity,* LXXXV (May 13, 1920), 170–1.

361. "A Pioneer Settlement," *ibid.,* LXXXV (June 10, 1920), 233–7.

362. "A Pioneer Philanthropist," Review of *Canon-Barnett,* by S. A. [sic] Barnett, *Yale Review,* n.s. IX (July, 1920), 867–72.

363. Memorial address for Judge Merritt W. Pinckney, *Unity,* LXXXV (July 1, 1920), 281.

364. "German Women Appeal from the Way of Violence," *World Tomorrow,* III (August, 1920), 251.

365. "Feed the World and Save the League," *New Republic,* XXIV (November 24, 1920), 325–7.

366. "Madeline McDowell Breckenridge," *Survey,* XLV (December 25, 1920), 469.

367. Testimony, in U.S. Senate, Committee on Banking and Currency, *Rehabilitation and Provisions for European Countries (Hearings Relative to Need of Assistance in Exporting our Goods and Rendering Financial Aid Generally in Rehabilitating European Countries),* 66th Cong., 3rd Sess., 1921.

368. "Some Phases of the Disarmament Conference," in Illinois Conference on Public Welfare, *Proceedings* (1921), pp. 11–4.

369. "Some Phases of the Disarmament Conference," in Illinois Department of Public Welfare, *Institutional Quarterly,* XII-XIII (September 30, 1921/June 30, 1922), 88–91. This is a reprinting of number 368.

370. The American Commission on Conditions in Ireland, *Interim Report* (n.p. [New York], n.d. [1921]). This is also signed by Frederic C. Howe, James G. Maurer, Oliver P. Newman, George W. Norris, Norman Thomas, and L. Hollingsworth Wood.

371. Presidential address, in International Congress of Women, *Report,* III [1921], 1–3.

372. Testimony, in *Evidence on Conditions in Ireland: Comprising the Complete Testimony, Affidavits and Exhibits Presented before the American Commission on Conditions in Ireland, Transcribed and Annotated by Albert Coyle, Official Report to the Commission* (Washington, n.d. [1921]).

373. "What is the Practical Ideal of Protection and Care for Children Born Out of Wedlock?" in U.S., Children's Bureau, *Bureau Publications,* LXXVII (1921), 35–7.

374. "Chicago's School of Social Service Administration," *Survey,* XL VI (May 21, 1921), 220–21.

375. "Potential Advantages of the Mandate System," *Annals,* XCVI (July, 1921) , 70–4.

376. "Disarmament and Life," *Church Militant* (October, 1921, Supplement), pp. lv–lvi. This is a reprinting of number 368.

377. "Disarmament and Life," in National Peace Council, Joint Disarmament Committee, *Disarmament Pamphlet,* II (October, 1921). This is a reprinting of number 368.

378. "The Attack on War," *Christian Century,* XXXVIII (October 13, 1921), 10–12. This is a reprinting of number 368.

379. "Peace and Bread, I. A Speculation on Bread-Labor and War Slogans," *Survey,* XL VII (December 31, 1921), 527–30.

380. *Peace and Bread in Time of War.* New York, 1922. Chapter V, includes material published in number 379.

381. "Aftermath of the War," *Christian Century*, XXXIX (January 5, 1922), 10–2. Excerpted from number 380, Chapter IX.

382. "Why the League Limps," *ibid.*, XXXIX (January 19, 1922), 71–4. This is excerpted from number 380, Chapter X.

383. "Peace and Bread, II. President Wilson's Policies, III. Personal Reactions during the War," *Survey*, XLVII (January 28, 1922), 659–63. This is excerpted from number 380, Chapters III and IV.

384. "What I Saw in Europe," *La Follette's Magazine*, XIII (February, 1922), 20–1.

385. "Peace and Bread, IV. Witness Borne by Women," *Survey*, XLVII (February 25, 1922), 842–4. This is excerpted from Chapter IV of number 380.

386. "The Threat of World Starvation," in Kansas State Board of Agriculture, *Report*, X (January-March, 1922) , pp. 75–9.

387. "Washington's Birthday," in Ashley H. Thorndike (ed.), *Modern Eloquence* (New York, 1923), 1, 16–9. This is a reprinting of number 71.

388. "Seconding the Nomination of Roosevelt for President, 1912," in *ibid.*, VIII, 1–2. This is a reprinting of number 216.

389. "In Memory of Henry Lloyd," in *ibid.*, IX, 1–5. This is a reprinting of number 76. Subsequent revised editions of *Modern Eloquence* published in 1928, 1936, and 1941 contain numbers 387, 388, and 389 with the same volume and page numberings.

390. *Christmas Message for* 1923 (n.p., n.d.).

391. Speech, *City Club [of Chicago] Bulletin*, XVI (October 22, 1923), 117–8.

392. "A New Political Method Emerging in the Orient," in Illinois League of Women Voters, *Bulletin*, III (December, 1923), 11.

393. "International Co-operation for Social Welfare," in National Conference of Social Work, *Proceedings* (1924), pp. 107–13.

394. *Opening Address as President of the Women's International League for Peace and Freedom, at the Fourth Biennial Congress, Washington, May 1–8, 1924* (Geneva, n.d. [1924]).

395. Preface; Women's International League for Peace and Freedom, *Congress Report*, IV [1924], vii–xi.

396. "Opening Address," *ibid.*, pp. 1–3. This is a reprinting of number 394.

397. "Whoso Liveth to Himself," *Survey*, LI (January 15, 1924), 373. This is a reprinting of number 390.

398. "Intimate Glimpses," *City Club of [Chicago] Bulletin*, XVII (February 11, 1924), 22–3.

399. "Is Woman Suffrage Failing? "*Woman Citizen*, VIII (April 19, 1924), 15–6.

400. "Why I Shall Vote for La Follette," *New Republic*, XL (September 10, 1924), 36–7.

401. Introduction, in *The Child, the Clinic and the Court; a Group of Papers* (New York, 1925), pp. 1–2.

402. "Impressions of Mexico," in Women's International League for Peace and Freedom; United States Section, *Bulletin,* XIV (April/May 1925), unpaged.

403. "How Much Social Work Can a Community Afford?" in National Conference of Social Work, *Proceedings* (1926), pp. 108–13.

404. "New Methods of Procedure," Women's International League for Peace and Freedom, *Congress Report,* V (1926), 63–5.

405. Foreword, in Winthrop D. Lane, *Military Training in Schools and Colleges in the United States, the Facts and an Interpretation* (n.p. [New York], n.d. [1926]), pp. 3–4. The foreword is co-signed by fifty-seven other people.

406. "The World Court," *Republican Woman,* III (February, 1926), 7–8.

407. "My Greetings to the Youth's Companion," *Youth's Companion,* C (February 4, 1926), 90.

408. Letter to the editor, *Pax International,* I (June, 1926), unpaged.

409. "New Methods of Procedure," *ibid.,* I (August, 1926), unpaged. This is a reprinting of number 404.

410. "Generous Impulses in Politics," *ibid.,* I (September, 1926), unpaged.

411. "New Methods of Procedure," *Unity,* XCVIII (September 6, 1926), 15. This is a reprinting of number 404.

412. "How Much Social Work Can a Community Afford? " *Survey,* LVII (November 15, 1926), pp. 199–201. This is a reprinting with minor deletions of number 403.

413. "Problem of Crime Unsolved, Let Us Start Anew," in American Crime Study Commission, *The Prevention and Cure of Crime* (n.p., 1927), pp. 26–8.

414. "The Hopes We Inherit," in *Building International Goodwill* (New York, 1927), 3–18. This is co-authored by E. G. Balch.

415. "Social Consequences of the Immigration Law," in National Conference of Social Work, *Proceedings* (1927), pp. 102–6.

416. "A Book that Changed My Life," *Christian Century,* XLIV (October 13, 1927), 1196–8.

417. "Chicago's Mayor Turns Censor," *Woman Citizen,* XII (December, 1927), 15, 39.

418. "Introduction," in Abraham Epstein, *The Challenge of the Aged* (New York, 1928), pp. xi–xiii.

419. Statement, in *Liber Amicorum Romain Rolland* (n.p. [Zurich], n.d. [1928]), pp. 9–10.

420. Foreword, in Howard E. Wilson, *Mary McDowell, Neighbor* (Chicago, 1928), pp. ix–xi.

421. Preface, in Giovanni Ermenegildo Schiavo, *Italians in Chicago, a Study of Americanization* (Chicago, 1928), p. [5].

422. "Social Attitudes and Character," in *Building Character: Proceedings of the Mid-West Conference on Parent Education, February 1928* (Chicago, 1928), pp. 291–5.

423. Presidential address, in Pan-Pacific Woman's Conference, Honolulu, *Women of the Pacific, Proceedings of the Pan-Pacific Woman's Conference,* I (1928), 13–4.

424. "Sailing Orders," *Neighborhood,* I (January, 1928), 3.

425. "The Importance to America of the Josephine Butler Centenary," *Social Service Review,* II (March, 1928), 10–23.

426. "Pioneers in Sociology," *Neighborhood,* I (July, 1928), 6–11.

427. "What to Do Then," *Russian Student,* V (September, 1928), 19–22. This is a revision of number 416.

428. "Tolstoy, Prophet of Righteousness," *Unity,* CII (September 10, 1928), 11–2. This is a reprinting of number 427.

429. "Address to the Pan-Pacific Women's Conference, *Pax International,* III (October, 1928), unpaged. This is a reprinting of number 423.

430. "The Opening of a Women's Congress," *Mid-Pacific,* XXVI (October, 1928), 303–6.

431. "Graham Taylor—Pioneer in Sociology," *Chicago Theological Seminary Register,* XVIII (November, 1928), 17–28. This includes number 426.

432. President's Address, in Women's International League for Peace and Freedom, *Congress Report,* VI (1929), 13–5.

433. "Women and War," in F. C. Hicks (ed.), *Famous Speeches by Eminent American Statesmen* (St. Paul, 1929), pp. 439–43. This is a reprinting of number 283.

434. Statement, in Anna Morgan (comp. and ed.), *Tribute to Henry B., from Friends in Whose Minds and Hearts He Will Live Always* (n.p., 1929), p. 129.

435. Address, in Illinois Conference on Public Welfare, *Proceedings* (1929), 10–1.

436. "Law—Not War," review of *Law or War,* by Lucia Ames Mead, *World Tomorrow,* XII (April, 1929), 183.

437. "After Sixty-Five," *Survey,* LXII (June 1, 1929), 303.

438. "The Settlement as a Way of Life," *Neighborhood,* II (July, 1929), 139–46.

439. "The Pageant of Emancipation," *Woman's Press,* XXIII (August, 1929), 525–8.

440. "Opening Speech at Prague Congress," Pax International, IV (September, 1929), unpaged. This is a reprinting of number 432.

441. "Decade of Prohibition," *Survey,* LXIII (October 1, 1929), 5–10.

442. "Prohibition as Seen from Hull House," *Literary Digest,* CIII (October 19, 1929), 22–3. This is excerpted from number 441.

443. "Safety in the Home," in National Broadcasting Company, *Second Universal Safety Series* (October 23, [1929]), unpaged.

444. "Immigrants under the Quota," *Survey,* LXIII (November 1, 1929), 135–9.

445. "Toast to John Dewey," *ibid.,* LXIII (November 15, 1929), 203–4.

446. "Safety in the Home," *American Labor Legislation Review*, XIX (December, 1929), 409–10. This is excerpted from number 443.

447. "Immigrants under the Quota," *Review of Reviews*, LXXX (December, 1929), 94–5. This is excerpted from number 444.

448. "Appreciation of A. S. B. [Alice Stone Blackwell]," *Woman's Journal*, n.s. XIV (December, 1929), 10.

449. "Efforts to Humanize Justice," *Survey*, LXIII (December 1, 1929), 275–8.

450. Memorial address, in *Helen Castle Mead* (n.p., n.d. [1930]), pp. 19–13.

451. "Jane Addams," in Helen J. Ferris (ed.), *When I Was a Girl; the Stories of Five Famous Women as Told by Themselves* (New York, 1930), pp. 167–222. This is excerpted from number 180.

452. "Reflections on the First Pan-Pacific Women's Conference," in Pan-Pacific Women's Conference, Honolulu, *Record of Proceedings*, II (1930), ix–x.

453. "Social Workers and the Other Professions," in National Conference of Social Work, *Proceedings* (1930), pp. 50–4.

454. "John Dewey and Social Welfare," in Henry W. Holmes (ed.), *John Dewey: the Man and His Philosophy* (Cambridge, Mass., 1930), pp. 140–52. This is a reprinting of number 445.

455. *The Second Twenty Years at Hull-House, September 1909 to September 1929, with a Record of a Growing World Consciousness* (New York, 1930). Chapter IV includes a reprinting of number 452. Chapter VI includes a reprinting of number 390. Chapter VIII includes a reprinting of number 441. Chapter IX includes a reprinting of number 444. Chapter X includes a reprinting of number 449.

456. "What Is Security? How Does Each Naval Power, Including Germany, Define Security; and What Agreements or Armaments Does Each Believe Necessary to Maintain Peace? How Far Does Each Country Depend upon Political Agreement; How Far upon Armaments Held in Readiness for War?" *Conference on the Cause and Cure of War*, VI (1930), 33–40.

457. "Widening the Circle of Enlightenment, Hull House and Adult Education," *Journal of Adult Education*, II (June, 1930), 276–9.

458. "Aspects of the Woman's Movement," *Survey*, LXIV (August 1, 1930), 384–7. This is a reprinting of Chapter IV of number 455.

459. "Education by the Current Event," *ibid.*, LXIV (September 1, 1930), 461–4. This is a reprinting of Chapter XII of number 455.

460. "Contrasts in a Post-War Generation," *ibid.*, LXV (October 1, 1930), 21–5. This is a reprinting of Chapter VII of number 455.

461. "The Post-War Generation," *Pax International*, VI (November, 1930), unpaged. This is excerpted from Chapter VII of number 455.

462. "The Play Instinct and the Arts," *Religious Education*, XXV (November, 1930), 808–19. This is a reprinting of Chapter XI of number 455.

463. Statement, in Ramananda Chatterjee (ed.), *The Golden Book of Tagore, a Homage to Rabindranath Tagore from India and the World in Celebration of His Seventieth Birthday* (Calcutta, 1931), p. 19.

464. Introduction, in Victor Lefebure, *Scientific Disarmament* (New York, 1931), p. 8.

465. "Tribute," in Sydney D. Strong (ed.), *What I Owe to My Father* (New York, 1931), pp. 1–8. This is an excerpt from number 180.

466. *Social Consequences of Business Depressions* (Chicago, 1931).

467. "Twenty Years at Hull House," in Clara L. Myers (ed.), *Readings in Biography* (New York, 1931) , pp. 277–92. This is excerpts from number 180.

468. "Casting Out Fear," *Pax International,* VI (February, 1931), unpaged.

469. "Reply," *Bryn Mawr Alumnae Bulletin,* IX (June, 1931), 5.

470. "A Needed Implement to Social Reform," *Unitarian Register and Newsletter,* CX (June 4, 1931), 464–5.

471. "A Needed Implement in Social Reform," *Christian Leader,* XXXIV (June 20, 1931), 778–80. This includes the material in number 470.

472. "Through Disarmament Nations Will Substitute Political for Military Arrangements," *International Disarmament Notes,* IV (August 17, 1931), [1].

473. "Not Afraid of Unpopular Causes," *Progressive,* II (November 7, 1931), 3.

474. "Tolstoy and Gandhi," *Christian Century,* XLVIII (November 25, 1931), 1485–8.

475. "The Process of Social Transformation," in Charles A. Beard (ed.), *A Century of Progress* (New York, 1932), pp. 234–52. A revised edition which was published in 1933 retained the same pagination.

476. *The Excellent Becomes the Permanent* (New York, 1932). The memorial to Sarah Rozet Smith is a reprinting of number 82. The memorial to Henry Demarest Lloyd is a reprinting with a small deletion of number 76. The memorial to Judge Murray F. Tuley is a reprinting with slight changes of number 116. The memorial to Mary Hawes Wilmarth is an excerpt with many revisions of number 345. The memorial to Canon Samuel A. Barnett uses excerpts from numbers 334 and 362. Chapter XII is a reprinting of number 270.

477. "Social Consequences of Business Depressions," in Felix Morley (ed.), *Aspects of the Depression* (Chicago, 1932), pp. 12–21. This is a reprinting of number 466.

478. "The Friend and Guide of Social Workers," in *Ernest Freund, 1864–1932* (n.p., n.d. [1932]), pp. 43–5.

479. "Social Consequences of the Depression," *Survey,* LXVII (January 1, 1932), 370–1. This is a reprinting of number 466.

480. "Disarm and Have Peace, a Pacifist Plea to End War," *Liberty,* IX (March 12, 1932), 25.

481. "The Excellent Becomes the Permanent," *Illinois Voter,* XII (June, 1932), 3.

482. "A Great Public Servant, Julia C. Lathrop," *Social Service Review,* VI (June, 1932), 280–5. This is an expanded version of number 481.

483. "How to Build a Peace Program," *Survey,* LXVIII (November 1, 1932), 550–3.

484. "Social Deterrent of Our National Self-Righteousness; with Correctives Suggested by the Courageous Life of William Penn," *Friends' Intelligencer,* LXXXIX (Eleventh month 5, 1932), 890–5.

485. "The Education of Negroes," *Opportunity,* X (December, 1932), 370–1.

486. Introduction, in Leo Tolstoy, *What Then Must We Do?* trans. Alymer Maude (Oxford, 1933), pp. vii–xiii. This is a revision with additions of number 416.

487. "The Philosophy of a New Day," in *Our Common Cause—Civilization, Report to the International Congress of Women, Chicago, 1933, Including the Series of Round Tables, 16–22 July 1933* (New York, 1933), pp. 65–8.

488. "Introduction to the Forum," "Response," and remarks, in *ibid.,* pp. 185, 203, 204, 210, 213, 216, 218, 242–3.

489. Discussion, in Thomas H. Reed (ed.), *Legislatures and Legislative Problems* (Chicago, 1933), pp. 1–9.

490. "The Rise in Negro Education," *School Life,* XVIII (January, 1933), 98. This is excerpted from number 485.

491. "Friend and Guide of Social Workers—Ernest Freund," *University [of Chicago] Record,* XIX (January, 1933), 43–5. This is a reprinting of number 478.

492. "The Social Deterrent of our National Self-Righteousness with Correctives Suggested by the Courageous Life of William Penn," *Survey Graphic,* XXII (February, 1933), 98–101. This is a reprinting with a few deletions of number 484.

493. "Our National Self-Righteousness," *University [of Chicago] Magazine,* XXVI (November, 1933), 8–10. This is a reprinting with several deletions of number 484.

494. "Pioneering in Social Work," *Federation News,* I (November, 1933), 1–2.

495. "Exaggerated Nationalism and International Comity," in William H. Cordell (ed.), *Molders of American Thought, 1933–1934* (New York, 1934), pp. 43–51.

496. "Is a United Peace Front Desirable ?" *Survey Graphic,* XXIII (February, 1934), 60. This is co-authored by Emily Greene Balch.

497. "A Feminist Physician Speaks: a Review of Rachelle S. Yarros' *Modern Woman and Sex,*" *Survey,* LXX (February, 1934), 59.

498. "Exaggerated Nationalism and International Comity," *Survey Graphic,* XXIII (April, 1934), 168–70. This is a reprinting of number 495.

499. "Letters of Julia Lathrop," *Survey,* LXX (May, 1934), 174. This is co-signed by Grace Abbott.

500. "Because Wars Interfere with the Normal Growth of Civilization," in Rose Young (ed.), *Why Wars Must Cease* (New York, 1935), 129–39. Much of this material is reprinted from number 495.

501. Statement, in Herman Bernstein, *Can We Abolish War?* (New York, 1935), pp. 30–1. This is excerpted from number 414.

502. "Opening the First Session, June 18, 1933," in Charles Frederick Weller (ed.) , *World Fellowship, Addresses and Messages by Leading Spokesmen of All Faiths, Races, and Countries* (New York, 1935), pp. 11–2.

503. *My Friend, Julia Lathrop* (New York, 1935). Material originally published in numbers 481 and 482 is included in this book.

504. "Julia Lathrop and Outdoor Relief in Chicago, 1893–1894," *Social Service Review,* IX (March, 1935), 24–33. This is a reprinting of Chapter V, number 503.

505. "Child Labor Amendment—Yes," *Rotarian,* XLVI (March, 1935), 12–5.

506. "Old Age Security," *Booklist,* XXXI (March, 1935), 215.

507. "In Memoriam," *National Parent Teacher,* XXIX (May, 1935), 24.

508. "Julia Lathrop's Services to the State of Illinois," *Social Service Review,* IX (June, 1935), 191–211. This is a reprinting of number 503, Chapter VII.

509. "There Is a River," *Advance,* CXXVII (June 6, 1935), 444.

510. "The Home," *Unity,* CXV (July 15, 1935), 186.

511. "Julia Lathrop at Hull House," *Survey Graphic,* XXIV (August, 1935), 373–7. This is excerpted from number 503.

512. "Julia Lathrop at Hull House, II, Women and the Art of Government," *ibid.,* XXIV (September, 1935), 434–8. This is excerpted from number 503.

513. "Julia Lathrop at Hull House, III, Young People and Old Laws," *ibid.,* XXIV (October, 1935), 488–92. This is excerpted from number 503.

514. "The Profession of Social Service," in Earl G. Lockhart (comp.), *My Vocation, by Eminent Americans: or W hat Eminent Americans Think of Their Callings* (New York, 1938), pp. 311–23. This is co-authored by Edith A. Abbott.

INDEX